Critical Thinking and Communication

The Use of Reason in Argument

Second Edition

Barbara Warnick
University of Washington

Edward S. Inch
Pacific Lutheran University

Macmillan Publishing Company
New York

Maxwell Macmillan Canada
Toronto

Maxwell Macmillan International
New York Oxford Singapore Sydney

To Michael and Pamela

Cover art: Marsha McDevitt
Editor: Kevin M. Davis
Production Editor: Julie Anderson Tober
Art Coordinators: Peter A. Robison, Vincent A. Smith
Artist: Jane Lopez
Cover Designer: Thomas Mack
Production Buyer: Jeff Smith
Electronic Text Management: Ben Ko, Marilyn Wilson Phelps

This book was set in Garamond by Macmillan Publishing Company and was printed and bound by R. R. Donnelley & Sons Company. The cover was printed by Phoenix Color Corp.

Macmillan Publishing Company
866 Third Avenue
New York, New York 10022

Macmillan Publishing Company is part of the
Maxwell Communication Group of Companies.

Maxwell Macmillan Canada, Inc.
1200 Eglinton Avenue East, Suite 200
Don Mills, Ontario M3C 3N1

Library of Congress Cataloging-in-Publication Data
Warnick, Barbara
      Critical thinking and communication : the use of reason in argument / Barbara Warnick,
   Edward S. Inch. —2nd ed.
        p. cm.
   Includes bibliographical references and index.
   ISBN 0-02-424742-1
   1. Reasoning. 2. Critical thinking. 3. Communication. I. Inch, Edward S. II. Title.
BC177.W35 1994
168—dc20
                                       93-25171
                                           CIP

Printing: 1 2 3 4 5 6 7 8 9   Year: 4 5 6 7 8

Preface

Since the appearance of the first edition of this text, the Cold War ended; the Soviet Union ceased to exist; and significant changes in government and international politics occurred. These developments contributed substantially to increased interest in argumentation and political communication in Western and Eastern Europe as well as Asia. In the past ten years, new journals and international conferences in argumentation have been organized.

Furthermore, public concern about the basic competencies of college graduates has focused attention on critical thinking and reasoning. Critical thinking researchers agree that critical thinking involves more than knowing the validity conditions for the syllogism. Expert thinkers know how to select the strongest arguments from possible candidates, how to systematically defend their positions on issues, how to anticipate and respond to possible objections, and how to adapt their presentation of claims and evidence to the beliefs and expectations of their audiences. These macrolevel analytical and argumentation skills are emphasized in this text and are best developed in argumentation courses such as those for which this text is intended.

This text examines the forms of practical reasoning used in persuasive communication (speeches, conversations, essays, group deliberation, and other situations in which argument occurs). We believe that students learn by doing—by analyzing topics for argument, conducting research, constructing cases, and analyzing and refuting others' arguments. We therefore emphasize examples and exercises that require active student involvement. Our view is that by producing and evaluating argumentation on topics of interest to them, we will help students to effectively develop their critical thinking skills.

As in the first edition, we have produced a flexibly organized text. The first five chapters provide an orientation to argument and its basic elements and should come early in the course. The remaining chapters can be read and studied in any order depending on student need and teaching interest. We have also provided many study supplements—lists of key concepts, chapter summaries, a bibliography, and exercises that require students to apply chapter concepts. These aids should enable students to review for exams, to do further reading, and to have handy references when reading text material. We have used a variety of examples from law, education, ethics, business, and other fields to illustrate the argument concepts introduced in the text.

The text treats many topics that are standard in argumentation courses—reasoning types, fallacies, tests of reasoning and evidence, case construction, and, for courses including debate assignments, a debate appendix. The text is also innovative in three ways. First, the focus is not exclusively on speeches or on debate. Our view is that argument occurs in many settings including interactive and written communication. We have designed a text in general argumentation that has applications across a broad range of discourse. Second, we have used multiple argument models in Chapter 7 on argument analysis and diagramming. Developed by philosophers Stephen Toulmin, Michael Scriven, and Irving Copi, these models have been highly useful to our students in understanding how arguments work. Third, Chapter 8 contains extensive explanation of value argument and of how to construct a value case. Until recently, students who sought to construct cases on nonpolicy claims had little guidance on how to organize their arguments. Chapter 8 offers concrete suggestions concerning the organization of value arguments.

We would like to conclude by thanking the individuals who assisted in the development of this text. We would again like to thank Susan L. Kline of Ohio State University and Joseph W. Wenzel of the University of Illinois. Both of these individuals contributed substantially to this project through their detailed and theoretically germane critiques and suggestions. We would also like to recognize the reviewers for the second edition: Robert D. Kully, California State University, Los Angeles; David E. Williams, Texas Tech University; Beth M. Waggenspack, Virginia Polytechnic Institute and State University; Joseph W. Wenzel, University of Illinois; Mike Bauer, Ball State University. Finally, we thank our editor, Kevin Davis of Macmillan Publishing Company, for his advice and support.

B.W.
E.S.I.

Chapter 4   Evidence: The Foundation for Arguments   73
   The Nature of Evidence   74
   Types of Evidence   76
   Evaluating Fact and Opinion Evidence   78
          Reliability   79
          Expertise   79
          Objectivity   80
          Consistency   80
          Recency   81
          Relevance   82
          Access   82
          Accuracy of Citation   83
   Evaluating Statistical Evidence   85
   Locating Evidence   88
          Books   88
          Periodicals   89
          Newspapers   91
          General Reference Works   92
          Government Documents   93
          Other Sources of Information   95
   Recording and Organizing Evidence   96
   Summary   98
   Exercises   99
   Notes   104

Chapter 5   Reasoning: Making Inferences   107
   The Usefulness of Formal Logic   109
   Reasoning as Inference Making   112
          Quasi-Logical Arguments   113
          Analogy   115
          Generalization and Argument from Example   118
          Cause   120
          Coexistential Arguments   122
          Dissociation   125
   Summary   127
   Exercises   128
   Notes   132

Section 3   *Criticizing and Analyzing Arguments*   135

Chapter 6   Fallacies: The Detection of Faulty Arguments   137
   The Nature of Fallacies   139
   Fallacies of Faulty Reasoning   140
          False Analogy   141
          Hasty Generalization   141
          False Cause   142
          Slippery Slope   144

Contents

Section 1   *Introduction*   1

Chapter 1   Arguments and Argumentation   3
 A Definition of Argument   6
 Argumentation and Critical Thinking   10
  Perspectives on Argumentation   12
 An Argument Model   15
 Summary   20
 Exercises   21
 Notes   24

Chapter 2   Arguments in Context   27
 Context Element 1: Culture   29
 Context Element 2: Argument Fields   35
 Context Element 3: Argument Occasion   37
 Context Element 4: Ethics   39
 Summary   42
 Exercises   44
 Notes   47

Section 2   *The Anatomy of Argument*   49

Chapter 3   Argument Claims and Propositions   51
 Claims and Propositions   52
 Formulating a Proposition   57
  Controversiality   58
  Clarity   58
  Balance   61
  Challenge   62
 Types of Claims   63
  Factual Claims   64
  Value Claims   66
  Policy Claims   66
 Summary   67
 Exercises   68
 Notes   71

Fallacies of Grounding   145
    Begging the Question   146
    Non Sequitur   146
Fallacies of Misdirection   147
    Ad Hominem   148
    Ad Populum   149
    Appeal to Tradition   150
    Straw Arguments   151
Fallacies of Language Use   152
    Equivocation   153
    Amphiboly   153
    Emotive Language   154
Summary   156
Exercises   158
Notes   160

Chapter 7   Argument Analysis and Criticism   163
Benefits of Argument Analysis   164
A General Model for Argument Analysis   166
    Analysis of Simple Arguments   166
    Analysis of Other Structural Patterns   171
    An Application   175
The Toulmin Model   179
    The Nature and Background of the Toulmin Model   179
    Six Parts of the Model   179
    Difficulties in Applying the Model   184
    Argument Chains and the Toulmin Model   186
Comparison of the Two Models   187
Summary   188
Exercises   189
Notes   195

Section 4   *Constructing Argumentative Cases*   197

Chapter 8   Principles of Case Construction   199
Values and Policies   200
Constructing Argumentative Cases   202
Refutation   205
Summary   207
Exercises   208
Notes   210

Chapter 9   Arguing About Values   211
Values and Value Systems   213
The Process of Value Change   215
Values and Argumentation   216

Stock Issues for Value Arguments   218
    Definition   219
    Field   219
    Criteria   220
    Application   221
    Hierarchies   222
The Issues Brief   223
Summary   226
Exercises   227
Notes   231

Chapter 10   Arguing About Policies   233
Policy Arguments and Policy Systems   235
Stock Issues in Policy Arguments   237
    Ill   238
    Blame   240
    Cure   241
    Cost/Benefits   242
Issues Brief   243
Alternative Formats for Arguing Policies   248
    Comparative-Advantages Case   249
    Goals Case   252
Alternative Formats for Refuting Policy Arguments   254
    Strategy of Defense of the Present Policy System   254
    Strategy of Defense of the Present System with Minor Repairs   255
    Strategy of Counterproposals   256
Summary   257
Exercises   258
Notes   261

Section 5   *Communicating Arguments*   263

Chapter 11   Language and Argument   265
The Nature of Language   267
    Language and Meaning   267
    Language and Abstraction   268
    Connotations and Denotations   271
Language in Argument   273
    Language, Thought, and Perception   273
    Functions of Language   275
    Using Language in Argument   278
Summary   283
Exercises   285
Notes   287

Chapter 12   Arguers, Recipients, and Argumentation   289

The Audience and Argumentation   291
Selecting the Starting Points   292
Supporting Reasoning   293
Using Evidence   294
Organizing Arguments   296
Additional Concerns about Audience   298
Analyzing the Audience   299
The Arguer and Argumentation   300
Message Sources and Their Influence   302
Enhancing Credibility Through Argument   305
Summary   308
Exercises   310
Notes   314

Appendices

Appendix A   Basic Debate Theory and Practice   317

The Nature of Debate   318
The Debate Proposition   320
Analyzing Debate Propositions   322
Debate Pragmatics   325
Conclusion   330

Appendix B   Answers to Selected Exercises   331

References   347

Index   353

SECTION

1

Introduction

■

CHAPTER *1*

Arguments and Argumentation

CHAPTER OUTLINE

- **A Definition of Argument**
- **Argumentation and Critical Thinking**
  Perspectives on Argumentation

- **An Argument Model**
- **Summary**
- **Exercises**

KEY CONCEPTS

argument
claim
evidence
reasoning

argumentation
critical thinking
level of dispute
argument chain

7:00 a.m.   Cindy plans to get to school early so she will have a couple of hours in the library to study for her geology exam. While she awaits for her tea to steep, she eyes the editorial page of the morning paper. One letter to the editor, in particular, catches her attention.

Fetal Tissue Research Degrades Science, Life

Your editorial advocates transplanting fetal tissue.

The notion of harvesting and commercially exploiting tissues and organs from millions of human fetuses should be abhorrent and contrary to the ethical canons of a civilized culture.

In any case, there is tremendous disagreement over whether there is any reliable, scientific evidence to back up the claims of patient improvement after the injection of fetal tissue. In May 1991, Professor Robert J. White, Case Western Reserve University, wrote: "The clinical studies so far conducted in transplanting human fetal brain tissue into the cerebral hemisphere of patients with Parkinsonism have demonstrated little evidence of measurable, lasting improvement in neurological dysfunction."

Dr. Adrien Williams, a professor of clinical neurology at the University of Birmingham, wrote in a British journal, August 1990, that so far probably more patients have been harmed by the procedure than have benefited.[1]

As Cindy sips her tea, her housemate, Karen, wanders sleepily into the kitchen. "You should read this editorial on fetal tissue research," says Cindy. "Oh, *please!*" responds her housemate. "I don't even know what day it is yet and you want to discuss current events. You're such a *morning* person!"

Figuring that conversation with Karen is a lost cause, Cindy quickly slips out of the kitchen and heads up to her room to get dressed. As she gets ready for school, she absentmindedly listens to an early morning talk show on women's efforts to advance in the business world. Three female panel members—an account executive, a stockbroker, and the head of a public relations firm—are discussing the problem, with participation from the audience.

ACCOUNT EXECUTIVE:	One of the major problems facing women who want to advance is the resistance to having a female boss supervising men.
FIRST AUDIENCE MEMBER:	That's right. I work for two women and I enjoy it. They are both easygoing and have a sense of humor. But my husband feels very uncomfortable working for a female supervisor.
STOCKBROKER:	I hear resentment here against women succeeding. There seems to be a feeling that we live in a sexist society, or a fear of women succeeding.
SECOND AUDIENCE MEMBER:	Look, we're our own worst enemies. We'd rather sit around complaining than do something about it.

THIRD AUDIENCE MEMBER:	That's absolutely right. I'm a nurse and I tried to get the women I work with to stand up against management. None of them would.
MODERATOR:	Why not?
THIRD AUDIENCE MEMBER:	Oh, they're married and it's their second income. They're afraid of losing their jobs. They won't stand up for themselves.
PUBLIC RELATIONS HEAD:	Yes, but women who do put themselves forward are often successful. My secretary came in and asked for a raise. She had her case together, knew what other secretaries in similar jobs were making. I thought about it and she was right, so she got the raise.

7:45 a.m. Cindy picks up her bus pass and heads downstairs where she finds Karen in a more conversational mood.

KAREN:	Listen, do you have a few minutes before your bus leaves?
CINDY:	Yeah. About ten. Why?
KAREN:	Well, I've been thinking about transferring to the main campus at the end of the term. What do you think?
CINDY:	Why do you want to do that?
KAREN:	I could start taking my premajor coursework and maybe finish more quickly.
CINDY:	Look, if you really want my opinion, I think it's a bad idea. I already looked into early transfer myself, and I decided against it. Have you checked out the main campus? The classes are *huge,* and they're so impersonal! You'd never get to know your teachers. And, besides that, it's more expensive. Tuition is higher, not to mention the living expenses. You should really look into it before you make any hasty decisions.
KAREN:	But they don't offer the premajor coursework I need at the community college. Just getting *into* my major after I transfer will take an extra quarter, or maybe two. I'd really like to finish school as quickly as possible.
CINDY:	I still think you should put it off. As long as you stay here, you'll stay even on your expenses. You're in no better financial shape than I am to make the change now. Besides you like a more personal learning environment. I think you should reconsider.

KAREN: But consider the extra terms I'll have to spend when I get there.

CINDY: Hey, you asked my opinion, and you got it. I've got to run; my bus leaves in three minutes.

Between the time she woke up and the time she left the house, Cindy heard, read, or produced arguments about fetal tissue research, job discrimination, and college transfers. When she arrives at school, Cindy will continue to listen to and make arguments in her classroom discussions and at her part-time job. Her ability to make good decisions and to coordinate her goals and needs with others will depend on whether she can provide good reasons for her proposals, detect weaknesses in others' proposals, ask needed questions, and tell the difference between fact and opinion.

Cindy's experience illustrates the pervasiveness and importance of argument in daily life. This book will focus on the processes of understanding, interpreting, criticizing, constructing, and communicating arguments. By studying how arguments work, you will learn how to seek pertinent information on a topic; weigh and test alternative proposals; avoid stereotypes, prejudices, and misinformation; present well-organized proposals; and respond to objections when challenged. This chapter will begin this process by defining the terms *argument* and *argumentation* and by discussing their relationship to critical thinking and to various forms of communication.

■ *A Definition of Argument*

In everyday language, the term *argument* is used in various ways in different contexts. Sometimes it refers to a type of interaction, as when we say "they were having an argument" or "Cindy and Karen were arguing about whether Karen should transfer to another school." Sometimes described as "quarrels" or "squabbles," these kinds of arguments usually involve two or more persons engaged in extended overt disagreement with each other. Research in interpersonal argument of this kind has focused on the interaction process—the means by which disputes arise, take place, and are resolved. The emphasis is on how one utterance leads to another.[2]

Another concept of argument refers to "making an argument," offering a claim and giving support for it, as in "Cindy argued that Karen might not adapt well to an impersonal learning environment." This view considers whether an argument is sound and effective; it emphasizes argument as a *reasoning process* and considers arguments as units rather than as interactive processes. In this book, we will emphasize argument in this second sense, as a set of statements produced when one attacks or defends a proposal.[3] *An argument is a set of statements in which a claim is made, support is offered for it, and there is an attempt to influence someone in a context of disagreement.* This definition emphasizes the content of what is said and the connections made among the statements making up an argument.

Arguments are only one kind of communication. When we greet someone ("Hello, how are you?"); issue commands ("Shut the door."); vent our emotions ("I hate it when you do that!"); make promises ("I'll return your book tomorrow."); and so forth, we do not produce arguments. To clarify the differences between arguments and nonarguments, we will describe the important features of arguments and arguing that make them different from other forms of communication.

First, to be considered an argument, a statement generally should make a claim. *A claim is an expressed opinion or a conclusion that the arguer wants accepted.* In the arguments addressed to Cindy in examples earlier in this chapter, some of the claims were:

> There is disagreement over whether there is reliable scientific evidence supporting fetal tissue transplant.
>
> Resistance to having a female boss shows a fear of women succeeding in our society.
>
> Women are their own worst enemies.
>
> It would be a good idea for Karen to transfer to the main campus.

Claims take on various forms and labels depending on the circumstances and situations in which they are made. Furthermore, the term *claim* can refer to the particular claim advanced in an individual argument or to the main claim made in a more lengthy argument. For example, in writing, the thesis statement may serve as the claim; in debate, the resolution functions as a claim; and in criminal law, the charge brought against the defendant may be viewed as a claim. In extended arguments, the claim is often labeled a *proposition.* In making claims, arguers advance statements with which they believe others will disagree. Those to whom the claims are addressed expect arguers to offer further support beyond the claim itself.

Because claims challenge the beliefs or opinions of others, they require support in the form of reasons and information, whereas other kinds of statements do not. When we command someone to do something ("Open the window."), he or she does not expect us to offer support or reasons for the command. When we make a promise ("I'll be there tomorrow."), we commit ourselves by making the statement and no further proof is necessary.[4] Likewise, pure description ("The setting sun was reflected in a rosy haze."); small talk ("Things are so-so; could be better."); and other neutral statements generally do not make claims—they do not advance statements on which there is disagreement.

Sometimes we can only tell whether or not a statement is a claim by considering its context. Arguers often leave their evidence, reasoning, or claim unstated. Do the following examples contain claims?

> When guns are outlawed, only outlaws will have guns.
>
> It was a rare morning. The snow-topped mountains shone through the clouds and the moon could still be seen.
>
> Every time I'm nice to him, he ignores me.

If we learn that the first statement is a bumper sticker displayed by an opponent of gun control, we can figure out the claim: "Making guns illegal means that only those who circumvent the law will have guns." In the second example, are we to view the statement that it's a rare morning as a claim and the sentence that follows it as support, or are we to view the entire passage as a description? Knowing argument structures might help us here. Since the statement that it's a rare morning is disputable and since the scene described is visible to all, the first sentence could be viewed as a claim and the second sentence as a statement offered to support it. Is the author of the third sentence making a claim about her friend's behavior, or is she merely asking for sympathy? Knowing more about the context in which she made the statement and about her relationship with her friend might enable us to answer this question. Some claims can be recognized as claims only when we know about the speaker's intention, the claim's relation to other statements made along with it, or the situational context in which a claim is made.

The second characteristic of an argument is that support is offered for the claim. Claims are supported by evidence and by the reasoning or inferences that connect the evidence to the claim. Evidence comes in many forms, but it always functions as the foundation for argument or the grounds on which argument is based.[5] When we make an argument, we move from statements we believe our receivers will accept (evidence) to statements that are disputable (claims). *Evidence consists of facts or conditions that are objectively observable, beliefs or statements generally accepted as true by the recipients or conclusions previously established.*[6] In the arguments Cindy heard, read, or participated in, the following statements served as evidence.

> Medical researchers White and Williams found no evidence of benefit from fetal tissue transplants.
>
> My husband feels very uncomfortable working for a female supervisor.
>
> I'm a nurse and I tried to get the women I work with to stand up to management. None of them would.
>
> The classes are huge. . . .You'd never get to know your teachers. . . .Tuition is more expensive. . . .

To be counted as evidence, statements should be generally accepted and viewed as relevant by all parties to the dispute or audiences to whom arguments are addressed. (If a statement is accepted by only one party—the arguer—then it is a *claim,* not evidence.) Karen has to agree with Cindy's description of life at the big university in order for Cindy's statement to function as evidence for her. The arguer who begins establishing a claim on grounds that are not accepted will not get far. Furthermore, for evidence to provide reliable grounds for claims, it must conform to what actually is the case. If Karen could show that classes at the university were actually small, Cindy's description would be viewed as defective because it was based on evidence that turned out not to be true.

Claims are also supported by the link that the arguer makes between the evidence and the claim. The part of the argument containing *reasoning* is frequently called the *inference.* Reasoning can take various forms. Those which occur most frequently will be described in Chapter 5, and you will become experienced at identifying them. *Reasoning constructs a rational link between the evidence and the claim and authorizes the step we make when we draw a conclusion.* Reasoning answers the question "How did you get from the evidence to the claim?"[7] It consists of general principles that say how the evidence and the claim are connected.

The study of argument is made all the more interesting because arguers often do not explicitly state their inferences. They provide evidence and make claims, but often one can only guess how the link between the two was made. For example, consider Cindy's claim that transferring to the main campus would be a bad idea. Part of her evidence is that she herself looked into transferring and decided against it. Her reasoning in making this connection is not stated. Can you supply it? If you concluded that Cindy assumed that Karen would reach the same decision about transferring that Cindy did, you are right. The inferences for the other three arguments isolated earlier in this chapter were also not supplied by the arguers who made them but were left unstated. If supplied, they might be the following:

Qualified medical authorities have challenged scientific evidence supporting fetal tissue transplant.

Discomfort about working with a female supervisor is a sign of fear in our society.

People who do not stand up for themselves are their own worst enemies.

Supplying unstated reasoning is difficult. To do it well, one must have a thorough knowledge of the structure and function of arguments and be able to interpret the argument accurately. We will discuss and illustrate various types of inferences and argument structures in Chapters 5 and 7.

The third and last characteristic of arguments is that they are *attempts to influence* someone in a context where people disagree with each other. The phrase "*attempts* to influence" is important because the arguer may or may not succeed. The recipient of the argument is free not to agree with the expressed opinion of the arguer. The person to whom the argument is addressed may accept the claim, reject it, or continue to express doubts about it.[8] In the examples at the beginning of this chapter, certain audience members accepted the claim that women are their own worst enemies; Karen apparently rejected Cindy's argument that tuition costs and the learning environment were the most important factors in deciding whether to transfer. In complex disputes, parties to an argument may also compromise, with each arguer accepting only a portion of the other's expressed opinions.[9]

To say that arguments are "attempts to *influence*" means that there must be a recipient, or "arguee," to whom the argument is addressed who is capable of responding to it. The arguee must be open-minded and able to change her beliefs or actions because of the argument. Furthermore, in choosing argument instead of command or coercion, the arguer recognizes that the process of argument is reciprocal, that initiative and control pass back and forth as the arguer states his viewpoints and the recipient weighs his support and decides whether to accept his argu-ment.[10] As she listens to arguments, the recipient retains her option of challenging, questioning, criticizing, or countering the expressed opinions of the arguer.

The influence that arguments aim to bring about assumes many forms. Arguers may wish to cause recipients to become concerned about an issue on which they are ambivalent or neutral, to change favorable to unfavorable attitudes or vice versa, or to change behavior. Consequently, arguers often begin deciding how to phrase argu-ments by asking such questions as: What evidence will the other person accept? What are the beliefs, attitudes, and values of the recipient? What will gain attention? What authorities will be accepted? How much does the recipient know about argu-ment? What response is being sought?

Arguments are attempts to influence *someone.* An argument may be addressed to oneself, to another person, to a small group, to an audience of individuals, or to multiple audiences. Arguments occur in writing, in conversation, in public speeches, and in all forms of communication. In the examples of arguments earlier in this chapter, the letter about fetal tissue transplants was addressed to the editor as well as to the newspaper's readers and the general public. The panel participants on the talk show discussing job discrimination were talking to each other, the audience members who were present, and the television audience. Argument is a complex phenomenon that occurs in numerous forms and media of communication and that is addressed to many different kinds of audiences.

Finally, to say that argument occurs only when there is disagreement or the potential for disagreement means that the topic addressed must be controversial, capable of inciting opposing opinions from the parties involved. For example, con-sider the following dialogue:

JOHN:	Should we go to the movies this evening?
MARY:	Fine, what would you like to see?
JOHN:	How about *Attack of the Killer Bees?*
MARY:	OK. Do you want to go to the 7 o'clock showing?
JOHN:	Sure.

There is no argument here because there is no opposition. If Mary had rejected the whole idea of going to the movies, or if she had proposed another film and given reasons for preferring it, argumentation would have occurred. But as long as parties to a discussion agree with the opinions expressed, they will not produce arguments.

■ *Argumentation and Critical Thinking*

In addition to individual arguments made by arguers, the serious student of argu-ment should also be interested in *argumentation—the process of making argu-ments intended to justify beliefs, attitudes, and values so as to influence others.* Individual, microlevel arguments such as those described in the last section do not exist in isolation; they are part of a larger process of defending a position—advancing a thesis, offering arguments in support of it, refuting opposing views, and responding to criticisms of one's own view. As a process essential to reaching rational and well-founded decisions, argumentation is significant to the development and maintenance of a healthy society.

Argumentation is only one part of the persuasive process. Its role is to convince others through sound reasoning and good evidence that a particular value or viewpoint should be adopted. Persuasion as a whole has other dimensions besides argument. One of these is source credibility, or whether the audience perceives a message source to be competent and trustworthy. Other dimensions of persuasion relate to emotional appeals and the use of style. Although these factors are important, the focus of this text will be on the use of reasoning and evidence in argument, or what has traditionally been called *invention*.

Argumentation as a process operates on the "macro" level; rather than dealing with individual arguments, argumentation deals with the construction of cases or overall positions. It is used in selecting government policies in legislatures and parliaments, deciding upon guilt or innocence in the courts, making important decisions in our personal lives, selecting strategies in business, conducting campaigns for public office, and performing many other personal and social functions. When someone constructs a case for the prosecution or defense, proposes and defends a marketing plan, delivers a state of the union address, or introduces and justifies a new bill or piece of legislation, that person has engaged in argumentation.

When parties engage in argumentation, they agree to certain conventions and tacit principles. They consent to listen to what others have to say; they agree to rules for conducting the discussion; they make contributions as required; and they seek the approval of the other parties involved.[11] Sometimes people refuse even to listen to or discuss a problem. In these cases, argumentation is not possible because there is no agreement to engage in an argumentative dispute.

The practice of argumentation has been linked with a set of skills that educators have labeled "critical thinking." *Critical thinking involves the ability to explore a problem, question, or situation; integrate all the available information about it; arrive at a solution or hypothesis; and justify one's position.*[12] Critical thinking includes many specific skills, such as analyzing and evaluating evidence, identifying relevant questions, drawing sound inferences, generating plausible solutions and hypotheses, detecting errors in others' reasoning, stating implicit assumptions, and understanding the implications of an argument.

Some researchers who have studied critical thinking and how it is taught and learned have divided these skills into two large groups—the skills of discovery and the skills of justification. The first group is generally made up of *receptive* skills—identifying evidence, evaluating arguments, judging relevance of evidence and reasoning, and understanding how inferences work. The second group is made up of skills an arguer must have to successfully *defend* a position—selecting the best possible evidence to support one's position, choosing the best solution from many alternative solutions, anticipating and countering objections to one's view, and employing sound reasoning. While both sets of skills are necessary, researchers have found that receptive skills (by which one evaluates the arguments of others) must be complemented by experience in justifying one's own position to fully develop critical thinking ability.[13] "Novice thinkers" look for quick solutions, fail to consider audience objections or interests, and employ a limited repertoire of argument strategies. "Expert thinkers" thoroughly interpret and analyze problems before posing solutions, monitor their own effectiveness, anticipate objections, and choose the most effective from a wide range of argument strategies.

We believe that experience in the process of argumentation such as that provided in this book will develop both the skills of justification and the skills of reception. For example, Chapter 4 poses criteria to evaluate evidence; Chapter 5 describes inference patterns that can be used to analyze and construct arguments; Chapter 6 considers errors in reasoning; and Chapters 8 and 9 focus on case construction of macro arguments intended to justify and defend value and policy proposals. The activities and assignments suggested in these chapters should lead to classroom speeches, discussions, and debates in which students systematically and progressively practice and apply critical thinking and argumentation skills.

Perspectives on Argumentation

Argumentation is a complex process with many dimensions. Scholars therefore disagree about how it should be described and explained. Some believe arguers have an obligation to determine truth through the use of true premises and sound reasoning.[14] Others argue that the "truth" frequently cannot be decisively determined and that argumentation should be studied as a means of influence in the social and political marketplace.[15] Still others, noting the tension between rational and nonrational factors of influence, have concluded that "a central focus of argumentation is on discovering and applying the general standards for determining what is true or reasonable."[16]

Joseph W. Wenzel recently summarized the various perspectives on argument and concluded that they could be put into three categories—*logical, dialectical,* and *rhetorical.*[17] These are not three different kinds of argument; they are three different ways of looking at argumentation. Each perspective emphasizes a different set of functions and features of argumentation. They best might be understood if we examine the following argument from each of the three perspectives. This argument, which appeared in the conservation column of a wilderness organization's monthly newsletter, argues that the spotted owl, an endangered species that the U.S. Forest Service is mandated to protect, is being ill-served by Forest Service policies.

> The Forest Service wants to save only 1,000 acres per breeding pair, but scientists think they require an average of over 2,000 acres. The discrepancies between USFS acreage allowances and biologists' minimum recommended acreage has meant further study and a supplemental environmental impact statement to be issued sometime this summer. . . .
> Spacing of spotted owl management areas is also controversial. Scientists think they should be spaced from 1–6 miles apart, and the Forest Service plans to place them at the

maximum of this range—6 miles apart, which will make it difficult for young owls to disperse from their original nest sites. . . .

If scientists' recommendations and Forest Service plans are so disparate, perhaps there should be a moratorium placed on all harvest of spotted owl habitat. The burden of proof that harvest can continue without endangering the survival of the species should rest on the Forest Service.[18]

The author here presents two sets of evidence—Forest Service recommendations and scientists' findings regarding the spotted owl. She then shows that the two are not in agreement—that there are discrepancies that might affect the owls' well-being and even their survival. From this she concludes that a moratorium on habitat harvesting should be declared until the discrepancies can be resolved and there is agreement about what measures are needed to ensure the owls' survival.

The logical perspective asks, Is the argument sound? The dialectical perspective asks, Has the discussion been handled so as to achieve a candid and critical examination of all aspects of the issue in question? And the rhetorical perspective asks: Has the arguer constructed the argument so as to successfully influence a particular audience? All three perspectives are useful and necessary, and the significance of any one perspective at any time depends on the arguer's purpose and the situation in which the argument is made.

If we are to use a *logical* approach to this example, we will view it as a set of statements made up of premises and a claim or conclusion. The logical perspective emphasizes the accuracy of the premises and the correctness of the inferences linking premises and evidence to the claims they support. An argument favorably evaluated from the logical perspective will be based on correct evidence and will use reasoning that is sound according to the standards of logic. Dividing the preceding argument into its parts—claim, evidence, and inference—we might ask:

Is the evidence correct?	• Are scientists' recommendations accurately summarized?
	• Do the recommendations reported cover all the studies that have been done?
Does the inference justify the move to the conclusion?	• Will maximum placement of the management areas actually interfere with dispersal?
	• Will placing a moratorium resolve the discrepancy between the scientists' recommendations and the Forest Service's plans?

The logical perspective views argumentation as addressed to an audience of rational individuals well informed on the topic of the dispute.[19] It removes arguments from their situational contexts and considers them primarily as statements connected by logical inferences. The inferences are identified, classified, analyzed, and critiqued by comparing their structure and adequacy with prescriptions from logical theory.

Viewing the example from the *dialectical* perspective leads us to consider this argument as one move in an ongoing process of inquiry about policies concerning the spotted owl. By refraining from deciding on a position or course of action until all aspects of the question have been thoroughly explored, a dialectical approach to argumentation searches for significant issues, identifies alternatives, generates standards or criteria for selection, and uses them to test proposals. The dialectical perspective focuses on and enhances a candid, critical, and comprehensive examination of all positions relevant to the topic. It makes a concerted effort to seek out *all* points of view. In the spotted owl controversy, the arguer articulated the environmentalist position on the issue. A dialectical perspective on the argument would seek out the viewpoints of the scientific community, the Forest Service, and the timber industry. In regard to the argument in the example, we would be led to ask such questions as:

- What is the spotted owl's present situation? Is it in immediate danger? Is the decline in old growth forests the primary threat to the species, or are there other threats?
- What will be the impact of a harvest moratorium on the timber industry?
- Will the promised supplemental environmental impact statement provide information to resolve the disparity?
- Are there alternatives to the proposed moratorium?

Argumentation viewed from a dialectical perspective focuses primarily on the process of reaching the best conclusion. The assumption is that the "best" conclusion will be accepted if all points of view and issues have been carefully considered and discussed.

Viewing the example from a *rhetorical* perspective means that we see it as addressed to a particular audience in a social and political context in which recipients are to be influenced by the author's position. In the rhetorical perspective, arguments are viewed as appeals to an audience and we must take account of the circumstances in which the argument was made and the strategies used to influence its audience. Considering the argument this way might lead us to ask:

- Is the author aware of the interests and values of the newsletter's readers?
- What strategies does she use to structure and present the argument?
- Are there other arguments that might appeal to the readers' values and interests more successfully?
- Does the author appear knowledgeable and trustworthy? Will the readers believe her?

The rhetorical perspective on argument is important because of its emphasis on arguments as forms of communication. By taking account of the circumstances in which the argument was produced, the arguer's intent, and the beliefs and values of those to whom arguments are addressed, the rhetorical perspective enables one to interpret and evaluate the content of the arguments themselves.

Understanding that any argument can be viewed from any of these three perspectives is important. Each of the perspectives implies a different purpose and a different emphasis when one considers an argument. The logical perspective focuses on the structure of an argument and on its logical soundness when removed from a context. (This is the perspective of many courses in formal and informal logic.) The dialectical perspective considers especially the capacity of any given procedure for argumentation to contribute to reasoned and careful deliberation about an issue. The rhetorical perspective emphasizes the argument's *effectiveness* in persuading its audience. When individual arguments and argumentation are viewed from each of these three perspectives, different dimensions of the process of arguing are featured.

We will use all three of these perspectives—the logical, the dialectical, and the rhetorical—in various places in this book. For example, in Chapters 5 and 7 when we discuss forms of reasoning and argument analysis, we will focus on the logical perspective. In Chapters 8, 9, and 10, when we discuss analysis and the construction of argumentative cases, we will emphasize the dialectical perspective and its usefulness in discovering vital questions on a given topic. In Chapters 11 and 12, we will be particularly concerned with the kinds of questions raised by a rhetorical perspective, which is concerned with the arguer's relationship to other parties and with how arguments are expressed in everyday language.

■ *An Argument Model*

An individual argument, then, can be viewed as a set of logically connected statements, as part of a larger process of inquiry and proof, or as a unit of persuasive communication addressed to an audience. Even though arguments will be considered individually in Chapters 5 and 7 of this book when their inferences and logical patterns are studied, it is important to remember that arguments do not occur in isolation but function as a whole to influence their listeners. The content and interpretation of arguments should therefore be understood in terms of the predispositions and experiences of the recipients who hear and read them, the language in which they are expressed, and the context in which they arise.

One aspect of argument that is influenced by all these factors, but most particularly by the attitudes and beliefs of recipients, is the level of agreement that separates premises from claims and allows certain statements to be accepted without further support as evidence. To clarify the importance of this aspect in the conduct of argument, this section is devoted to developing a model of argument that illustrates the interrelationship of its parts.

Let us begin by considering the relationship of the three components of an argument that we have already defined. Visually represented, their relation can be seen in Figure 1–1.

Figure 1–1
A Model of an Argument

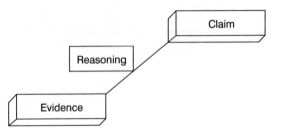

An example will illustrate how these three elements work together in an argument. On March 31, 1992, James S. Brady appeared in a newspaper announcement urging people to call their congressional representatives about tougher gun control laws. He made many arguments supporting his central claim that we should pressure Congress to act. For example, he said:

> Please help me save lives. Add your voice to mine. Help stop random gun violence. . . . I'm calling on Congress to enact a common sense law—the Brady Bill—requiring a "cooling-off" period before the purchase of a handgun so police can run a thorough background check on the buyer. Time to cool off a hot temper. Time to screen out illegal purchasers.[20]

In this argument, Brady appealed to his audience to help stop random gun violence. His evidence was that the Brady Bill would require a "cooling-off" period before purchase of a handgun so police could run background checks on the buyers. The parts of his argument are linked together by the idea that police checks would allow "time to cool off a hot temper" and "time to screen out illegal purchasers." Using our argument model, the relationships between the parts of the argument could be displayed as in Figure 1–2.

In the same advertisement, Brady used other arguments that could be diagrammed using this model. Diagramming makes it easier to see how the parts of an argument function in relation to each other. As discussed in Chapter 7, diagramming

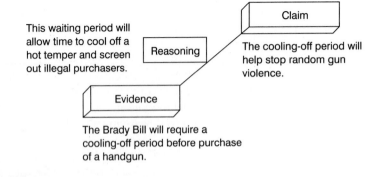

Figure 1–2
A Diagrammed Argument

is an important critical step that helps us to describe and evaluate arguments. Similarly, the other arguments Brady used to support his primary claim can be diagrammed. Using this model to diagram his arguments makes it easier to see how the parts of the argument function.

Arguments occur in contexts which give rise to agreement and disagreement about the topic of the argument. Since arguments occur only when people disagree with each other, we can imagine a line which separates the statements of belief and value with which an audience agrees from those with which it disagrees. In other words, for any issue we can think of, there is a line which separates what we are willing to accept from what we are unwilling to accept initially. For instance, we might discuss the relative strengths of President Franklin D. Roosevelt and the four-term presidency. Even if you were a staunch political conservative and truly believed Roosevelt almost destroyed American freedoms through a strong centralized government, there is some aspect of Roosevelt's presidency you would accept. You might not agree with the arguer who says Roosevelt was the best president, but you would probably accept that he was president. You would also probably accept that he was elected for four terms and that under Roosevelt many government programs for economic reform were passed. While you might not accept the value of such programs you would probably agree with the facts of his administration (the WPA was established; the United States entered World War II). The point to be made here is that for any issue you can think of, there is a level of agreement on facts.

This level or imaginary line which separates what is accepted by the audience from what is not accepted we will call the level of dispute.[21] Arguments that occur below the line are already accepted by the audience and those that occur above it are not accepted. The term *line* may be a little misleading here. We are not suggesting that all issues have clearly demarcated lines that all recipients of argument acknowledge. Such a position would fail to recognize that people do not have their minds made up on all issues. Rather, we can think of this line or level of dispute as a not clearly defined area in which people neither accept nor reject arguments immediately. Therefore, the level of dispute is the lowest common level which an audience is willing to accept. The claim of an argument must always fall above the level of dispute. Otherwise, the argument is already accepted.

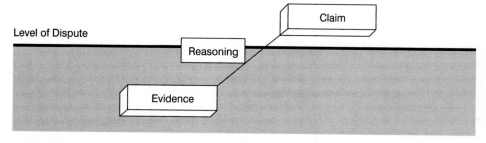

Figure 1–3
The Level of Dispute

Figure 1–3 helps to illustrate the role played by the level of dispute. Evidence in this model falls below the level of dispute because if evidence were disputed and fell above the line, then the evidence itself would need to be proved and anchored to the audience's accepted knowledge. In other words, the evidence would become the subject of an argument. The key is simply that arguments seek to move the audience from positions already accepted to new and different positions. An advocate, then, seeks to use acceptable evidence in order to reason with the audience to accept a new claim. For example, Jim Brady made the argument:

> Add your voice to mine. Help stop random gun violence.
>
> I know firsthand the daily pain of a gunshot wound. And I'm one of the lucky ones. I survived a bullet to the head. Since I was shot eleven years ago, more than 220,000 men, women, and children have been killed in handgun fire. Each night's news seems to bring a more horrible story. Shots fired in a classroom. Two students killed in a high school hallway. Woman shot in the head while driving on a freeway. America's epidemic of random gun violence rages on. . . .
>
> Let your Senators know you want action on the Brady Bill now—before you or someone you love becomes a victim.[20]

Throughout the advertisement, Brady used the audience's knowledge of accidental and deliberate gun deaths and injuries as support for handgun control laws. His examples depended on audience recollections of the attempted assassination in which Brady was injured, reports of handgun violence in the nightly news, and reports his readers have read in their local newspapers. The advertisement assumed an audience sympathetic to gun control. The incidents referred to by Brady that function as evidence fell below the level of dispute; his claims fell above the line; and his reasoning acted as a bridge between what was known (below that line) and what was not known (above the line).

What would happen to the argument if the evidence were not accepted as true by the audience? If the advertisement's readers were unaware of incidents such as those Brady described, he would have to prove that such incidents actually happened. Similarly, the National Rifle Association might object to Brady's evidence that said every police group supported the Brady Bill. If the evidence is not accepted, it becomes an issue for dispute and will itself become a focus for argument.

The level of dispute exists and is drawn in the minds and perceptions of argument recipients. An arguer's objective is to adapt the evidence, reasoning, and claims to the recipient's understanding of the subject being argued. While this may appear to be a relatively straightforward task, it can become more complex as the number of listeners increases. Someone with a great deal of experience in one area may have a relatively high level of dispute. Someone with little knowledge of the area will have a relatively low level of dispute. When these two people are in the same audience, the arguer has the difficult task of adapting to the different levels of dispute of the different individuals. Often the result is argument directed toward the lowest common denominator that everyone in the audience can understand and agree with. While the lowest common denominator approach may appeal to some, it is just as likely to bore the other recipients.

The arguer chooses and adapts the level of dispute to the audience. This is a choice unique for each situation and audience. If an arguer receives feedback indicating confusion or disagreement, he or she may decide to raise or lower the level while arguing. For a critic examining the argument, understanding the level of dispute is important because its location implies the type of recipients assumed by the arguer and offers a better understanding of the argument context.

The third component of the argument, reasoning, connects the evidence and the claim. This is because reasoning serves as a logical and persuasive bridge between the two ends of an argument. By means of the inferences made, reasoning acts to draw a strong relationship between that which is known and accepted and that which is unknown or unaccepted. The reasoning implied in Brady's argument is that a "cooling-off period" will prevent irresponsible persons and criminals from obtaining guns and that public pressure on Congress will promote passage of gun control measures.

Once an argument is proven, what happens to the level of dispute? Logically, if the claim is proven and those to whom it is addressed accept it as a valid conclusion, then the level of dispute rises such that the claim now falls below the line. See Figure 1–4. This means that an advocate can now use a proven argument as evidence for another argument. The process of linking proven claims to unproven claims is called chaining, and is demonstrated in Figure 1–5. *An argument chain simply uses a proven argument as evidence for an unproven claim.* The argument advanced by Jim Brady helped to illustrate this concept. He began with evidence below the level of dispute. He said, "More than 220,000 men, women, and children have been killed. . . . Each night's news seems to bring a more horrible story. Shots fired in a classroom. Two students killed in a high school hallway. Woman shot in the head. . . ." Using this as evidence, Brady advanced the claim "America's epidemic of random gun violence rages on." He then used the audience's acceptance of this claim as evidence for his next claim, "I'm calling on Congress to enact a common sense law—the Brady Bill. . . ." The initial claim about random gun violence was thus used to support the further claim that Congress should enact the Brady Bill.

Level of Dispute

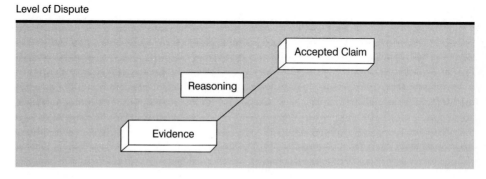

Figure 1–4
Level of Dispute in a Proven Argument

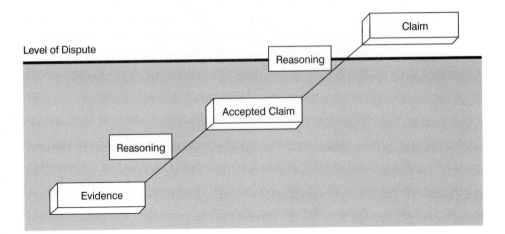

Figure 1–5
An Argument Chain

The concept of chained arguments holds many important implications for building *macro arguments* or argumentative cases. For example, the arguer's central thesis or claim in a macro argument may lie far above the level of dispute and many preliminary claims may have to be established before the central claim is adequately supported. If the arguer begins with facts and premises accepted by everyone to whom the argument is addressed and builds arguments one step at a time, the level of dispute can be raised in increments until the central claim is proven. An extended example illustrating chained claims will be provided in Chapter 3.

■ *Summary*

This book emphasizes arguments and argumentation. An argument is made up of a claim and support. The support for the claim is an attempt to influence someone in a context of disagreement. Arguments are different from promises, commands, or emotive expressions because they offer a claim or expressed opinion for which the arguer seeks acceptance. The support offered for a claim takes the form of evidence and reasoning. Evidence consists of facts or premises accepted by the arguer's audience, while reasoning constructs a rational link between that evidence and the claim for which the arguer seeks acceptance.

Argumentation is the process of making claims intended to justify beliefs, attitudes, and values so as to influence others. Argumentation, which is comprised of individual arguments, is the process by which we reach reasoned decisions regarding laws, policies, and personal matters. Argumentation is based on a common understanding of how reason operates and how arguments are conducted. Argumentation involves critical thinking—the ability to explore a problem, integrate information about it, arrive at a solution, and justify one's considered opinion. Skills involved in critical thinking include collecting, analyzing, and evaluating evidence; identifying relevant issues; drawing sound inferences; detecting fallacies; understanding the implications of an argument; and constructing a case for one's position or proposal.

Argumentation can be viewed from three different but complementary perspectives, each of which emphasizes different aspects of argument. The logical perspective views an argument as a set of premises and a conclusion and is primarily concerned with whether the premises are true and the inference is correctly stated. The dialectical perspective describes argumentation as a process of discovering issues, generating alternatives, establishing standards for judgment, and withholding a decision until all viewpoints have been stated and tested. The rhetorical perspective emphasizes argumentation as a method of influence and considers whether arguers seem aware of the interests and values of the audience and state their arguments appropriately and effectively.

The chapter concluded with an argument model that was intended to illustrate the workings of individual arguments. Arguments are based on statements accepted by their recipients and for which no further support is needed. Because these statements provoke no disagreement, they fall below the level of dispute. When they are successively and successfully used to support new claims, the level of dispute rises and the formerly contested claim becomes a premise for a new argument. When a proven argument is used as evidence for an unproven claim, the result is an argument chain. The concept of a level of dispute is useful because it illustrates how the extent of the recipients' agreement with the arguer's claims may vary as the argument is being made.

This book will focus on argumentation (the process of making reasoned arguments) and on the arguments themselves. It will consider the ethical standards for good argument, the methods of judging the quality of evidence and reasoning, the means for analyzing arguments, the methods of case construction, and the ways in which arguments are effectively communicated. Studying and implementing these skills will improve critical thinking as well as one's ability to provide reasoned justification for one's position on controversial topics.

Exercises

Exercise 1   In defining what an argument is and in comparing arguments to other forms of communication, Chapter 1 identified four arguments in the examples at the beginning of the chapter. Try to identify four more arguments from the same examples. For each argument you can identify, state the claim and the evidence. Remember that the claim and evidence will not always be explicitly stated, although they often are. For example, an additional argument in the editorial on fetal tissue research was:

Implicit Claim: There is disagreement over whether there is reliable scientific evidence supporting fetal tissue transplant.

Evidence: Medical researchers White and Williams found no evi-
                                 dence of benefit from fetal tissue transplants.

Can you locate four other arguments from the discussions that Cindy heard or participated in?

Exercise 2   Can you distinguish a statement that is an argument from one that is
not? Remember that an argument

   a. puts forth a claim,

   b. offers support for it, and

   c. makes an attempt to influence someone.

Now, consider the following statement:

   If it rains tomorrow, I'm going home.

This is not an argument because the speaker offers neither a claim nor support for it.
Rather, he merely states his intention which does not depend on the other person's
acceptance. Furthermore, the speaker does not explicitly try to influence anyone
else but merely states what he himself intends to do. Consider the following statements, decide whether or not they are arguments, and explain the reasons for your
decision. Remember that statements of one's emotional state or pure descriptions
are not generally viewed as arguments.

✳ 1. Monday's unanimous Supreme Court ruling on a St. Paul, Minn., hate-crimes law must
      be recognized not as a ground-breaking victory for the most loathsome among us and
      their hateful, hurtful screed. Rather it should be recognized as yet another in a series
      of reasoned, constitutionally anchored defenses of the basic, precious right of free
      speech.

                                 "A Sound Ruling on Free Speech," *Seattle Times*,
                                 June 24, 1992, A8.

   2. FRED: Why are you leaving so early for the meeting?

      GALE: Sue asked me to pick her up on the way. Are you going
                      to watch that movie at 8 o'clock?

      FRED: Yeah. It lasts until 10 and then I thought I'd go to bed
                      early.

      GALE: Fine. I'll see you in the morning.

   3. Because surgeon's work is more tangible and precise, surgery was the first area of
      medicine to come under critical scrutiny. For a half century, the American College of
      Surgeons has condemned operations by insufficiently qualified surgeons, fee soliciting
      between surgeons and the physicians who send them patients, and needless surgery.

                                 "TIME Essay," *Time*, December 17, 1973, 56.

4. I try to remember when this rivalry between my daughter and me first began. I can't. It sometimes seems that we have always been this way with each other, that we have never gotten along any better or differently, I would like to make my daughter less miserable if I can, to help her be happier and much more pleased with herself, I don't know how.

> Joseph Heller, *Something Happened* (New York: Ballantine Books, 1974), 179.

✳ 5. JOHN: Should we figure the raises on a 3 percent cost of living increase plus merit?

   JUDY: That will work as long as we have enough in the budget to cover it. How much is available to us?

   DAN: Well, we do have a reserve fund to cover any excesses. I think we should start out with what the staff ought to receive and concern ourselves with what's available later on.

   JUDY: That sounds fine to me, as long as we have some excess.

6. For twelve years I served as a faculty member and principal academic/administrative officer of a small liberal arts college which made an effort to reach a larger number of minority students, eventually reaching 48 percent of our total enrollment. In addition to increasing their numbers, we endeavored to get more of them to major in the natural and physical sciences rather than to follow the tendency of earlier entrants toward the social sciences.

> J. Herman Blake, "Approach Minority Students as Assets," *Academe,* November–December 1985, 19.

7. The immense suffering by animals in connection with the fur industry is staggering and it pains me that so many men and women seem to be so totally indifferent to this fact. Maybe someday people will wake up and remember what Jesus said about the animals: "What you do unto them, you do unto me."

> Letter to the Editor, *Seattle Times,* December 29, 1985, A19.

8. In order to save the most-endangered species, The Endangered Species Act diverts attention and money from the much more crucial goal of preserving biological diversity—that is, preserving the maximum number of healthy species in ecosystems that require a minimum of maintenance. The way to save species is to save the places where they live.

> Suzanne Winckler, "Stopgap Measures," *The Atlantic* (January 1992): 78.

✳ ***Exercise 3***   This chapter introduced you to an advertisement featuring James Brady. The following is the complete text of the ad. The chapter developed this example extensively; now see if you can read the full advertisement and accomplish the following objectives without referring back to the explanations.

   1. Locate all the claims, reasoning, and evidence in the ad. Draw a line under each one and label it as claim, evidence, or reasoning.

2. Explain the meaning and implications of this ad using a logical, a dialectical, and a rhetorical perspective. How do they differ? How does shifting from one perspective to another change the way we look at the arguments?

3. What critical conclusions can you reach about the argument? Does it seem sound? How might Brady have improved the argument?

James S. Brady, President Reagan's Press Secretary, shot on March 30, 1981 by John Hinckley

Please help me save lives. Add your voice to mine. Help stop random gun violence.

I know firsthand the daily pain of a gunshot wound. And I'm one of the lucky ones. I survived a bullet to the head. Since I was shot eleven years ago, more than 220,000 men, women, and children have been killed in handgun fire. Each night's news seems to bring a more horrible story. Shots fired in a classroom. Two students killed in a high school hallway. Woman shot in the head while driving on a freeway. America's epidemic of random gun violence rages on.

I'm calling on Congress to enact a common sense law—the Brady Bill—requiring a "cooling-off" period before the purchase of a handgun so police can run a thorough background check on the buyer. Time to cool off a hot temper. Time to screen out illegal purchasers. Every major police group in America supports this public safety measure.

So why hasn't Congress passed the Brady Bill? Because too many Members of Congress are either afraid of the hardcore gun lobby or pocket the gun lobby's PAC money. Like Senator Phil Gramm (R-TX) who has received more than $349,000 in campaign support from the NRA since 1984.

Right now, the Brady Bill is being blocked from final passage by Senator Gramm and a few others controlled by the gun lobby. We need to send these politicians a message. It's time to put public safety ahead of politics. If our legislators really care about saving lives, they will pass the Brady Bill.

Let your Senators know you want action on the Brady Bill now—before you or someone you love becomes a victim.[20]

Notes

1. Elenor Loarie Schoen, "Fetal Tissue Research Degrades Science, Life," *Seattle Times,* April 4, 1992, A7. Used by permission.

2. Daniel J. O'Keefe, "Two Concepts of Argument," *Journal of the American Forensic Association* 13 (1977): 121–28; and "The Concepts of Argument and Arguing," in J. Robert Cox and Charles Arthur Willard, eds., *Advances in Argumentation Theory and Research* (Carbondale, Ill.: Southern Illinois University Press, (1982): 3–23.

3. For studies of interpersonal argument, see Sally Jackson and Scott Jacobs, "Structure of Conversational Argument: Pragmatic Bases for the Enthymeme," *Quarterly Journal of Speech* 66, (1980): 251–265; and "Conversational Argument: A Discourse Analytic Approach," in Cox and Willard, *Advances in Argumentation Theory and Research,* 205–37.

4. Frans H. van Eemeren and Rob Grootendorst, *Speech Acts in Argumentative Discussions* (Dordrecht, Netherlands: Foris Publications, 1984), 97–108.

5. The term "grounds" is applied to the original data or evidence upon which an argument is based in Stephen Toulmin, Richard Rieke, and Allan Janik, *An Introduction to Reasoning,* 2nd ed. (New York: Macmillan Co., 1984), 37–44.

6. Evidence does not consist only of facts. From a *rhetorical* point of view (i.e., that arguers seek acceptance for their claims *from audiences*), it makes sense to regard any proposition or belief *accepted by everyone in the audience* as a starting point for argument. There are many statements ("A person is innocent until proven guilty"; "One ought to keep one's promises") that are *not* facts but that could function as evidence in relation to a claim.

7. Stephen Toulmin, *The Uses of Argument* (Cambridge: Cambridge University Press, 1969), 98.

8. van Eemeren and Grootendorst, 79.

9. Douglas Ehninger and Wayne Brockreide, *Decision by Debate,* 1st ed. (New York: Dodd, Mead, & Co., 1963), 7.

10. Ehninger, "Argument as Method: Its Nature, Its Limitations, and Its Uses," *Speech Monographs,* 37 (1970): 102–03.

11. H. P. Grice, "Logic and Conversation," in Peter Cole and Jerry L. Morgan, eds., *Syntax and Semantics: vol 3. Speech Acts* (New York: Academic Press, 1975) 45.

12. Joanne G. Kurfiss, *Critical Thinking: Theory, Research, Practice, and Possibilities* (Washington, D.C.: Association for the Study of Higher Education, 1975), 2.

13. Kurfiss, 2–3; see also James H. McMillan, "Enhancing College Students' Critical Thinking: A Review of Studies," *Research in Higher Education* 26 (1987): 3–29.

14. Glen E. Mills and Hugh G. Petrie, "The Role of Logic in Rhetoric," *Quarterly Journal of Speech* 54 (1968): 260–67; and Hugh G. Petrie, "Does Logic Have Any Relevance to Argumentation?" *Journal of the American Forensic Association* 6 (1969): 55–60.

15. Ray Lynn Anderson and C. David Mortenson, "Logic and Marketplace Argumentation," *Quarterly Journal of Speech* 53 (1967): 143–151.

16. George Ziegelmueller, Jack Kay, and Charles A. Dause, *Argumentation: Inquiry and Advocacy* (Englewood Cliffs, N.J.: Prentice-Hall, 1990), 3.

17. Joseph W. Wenzel, "Three Perspectives on Argument," in Robert Trapp and Janice Schuetz, eds., *Perspectives on Argumentation* (Prospect Heights, Ill.: Waveland Press, 1990), 9–26.

18. Joan Burton, "The Spotted Owl: A Victim of Forest Plans?" *The Mountaineer* 80, no. 7 (July 1986), 8. Used by permission.

19. Chaim Perelman and Lucie Olbrechts-Tyteca, *The New Rhetoric: A Treatise on Argumentation,* trans. J. Wilkinson and P. Weaver (Notre Dame: University of Notre Dame Press, 1969), 34.

20. James S. Brady, "Please Help Me Save Lives" [advertisement], *New York Times,* March 31, 1992. Used by permission of Handgun Control, Inc., Washington, D.C.

21. J. Michael Sproule, *Argument: Language and Its Influence* (New York: McGraw-Hill, 1980), 7. Sproule develops the concept of "surface of dispute" and uses a diagram similar to our argument chain diagram to illustrate visible arguments and assumed arguments.

CHAPTER 2

Arguments in Context

CHAPTER OUTLINE

- Context Element 1: Culture
- Context Element 2: Argument Fields
- Context Element 3: Argument Occasion
- Context Element 4: Ethics
- Summary
- Exercises

KEY CONCEPTS

culture
field-dependent standards
argument occasion
exigence

argument fields
field-invariant standards
rhetorical situation
ethics

Arguments are a pervasive and common part of our lives. We make arguments, listen to them, evaluate them, and based on our understanding of them, we choose to act or think in different ways. Arguments are very powerful. With our words, we have the potential to shape our own lives as well as the lives of those around us.

When we use arguments well, we can help our audiences think of alternatives they may never have considered and we might help them evaluate their decisions in better ways. At the same time, if we use arguments improperly or deceitfully, we have an equal opportunity for clouding issues, concealing the best choices, and leading our audiences to the wrong decisions.

The power of argumentation and its influence on people is considerable. We should not take our arguments for granted but should understand their effects. Given the context in which they are made, we should be able to evaluate whether our arguments are appropriate, reasonable, and ethical. Although these might seem like intuitive and obvious considerations for any arguer, the means for making reasonable and ethical arguments are not always apparent. Discovering the "right" arguments and still being able to make our points is often as difficult as constructing the arguments themselves. Furthermore, the appropriate argument is not always apparent and may change as our recipients change their attitudes, beliefs, values, and actions.

This chapter focuses on argument contexts and how contexts influence the way arguers and recipients make choices about argument construction and evaluation. Understanding how argument contexts influence the production and evaluations of arguments is important as argumentation theorist Joseph Wenzel explained when he wrote:

> In the course of social life, we pass through innumerable contexts in which arguing may occur. All of these are framed by the general matrix of our sociocultural system as well as by special features of each occasion.[1]

Argument contexts are comprised of four elements: culture, field, occasion, and ethics. This chapter will examine each of these elements and their importance for understanding how arguments function. Figure 2–1 presents a model of argument context. In this model, the common area that is created by overlapping culture, field, occasion, and ethics represents an ideal locus or point for argument. It is the realm within which advocates should strive to place their arguments. When speakers present their arguments, they should attempt to make arguments that are appropriate for their culture, field, occasion, and ethical context; in other words, arguers should make arguments within the locus for argument. Arguments not situated in this locus will not be adequately adapted to the situation or to the audience.

The following sections of this chapter will detail each of the elements of argument contexts. It is important for arguers to understand how contexts function and appreciate how differences in the four context elements can change or alter argument contexts. As you read this chapter, you should try and develop an understanding and sensitivity about how pervasive and influential argument contexts are.

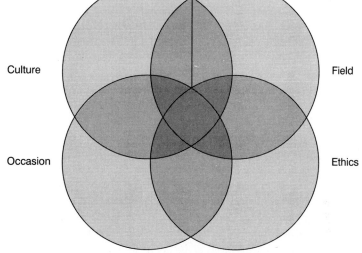

Figure 2–1
The junction of culture, field, occasion, and ethics is the locus for argument.

■ *Context Element 1: Culture*

Culture has been the subject of much controversy because while we all know that we belong to a culture, what defines any given culture is often difficult to describe or understand. Generally, however, culture can be defined as *systems of shared meanings that are expressed through different symbolic forms such as symbols, rituals, stories, and myths and that hold a group of people together.*[2] This is a fairly complex definition that requires some explanation.

First, culture requires systems of shared meanings. This means simply that for a culture to exist, people must have a way of understanding one another. This idea is developed in greater detail in Chapter 11 when we discuss the uses of language and the development of meaning. But, at its root, culture requires some communication form. If you have ever met someone unable to understand English, you appreciate why this is an important consideration for culture. When we cannot communicate verbally, we often seek to communicate with one another nonverbally by drawing pictures, making gestures, or pointing. Our goal is to understand one another and the only way culture is possible is when we each have a system that allows us to share our meanings so we can reach mutual understanding.

Communication patterns can set distinct cultures apart and can unite the members of a culture. In his book *Coming Apart*, William O'Neill wrote that during the late 1960s music became a medium for communication that identified a youth culture and made arguments for philosophical and ideological perspectives.[3] O'Neill wrote:

> Where once entertainers were content to amuse for profit, many began seeing themselves as moral philosophers. Music especially became the medium of propaganda, identifying the young as a distinct force in society with unique values and aspirations.[4]

Specialized communication can bring people together and identify them with a culture or it can separate and segregate them. In this role, arguments are a powerful cultural force.

Second, cultures contain symbolic forms such as rituals, stories, specialized language, and myths. They give us a shared history and mythology that helps provide a common framework or understanding of one another.

Our cultural mythology takes many forms. It may consist of historical accounts of significant events, it may be largely fictitious legends, or it may be entirely imagined fables. Similarly, rituals are common cultural practices and consist of such things as initiations, rites of passage, religious ceremonies, and the like. All these elements of our mythology and cultural heritage serve to provide the members of a culture with a common understanding of cultural purpose and unity.

The truthfulness of our cultural mythology is less important than that the members of a culture understand these stories and use them as part of a common experience that binds the membership together. For example, if asked who the first president of the United States was, a member of the United States' culture would probably respond, "George Washington." In fact, most of us may be able to recount a variety of stories about Washington: He told the truth about chopping down a cherry tree, he crossed the Delaware to attack the Hessians, and he threw a dollar across the Potomac River. Yet, there is fair evidence that some of these stories are not true. For instance, Washington was not really the first president of the United States. A man by the name of John Hanson from Maryland served as the first president of the United States under the Articles of Confederation. And, according to Tad Tuleja, author of *Fabulous Fallacies*, there were seven other presidents before Washington was elected.[5] Regardless of the historical accuracy of the traditional and commonly understood account, however, Washington serves as a cultural icon that represents a common thread of understanding for members of the United States' culture. All Americans identify with the myth and that provides a common framework for understanding.

For an arguer, understanding the culture in which the argument is developed is important. Different cultures, with their different experiences and frameworks for interpretation, understand and evaluate arguments differently. In the United States, for instance, we are surrounded with arguments about whether abortion is right or wrong. Members of the pro-choice movement argue that women should have the right to choose and to control their own bodies and that abortion decisions should not be left to the government. On the other hand, members of the pro-life movement argue that human life begins with conception and that the choice to abort a pregnancy is tantamount to murder. While this remains a controversial issue decades after the Supreme Court handed down the *Roe v. Wade* decision that legalized abortion, few Americans would argue that abortion should be used as a preferred means of birth control.

While members of both sides of the issue might agree on this simple premise, the normative standards imposed by each movement's culture for evaluating arguments would be different. For example, cultural assumptions about when life begins would change the way arguments are evaluated in the context. If the cultural understanding is that life begins at conception, then the argument that abortion through the first trimester is warranted or justifiable would be equated with an argument for murder. Similarly, if the cultural understanding of life presumes that life does not begin until the fetus is viable outside the womb, then abortion could not be considered murder. Understanding and criticizing the two arguments depends on the cultural context in which they are placed.

Culture provides us with a framework for understanding and interpreting arguments and helps us evaluate their appropriateness. As people become adjusted to a culture, they learn the basic assumptions of that culture so that they can perform their roles and abide by its rules, values, and morality. When we make an argument, our recipients understand our basic cultural assumptions and use them as a framework for evaluating ideas and arguments. For instance, Western European and American cultures, among others, hold cultural assumptions about the value of life, truth telling, hard work, and family.

Cultural standards constantly evolve as the social groupings and institutions change. As difficult as it might be to accept now, slavery was once accepted in some segments of American culture as an economically necessary and socially justifiable practice. Now slavery is viewed as reprehensible, and many Americans have fought institutions such as South African apartheid that contained elements of slavery or racism. Similarly, at end of the nineteenth century it was common to hear people argue against women's right to vote. It is difficult to imagine anyone arguing for denying women the right to vote now.

Arguers are faced with two challenges in understanding how culture affects arguments. First, cultural rules and norms are not always obvious. Many cultural themes, myths, and stories that provide arguers with a common framework for understanding arguments are unstated and just "understood" by the members of the culture. This means that arguers need to be sensitive and observant so as to understand how arguments "fit" within a particular cultural framework without violating generally held cultural rules or norms.

The second challenge faced by arguers is that cultures have depth. In other words, cultures are not large homogeneous groups of people but are subdivided into many groupings of specialized cultures called subcultures. Subcultures possess their own traditions, beliefs, and values and at the same time are a part of the traditions, beliefs, and values of the host culture.

Within the American host culture, there are many subcultures. For instance, African-American, Asian, and Native American cultures are all members of the American host culture but have their own traditions, rituals, and norms that bind them together. Furthermore, each subculture may be further divided into additional subcultures with unique cultural characteristics.

The civil rights movement of the 1960s provides a good example of divided subcultures. During that decade, African-Americans constituted a subculture that sought racial equality. Their history, traditions, and basic cultural assumptions defined a community that was unique from the host American culture. Yet, even the African-American subculture was further divided into subgroups that prized nonviolence and followed the teachings of Dr. Martin Luther King, Jr., and those that followed a more militant segment of the subculture such as Stokely Carmichael and his followers. While King preached nonviolent resistance and integration, Carmichael preached violence and separatism. He said:

> It seems to me that the institutions that function in this country are clearly racist, and that they're built upon racism. . . . How can we begin to build institutions that will allow people to relate with each other as human beings? This country has never done that. . . . Now several people have been upset because we've said that integration was irrelevant when initiated by blacks and that in fact it was a subterfuge, an insidious subterfuge for the maintenance of white supremacy. We maintain that in the past six years or so this country has been feeding us a thalidomide drug of integration, and that some Negroes have been walking down a dream street talking about sitting next to white people. . . . We were never fighting for the right to integrate, we were fighting against white supremacy. . . . We are tired of trying to explain to white people that we're not going to hurt them. We are concerned with getting the things we want, the things that we have to have to be able to function. The question is, can white people allow for that in this country? . . . If that does not happen, brothers and sisters, we have no choice, but to say very clearly, move on over, or we're going to move on over you.[6]

Within any culture or subcultures, separate groups look for identity and recognition. We can visualize the relationship between host cultures and subcultures as illustrated in Figure 2–2. In this figure, the larger circle represents the dominant culture. Its basic assumptions (listed as A, B, and C) may be subscribed to by each of the smaller subcultures within it. Yet, the smaller subcultures have their independent traditions and institutions (shown with additional letters). For instance, consider the many different subcultures that function within the United States. Richard E. Porter, an intercultural communication scholar, wrote that:

> Today in the United States we find many cultures. Some are based on race. . . . Others are based on ethnic differences. . . . There are also cultures based on socioeconomic differences. . . . And, finally, cultures develop around ways of life and values systems. Members of the drug culture share perceptions of the world and values that are vastly different from those shared, for example, by members of the John Birch Society or the Ku Klux Klan. Or there are followers of Reverend Moon, members of the gay community, or activists in the feminist movement who all have different perceptions and belief-value structures.[7]

For any of these subcultures within the United States, we could make the following statements about their membership:

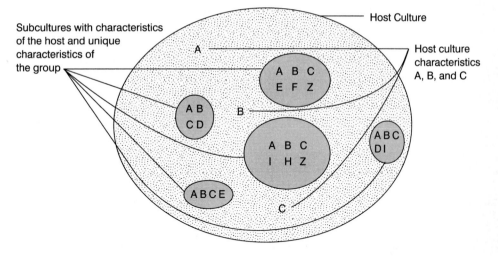

Figure 2–2
Within a dominant culture are subcultures with independent traditions and institutions.

1. We all share a common U.S. history and U.S. government.
2. We are all subject to the provisions of the Constitution, Bill of Rights, and other federal and state laws.

Of course, there are many other rules and conventions that members of our culture adhere to that are given to us from the host culture. At the same time, however, there are unique norms and rules that guide each of the subcultures. These might include:

- values and expectations for education, career, and social choices
- attitudes about government, law, or other cultures

Again, these are only two among many possible unique characteristics possessed by subcultures. Subcultural differences distinguish the subculture from the host culture, and serve to specify a unique grouping of people within the culture.

Arguments made in one subculture draw on the assumptions, evidence, and reasoning recognized by the cultural grouping for which they are presented. Further, the members of one group would evaluate arguments differently from members of another group based on cultural differences. The distinction between cultures and successful argument was made by K. S. Sitaram when he said:

> What is an effective communication symbol in one culture could be an obscene gesture in another culture. The communication technique that makes a person successful in New York could kill him in New Delhi.[8]

While Sitaram's conclusion may seem extreme for an arguer, it points out that arguments can have different effects in different cultures. At some point in our lives, most of us will make an argument for why a prospective employer should hire us. With our resumes and our interviews we will provide evidence and claims about our abilities and future promise. But the kinds of arguments an American might use to secure a job are different from the arguments used by other cultures. This was the lesson learned by many workers in the former Soviet Union as they began to apply for jobs in Western-owned businesses after the fall of the Soviet Union. A Russian, Vladimir Soloviev, recognizing that most Soviet citizens never had to interview or prepare a resume to secure employment, conducted classes to train people for the Western job market. *The Wall Street Journal* provided an interesting description:

> "People at McDonald's smile a lot," Mr. Soloviev says. "Russian workers don't. That's how we differ from the West." For the uninformed, Mr. Soloviev offers a helpful demonstration: "A smile is when both corners of your mouth go up at the same time." Several students scribble in their notebooks. . . .
>
> For many Russians, job hunting is a process full of mystery and fraught with anxiety. Few have ever gone to a job interview. . . . In the past, jobs were either assigned by the state or arranged through personal connections. Resumes were meaningless. The document that mattered was the Communist Party's dossier, which followed an employee from one workplace to another.
>
> "Most Russians don't know the basics of how to make themselves attractive to an employer," says Mr. Soloviev. . . . "They're shocked to learn that there are certain ways to dress or act."
>
> As an illustration, he recalls a female applicant who was interviewed by Coca-Cola. . . . When the representative offered her a can of Coke, "she told him, 'I don't drink this trash.' . . . End of interview."
>
> . . .students should think about wardrobe. Women. . .should not look sexy. Men should wear a standard dark suit with a single-color tie—"not some Chinese jungle tie," he says. "You go to Coca-Cola with a leather jacket and you're dead meat. You go to a British company wearing funny stuff, forget it. And the most important thing: Never, never wear white socks with a dark suit."[9]

Different cultures prescribe different norms for argument. The way we understand and interpret arguments changes as the cultural expectations change. Although the plight of former Soviet citizens in the Western job market may seem humorous, it illustrates that the basic cultural assumptions that people take for granted are not present in other cultures. The result is that people don't understand the context of argument they operate within.

Perhaps this was nowhere more evident than in the October 1991 confirmation hearings for Supreme Court Justice nominee Clarence Thomas. Law school professor Anita Hill alleged that while she worked for Thomas he had sexually harassed her by repeatedly pressuring her to go to dinner or engage in other social activities and by telling her inappropriate or lewd jokes. The Thomas/Hill hearings prompted a nationwide debate about sexual harassment and the relationship between men and women. What became evident from both the hearings and following discussions is that what men perceive as harassing and what women perceive as harassing is different.

■ *Context Element 2: Argument Fields*

Argument fields are similar, in many ways, to culture. They provide arguers with a context for making and interpreting arguments and they provide arguers with a common ground or framework for conducting disputes. The very fact that an argument takes place in a law court, a corporate board room, a medical care setting, or an art class may influence the procedures that are used, the conventions employed, and the standards that are applied to make judgments about arguments. Perhaps argumentation theorist Joseph Wenzel put it best when he said that although fields can be very difficult to define, they do refer to "*some* sort of universe of discourse."[10] Without an understanding of argument fields, we would have a difficult time producing or evaluating arguments.

In *The Uses of Argument* and subsequent works, the philosopher Stephen Toulmin termed such argument universes or argument situations as *argument fields*.[11] Although Toulmin's description of fields was ambiguous, he offered them as a way to better understand both the "form and merits" of argument.[12] Based on Toulmin's analysis and subsequent scholarly discussion, we can define the fields as follows: *Argument fields are the sociological contexts for arguments bound together by recurring patterns of communication and commonly accepted by participants in argumentative disputes.* The arenas in which arguments are developed influence the forms of argument, the bases on which inferences are made, and the means for deciding disputes. They are both social and communicative phenomena. In other words, fields for argument are made by people through interaction; they act as the source for the conventions and criteria used in conducting arguments and they are an important feature of arguments.[13]

Argument fields include such examples as law, ethics, medicine, science, and aesthetics. Furthermore, each of these fields has subfields (e.g., tort law, family law, criminal law) that themselves function as fields of argument. Describing what fields exist at any given moment can be difficult because we are constantly surrounded by and involved in many different fields. Nevertheless, the field in which arguments are produced affects the nature of the argument; as the field changes so does the way the argument is constructed. Robert Rowland made the point that it "seems obvious that arguments vary by field."[14]

Although fields can be complex and difficult to isolate, generally, fields share five common characteristics. First, they are a human creation.[15] This means that fields develop over a period of time through social interaction. Second, fields are developed by people with shared goals.[16] People sustain interaction and develop fields when they share objectives and purposes. In science, for example, the purpose is to identify the laws of nature; in ethics, the purpose is to distinguish what is good and morally right from what is not; and in medicine, the purpose is to promote health by preventing and curing illness. Third, fields develop specialized language and rules.[17] When people converse to achieve their objectives, there are certain rules of conduct as well as language that facilitate their objectives. We may call such specialized language *jargon* but for the members of a field, the language carries unique meanings. Fourth, people may belong to many fields.[18] Humans share many different objectives and adhere to many different sets of rules. Therefore, we can be members of as many fields as serve our interests or objectives. Fifth, a field will survive only as long as the field serves the common purpose of its members and as long as it can adapt to changing objectives.[19] When a field no longer serves its members and cannot adapt to meet their needs, it will disappear.

Any field can be characterized by these five dimensions. For example, if we look at the field of politics, we could say first that politics is a human creation. Politicians were not needed until human beings perceived the need for them. Second, politics consists of people with shared goals. Some might say politicians simply want to exercise power and others might say that politicians want to make a better and more just world. In either case, politicians become politicians to achieve similar and shared goals, namely, to provide leadership for their country. Third, politicians develop their own specialized language to describe the activities and directions in their field. They can talk about a resolution, censure, election return, impeachment, electoral college, caucus, primary, or hearings. In each case, these words when used by politicians have specialized meanings and connotations that are peculiar to their use in the field of politics. Fourth, politicians may belong to many other fields. Some politicians may be lawyers and share legal field objectives and language. Finally, politicians need to be able to adapt to changing conditions and times for the field to survive. Public disillusionment with political perquisites and privileges threatens the political field. Unless the members can adapt to their constituents' needs, there may arise term limitations, salary caps, and other restrictions that will force members from the field or cause voters to redefine the field.

Toulmin, among others, has concluded that arguments are judged according to the standards of the field for which they are produced.[20] Different standards are applied in the field of law, for example, than in the field of politics. The legal field's standards for regulating the use of evidence and determining the charge to be brought against a defendant are much more precise and clearly defined than the political field's standards for deciding what policy should be implemented to address a social problem.

Argument fields are important for arguers and critics alike because they provide us with a means of judging arguments. When we evaluate arguments to determine whether they are true or false, good or bad, valid or invalid, we apply two sets of tests: field-dependent standards and field-invariant standards.[21] *Field-dependent standards are the rules, norms, and prescriptions guiding the production of arguments in a particular field.* These are the standards that the particular field identifies as appropriate for evaluating arguments. Therefore, legal standards pertaining to hearsay evidence applied to legal arguments would constitute field-dependent standards.

Field-invariant standards apply generally, regardless of the field of argument. All arguments must have the required parts of an argument: claim, evidence, reasoning, and attempt to influence. This requirement is invariant, in other words, regardless of the field, an argument should have these parts. Similarly, if evidence and reasoning are used inappropriately (perhaps the evidence is fabricated) or the audience's emotions are played upon by the arguer to avoid criticism or thoughtful judgment, then the argument would be considered fallacious regardless of the field.

Arguers should be aware of the requirements of the fields in which they argue. The selection of a field for argument implies the grounds to be used in making a decision. The legal field uses precedent (decisions rendered in earlier, similar cases) and various types of charges (extortion, property damage, manslaughter, and so forth) to judge issues supporting the claim. Argument fields also imply certain peculiar burdens or requirements that must be addressed. A jury, for instance, must believe a defendant guilty beyond a reasonable doubt. Furthermore, the legal field implies specific rigorous rules of evidence (hearsay is inadmissible, affidavits must be notarized, testimony must come from witnesses or disciplinary experts, and so forth). Yet, in other fields these rules may not apply at all.

The notion of an argument field is valuable because understanding fields helps arguers understand many of the rules and conventions for judging between competing claims in a controversy. Depending on which standards from which fields are applied to arguments, the results can be very different. This is why it is important for advocates to be aware of the fields from which they argue and to learn as much about the field for argument as about the subject they are arguing.

▪ *Context Element 3: Argument Occasion*

As with so many other human events, in argumentation timing is everything. Arguments (or any form of communication) may be interpreted very differently at different times. All communication is generally bound by its particular occasion. For example, the first edition of this text was published in 1989 and used many examples of arguments about the Soviet Union and the Cold War. If these same arguments were made today, they would be considered outdated and inapplicable given current events and the dissolution of the U.S.S.R. *Argument occasion refers to the rhetorical situation of the argument.* Perhaps the person most noted for his development of the "rhetorical situation" is a theorist named Lloyd F. Bitzer.[22]

The rhetorical situation is a natural context of persons, events, objects, relations, and an exigence which strongly invites arguments. Therefore, every argument exists in a particular and unique occasion. The occasion is made up of the audience, the arguer, the experiences of the audience and arguer, and what Bitzer refers to as exigence. *Exigence can be defined as "an imperfection marked by urgency; it is a defect, an obstacle, something waiting to be done, a thing which is other than it should be."*[23] In other words, arguments are not developed randomly but are instead called into existence by some exigence—there is some cause or reason for us to argue. When Martin Luther King, Jr., presented his "I Have a Dream" speech, he presented it to a particular audience at a particular time. He was responding to decades of discrimination and he was urging action on a pending comprehensive civil rights bill. His audience was comprised of more than 250,000 people who had come to Washington, D.C., to protest for civil rights. It was the largest demonstration ever held in the United States to that time and the situation required a cornerstone address. King's address met the exigence of the situation.

Not all exigencies, however, require such important arguments. Presenting an argument in class to fulfill the requirements of an assignment may address the exigence of the assignment, but it also addresses an exigence in a larger sense. *An exigence is also a contemporary problem or issue that needs to be addressed.* This is why classroom assignments address significant or important issues as opposed to the trivial. The exigence is like a question waiting for an answer. The point is simply that particular occasions call for particular arguments, and speakers who are able to identify and understand the requirements of the rhetorical situation may be able to develop arguments that "fit" the needs of the argument context.

Generally, argument occasions have four characteristics. First, the occasion invites arguments. Our arguments are in response to some problem, proposition, or other issue that we are attempting to address. Without a problem there is little reason for argument. King's "I Have a Dream" speech was designed in response to a problem of racial inequality. If the United States was truly integrated—if King's "Dream" had already been fulfilled—there would have been no need for the speech and it is unlikely King would have presented it.

Second, the argument must be fitting to the occasion. Even though arguers may be able to identify a problem, not just any argument will fit the situation. If King, for instance, had written a speech about the need for more space exploration or better pay for migrant farm workers, the speech would not have fit the situation because the audience and occasion would not have been appropriate for the subject. Similarly, if an advocate makes an argument that is not relevant or does not address the important issues of a dispute, then the argument does not fit.

Third, situations prescribe the criteria for a fitting response. If we agree that a response must fit the situation, the requirements for the fit should be clear. This means that if King's speech fit the situation, then the criteria for judging the fit must be identifiable such that King could have understood them and adapted the speech to them. King knew that he was expected to offer a message of hope to those engaged in the struggle for civil rights, acknowledge the sacrifices many had made, call for redress of discrimination against persons of color, and emphasize the importance of nonviolent protest. He did all of this so admirably and his speech so fit the occasion that it has always been regarded as a masterful speech.

Fourth, argumentative situations are impermanent. This means that just as situations arise and invite argument, they also dissolve or become unimportant. Just as some questions go unanswered, so do situations. Situations, then, are temporary and if unanswered will dissipate and lose their significance. Had King chosen not to speak during the demonstration, his opportunity for argument would have been lost and "I Have a Dream" might have been nothing more than a manuscript somewhere. Even if he had spoken a day later, the situation would have dissipated as the demonstration broke up and people went home.

■ *Context Element 4: Ethics*

Just as arguments can be used to help people make better decisions, arguments can also undermine and harm people. As with any tool, arguments have the capacity to improve our lives or to damage them. The difference rests in how the arguer selects to use arguments and how recipients evaluate them.

When arguers use arguments to oppress others, mislead their audiences, evade the truth, and deceive the public, the repercussions can be felt for generations. Millions of people in Europe died because the Nazis believed Adolf Hitler's argument that their misfortunes were caused by the Jewish people. Many lives and careers were ruined in the early 1950s when the public believed Joseph McCarthy's false claims and accusations about Communist infiltration. President Richard Nixon and his advisors sought to conceal illegal activities through half-truths and evasions during the Watergate cover-up. During President Reagan's administration, Oliver North, an aide to the National Security Council, admitted that he had lied and misrepresented the facts regarding the Iran/contra arms dealings in earlier testimony.

Because arguments have the potential to do great harm, people involved in arguments have a responsibility to be vigilant about the quality and integrity of arguments they present and receive. In other words, all people involved in arguments share an ethical responsibility. *Ethics is the study of what is morally right or just.* When we abide by the prescriptions of our ethics (for example, we do not lie, attempt to cause injury to others, or deceive) our arguments are considered ethical. However, when we use the power inherent in arguments to persuade people based on deception or argumentative trickery, then our arguments are considered unethical.

As citizens of a democratic society and as private individuals, we must be critical of the arguments addressed to us and scrupulous in presenting arguments to others. Evasion, deception, and misrepresentation cause public distrust, poor decision making, and occasionally outright harm and injury to individuals. We must, therefore, be aware of the quality of our arguments and knowledgeable about standards that will enable us to distinguish arguments that are ethically or morally right from those that are wrong. The remainder of this chapter, therefore, will consider the question, "What is an ethical argument?"

We are constantly influenced by ethical codes for conduct, whether they are formally stated or informally understood. Because ethics are often not formally stated, however, we are challenged with making the "right" decision based on what we believe is the correct action. For example, what would you do if you found a $100 bill on a sidewalk outside of a store? If there is no identification on the money, do you keep it? Do you give it to the clerk in the store? Do you take it to a police station? This can be a difficult choice and your decision will depend on what you believe to be the correct or just choice. Another ethical issue is raised by the *Mason Country Journal,* a newspaper in Shelton, Washington, that routinely publishes the names of rape suspects and victims alike (including juvenile rape victims). The paper's argument is that its job is to publicize the full record of Shelton and rapes are a part of that record. However, releasing the names has disrupted the lives of many women and young girls. Is that ethical? The answers are not always clear.

Ethicists have long considered the nature of ethical conduct and how different ethical requirements and rules emerge from a variety of fields. While understanding how ethics function in any given field can be difficult, ethics in argumentation generally operate at two levels: a content level and a relationship level.

First, some ethical principles govern the content of arguments. Such ethics evaluate whether the claim, evidence, reasoning, and attempt to influence are moral, good, or just. Such a position was taken by Wayne Minnick when he wrote that an ethical communicator should

> reject all frauds, deceptions, concealments, specious arguments; cultivate the capacity for careful investigation and judicial and reflective deliberation of controversies and problems; endorse only those positions whose truth-claim merits his advocacy; must use intrinsically sound methods; use ethically neutral methods in ways that are consistent and can be defended by reliable evidence and sound reasoning.[24]

Minnick's position seems reasonable enough. If we speak the truth and use care in selecting appropriate arguments, then we are behaving ethically.

Richard L. Johannesen wrote in *Ethics in Human Communication* that what is ethical or unethical can be evaluated from many different perspectives including religion, politics, and law.[25] From the religious perspective, arguments are evaluated by a series of "thou-shalt-nots" which prescribes the right from the wrong. For example, lying, slander, and deception are all considered unethical as described in a religious document such as the Bible. The political perspective derives its ethics from a set of values and criteria unique to the political system. Johannesen noted:

> Naturally each different political system could embody differing values leading to differing ethical judgments. Within the context of American representative democracy, for instance, various analysts pinpoint values and procedures they view as fundamental to optimum functioning of our political system. . . .[26]

These values include respect for the dignity and worth of the individual, fairness and equality, freedom, and the ability to understand and participate in democracy. Anything that enhances these values is viewed as ethical, and acts that undermine them are viewed as unethical. Yet, making such a clearly defined distinction is not always so easy. While the standards for determining what is ethical might seem simple and clear, often they are not—especially when different people hold widely different values and views of what is ethical or not.[27]

For example, take the case of Dr. Jack Kevorkian, also known in media circles as Dr. Death. Between June 1990 and February 1993, he assisted fifteen people in taking their own lives through the use of his "suicide machine" and the use of carbon monoxide poisoning. Each of his patients wanted to die and had asked for help. Kevorkian assisted them in fulfilling their wishes. Were his actions ethical and moral? From a legal point of view, what he did was not wrong, and although Michigan passed several injunctions barring Kevorkian from assisting in further suicides, at the time he helped with the suicides, there was no law forbidding it. So, if one considers the standards for what is deemed ethical, the question becomes "Did Kevorkian show respect for the dignity and worth of the individual, was he fair and equal, did the people have the right to make their own choice?" These are important issues and ones that cannot be easily decided depending on the field used for examination.

It should be clear from the preceding discussion that ethics are difficult to define and describe because, in part, they can change so dramatically from field to field and perspective to perspective. What remains constant is that each perspective imposes restrictions on the content of the argument. Almost every field has some type of code of ethics. Ethical codes prescribe what can and cannot be argued, and what is and what is not ethical.

The relational level, the second level of argument ethics, focuses on whether an arguer has enhanced or diminished the relationship among the arguer, recipient, and field. If an arguer seeks to harm the intellectual integrity of the recipient or covertly seeks to damage or undermine the relationship with the recipient, the arguer has acted unethically.

Whenever a person engages in arguments with another, a relationship is created and that relationship is an important part of the process of argumentation. Wayne Brockriede put the relational level in perspective when he wrote an article called "Arguers as Lovers."[28] Brockriede noted that beyond the content of argument transactions, "the relationship among the people who argue may afford one useful way of classifying argumentative transactions."[29]

Brockriede, as the title of his article suggests, takes the position that arguers, in their attempt to influence and relate to their recipients, should act as lovers toward their audiences and need to respect and understand the needs of their recipients. The goal or ethically correct choice for the arguer is to "love" the audience.

Brockriede wrote that the relationship between arguers and their audiences can be classified as three different types: rapist, seducer, and lover. When arguers rape, they view their relationship with the audience as a unilateral one. The arguer will tend to objectify the audience and will seek to manipulate the recipients. As Brockriede claimed, "The rapist wants to gain or to maintain a position of superiority—on the intellectual front of making his case prevail or on the interpersonal front of putting the other person down."[30]

Whether or not we like to admit it, argument rape is a common practice and many people engage in it without even thinking. But we live in an adversarial society in which one person's success often means another's failure and where success at whatever cost is prized over failure. It can be easy for arguers—who may not even be aware of their actions—to "rape" their recipients. Even our language describing arguments suggests this. We often say:

> I beat their arguments.
>
> I destroyed their position.
>
> I demolished the competition.

Yet, each of these examples points to our tendency to objectify and treat people who oppose us as less than human.

A second type of relationship between arguer and recipient is seducer who seeks to win covertly through charm or deceit. As Brockriede noted:

> The seducer's attitude toward co-arguers is similar to that of the rapist. He, too, sees the relationship as unilateral. Although he may not be contemptuous of his prey, he is indifferent to the identity and integrity of the other person. Whereas the intent of the rapist is to force assent, the seducer tries to charm or trick his victim into assent.[31]

There are many ways for arguers to trick their recipients. In Chapter 6, for instance, you will be presented with different types of fallacies that make faulty arguments appear reasonable and believable. When employed by a crafty arguer, fallacies may cause audiences to believe in faulty arguments. Similarly, withholding information, telling half-truths, taking evidence out of context, fabricating evidence, among other deceptions, all provide arguers with the means of fooling audiences.

The third type of relationship between arguer and recipient is that of lover. The arguer as lover seeks to empower the recipient through argument and to expand and enlighten the recipient. The lover, according to Brockriede, wants "power parity" in which arguer and recipient share equally in the exchange of arguments. Brockriede noted: "whereas the rapist and seducer argue against an adversary or an opponent, the lover argues with his peer and is willing to risk his very self in his attempt to establish a bilateral relationship."[32]

The arguer-as-lover relationship views the process of giving reasons in argument as a person-centered enterprise. Its central tenet was summarized by Thomas Nilsen when he concluded that: "Whatever develops, enlarges, enhances human personalities is good; whatever restricts, degrades, or injures human personalities is bad."[33] For Nilsen, this meant that arguers should always give their recipients a "significant choice," which means that arguers should provide their audiences with enough information to draw their own conclusions.

The arguer-as-lover relationship can enhance personal development and improve the quality of life. The relationship is based on the arguer's candidness and efforts to preserve free and well-informed choices by all parties to an argument.

■ Summary

Arguments occur in context and are understood by audiences as a part of their context. This chapter examined how argument contexts influence the way arguments are created, understood, and evaluated. Generally, argument contexts consist of four parts: culture, field, occasion, and ethics. These four elements converge to create an argument locus, or a point for argument, in which arguers strive to locate their arguments.

Culture refers to the system of shared meanings that people use to interpret and understand their environment. Advocates build their arguments by using culture as a frame of reference or common ground for their arguments, and audiences come to understand arguments, in part, through the understanding of the culture.

For a culture to function it must first have a system of shared meanings. Without a common framework for people to understand one another, higher forms of communication, such as argument, are not possible. Second, cultures have their own mythologies that may consist of shared historical accounts, rituals, rites of passage, or other shared events and points of reference. Culture is not a static entity, but rather evolves as its membership evolves. Often, cultures will divide into subcultures with each segment serving a separate subgroup of people.

Arguers are faced with several challenges posed by culture. First, cultural rules and expectations are not always clearly stated and arguers must be sensitive to how cultural expectations should affect their use of evidence, language, and reasoning. Second, arguers should understand that subcultures have expectations and norms beyond those of the host culture. Knowledge of cultural differences and an understanding of cultural points of reference can help an arguer develop arguments that fit the cultural context.

Argument fields are similar to culture in many ways. They also help provide a context for making and interpreting arguments. However, fields are more than cultural contexts, they are the specialized contexts that determine the rules for acceptable evidence, the types of issues to be considered, the rules or procedures for conducting argument, the requirements for proving a case, and even the specialized language in which arguments are expressed. Examples of such fields are law, medicine, and science. Fields are important in judging between competing claims because they provide the basic principles on which many forms of reasoning are based. Some standards for judging arguments are field-dependent and arise from the particular context in which the argument is made. Other standards are field-invariant and apply to all arguments regardless of their contexts.

Argument occasion refers to the rhetorical situation of the argument. Bitzer contended that a rhetorical situation arises from the context of persons, events, objects, relations, and exigence which together call for an argument to be produced. Argument occasions have four characteristics. First, the occasion asks for an argument to be offered. Just as a question invites an answer, an argument occasion invites an argument. Second, the argument must be a fitting answer to the occasion. The answer offered should be relevant to the question asked. Third, the standards for judging a fitting response should be embodied in the situation. The arguer should know how to adapt the arguments to the occasion. And fourth, argument occasions are temporary. Situations arise, they exist, and if left unanswered, they disappear.

Argument ethics involves the study of making moral and just arguments. Arguments are powerful and if used justly, they can enhance and promote the quality of life. But if used deceitfully, they can just as easily undermine or destroy life. Argument ethics involve two considerations: content ethics and relationship ethics. Content ethics refers to the truth and validity of the argument. Relationship ethics refers to how arguers treat their audiences.

Exercises

Exercise 1   In 1987, in an attempt to promote AIDS awareness, a pamphlet was widely distributed at a small, liberal arts, religious university. The pamphlet briefly discussed AIDS and AIDS prevention and, with the use of a cartoon figure, it demonstrated the correct way to put on a condom. After an initial campuswide distribution, the university administration restricted its distribution. The following editorial appeared in the school's student newspaper protesting the decision. It presents an argument and supports its claims with evidence and reasoning. As you read the editorial, try and answer the following questions:

1. What culture(s) operate in the editorial? Do you think you are currently in a different culture or is your culture different? How?

2. What field(s) operate in the editorial? Can you identify the field-invariant and field-dependent standards that were used in the argument to restrict the pamphlet? Can you use your understanding of fields to explain why the students were upset with the decision?

3. What role did argument occasion play in the restriction of the pamphlet? What was the exigence in the situation?

4. In the chapter we presented four characteristics of an argument occasion. These were:

   a. The occasion invites arguments.

   b. The argument must be fitting.

   c. Situations prescribe the criteria for a fitting response.

   d. Argumentative situations are impermanent.

   How well do you think this editorial and its surrounding situation meet these criteria? If your university administration decided to ban a controversial pamphlet, what would be the characteristics of your situation?

5. Was it ethical for the administration to restrict the pamphlet? Why? What ethical criteria should be used to decide when censorship is appropriate or inappropriate? Is censorship ever appropriate?

Focus on banning sexual disease, not condom pamphlet[34]

(Author's Note: The brackets [ ] have been inserted to indicate a change of name or place.)

   In an age where sex and sexually related diseases have been a major focus of nationally affiliated health care organizations, it seems rather ironic that the [Northern] University administration is hung up on distributing informational material on safe sex.

It's especially ironic when one considers the attention sexual attitudes have received this semester. Just six weeks ago, the Office of the President and [Alumni] co-sponsored a Presidential Forum aimed directly at educating the student community on the facts and figures of sexual relations between college students and the risks involved.

A state-produced pamphlet entitled, "Using a Condom" was banned from all public distribution sites at [NU] except for the health center on Nov. 9. [NU] president [James A. Smith] issued a restriction on the material after fielding complaints from two students during a dorm visit.

Now certain health center employees are arguing against the ban. We support this argument.

[Arthur L. Hamber], [NU]'s Vice President and Dean for Student Life, said the brochure was banned because the material in the supplement was presented poorly, saying that it dealt with a serious topic in a playful fashion.

There's no argument that the material was presented playfully. That was the point of the brochure. The real point is, however, sometimes referring to a very serious topic in a non-serious manner is one way to break the ice with students who may really have questions about safe sex but are too embarrassed or afraid to ask them in public. Students joke about a comic strip penis with feet in the brochure, but those same students are the ones who are reading these pamphlets word for word.

It is important to note that the pamphlet, written and developed by the Oregon Health Division's AIDS Education Program does not encourage promiscuity—it just informs students on how to use birth control. It is free, available in quantity and lauded by Health Center personnel as being concise, accurate and eye-catching.

While administrators insist that [NU] is an institution with bright and capable students with a cognitive level about that of the material contained in the pamphlet, we maintain that banning the publication does more harm than good. It sets a precedent for bans of other informative supplemental information which could be shelved based on the objection of a handful of people. [Northern] University does have many bright and capable students—students who should have the ability to decide for themselves whether or not a pamphlet is garbage. If the brochure does indeed educate even one student on the importance of safe sex, then the cost of producing and distributing the supplement is money well spent.

We urge the administration to reconsider the ban and instead concentrate its efforts on how we can teach the students of this institution more about sexual relations, birth control and sexually related diseases by offering as much information as possible on these topics.

Let's stop worrying so much as to how we get to the directed goal of educating students and start focusing instead on getting the message itself across—using whatever method it takes.

Exercise 2   We have discussed the role of argument fields in

- providing grounds for decisions
- implying requirements for what audiences expect from argument
- implying rules arguers will follow in conducting arguments

One example of a field in which argument occurs is education. How does the milieu for educational discourse operate to influence lectures or other persuasive speeches? What forms of grounding are implied? What are audience expectations in this field? What are some conventions or rules for giving lectures or other persuasive speeches?

Exercise 3   What fields are you associated with? Using the description of fields presented in the text, how would you characterize these fields?

Exercise 4   Almost daily we are faced with decisions that have a moral or ethical character. Consider the following example and decide what the most ethical course of action is.

> What should we do when bad money supports good causes? If, for instance, organized crime offered the Scouts a million dollars, should the Scouts take the money? Should they publicize it or should they keep it secret? While this may seem far fetched, it really isn't. While tobacco companies are not the same as organized crime, their products contribute to more than 440,000 deaths a year to say nothing of the suffering inflicted on surviving family members. Yet, tobacco companies support good causes. Consider:
>
> - Many sporting events are sponsored by tobacco companies and some would argue that women's tennis would never have become a high-profile, high-paying sport if it were not from the support of companies such as Virginia Slims.
>
> - Tobacco companies support political candidates and give Democrats and Republicans alike large amounts of money for their campaigns.
>
> - The Partnership for a Drug-Free America receives large financial support from the tobacco industry enabling it to get its message and programs across.
>
> - Tobacco money also supports the American Civil Liberties Union, the NAACP, the Urban League, the National Women's Political Caucus, and the Poetry Society of America. Beyond that, tobacco money supports many different children's charities, environmental groups, and even some health organizations.

There are many more examples. The problem is that money is tight and budgets are being cut and when the tobacco industry offers to help, then good programs survive and flourish. But is there a larger issue at stake? For instance, the Coalition for the Homeless no longer takes money from the tobacco industry because of its source. Amnesty International USA no longer takes money from the industry. Yet, the ACLU has no difficulty taking money from the industry because it allows the organization to survive and do good work to help people.

And the tobacco industry is only one example. There are many other instances of foreign industries and organizations supporting specific candidates for office in the United States. Is there a problem when bad money allows good organizations to be effective?

Consider the following issues:

1. What are the ethical considerations inherent in bad money supporting good causes?

2. Formulate an argument on both sides of the issue. Why is it all right to take the money and why should we reject the money?

3. Considering all the information you have been presented, should "good causes" take the money?

4. Do cultural considerations play a role in the decision to take the money or not?

5. In general, are there some basic ethical guidelines that might help us decide when to accept money and when not to? What might these criteria be?

Notes

1. Joseph Wenzel, "On Fields of Argument as Propositional Systems," *Journal of the American Forensics Association,* 18 (1982): 204.

2. Charles Conrad, *Strategic Organizational Communication,* 2d ed. (Fort Worth: Holt, Rinehart, & Winston, 1989), 4.

3. William L. O'Neill, *Coming Apart: An Informal History of America in the 1960's* (New York: Times Books) 233–271.

4. O'Neill, 233.

5. Tad Tuleja, *Fabulous Fallacies,* (New York: Harmony Books, 1982), 1.

6. Stokely Carmichael, "Black Power," in *Black Protest: History, Documents and Analysis.* Joanne Grant, ed. (New York: Fawcett Premier, 1968), 459.

7. Richard E. Porter, "Intercultural Small Group Communication" in *Small Group Communication: A Reader,* (5th ed.), Robert S. Cathcart and Larry A. Samovar, eds. (Dubuque: Wm. C. Brown, 1988), 155–56.

8. K. S. Sitaram, "What is Intercultural Communication?" in *Intercultural Communication: A Reader,* L. Samovar and R. Porter, eds., (Belmont, Cal.: Wadsworth, 1972), 166.

9. Adi Ignatiub, "Russians Who Wear Jungle Ties Need Not Apply," *The Wall Street Journal,* June 19, 1992, A1:4. Reprinted by permission of *The Wall Street Journal,* ©1992 Dow Jones & Company, Inc. All Rights Reserved Worldwide.

10. Wenzel, 204.

11. Stephen Toulmin, *The Uses of Argument,* (Cambridge, Mass.: Cambridge University Press, 1958), 13–15. Further information can be found in Charles A. Willard, "Argument Fields and Theories of Logical Types," *Journal of the American Forensic Association,* 17 (1981), 129–145.

12. Toulmin, 15.

13. Charles Kneupper, "Argument Fields: Some Social Constructivist Observations" in *Dimensions of Argument: Proceedings of the Second Summer Conference on Argumentation,* George Ziegelmueller and Jack Rhodes, eds. (Communication Association/American Forensic Association, 1981), 80–87.

14. Robert Rowland, "The Influence of Purpose on Fields of Argument," *Journal of the American Forensic Association,* 28 (1982): 228.

15. Charles A. Willard, "Argument Fields" in *Dimensions of Argument,* 21–42.

16. Willard, 41.

17. R. Rowland, "Argument Fields" in *Dimensions of Argument,* 56–79; and "The Influence of Purpose on Fields of Argument," 228–45.

18. Rowland, 64.

19. Kneupper, 82.

20. Toulmin, 33.

21. Toulmin, 33.

22. Lloyd F. Bitzer, "The Rhetorical Situation," *Philosophy and Rhetoric* 1, (1968): 1–15.

23. Bitzer, 4.

24. Wayne L. Minnick, "The Ethics of Persuasion" in *Ethics and Persuasion: Selected Readings,* R. Johannesen, ed., (New York: Random House, 1967), 38.

25. Richard L. Johannesen, *Ethics in Human Communication* (Prospect Heights, Ill.: Waveland Press, 1981).

26. Johannesen, 20–21.

27. An interesting discussion of how ethics change and develop over time can be found in Johannesen, 17.

28. Wayne Brockriede, "Arguers as Lovers," *Philosophy and Rhetoric,* 5 (1972): 1–11.

29. Brockriede, 2.

30. Brockriede, 3.

31. Brockriede, 4.

32. Brockriede, 5.

33. Thomas R. Nilsen, *Ethics of Speech Communication,* 2d ed. (Indianapolis, Ind.: Bobbs-Merrill, 1974).

34. Clayton Cowl, "Focus on Banning Sexual Disease, Not Condom Pamphlet," *Mooring Mast*, December 11, 1987. Used with permission of Pacific Lutheran University, Department of Communication.

SECTION

2

The Anatomy of Argument

■

CHAPTER *3*

Argument Claims and Propositions

■

CHAPTER OUTLINE

- **Claims and Propositions**
- **Formulating a Proposition**
  Controversiality
  Clarity
  Balance
  Challenge

- **Types of Claims**
  Factual Claims
  Value Claims
  Policy Claims
- **Summary**
- **Exercises**

KEY CONCEPTS

propositions
controversiality
double-barreled
challenge
presumption
relational claim
claim of historical fact
policy claims

issues
clarity
balance
burden of proof
factual claims
value claims
values

In all situations in which disputes arise and arguers argue, claims are made. As we said in Chapter 1, a claim is the end point of an argument: "an expressed opinion or conclusion that the arguer wants accepted." Usually, before an argument is made, the arguer has made a decision and is committed to a position that the arguer is prepared to support and defend. Being able to identify an arguer's claim and to distinguish it from the evidence and reasoning used to support it will enable you to analyze and criticize competently the arguments of others.

Knowing the characteristics of well-stated claims will enhance your ability to construct arguments yourself. This chapter will discuss the nature and characteristics of claims and propositions, suggest criteria which distinguish good claims and propositions from bad ones, and identify the various types of claims and propositions.

■ *Claims and Propositions*

Whenever we argue, we use claims and propositions. Both serve an important function in argument because they help define and focus the direction of arguments. At this point, it is useful to make a clear distinction between claims and propositions. Argument claims, as they were defined in Chapter 1, are the end points of an argument. They are supported by reasoning and evidence and focus on a single issue or idea. When we argue, we may develop many different subarguments and each of those subarguments has a claim. Claims are relevant to the evidence and reasoning that serve to support them.

Beyond the claims of individual arguments, however, lie propositions. *Propositions are overarching or main claims which serve as the principal claim of an extended argument.* They define and limit the issues that are available to arguers in a dispute. For instance, if two advocates argue over the proposition that "The U.S. federal government should provide more financial aid for college students," the proposition includes some issues and excludes others. *Issues are the points of potential disagreement related to a proposition.* Propositions set the boundary of acceptable and reasonable issues. In other words, they create a propositional area that defines what issues are appropriate for the discussion. In the case of financial aid, several issues are apparent:

Is there enough financial aid currently?

Can the government afford more education money?

Are there sources of unused financial aid which could meet the need?

Do students forgo their educations because they cannot afford them?

Just as these issues might be included in a conversation about financial aid, this proposition also excludes other issues. For example, issues about space flight, the right to die, and health care have nothing to do with the area created by the proposition. Advocates, therefore, could not appropriately develop arguments that focus on issues beyond the scope of the proposition because such arguments would not be relevant.

Because propositions represent collections of issues, they indicate relevant arguments that both support and deny the proposition. If, for example, an advocate argued that American college students do not receive sufficient financial aid, an opponent could appropriately argue that there are millions of dollars of unclaimed scholarships each year and that additional aid is unnecessary.

Propositions are supported by collections of individual arguments that are developed from the issues within the propositional area. These individual arguments are all related in some way to the proposition and may either support or deny it. Propositions thus provide the framework for individual arguments in a question. See Figure 3–1. In this figure, all the potential and relevant issues for discussion are contained within the field. These include A, B, C, D, E, F, G, and H. In the financial aid example, such issues might include who can afford school, how much aid is available, how much more is needed, what is an appropriate amount of aid for a given student, and what criteria should we use to determine who receives aid and who doesn't.

Irrelevant issues are excluded by the proposition's boundary. In the figure, these issues are represented as I, J, K, L, and M. Examples of irrelevant issues might be whether students should work instead of attending college, whether universal military service would be beneficial, or whether conservation is a means of saving our resources. These issues do not address the central question advanced in the proposition. It is important for advocates to be clear as to what issues fall within the propositional area and are therefore relevant and what issues fall outside the proposition and are therefore irrelevant.

However, just because the proposition contains issues does not mean that an advocate constructing an extended argument has to address them all. Arguers select from the available issues and construct extended argument cases supporting or denying the proposition. Some issues may never be addressed. The choice rests with the advocate who decides what is appropriate for a given audience and situation.

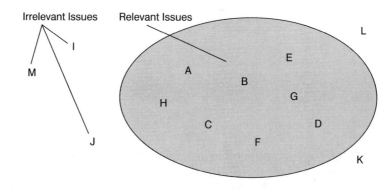

Figure 3–1
The propositional area includes relevant issues and excludes irrelevant ones.

Often, claims and propositions are explicitly stated; but not always. Occasionally, someone will ask, "What point are you getting at?" and arguers who want to be understood will respond by clearly and explicitly stating their claim or proposition. Consider the following example.

MARY:	You know the Campbells are coming over tonight?
DAN:	Of course I know! Why do you think I got out the grill and cleaned it?
MARY:	It's too bad Jimmy's gone this week.
DAN:	Why? I'm enjoying the peace and quiet.
MARY:	Yes, but I miss having him around to do certain chores.
DAN:	Like what, for instance?
MARY:	Like mowing the lawn, for instance.
DAN:	Oh, you want me to mow the lawn, is that it?

Mary wanted Dan to mow the lawn for two reasons: They had guests coming over for a cookout, and the regular lawn mower was out of town. But her statements made no sense to Dan until he discovered that her claim was "I think you should mow the lawn."[1]

In essays, speeches, and other forms of one-way communication, claims are usually stated at the beginning or at the end of the argument. This placement occurs because arguers like to either state their position and then support it or to present evidence or reasoning followed by a conclusion. Where are the claims in the following paragraphs?

Warnings of a great danger are everywhere: a global population that will double in fifty years, causing severe stresses on resources and resulting in increased human misery; a thinning of the ozone layer in the atmosphere over Antarctica and the rest of the planet; the hottest year on record in 1990; the largest oil spill in human history as the consequence of the 1991 war in the Persian Gulf. These and many other indicators, including the destruction of species and bioregions, are all linked to the same metaphor: we are fragmenting because we are afraid to trust wholeness.[2]

The labels we use affect how others perceive us and how we see ourselves; they shape how we see others and how we want to be seen by them; they are used by those in power to define the rest even as they struggle to define themselves. They shape who we are.[3]

The beginning sentence in the first paragraph put forward the claim that the remainder of the paragraph supported, and the final sentence in the second paragraph did the same. Someone wanting to identify the central claim in a paragraph can also watch for terms like "therefore," "then," and "so" that show the conclusion is coming.[4]

On the other hand, informally developed arguments—such as arguments developed among friends in a conversation—may not have clearly placed claims. This is because claims often emerge and develop as we argue. We tend not to begin discussions with a claim and proceed in a rationally considered development of the claim.

Propositions often emerge and are formulated over time. Initially, they are tentatively stated and then honed and refined as participants become knowledgeable about vital issues in a dispute. For example, prosecutors study the particulars of a case before bringing charges; legislators study and revise bills before they are introduced; doctors study a patient's symptoms before issuing a diagnosis; and most of us think and read about social and political problems before we venture to express opinions about them.

Long essays, speeches, extended discussions, and lengthy conversations, in which efforts to argue and influence are taking place, frequently contain a network of related claims that are combined to support a proposition. Figure 3–2 is an illustration of this.

Figure 3–2 displays a network of claims supporting the proposition "lack of a clear policy for dealing with patients in irreversible comas is a problem in our society." The claims supporting this proposition on the problems of euthanasia emerged in a 1983 group discussion[5]. (Policies concerning euthanasia and the right to die have changed substantially since then.) The proposition is supported by a hierarchy of subsidiary claims—principal subclaims, secondary subclaims, and sub-subclaims. The principal subclaims state four major problem areas—lack of a definition of "death," rapid technological advancement, physician liability, and inconsistent procedures for decision making. Each of these four principal subclaims is in turn supported by clusters of secondary subclaims and sub-subclaims.

In extended arguments such as the one illustrated in Figure 3–2, argument claims begin with assumptions or factual statements (in columns 1 and 2) that function as evidence because they are accepted by all parties to the discussion. They therefore fall below the level of dispute and act as starting points which are linked together through reasoning and evidence to support further claims. The network of claims as a whole in turn supports a main claim or proposition that possesses certain characteristics arising from its role as a central thesis. Because the proposition functions as it does within the context of an extended argument, it can be identified only within that context.

Depending on the field in which they occur, extended arguments supporting a main claim or proposition appear in many forms. In journalistic circles, they may appear as editorials; in criminal law, as cases constructed by the prosecution or defense; in business, as recommendations to management; in religious settings, as sermons and theological discussions; and in academic research as articles in scholarly journals.

The field of argument determines the form of proposition for an extended argument. In a parliamentary setting, propositions may appear as motions ("I move that we endorse the university's divestment in corporations with holdings in South Africa"). In argumentative discussions, they may be expressed as an opinion ("MTV is a menace to the morality of today's youth"). In legal cases, they appear as indictments ("The state charges John Smith with reckless driving"). In medicine, they take

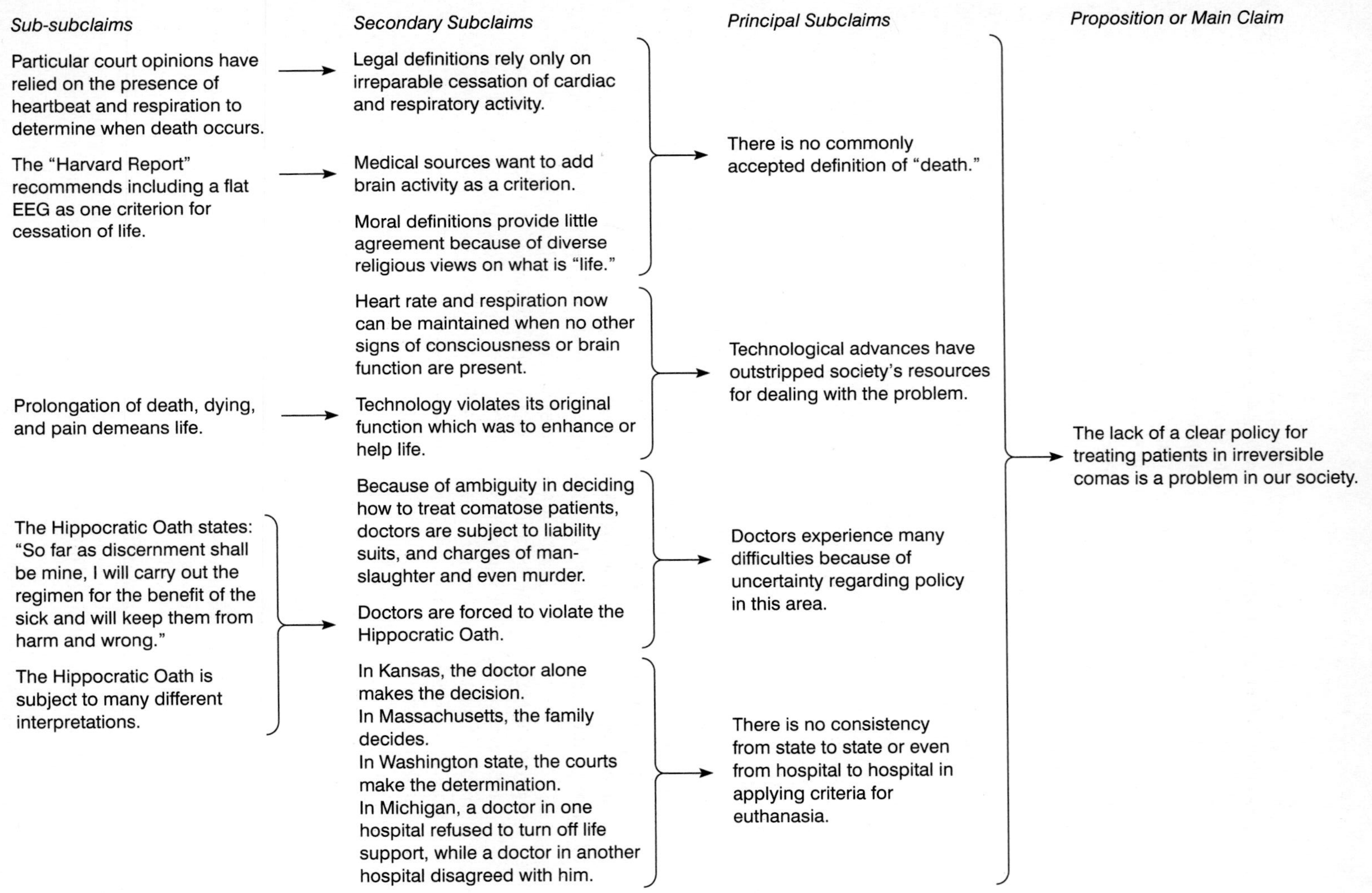

Proposition or Main Claim

Principal Subclaims

Secondary Subclaims

Sub-subclaims

The lack of a clear policy for treating patients in irreversible comas is a problem in our society.

There is no commonly accepted definition of "death."

Legal definitions rely only on irreparable cessation of cardiac and respiratory activity.

Particular court opinions have relied on the presence of heartbeat and respiration to determine when death occurs.

Medical sources want to add brain activity as a criterion.

The "Harvard Report" recommends including a flat EEG as one criterion for cessation of life.

Moral definitions provide little agreement because of diverse religious views on what is "life."

Heart rate and respiration now can be maintained when no other signs of consciousness or brain function are present.

Technological advances have outstripped society's resources for dealing with the problem.

Technology violates its original function which was to enhance or help life.

Prolongation of death, dying, and pain demeans life.

Doctors experience many difficulties because of uncertainty regarding policy in this area.

Because of ambiguity in deciding how to treat comatose patients, doctors are subject to liability suits, and charges of manslaughter and even murder.

Doctors are forced to violate the Hippocratic Oath.

The Hippocratic Oath states: "So far as discernment shall be mine, I will carry out the regimen for the benefit of the sick and will keep them from harm and wrong."

The Hippocratic Oath is subject to many different interpretations.

There is no consistency from state to state or even from hospital to hospital in applying criteria for euthanasia.

In Kansas, the doctor alone makes the decision.
In Massachusetts, the family decides.
In Washington state, the courts make the determination.
In Michigan, a doctor in one hospital refused to turn off life support, while a doctor in another hospital disagreed with him.

Figure 3–2

In a network of related claims, sub-subclaims support secondary subclaims, which support principal subclaims, which support the proposition or main claim.

the form of diagnosis and recommended treatment ("The patient appears to have a uterine fibroid tumor; surgery to remove it is recommended").

Failure to identify a proposition can cause an extended argument to become confused and unprofitable. Russel R. Windes and Arthur Hastings provided an excellent historical example of a public argument that became muddled because no central thesis was identified. Referring to criticisms of public education that were made in the 1950s and 1960s, Windes and Hastings wrote:

> Rightist groups have launched what amounts to a concealed and nationwide attack on public education. Their general proposition is difficult for the observer to state and seemingly impossible for them to state themselves. But it is probably similar to the following: Contemporary public education is failing to preserve the "American way of life". . . .Unfortunately . . .rather than debating the real issues in education—financing, teacher training, and curriculum—these advocates have concerned themselves with pseudo-propositions. . . .In public meetings, rightist advocates deliberate over the censorship of textbooks, the indoctrination of students, what is to be done about teachers and administrators who are "soft on subversives," and how to make schools more patriotic.[6]

Because the advocates in this example had not formulated a coherent statement of what they proposed and because the public and school administrators were unsure of exactly what it was they wanted, they had difficulty accomplishing anything concrete.

In this case, then, there was controversy but no specifically stated proposition. Since a proposition provides the focal point for issues in a dispute, the absence of a clearly formulated statement of the main claim to be argued is problematic. In some situations in which you will argue, the proposition will be formulated by another party to the dispute or by some agent authorized to state it in advance. At other times, however, you yourself will be able to state the proposition to be supported. Such an opportunity might arise in interpersonal argument when no one has clearly formulated the central question to be discussed. You may also need to formulate a proposition for an essay or speech you plan to make. The next section, therefore, discusses the criteria for clear, precise propositions.

◼ *Formulating a Proposition*

People who engage in argument expect certain things to happen. Their expectations grow out of the conventions or implicit "rules" for conducting arguments that influence argumentative discussions in our society.[7] Because people expect that arguments are made for specific purposes and are directed toward specific goals, arguers need to formulate their propositions and statements of opinion to meet others' expectations. This section will consider the basic requirements for expressing well developed propositions and claims. Claims and propositions need to be both controversial and clear. In addition, propositions need to be balanced and challenging.

Controversiality

All claims and propositions should be controversial. *If a claim or proposition is controversial it states a position that is not currently accepted or adhered to by the audience.* As we noted in Chapter 1, argumentative theses are concerned with matters that are controversial. After all, if the parties to an argument already agree to the claim, what need is there to argue? In fact, claims that are not controversial probably serve the function of evidence. People do not argue about things such as whether the earth is round or whether murder is wrong. Instead, we use our understanding of these accepted claims as evidence to ground other claims. In deciding upon a topic or a thesis to defend, the advocate should select something that will be important and controversial to an audience. For example, if you addressed students in the United States and decided to defend the proposition, "Education is beneficial to society," or to argue that "Freedom is important in a democracy," you might be met with ambivalence or disinterest from your readers or listeners. They might wonder why you felt such a thesis needed to be defended since everyone already agreed with it.

In deciding upon a proposition for discussion or debate, it is wise to canvass newspapers and other current periodicals. What is controversial and the subject of public attention at one time may be of little interest later on because the matter has been settled or because other issues seem more pressing. The questions of what was to be done about the polio epidemic or of whether we should have a national draft were very controversial at one time. But a vaccine was found for polio and the all volunteer army seems to be working well at present. The controversiality of a proposition may depend on what issues are timely and of significant public interest.

Clarity

When people engage in argument, they expect to know what the goal of the argument is and how they will know when the dispute is resolved. As we observed in the last section of this chapter, ambiguous, unclear, muddled claims and propositions generally lead to muddled argumentation. *Clarity refers to how well a claim focuses arguments on a particular set of issues.* People need to know where they are starting in order to decide when they have finished. If, through ambiguous wording, the claim allows multiple interpretations or fosters misunderstanding, then it is not clear. Consider Figure 3–3. If a proposition is stated clearly, the relevant issues included in the propositional area are focused; it is clear which issues are relevant to the proposition and which are not. But if a proposition is ambiguous, the relevant issues are less apparent and arguers may find themselves discussing extraneous matters or tangential issues.

One major source of confusion in stating propositions is the use of ambiguous terms that are interpreted one way by one party to the dispute and another way by the other. Since each party is interpreting the proposition differently, each arguer has a different starting point and is probably going in a direction unanticipated by the other. For example, consider a dispute between two professors discussing the

Figure 3–3
Ambiguously Worded Claims

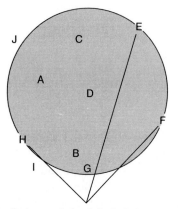

Issues that are not clearly included or excluded

merits of nongraded credit options for students. Both are unaware that there are actually *two* such options at their university. One option (Credit/No credit) is offered on a classwide basis. (All students take the class on a Credit/No credit basis.) The second option is Satisfactory/ Nonsatisfactory, which can be elected by individual students in courses where other students take the course for a grade. Professor Jones, who teaches a Credit/No credit course, is talking with Professor Smith.

PROF. S.:	I think the pass/fail grading system is just a way of letting students goof off.
PROF. J.:	That's not true! The students in my class work just as hard as they would for a grade!
PROF. S.:	Oh, come on! They just use pass/fail grading to make life easier for themselves. It's the easy route to accumulating credits.
PROF. J.:	That would only be true if students worked only for grades. Some are motivated more by the subject matter and the pleasure of learning.
PROF. S.:	You surely are an idealist. Everyone knows that it's the concrete payoffs which allow students to get ahead that really motivate them.
PROF. J.:	All I can speak from is my own experience.

This discussion is not going in a profitable direction, primarily because of the ambiguity of the phrase "pass/fail grading system." For example, if Professor Jones made it clear that he was speaking of the Credit/No credit designation that is mainly used for activity-based and performance courses (internships, readers' theatre, orchestra, etc.), his statements about motivation and the pleasure of learning might be more readily accepted by Professor Smith. Here are two more examples of ambiguous terms in propositions:

Euthanasia should be allowed when the patient and family consent to it.

Does "euthanasia" in this claim refer to removal of life support systems (passive euthanasia) or to administering drugs or other means to induce death (active euthanasia or "mercy killing")?

Grades are not an efficient means of determining a student's intelligence.

Does "determine" here mean "to obtain knowledge of" or "to bring about as a result?" Both are accepted dictionary definitions, yet they lend very different interpretations to the claim! Examples such as these show the desirability of using precise and exact terms when one states claims.

A second source of confusion and lack of clarity in stating claims is the "double-barreled" statement. *Double-barreled claims advance two or more claims simultaneously and, as with ambiguous terms, often lead arguers in separate directions because the relevant issues for each part of the claim are different.* Because double-barreled claims and propositions include issues from two or more propositional areas, arguers often find it difficult to focus on and define the area under dispute. If a proposition or claim has two different objectives, it is best divided by the arguer. Figure 3–4 illustrates the problems of double-barreled claims. In this diagram, the double-barreled claim encompasses issues that support one of the claims and not the other. The result is that an arguer is faced with confusion regarding which issues are relevant and which issues are not.

Confusion because of double-barreled claims has occurred in the example of the discussion between Professors Smith and Jones. Smith's claim really is that "opportunistic students exploit the pass/fail grading system." Consequently, Smith and Jones are actually discussing two issues simultaneously—whether nongraded options have an effect on student learning and performance and whether students are prone to take the "easy way out." If Smith had more clearly stated his claim and if

Figure 3–4
Double-Barreled Claims

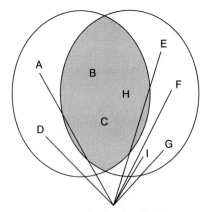

Issues that do not fit clearly within the proposition

Jones and Smith had agreed on what the main claim was to be, their discussion might have been less diffuse and more profitable. Here are two additional examples of double-barreled claims broken into two separate claims:

Double-Barreled Claim:	Congress should cut the federal budget to stimulate the economy.
Claim 1:	Congress should cut the federal budget.
Claim 2:	Cutting the budget will stimulate the economy.
Double-Barreled Claim:	If corporations test employees for drugs, they should also test for alcohol which is the biggest drug of all.
Claim 1:	Alcohol is the "biggest" (most frequently used) drug of all.
Claim 2:	Drug testing should be combined with alcohol testing by corporations that test for substance abuse.

The desirability of breaking double-barreled claims into separate claims is clearly illustrated by the rules of parliamentary procedure. As George W. Ziegelmueller and Charles A. Dause have observed,

> If someone proposes a motion with a dual idea, parliamentary procedure permits the division of the motion so that separate and distinct ideas can be considered separately. When an amendment to a motion is proposed, parliamentary procedure prescribes that the amendment must be considered and acted upon first before moving to the main motion.[8]

Dividing related but separate ideas allows participants in a discussion to recognize their starting point and to know when they have reached their goal. Stating individual ideas separately enables arguers to recognize the points on which they agree and the points on which they disagree, thereby conforming to the conventions of argument and promoting productive, orderly discussions.

Balance

A productive, fair discussion of the issues in a dispute can result only when the topic of discussion is stated in a form with which both parties feel comfortable. Recipients can only be drawn into a discussion and persuaded by the evidence an arguer offers when they are convinced that the arguer has a balanced perspective on the topic. *Balance is the requirement that the issues for and against a proposition be included equally in the propositional field.* When the topic is specifically and clearly stated in neutral language, the field is left open for both its proponents and its opponents to discuss it freely. In fact, a neutral, dispassionate statement of the proposition is a convention in many forums of argument. In law, the charges brought against a defendant are stated neutrally and are agreed upon before the trial can begin (Ms.

Jones committed libel against Ms. Davis; Mr. Smith is charged with driving while intoxicated). In business management, decision makers usually discuss a specific policy or course of action that has been recommended (Should we acquire the Widget Company as a subsidiary of our operation? Does the preliminary information we have on this product line indicate that it should be heavily promoted?).

When a proposition for discussion is stated in connotative or prejudicial language, however, the "deck is stacked" against the viewpoint that opposes the proposition because the issues available to the opposing arguers have been limited or tainted by the emotionally loaded language. Furthermore, speakers and writers who state their theses in ways that reveal personal biases cause their audiences to become suspicious. Consider, for example, the following propositions:

> The space race is the world's biggest money waster.
>
> Unprincipled recidivists should be put away for life.

Propositions such as these overstate one's case and close off rather than promote open discussion because extraneous language serves to limit the issues available to the arguers. Propositions that avoid connotative language, superlatives, and stereotypes encourage all parties to the dispute to consider all available options and decision proposals. The propositions given above could be rephrased so as to be more neutral. As a general rule of thumb, the wording of the proposition should be agreeable to all parties of a dispute.

> Funds invested in space exploration should be significantly reduced.
>
> Repeat offenders should receive life imprisonment.

Challenge

One of the characteristics of an argument that we discussed in Chapter 1 is that it is an attempt to influence someone else. *Challenge means that an arguer's claim confronts recipients' existing values, beliefs, or behaviors.* Generally, the arguer who initiates the dispute by stating the initial claim expresses dissatisfaction with a prevailing belief or state of affairs. The arguer tries to change the other's attitudes or behavior to something different from what the attitudes or behavior would be if no argumentation took place.

A proposition for argument or debate should, therefore, challenge what people already believe or do. This is more than the requirement of being controversial. Whereas controversy refers to how ready a recipient is to agree to or believe in a proposition or claim, challenge focuses on changing the recipient in some way. This convention is based on the principle that there is no reason to defend an already accepted practice or belief unless it is questioned or criticized. Richard Whately, a nineteenth-century educator and clergyman, described this convention and its implications for argument.[9] He observed that in most argumentation there was a *pre-*

sumption and a *burden of proof.* The presumption favors the position which, because it is already accepted, "preoccupies the ground" in a controversy until some challenge is made against it. The person initiating the dispute therefore has the burden of proof entailed in making such a challenge.

The metaphor of preoccupying ground that Whately uses is carried through in the associations we make when we hear the word "claim." A land claim is a claim to a parcel of land owned or possessed by someone else. The agency or the institution against which the claim is made enjoys no other advantage than the prerogative to retain the land if the claim is not upheld and accepted.

Therefore, the implication of Whately's concepts is that arguers who advance claims should challenge existing beliefs, policies, and states of affairs. Those who put forward proposals or advocate new ideas assume the *burden of proof which obligates arguers to provide good and sufficient reasons for changing what is already accepted.* Those who defend existing beliefs and practices enjoy the *presumption which is the predisposition to favor an existing practice or belief until some good reason for changing it is offered.* The following claims do not challenge existing beliefs and practices and thus do not fulfill the burden of proof requirement:

> School desegregation is desirable.
>
> Washington State should continue to rely on sales and property taxes for revenue.
>
> The legal drinking age should be left to the states to decide.

Propositions such as these do not advocate change, and if arguments supporting them were not made, the policies and conditions which they advocate would continue anyway. The following propositions, on the other hand, assume a burden of proof for the person who defends them because they challenge beliefs and policies that are presently accepted.

> A nationwide system of magnet schools is desirable.
>
> Washington State should implement an income tax.
>
> The legal drinking age should be set at 21 nationwide.

Because they raise the possibility of innovations and new policies, such propositions challenge the present system and fulfill our expectation that attempts at influence be necessary and justified.

Types of Claims

Both claims and propositions occur in various forms and types. Knowing which type of claim is in question helps the arguer decide what issues or questions to address. Some claims refer to sources or conditions which can be readily checked for verification. Other claims, such as those involving social values or policies, require more complex forms of support. For example, in Figure 3–2, the claim restating the Hippocratic Oath can be verified merely by referring to the text of the oath itself. If the group discussing euthanasia were to question whether "prolongation of death, dying, and pain demeans life," however, it would have to spend some time defining the terms of the claim and generating criteria to decide whether certain practices "demean life."

Many category schemes for classifying claims have been proposed.[10] The simplest and most frequently used scheme divides claims into the categories of fact, value, and policy. We will use this scheme here because it includes the major types of claims used as subjects of argument and because the sets of issues each type generates can be distinguished from the sets of issues generated by the other two.[11]

Factual Claims

Factual claims make inferences about past, present, or future conditions or relationships. In making such inferences, we reason from something that is known or assumed to be true to something that is unknown or disputable. These inferences occur in numerous forms and in Chapter 5 we will discuss these and explain how one makes the link from what is known to what is claimed. If a statement is about a condition or relationship that is already known and readily apparent to participants in the argumentation, it functions as *evidence,* or, in a network of claims, as a sub-subclaim used as a starting point for argument. (Remember from Chapter 1 that previously established claims can be used as evidence in new arguments that build on them.)

Some statements of fact are straightforward and easily established, therefore not disputable. For example,

> Mary weighs more than John.
>
> The flight cannot leave because of heavy fog.
>
> Central Airlines has the worst record for losing baggage in the United States.

Such statements are unlikely to serve as propositions for extended arguments because they are relatively easy to verify or prove. Claims of fact, however, are much more difficult to prove because the information we need to establish them is not available or because such information is subject to varying interpretations. Such claims could function as propositions and be supported and attacked in extensive argument.

One type of factual claim that states a controversial position is the relational claim. *A relational claim attempts to establish a causal relation between one condition or event and another.*

> Capital punishment deters crime.
>
> Smoking marijuana harms your health.

Violence on television affects children's behavior.

Researchers have completed many studies on each of these topics, and their results do not agree. Sifting through and comparing information on such topics is worthwhile because the inferences made in the claims are so controversial. We will discuss procedures for analyzing and supporting such claims in Chapter 5.

A second type of factual claim that makes an argumentative statement about what will happen is the predictive claim. *A predictive claim is based on the assumption that past relationships and conditions will be repeated in the future.* Because information that might prove such claims is often not available, predictive claims often serve as the subject of argumentation. For example,

A staffed space mission will reach Mars by 2010.

Our economy is headed for a massive depression.

A severe shortage of teachers will occur by the year 2000.

Such claims are usually supported by descriptions of long-term trends and statistically based projections; they also involve studying causal relationships that may be affected by unanticipated developments and events.

A third type of controversial factual claim is the *claim of historical fact, which rests on the strength of probable evidence to which we have access.* Because historical records and artifacts are damaged, destroyed, or lost as time passes, evidence supporting historical claims may be as unavailable as that supporting predictive claims. Extensive controversy has surrounded the following claims:

The Shroud of Turin was worn by Jesus in the tomb.

The author of *On the Sublime* was not Longinus.

Lee Harvey Oswald was the sole assassin of John F. Kennedy.

Supporters of such claims collect and describe as much circumstantial evidence as possible to convince skeptics that their claims are true. Historical claims cannot be positively proven because direct evidence to support them is unavailable.

Three types of factual claims that can serve as the subject of argument, then, are relational claims, predictive claims, and historical claims. Relational claims connect two conditions and infer that one of them has brought about or will bring about another. Predictive claims are grounded in the assumption that past events will be repeated in the future and make a claim about some future occurrence. Historical claims are descriptive and informational and are usually based on a preponderance of evidence that a particular account or interpretation of past events is the correct one. All three deal with matters that are disputable because the information we would need to establish them conclusively is insufficient or unavailable. They describe how or why something has come or will come about in ways that are controversial and subject to argument.

Value Claims

Value claims assess the worth or merit of an idea, object, or practice according to standards or criteria supplied by the arguer. The focus of argumentation about values is the values held by participants in a dispute. *Values are fundamental positive or negative attitudes toward certain end states of existence or broad modes of conduct.*[12] Such fundamental attitudes influence our conceptions of what is desirable or undesirable in a given situation. Joseph W. Wenzel has noted that "values exist in an intersubjective realm of agreements that are the fabric of a community; they exist in the actions and discourse of persons constructing, sustaining, testing, and revising the rules by which we will live and act together."[13] Examples of values expressing fundamental conceptions of desirable end states are equality, salvation, self-fulfillment, and freedom; those regarding models of conduct are courage, honesty, and loyalty.

Values govern our choice making and indicate to us what we ought to believe and do. When we make value claims by assigning a value to an object, practice, or idea, we are actually making recommendations to others. Following are examples of value claims:

> Capital punishment is beneficial to society.
>
> Private schools provide better elementary and secondary education than public schools.
>
> Degas's paintings are ethereally beautiful.

In each of these claims, a value judgment is made. The first deals with social benefit, the second with quality, and the third with aesthetic merit. The claims also involve an object of evaluation which may be an idea, a practice, a person, or a thing. Analysis of value claims must be located within some field or framework that implies the standards or criteria for the value judgment. For example, judging capital punishment according to its social benefits might involve a utilitarian standard whereby we try to determine whether capital punishment provides the greatest good for the greatest number of citizens. Criteria suggested by a utilitarian standard might include the following:

- Does capital punishment actually prevent capital crimes?
- Does implementing capital punishment save more lives than it takes?
- Does capital punishment discriminate against minorities?

More will be said about the analysis of issues in value claims in Chapter 9.

Policy Claims

Policy claims call for a specific course of action and focus on whether a change in policy or behavior should take place. Policy claims frequently deal with complex social, political, or economic problems, but they may also deal with actions on a much smaller scale. In the conversation between Dan and Mary with which this chapter began, Mary's implication that Dan should mow the lawn must be considered a policy claim. Other examples of policy claims are:

> The King County government should legalize prostitution.
>
> Sales of handguns to private citizens in the United States should be banned.
>
> You should not smoke cigarettes in public places.

When making policy claims, arguers express either a dissatisfaction with present practices or a belief that a change in practices or behavior would be an improvement. The types of issues generated in policy claims and methods for analyzing them will be explained in Chapter 10.

An important observation here is that the three types of claims—fact, value, and policy—are not discrete and separate. Like a pyramid, policies are based on values which, in turn, are based on facts. For example, discussing the claim "Sales of handguns to private citizens in the United States should be banned" might involve considering one or all of the following claims:

> The number of handgun deaths and injuries in our country is appalling. *(value claim)*
>
> The licensing and regulation of handgun sales is inconsistent from state to state. *(fact claim)*
>
> Eliminating handguns will decrease the number of unpremeditated and accidental gun injuries. *(predictive factual claim)*
>
> The "right to bear arms" is not as important as the public's right to safety and freedom from harm. *(value claim)*

An examination of the network of claims supporting policy propositions will always reveal subsidiary claims of fact and value. Furthermore, a value proposition such as "compulsory national service for all U.S. citizens is desirable" will involve decisions about policy (What is to be done to provide the needed service? Does "compulsory national service" mean a universal draft, required public service, or some other practice?). Claims of various types often occur in conjunction with each other and are interdependent. If arguers can identify and distinguish them, however, they will be able to focus on the issues and vital questions that the claims imply.

■ *Summary*

Claims and propositions serve important argument functions. They focus arguers' attention on the purpose of the argument and imply the issues that need to be decided before a dispute can be resolved. Extended arguments, whether they are in the form of conversations, discussions, speeches, or essays, include a network of claims that combine to support a proposition, or main claim. Skillful arguers should be able to identify the main claims and principal subclaims in the arguments of others. They should also be able to phrase their own claims so that they conform to others' expectations. By phrasing their claims appropriately, arguers will be more successful in constructing extended arguments.

People who participate in arguments expect the subject to be controversial or open to dispute. Anyone who advances a claim should be able to explain why it needs to be justified and supported. Arguers should therefore advance claims about which there is likely to be disagreement. People participating in arguments also expect them to be clear; that is, they want to know what the issues are and what is required to resolve them. Arguers stating claims should therefore avoid ambiguous terms, statements with multiple meanings, and statements that introduce multiple issues simultaneously. Furthermore, stating claims in a biased or prejudiced way forestalls open discussion of the options to be considered. Claims should therefore be stated objectively, and stereotypes and connotative terms should be avoided. Finally, people expect arguers to take issue with prevailing attitudes and practices. If an arguer attempts to influence someone, he or she must make a claim that would change what would continue to be done or believed had the argument not taken place. In presenting an argument for change, the arguer assumes the burden of proving there is good reason for the change to be made.

There are three major types of claims that are made in arguments. Each type of claim calls for a different type of analysis to identify the issues that the claim implies. Claims of fact make inferences about the past, present, or future conditions or relationships. Sometimes factual claims are readily verifiable and agreed upon by all parties to the dispute, or come to be agreed upon as the argument progresses. At other times, factual claims cannot be conclusively established because the needed information is unavailable, in conflict, or subject to conflicting interpretations. Value claims assess the worth or merit of something according to standards supplied by the arguer. The focus of disputes on value claims is on the fundamental attitudes (values) of participants in the argumentation. Value disputes may involve ethical, aesthetic, or moral judgments. Policy claims call for a course of action or change in the beliefs of others. They usually express dissatisfaction with present practices or a belief that a change in policy or behavior will bring improvement. Because considerations of fact, value, and policy are related to each other, the three types of claims are frequently interdependent.

Exercises

Exercise 1   In this chapter, four criteria were described that enable you to decide whether a proposition is well formulated. They are:

- *Controversiality.* The proposition should state a thesis that is potentially disputable rather than one about which most people would agree.

- *Clarity.* The proposition should be clearly and precisely stated; ambiguous terms and double-barreled claims should be avoided.
- *Balance.* The claim should be stated in objective, neutral language rather than in a way that reveals the personal biases or prejudices of the person making the claim.
- *Challenge.* The proposition should confront an audience's prevailing beliefs, values, or state of affairs.

Using these criteria, criticize the following propositions. Are they well formulated? If not, why not? How could they be reformulated so as to function more effectively?

✳ 1. Exercise is good for one's health.
 2. Plea bargaining is a good and essential means of case disposal.
 3. The United Nations should act as a world peacemaker.
 4. The United States should reduce its deficit by reducing its foreign military commitments.
✳ 5. Euthanasia is a desirable and necessary medical practice.
 6. People who are HIV-positive should not be allowed to attend public school.
 7. Women should be allowed to serve as officers in the military.
 8. Degenerate and perverted homosexuals should be removed from America's classrooms.
 9. Good salespeople are effective.
 10. The Florida State lottery taxes the poor and benefits the rich.
 11. Washington state should stabilize its revenues by imposing an income tax.
✳ 12. Women should have access to abortion on demand.
 13. Education is good.
 14. America's industries need to invest in manufacturing if the United States is to be internationally competitive in the twenty-first century.
 15. People who own large cars with eight-cylinder engines are wasteful, stupid, and trying to destroy our environment.

Exercise 2 Three types of claims have been identified in this chapter: fact, value, and policy. Fact claims make inferences about past, present, or future conditions or relationships; they can be explanatory, predictive, or historical. Value claims judge an idea, object, person, or practice by some value standard or set of criteria. Policy claims advocate a course of action that is not presently followed. Which of these three types describes the following claims?

✳ 1. Extraterrestrial beings visited Earth during prehistoric times.
 2. The state of Hawaii should require all teachers to pass a proficiency examination.
 3. Nuclear weapons are an efficient deterrent to enemy aggression.

4. Illegal immigrants generally take jobs United States citizens do not want.

5. Discrimination is never justified.

6. Marijuana should be legalized in the United States.

7. Mandatory seat belt laws violate our constitutional rights.

8. Polygraph evidence should be admissible in trials.

9. Pornography causes sex crimes.

10. Required automotive emissions tests are an inefficient means of ensuring clean air.

11. The U.S. welfare system has exacerbated the problems of the urban poor.

12. The disintegration of the Soviet Union freed the people of Eastern Europe.

13. Movies made in America have more graphic violence and gratuitous sex than they did ten years ago.

14. Higher education in America is the best in the world.

15. Colleges and universities in the United States should stress more technical and applied subjects.

Exercise 3 Select three topics on which you would like to develop an argumentative case. A list of suggested topics is given, but you may choose some other topic area. What is important is that you already know enough about the topic to construct claims related to it. Within each topic area, construct a proposition of fact, a proposition of value, and a proposition of policy. Be sure that the propositions you supply adhere to all the guidelines for wording propositions supplied in this chapter and listed in Exercise 1. Here is an example:

Topic area:	Alcohol Abuse
Proposition of Fact:	Alcohol-related accidents cause more deaths than any other cause in the United States.
Proposition of Value:	Alcohol is a more dangerous substance than marijuana.
Proposition of Policy:	The allowable BAC (blood alcohol content) in drivers should be significantly reduced.

Suggested topics (or select three of your own):

terrorism	the U.S. prison system
AIDS	drugs
inner cities	crime
censorship	political campaigns
environment	endangered species
abortion	gun control
consumer protection	religious cults
foreign policy	trade barriers
legalized gambling	capital punishment

Notes

1. Mary's original "claim" was actually a veiled request to mow the lawn. When requests are supported by reasons, they function as arguments. Study of such argument forms occurs in Sally Jackson and Scott Jacobs, "Structure of Conversational Argument: Pragmatic Bases for the Enthymeme," *Quarterly Journal of Speech* 66 (1980): 251–65; and Jacobs and Jackson's "Conversational Argument: A Discourse Analytic Approach," in *Advances in Argumentation Theory and Research,* J. Robert Cox and Charles Arthur Willard, eds. (Carbondale, Ill.: Southern Illinois University Press, 1982).

2. Adapted from Warren King, "Stalking the Killer," *Pacific,* July 20, 1986, 8.

3. Kevin P. Phillips, "Is the Party Over?" *Seattle Times,* July 20, 1986, A16.

4. More techniques for identifying claims and conclusions on the bases of contextual cues will be discussed in Chapter 7.

5. These claims are drawn from a group discussion of the topic "What policy should be enacted in regard to patients in potentially irreversible medical situations?" The discussion occurred at the University of Washington on May 8, 1983. Student participants were Steven McCornack, Ann Hurd, Leigh Chang, Anne Bigelow, Carrie O'Connor, Liza Thomas, and Margo Welshons. This discussion predated a significant Supreme Court decision that ruled that patients have the right to refuse medical treatment and to write living wills precluding extraordinary measures to prevent death.

6. Russel R. Windes and Arthur Hastings, *Argumentation and Advocacy* (New York: Random House, 1965), 51–2.

7. A good deal of work has been done in elaborating the conventions or "rules" of argument. By a rule, we mean "a regularity (formalized . . .written, understood, or tacitly observed) that defines an activity." See Gary Cronkhite, "Conventional Postulates of Interpersonal Argument," in *Argument in Transition,* David Zarefsky, Malcolm O. Sillars, and Jack Rhodes, eds. (Annandale, Va.: Speech Communication Association/American Forensic Association, 1983), 697. See also Frans van Eemeren and Rob Grootendorst, *Speech Acts in Argumentative Discussions* (Dordrecht, Netherlands: Foris Publications, 1984).

8. George W. Ziegelmueller and Charles A. Dause, *Argumentation: Inquiry and Advocacy* (Englewood Cliffs, N.J.: Prentice-Hall, 1975), 17–18.

9. Richard Whately, *Elements of Rhetoric,* Douglas Ehninger, ed. (Carbondale, Ill.: Southern Illinois University Press, 1963), 112–13.

10. For example, Ziegelmueller and Dause (pp. 14–15) describe two main categories—propositions of judgment and propositions of policy. Propositions of judgment are subdivided into descriptive, predictive, and evaluative propositions that deal with alleged facts, future facts, and value claims respectively. Church and Wilbanks describe another unique category scheme that divides propositions into those of inference, value, and policy, with the category of inference subdivided into trait, relational, historical, and predictive inferences. See Russell T. Church and Charles Wilbanks, *Values and Policies in Controversy* (Scottsdale, Ariz.: Gorsuch Scarisbrick, 1986), 35–42.

11. A fourth type of claim is the claim of definition or classification. Examples would be "This is an act of burglary" and "By 'euthanasia,' I mean the removal of life support from terminally ill patients." To support claims such as these, the arguer justifies the definition or classification by referring to a source which others find acceptable. The arguer may also have to show that the chosen definition is applicable. Only rarely do definitive claims serve as central theses in argumentation; they more frequently function as subsidiary claims when participants disagree about how to define a term in the main claim or proposition.

12. Daryl J. Bem, *Beliefs, Attitudes and Human Affairs* (Belmont, Cal.: Brooks/Cole, 1970), 16.

13. Joseph W. Wenzel, "Toward a Rationale for Value-Centered Argument," *Journal of the American Forensic Association,* 13 (1977): 153.

CHAPTER *4*

Evidence: The Foundation for Arguments

■

CHAPTER OUTLINE

- **The Nature of Evidence**
- **Types of Evidence**
- **Evaluating Fact and Opinion Evidence**
    - Reliability
    - Expertise
    - Objectivity
    - Consistency
    - Recency
    - Relevance
    - Access
    - Accuracy of Citation
- **Evaluating Statistical Evidence**

- **Locating Evidence**
    - Books
    - Periodicals
    - Newspapers
    - General Reference Works
    - Government Documents
    - Other Sources of Information
- **Recording and Organizing Evidence**
- **Summary**
- **Exercises**

KEY CONCEPTS

statistics
artifacts
opinion evidence
reliability
expertise
objectivity
sample

bias
external consistency
internal consistency
accessibility
primary source
secondary source
representative sample

As critics and consumers of argument, we should be aware of the vital role evidence plays in argumentation and decision making. Russel R. Windes and Arthur Hastings have suggested that the acceptance of conclusions and decisions in the absence of evidence "has resulted in decisions and actions which have led to indescribable human suffering and misery—to wars and material destruction, to political inequities and the suppression of human rights, to economic catastrophes, to unjust persecutions, to mob violence, and to superstition and prejudice."[1] If you believe that accepting unsupported or poorly supported claims is harmless, consider Nazi Germany.

The Nazi propaganda machine sought to isolate and ostracize the Jewish people. To do this, Nazi publications claimed that Jews had caused the country's economic ills, had committed atrocities against German women and children, and were devious and untrustworthy. In support of their claims, the Nazis presented either no evidence (only innuendo) or phony evidence. But if a claim is made often enough, people begin to believe it,[2] and the German people did. One result was the Holocaust in which millions of Jewish people were put to death.

Not only do we need to be aware of the absence or misuse of evidence in arguments we hear and read, but we also should be mindful of the need to use evidence in arguments we make. Particularly in situations in which an arguer is unknown to an audience or does not have an established reputation with them, evidence is vital in establishing the credibility of claims and arguments the arguer makes. Researchers who have studied the effect of evidence on the persuasiveness of arguments have found that speakers unknown to or only moderately respected by an audience will be more successful if they use evidence to support their claims.[3] As recipients, critics, and producers of arguments, then, it is important for us to be aware of the vital role played by evidence.

In Chapter 1, we defined evidence as "facts or conditions objectively observable, beliefs or premises generally accepted as true by the audience, or conclusions previously established." Evidence is what we produce whenever we are asked to prove something or when someone asks us "How do you know?" or "What have you got to go on?" This chapter will discuss the nature and types of evidence, procedures for locating evidence in libraries and resource material, and guidelines for the use of evidence to support arguments. After you have read this chapter, you should be able to recognize evidence, conduct research to find support for your arguments, and evaluate the quality of evidence used in your own and other's arguments.

◼ The Nature of Evidence

Our definition of evidence from Chapter 1 indicates that evidence is not simply concrete facts or observable behavior. Rather, the defining characteristic of evidence is that it is accepted by the audience and can be used to support statements (claims) that are not accepted. The three ways in which evidential statements can function will be discussed in this section so as to reveal the nature of various forms of evidence.

First, evidence can stem from objectively observable conditions in the world. For most people, this is what evidence is. Evidence is simply what we can see and hear, feel, touch, and smell. For instance, your desk can serve as evidence that is objectively observable; so can the color of the sky or the number of people in your argumentation class. These are things that can be seen or discovered by anyone looking for them.

Second, beliefs or premises generally accepted as true by the audience can function as evidence (as long as they do not clearly disagree with directly observable evidence). This view of evidence can be problematic for some people because it means that evidence is not always concrete. However, the concept of level of dispute introduced in Chapter 1 can provide a useful means for understanding this view of evidence. Evidence can be used as support because it lies below the level of dispute. If evidence fell above the line, then it would become a focal point for argument instead of support for a claim. For instance:

> Because we lost in Vietnam, we should not get involved in Central America because we will lose again.

> After all, Professor Jacobs is an expert in the mass media's effect on terrorism. Consequently, we can trust his argument that increasing media exposure results in increased terrorist activities. Therefore, to reduce terrorism, we should reduce media exposure.

In the first case, we rely on evidence that says that we lost the war in Vietnam. As long as the recipients of the argument accept that as true, then it provides partial support for the claim "we should not get involved in Central America," even though the claim is still controversial and the resemblance between Vietnam and Central America may be questioned. Likewise, in the second example, if we accept Professor Jacobs's assessment of terrorism, then the final claim is supported. However, suppose that the evidence in either case was disputed. Suppose that someone believed that we did not lose the war in Vietnam or that Jacobs is not an expert. Then the arguments' initial starting points would no longer serve as evidence because they fell above the level of dispute.

Third, conclusions that have been previously established can function as evidence. In the argument above, if you accept Jacobs as an expert and trust his argument that media exposure increases terrorism, then the arguer has established support for the claim that we need to control the media. Now, if you accept that claim as being true, the level of dispute rises until the proven claim falls below the level. The proven claim "the media should be controlled" can now be used as evidence for the next claim "we should black out media coverage for twenty-four hours after each terrorist act." This new claim depends on the audience's accepting both the previous claim and the original evidence. In Chapter 1, we called this an *argument chain*.

A prospective car buyer can provide a useful example of how people might commonly use evidence. There are many publications to help prospective car buyers choose from hundreds of makes and models. One of the most prominent of these is

Consumer Reports, which tests dozens of automobiles each year. These tests and surveys can provide the prospective buyer with a wealth of evidence: the price of the car and options, predicted reliability, comfort and convenience, ease of service, drivability, and performance. With the information from *Consumer Reports,* John, a prospective car buyer, goes looking for a new car. He drives many makes and models and notes the features in each of the cars he tests. With all of this information, he selects the car he wants and sits down to bargain with the dealer.

The *Consumer Reports* evidence is useful to John in making an argument with the dealer for a better price. He can tell the dealer that he likes the car but the $15,000 price is too high because the consumer magazines claimed that the dealer paid only $8,000 for the car in the first place. He can also claim that the car was not quite as comfortable, reliable, or gas-efficient as he had hoped, and perhaps he should look elsewhere for another car. In each case, John appeals to evidence to support his claims about the car.

Suppose, however, that the dealer rejected John's $8,000 figure and asserted that the particular car with its options cost him a good deal more. John's original evidence would then become a claim because it would be disputed and the subject of argument.

This illustration points to the nature of evidence. Evidence is not always concrete nor is it always certain. In fact, evidence can be placed on a continuum from concrete, objectively observable, certain evidence to evidence that is probably true. For instance, John knew the car existed. He could make an argument for the car's existence and have little difficulty getting people to agree with him. John could use any of the car's physical features as evidence without much fear of contradiction. On the other hand, suppose John argued that *Consumer Reports* conducted a reliability study on the car. Evidence from such a study is not directly experienced by the participants in an argument, and because neither party had a concrete experience with the evidence there is room for dispute. It could be that no such study was conducted or that John's interpretation of the study is wrong or that the study was biased. The results of the study and John's interpretation of them are probable but not certain. Sometimes evidence functions as fact; at other times it functions as opinions or premises accepted by the audience.

■ *Types of Evidence*

Evidence can be divided into two broad classifications—fact and opinion as to fact.[4] Facts may be thought of as things people believe to be the case either because they have experienced them firsthand or because they regard them as the truthfully reported experiences of others.[5]

Generally, there are two ways in which people come to believe something is a fact. First, they may verify it through their own observations or experiments. In other words, they can see, hear, feel, touch, or taste it. Most phenomena perceived by our senses are easily accessible, but some are not. Scientists seeking to prove the existence of atoms have conducted experiments allowing them to see the physical effects of atoms. They have used cloud chambers that help them trace atomic trails or computer simulations. If someone did not believe in the existence of atomic particles, their existence could be demonstrated by these or other methods.

A second way people come to believe in something as a fact is through common experience. We can talk about the history of the United States and the Civil War. While none of us have directly experienced the Civil War, it is part of our common heritage. We do not question it because we accept it as a fact, a historical occurrence well substantiated in many sources. Factual evidence can be further divided into types. Each type, in turn, can be verified by observations, experiments, or common experience.

1. *Reports and descriptions are nonnumerical or narrative accounts of some object or occurrence.* They often occur in arguments as examples and illustrations and may make a passing reference to something or describe it at some length. Here are two examples of this type of evidence from two midsummer newspaper articles on the hazards of fireworks set off on the Fourth of July:

> At noon on July 4, 1985, Seattle Fire Department Engine No. 2 left the station to respond to a call for help.
>
> For the next 14 hours, Engine No. 2 would race nonstop from one emergency to another. "That engine did not return to the station until 2 a.m." Fire Chief Claude Harris reports.[6]

> Last year, a few days before the holiday that some people equate with fireworks. . . .[J.R. "Don"] Schmidt lost portions of his thumb and two fingers on his right hand.
>
> The logger and some friends had gone to Hood Canal to discharge fireworks purchased from a stand on an Indian reservation.
>
> "My buddy lit a cherry bomb with a cigarette lighter, then handed it to me to toss. It had a short fuse. It went off too soon," Schmidt explained.[7]

Reports and factual descriptions such as these lend immediacy and vividness to many arguments. They help recipients identify with the characters and relate to the situations described. And they bring home or dramatize situations or conditions that might otherwise seem remote and unimportant.

2. *Statistics are facts and figures that have been systematically collected and ordered so as to convey information.* Generally, statistics provide a quantitative summary of the characteristics of a population or a sample (selectively chosen instances) of a population. Statistics may take the form of averages, numerical comparisons, percentages, totals, or estimates, for example. Here are some telling statistics from one of the articles on fireworks cited above:

> In 1985, our fire load was five times the normal load for July 4.
>
> In the 47-day period from June 15 through July 31 . . .fire departments responding to the survey devoted 4,509 man hours to fireworks problems, at an estimated cost of $169,200.
>
> States that allow a wide variety of fireworks to be sold for personal use have a rate of fireworks-related fires 50 times greater than states that strictly limit availability of fireworks.

Half of those injured were children under 15 years of age, and 11 percent of the injuries resulted in hospitalization.[8]

Statistics lend credence to arguments by showing that problems and conditions are not limited to isolated instances but instead affect many people in many different types of situations. The above statistics show that the experience of Fire Engine No. 2 is not limited to the Seattle area but occurs nationally and regionally in the areas surveyed. They also show that the kind of injury suffered by the logger who lost his fingers occurs to many children.

3. *Artifacts are physical evidence that helps to prove an argument.* An artifact is simply a physical object that a speaker might use to prove a point. For example, exhibits in a trial are artifacts. The article on fireworks just cited came as close as a printed medium can come to displaying physical exhibits. It was accompanied by a photograph of a fire marshal holding in his hands M-70 rockets of the kind that blew off the logger's fingers. Another photograph showed an explosion in which M-80 rockets were used to devastate the interior of a car. If we were able to observe it first-hand, this explosion (a demonstration by the Bellevue Police Department) would indeed be an effective "artifact" to prove the claim "These fireworks are dangerous!" Since we are influenced more strongly by what we see than by what we hear or read, artifacts can be a very effective form of factual evidence.[9]

The second broad type of evidence is opinion as to fact. *Opinion evidence is someone's interpretation of the meaning of factual evidence.* Whereas facts are based on direct or indirect experience, opinions are a judgment about how an event or state of affairs is to be understood, evaluated, or dealt with. In using opinion evidence, the advocate uses the statements of others' judgments and estimations to support his or her own claims. Consider the following opinion statement and the claim it might support:

Fire Chief Claude Harris has maintained that "Ideally, we should have a ban on private fireworks. . . .Even though this is Independence Day and we should recognize it, we don't have to have little kids running around with devices that are fire hazards and that have the potential to injure them."[10]

Claim: The dangers and injuries caused by fireworks should cause us to ban their use by private individuals.

Opinion evidence is frequently used by arguers who don't themselves have expertise in the topic of the argument. Guidelines for using this type of evidence will be presented later in this chapter and procedures for testing arguments based on this form of evidence will be presented in Chapter 5 and 6.

■ *Evaluating Fact and Opinion Evidence*

Just as a house or any structure is only as strong as the foundation on which it is built, so is an argument only as strong as the evidence used to support it. As arguers and as recipients of argument, we need to be aware of the quality of evidence so that we can judge others' arguments and select strong evidence to support our own arguments.

The remainder of this section will list and describe criteria to be applied to various types of evidence. Applying criteria such as reliability, objectivity, relevance, consistency, expertise, and recency to our own and others' evidence supplies us with a system for judging the quality of support provided for claims. The result can only be to make us better critics and users of argument.

Reliability

One question many audiences ask about a source is whether or not the source is reliable. *A reliable source is one that has proven to be correct many times in the past.* An excellent example of a reliable source is cited by Robert P. Newman and Dale R. Newman in their book on evidence:

> [Senator J. William] Fulbright's overall record of prophecy is pretty good. He warned President Truman that unless atomic energy were put under international control, there would be a monstrous arms race and proliferation. . . .He told Secretary [of State John Foster] Dulles that arms shipments to India and Pakistan would lead to war between the two. He . . .warned President Kennedy the Bay of Pigs would be a fiasco.[11]

Given Senator Fulbright's accuracy record for predictions, political leaders would have done well to attend to his opinions. People naturally trust sources and other people who have been proven right in the past. Thus we are likely to put our confidence in a Wall Street newsletter that accurately predicts stock market fluctuations or in *Consumer Reports* whose product assessments have repeatedly proven to be correct.

Expertise

Studies on factors affecting whether or not a source is believed have indicated that the most important factor is the recipients' perception of the source's competence.[12] *Expertise is the possession of a background of knowledge and information relevant to the subject matter under discussion.* Generally, we determine whether or not someone is an expert in a subject area by examining or considering the nature and extent of his or her experience with the topic. Education and formal training in a subject are one index as to whether a person is qualified. Experience may be gained in other ways, however. Any given senator would not be necessarily considered an expert on the conduct of Pentagon business, whereas a senator who had chaired the Senate Armed Services Committee for a number of terms would probably be considered an expert on the status of American armed forces. Any person who has published favorably reviewed books or articles on a subject is generally accepted as an expert on that subject. Furthermore, people who hold elective offices in professional organizations are highly regarded because it is assumed that they are respected by their peers.

Because of the importance of expertise in establishing the acceptability of evidence with most audiences, it is vital for arguers to fully cite their source's qualifications and experience with the topic. Instead of saying "Jon Smith concluded that NutraSweet should have been more thoroughly tested before it was approved by the Food and Drug Administration," an advocate should say "Dr. Jon Smith, a nutritionist at the University of Florida, recently reported in the *New England Journal of Medicine* after twelve years of investigation that. . . ." Unless the source's qualifications and experience with the topic are fully reported to recipients, they will have no way of making any judgment about the source's expertise. Emphasizing the source's credentials can enhance the argument's persuasiveness by showing that evidence is taken from someone whose knowledge and experience can be trusted.

Objectivity

Recipients feel confident in trusting sources they believe are objective about the topic of the argument. *Objectivity refers to a source's tendency to hold a fair and undistorted view on a question or an issue.* An objective source does not have views strongly colored by a personal emotional investment in one ideological viewpoint on the topic. We can hardly expect a member of the John Birch Society to provide a well-balanced discussion of the influence of the political left on contemporary American society. Nor can we expect a union leader to provide a complete account of corruption within his organization. We should not expect all sources to be completely impartial in their analyses of issues. After all, if they did not have a viewpoint to argue, they would not be making a claim or supporting a point of view. We should expect sources to be unbiased, however. *A bias is an unreasoned distortion of judgment or a prejudice on a topic.* A biased source often has a personal stake in the outcome of an argument and thus is unlikely to provide a fair account of differing points of view. A representative of the American Tobacco Institute (which is funded by tobacco companies) is unlikely to openly acknowledge the health hazards of smoking cigarettes. Nor is the National Rifle Association objective on the subject of gun control. Arguers using such sources are likely to discover that their recipients are aware of the biases of such groups and suspicious about any information taken from them.

Consistency

Recipients of an argument expect evidence used to be consistent with other information and with itself. Consistency with other information is called external consistency. *External consistency is the agreement of evidence with sources of information other than the source being used.* Concerning this form of consistency, Douglas Ehninger once remarked:

Because nature is not uniform and because people's actions are often unexpected or unpredictable, the fact that a given piece of evidence differs in form or content from other evidence bearing on the same point does not necessarily mean that it is false or inaccurate. Such deviation from the norm is, however, a justifiable cause for suspicion.[13]

A piece of evidence that runs counter to what is already believed or known about a topic is therefore not necessarily wrong, but the arguer using it has the burden of proving that the evidence is correct and can be reconciled with other seemingly incompatible facts the audience already believes or accepts. After all, the mainstream of opinion, or even of what is thought to be "knowledge" is not always correct. For example, Galileo argued that the earth revolved around the sun at a time when most people believed the sun revolved around the earth. Columbus believed that one could reach the East by sailing west at a time when most people thought someone attempting that would fall off the edge of the earth. However, when evidence fails to agree with other credible facts and sources, it can be detrimental to acceptance of an argument.

Advocates can increase the acceptability and believability of their arguments by using a sufficient amount of evidence from different sources to show that their support is externally consistent. Recipients of arguments can assure themselves that evidence is externally consistent by comparing it with facts they already know or information to which they have access.

Evidence should also be internally consistent. *Internal consistency is the absence of self-contradiction within information provided by a source.* When political leaders and other public figures contradict themselves, the media and the public take delight in pointing this out. For example, President George Bush was famous for his 1988 campaign pledge not to raise taxes ("Read my lips: No new taxes."). When he subsequently embraced a $137 billion tax increase as part of a 1990 plan to reduce the federal deficit, a *New York Post* headline read "Read my lips: I lied." In a 1992 address to the Republican Party convention, Bush attempted to resolve his inconsistency by blaming Congress for the increase, calling it "the Democratic tax increase."[14] Few things are more damaging to an arguer's credibility than the appearance of inconsistency or self-contradiction in statements that are made. Incidents such as Watergate and the Iran/contra arms deal have provided numerous examples of the need for internal consistency in statements an individual makes.

Recency

As a general rule, arguers should be aware of whether their evidence is or is not sufficiently current on the topic of their argument. The extent to which evidence must be recent varies with the topic under discussion. Advocates examining foreign policy, AIDS research, or international terrorism should rely on the most recent evidence available because our knowledge about such topics and the events that bring them to our attention change almost daily. Evidence about the world, objects, people, or anything else which changes needs to be current.

Other topics may be less affected by the comparative recency of evidence. Evidence relating to human rights or capital punishment, for example, may be of more enduring usefulness because conditions and values relating to these topics are less subject to change. Consequently, speakers appealing to values such as "life, liberty, and the pursuit of happiness" are arguing from safe ground because such values are an enduring part of American political life regardless of when the appeal was made.

Relevance

It is not uncommon for an arguer to present something that *sounds like* evidence and to connect it with a given claim when, in fact, the evidence is unrelated to the claim as made. Consider the following example of an ad for pain relief medication.

Evidence: Nine out of ten doctors recommend aspirin for headaches.

Claim: Aspirin is a powerful all-purpose medication.

A close examination of these two statements quickly reveals that the claim goes well beyond what is warranted by the evidence. First, the doctor stipulated a specific purpose for aspirin use and did not say it was "all-purpose." Second, the doctor made no statement about the aspirin's potency. So the evidence as stated does not relate to the claim as made.

One might think that irrelevant or unrelated evidence would be obvious, but often it isn't. The evidence is frequently somewhat related but does not directly support the claim because of the way it is worded or qualified. To detect this problem, we should be aware of the way the language and focus of the claim relate to the language and focus of the evidence. The following excerpt from a student's paper will illustrate how irrelevant evidence might *appear* to support a claim when, in fact, it does not.

A 1982 Safe Schools study showed that 36% of all secondary schools paddle children in a typical month. For junior high schools the figure jumps to 61%. Children all across the United States are being legally beaten under our laws.

The arguer uses a very connotative term—"beaten"—in her claim. Is this term, normally associated with child abuse which is illegal, to be equated with paddling? Furthermore, do the arguer's statistics show that this is happening "all across the country?" The answer to both of these questions is "probably not." The study makes no mention of geographical location, and punishment deemed legal by the courts should not be equated with abuse. Therefore, the claim departs from and exaggerates the evidence given to support it.

Access

When an arguer cites opinion as to fact about a situation or event, recipients should expect the source of that opinion to have been in a position to observe directly the matter in question. *Accessibility depends on whether or not someone offering an opinion is or has been in a position to observe firsthand the matter being disputed.* A person who has not directly experienced something must rely on reports or summaries provided by others or on impressions based on limited information. But any time we hear or read something secondhand, certain features and aspects are filtered out by the perspective and viewpoint of the person who reports it to us. The features identified and reported may not at all be the ones we would notice if we had an opportunity to observe the situation ourselves firsthand. The further we move from the original situation as directly observed by eyewitnesses, the greater the possibility for misinterpretation or error.

Newman and Newman emphasize the importance of accessibility to a reporter's ability to collect accurate and credible evidence.[15] They argue that we can be much less sure of reports coming from geographically remote foreign-language–speaking countries than we can of information from English-speaking countries. Their reason is that many reporters and observers in the foreign countries can observe only what local governments want them to see and can hear only about what the local governments want them to be told (particularly if the reporters or observers do not speak the host country's language). Furthermore, a senatorial junket or a two-week assignment in a country does not provide a congressperson or a reporter with sufficient exposure to situations to make accurate judgments. An important question to ask when we judge opinion evidence, then, is "Has the source had an opportunity to observe directly the matter in question, as well as the knowledge and experience to interpret competently what he or she has observed?"

Accuracy of Citation

When we make a decision on the basis of someone else's argument, we generally have certain expectations about the evidence presented to us. We hope it has been fully reported, is of the best possible quality, and is not misrepresented or intentionally distorted. Information that is second-rate or distorted does not provide reliable grounds for decision making. Arguers and recipients of argument should be aware of the ethical obligation to cite accurately the sources used to support arguments. There are many ways to interpret and communicate evidence so as to mislead recipients about its nature or quality, and not all involve deliberate falsification. Everyone would agree that adding to or altering a source's words is unethical, but often selectively omitting words or sentences is also ethically questionable. The overarching question is "Does the manner in which an arguer cites a source give recipients an accurate and faithful picture of the nature and intent of the evidence?" To clarify the implications of this question, we will consider *some* of the practices to be avoided.

1. *Omitting words to make the evidence more favorable to the arguer's claim.* Quotations from sources should be faithful to the context from which they are taken. If the citer of the source omits qualifying words or phrases or otherwise alters the meaning of the original, the practice is unethical. It is not difficult to completely

reverse the meaning of a quotation by leaving part of it out. For example, an arguer once claimed that

> For a man who is supposed to be a champion of democracy, it is odd that Lincoln said: "You can fool all of the people some of the time." This doesn't show much faith in the judgment of the people.

While this claim uses Lincoln's words, its interpretation was flawed because it does not address the remainder of Lincoln's statement, which was

> You can fool some of the people all the time and all the people some of the time, but you can't fool all the people all the time.

A practice of misrepresentation through omission with which we are all familiar is the movie advertisement that quotes movie critics' statements. For example, the *Boston Tribune* recently reviewed *Attack of the Killer Ants,* a horror film aimed at the teenage audience. The reviewer reported that "The only way this movie could be best picture of the year is if children under the age of sixteen are the only people allowed to vote for best picture this year." Yet, within three days the movie marquee announced "According to *Boston Tribune*— . . .Best Picture of the Year. . . ." Omitting statements from quotations to make them support one's point is easy to do but is wrong because it misleads and deceives the audience.

2. *Failing to distinguish between primary and secondary sources. A primary source is the original source of the evidence.* The primary source is the source in which the evidence first appeared. Eyewitness accounts; original documents (letters, diaries, personal notebooks); and transcripts of speeches as originally delivered are examples of primary sources. Primary sources provide the most immediate possible account of what was said by the source at the moment it was uttered.

Secondary sources are sources that compile, analyze, or summarize primary sources. Secondary sources often provide an interpretation or a restatement of what was originally said. For example, Thomas Jefferson's own correspondence about events leading to the Declaration of Independence is a primary source; an account of the Revolutionary War period in a history book is a secondary source. An original editorial is a primary source; a reprinting or summary of that editorial is a secondary source.

Arguers should use primary sources whenever possible because they are authentic and there is less possibility for error when they are used. When original or primary evidence is unavailable, arguers may use secondary sources, but they should always report that the information was cited in a secondary source and give the secondary source credit. Information in a secondary source may have been shortened, changed, or edited. For example, the *Reader's Digest* often changes and alters the articles it republishes. It is therefore important for recipients to know that the arguer is not citing the original source.

3. *Failing to give all relevant information about the source from which the evidence was taken.* When sources are cited, complete information about where the evidence was found and the qualifications of the sources should be given. This

includes the name of the author (if one is available), his or her qualifications, the date the statement was made, and the place of publication.

> Dr. James I. Brilhart, professor of anthropology at the University of California at Berkeley, argued in the January 12, 1980, issue of *Time* that "There is no such thing as a primitive language."

The arguer should provide enough information about the source that the recipients could track down the information and read it themselves if they wanted to. Fully disclosing the sources of one's information makes the argument appear credible and the arguer trustworthy.

Alluding to one's sources vaguely ("according to several articles that have appeared recently") is unacceptable. Not openly dating the information is deceptive. What if an arguer decided to leave out the date in the statement about primitive language cited above? A good deal of research has been done on language behavior recently and, if the recipients thought the comment was current, they would be deceived.

Ethical requirements for using evidence, then, include citing the words of the author so the citation conforms to his or her intentions and to the context, distinguishing between primary and secondary sources, and providing recipients with complete information about the source's qualifications and where the evidence was found. Omission or addition of words or information to make the evidence appear more favorable to one's claim is unacceptable.

■ *Evaluating Statistical Evidence*

One should keep in mind the adage "Figures lie and liars figure." All of the standards we have just proposed for fact and opinion evidence apply equally well to statistics. Statistics are the end result of a process subject to human bias and human error. Questions on a survey can be loaded; the people surveyed can be subjectively chosen; comparisons may be made of noncomparable units; and reports of findings can be slanted. Actually, statistics are often no more reliable than other forms of evidence, yet people often think statistics are true. As Newman and Newman laconically observed,

> If you would not believe a man who testifies that he has seen a flying saucer, do not believe him when he claims to have seen fourteen flying saucers each measuring twenty-two feet in diameter and weighing eleven tons.[16]

Gathering, using, and assessing statistics nevertheless present problems and challenges different than in other forms of evidence. This section will alert you to difficulties that frequently arise when arguers use statistics to support their claims. As an advocate, you should take care to avoid these pitfalls in conducting your own research. As a recipient of argument, you should scrutinize the statistics you hear and read and be alert to some of these practices.

1. *Using pseudo-statistics.* Sometimes we hear statistics applied to phenomena and situations in which it is difficult if not impossible to imagine how the statistics could have been compiled using good statistical methods. Here are three examples:

> According to *Esquire* magazine, February, 1964, Judy Garland sang "Over the Rainbow" 1,476 times.
>
> Seven out of every ten Americans cheat on their income taxes.
>
> *Mega Foods* has developed a revolutionary line of *Food* Vitamins and *Food* Minerals that are up to sixteen times more effective than the so-called "natural" vitamins and we can prove that with scientific research.

While the first case appears innocent enough, a closer look invites criticism. Specifically, how does anyone know precisely how many times Garland sang "Over the Rainbow"? Did someone count every time the song was sung in rehearsal, on stage, and in the shower? It is unreasonable to assume that this statistic could be accurate because there is almost no way it could have been collected. Similarly, the second piece of evidence would be difficult to arrive at reasonably. In order to collect the figure seven out of ten, what would a researcher have to do? Ask a group of people which one of them cheats? How would each of the respondents interpret what is meant by "cheat"? Given people's concern about tax audits, how many would honestly say they cheat? And how would "scientific research" determine that a certain brand of vitamins and food supplements is precisely sixteen times more effective than the natural alternative? Would respondents have to feel sixteen times better? Would they need to be sixteen times more resistant to disease? Was the study based on the self-reports of people taking the vitamins and supplements or on some other measure? We don't know.

2. *Comparing noncomparable units.* In essence, this practice, which emerges most frequently when longitudinal trends are reported, involves comparing dissimilar items while assuming they are the same. For example, due to inflation, the value of the dollar has declined. The 1993 dollar does not have the same value that the 1963 dollar did. This is why salary comparisons and commodity prices are always "corrected for inflation" when across-time comparisons are made. A similar problem arises when advocates use the federal government's crime statistics. The definition of what constitutes a felony or a misdemeanor varies from one time or location to another. When new types of crimes are included in the class of felonies, the felony rates appear to increase simply because the method of classification has changed.

3. *Using an unrepresentative sample. A sample is a population or group of people or objects that researchers survey when a study is conducted.* Most researchers do not have the time, money, or ability to survey or study every individual in a given state or the country. Consequently, researchers must draw upon a group or sample of people small enough to work with. Conclusions about their sample are then generalized to a broader group. One example is the studies of college

students that conclude that seventy percent will graduate after four years and find employment in their chosen field. This statistic was arrived at by surveying a group of students and then generalizing the conclusions to all other students. Certain questions need to be answered before such evidence should be used or accepted. Was the sample representative? Was the sample too small? Was the sample randomly selected?

A representative sample is one that possesses all the characteristics of the larger group from which it is drawn. For example, if the general population of college students on which a study is done is 35 percent college freshmen, 20 percent college sophomores, 10 percent juniors, and 35 percent seniors, then a representative sample is one made up of approximately the same proportion of individuals. In this sense, a representative sample is a group drawn from a larger group that shares most of the larger group's characteristics.

One of the best-known examples of use of an unrepresentative sample is the *Literary Digest*'s 1936 poll of voters that showed that Republican Alfred Landon would defeat Franklin D. Roosevelt by winning 57 percent of the vote. When Roosevelt won and Landon's share was only 37.5 percent, the *Digest* was so discredited that it had to cease publication. The problem with the *Digest* poll was it was based on an unrepresentative sample. The *Digest* mailed postcard ballots to people listed as owning automobiles and having telephone service. But the poorer classes who supported Roosevelt did not have such luxuries and thus were not included. This is why the poll results were so skewed in favor of Landon and so misleading.[17] The *Digest* should have sampled registered voters to get its results.

4. *Using poor statistical methods.* Sound methods for gathering statistical information should guard against redundancy and bias when responses are counted. For example, surveys that count some of the respondents twice or those that count only people who are highly motivated to respond are using poor statistical methods.

One example is the compiling of casualty statistics during the Vietnam war. Officers in the various services frequently sought totals of the number of enemy dead after battles. Various platoons were dispersed to conduct body counts, but there was no way to ensure that one platoon would not duplicate another's count. Furthermore, it was difficult to distinguish civilians from soldiers because many Vietnamese soldiers did not wear uniforms. Combat conditions also made counts very difficult to conduct. Nevertheless, casualty totals, however inaccurate, were reported.[18]

Another example is the media polls that ask viewers to call a toll-free number to express support for or opposition to an idea. One Seattle television station recently asked viewers to phone one of three numbers to express support for one of three potential state songs the legislature was considering. "Roll On Columbia" received the largest number of votes. The station projected a winning song based on the assumption that those who were motivated enough to call in were representative of the state population—a shaky assumption at best.

Remember that statistics can be erroneous, misleading, or biased. The adequacy of methods used to compile them should be carefully considered. In addition, the standards for other types of evidence, particularly objectivity and recency, should be applied to statistics as well.

■ *Locating Evidence*

The purpose of this section is to assist you in finding the evidence you need to support individual arguments and to build an extended argument for a proposition of fact, value, or policy. When you are conducting research on your topic, it is important to keep in mind all the criteria we have just provided for assessing the *quality* of evidence. All information sources are not equal. Some are more objective, more authoritative, or more scholarly than others. As you locate, read, and record information, remember to regard your sources with a critical eye.

Popular magazines and books that do not require extensive prior knowledge of a topic and that are intended for a mass audience can be contrasted with scholarly journals and books that assume a higher level of reader knowledge and sophistication and that are intended to provide in-depth analysis of a question or issue. Popular publications include news magazines such as *Time, U.S. News & World Report,* and *Newsweek*; magazines such as *Psychology Today* and *Ladies Home Journal*; and popular trade books. While your search for evidence can begin with the popular publications, it should not stop there. Having gained basic information on a subject, you should move on to scholarly sources that provide in-depth analysis of and detailed information on major issues in your topic area. Scholarly sources include professional journals and scholarly books. They are generally written by experts and reviewed by authorities.

Furthermore, you can ensure that you have a complete complement of thorough, reliable, objective, and authoritative information by seeking out a *variety* of sources of information from current publications. As you will see in this section, each type of source offers a different type of information and a different slant on the topic. By examining sources of different kinds, you will get a broad range of viewpoints and information of many varieties. The student who consults two journals, two books, and an encyclopedia on a topic will probably have more information of better quality than the student who reads three news magazines and two brief newspaper articles. Because the quality of your argumentative speech or essay depends *directly* on the quality of the evidence used to support your claims, it is in your interest to seek out high-quality sources. The remainder of this section will provide a brief discussion of sources of various kinds.[19] It is hoped that this list will be enough to get you started. If you conduct research on a regular basis, however, your own knowledge of the library will soon outstrip what is offered in this chapter.

Books

A logical place to begin your research might be the books on the topic. Your college or university library has a computerized catalog and/or a card catalog that index books by author, subject, and title. Such catalogs are usually quite easy to access and to use, and books can be located on many topics related to public policy and decision making. There are a few cautions to keep in mind about books, however.

First, book production takes time. From the time a book is written until it actually appears in print, two to five years can elapse. (This textbook, for example, was revised in 1992 but was published in late 1993.) Once the book has actually been published, it takes time for libraries to acquire and catalog the book. Consequently, information about a topic contained in books is somewhat dated. If your topic requires that you have recent information (within the last two years), then the card catalog might not be the best place to start.

Second, book-length studies of a topic take time to read. Investing the time takes time away from reading a variety of other sources. This is not to say that you should not consult books but rather that you should be relatively certain the book you are reading is a good source; perhaps that you should read it selectively, avoiding chapters and sections that appear to be only marginally relevant to your topic.

Third, information regarding a book's authoritativeness can and should be obtained, particularly if you intend to cite the book frequently in your argument. There are many reviews of books available. Book reviews are indexed in guides to periodicals, and there are many types of indexes to book reviews. One particularly well-known index is the *Book Review Index* that contains an author listing with abbreviated citations to reviews in over 450 publications in the fields of general fiction and nonfiction, humanities, and social sciences. If you have trouble locating a review of a book you want to use, ask the librarian for help. Also, you should ascertain the professional qualifications of the book's author. This information may appear in the front matter of the book. You may also find out something about the author in biographical dictionaries, a type of source we will discuss later in this section.

Periodicals

Periodicals are sources published periodically—weekly, monthly, quarterly, semiannually, and annually. They include popular magazines as well as professional journals. Periodicals are important sources of information because they are often up-to-date on topics of current interest. In addition, although you may have trouble locating books on certain topics, you will often succeed in finding periodical articles on them. Periodicals offer contemporary opinion on current events and issues as well as chronologies and relevant facts.

Like other sources, periodicals can be biased, unauthoritative, or otherwise inadequate. When you read a periodical, be aware of the credentials and background of the author. Does he or she have extensive background or knowledge of the topic, or is the person a journalist who is trying to meet a deadline? Sometimes, information about the author's identity and credentials may not be available; if so, the source may be a useful one on facts about the topic, but should not be used for opinion evidence. The fact that a source appears in print does not mean the source is qualified.

You should look for lengthy and in-depth articles on your topic. The kind of coverage provided by popular magazines intended for a mass audience (like news magazines) is often superficial and brief. Periodicals of general interest on current events that include lengthy articles by experts in various fields are to be preferred. Examples include *Congressional Digest, Congressional Quarterly, Current History, Commentary, Harper's, Fortune, The Atlantic,* and *The Progressive.*

Some magazines have a definite editorial slant. They may be liberal, conservative, socialist, or libertarian. *The Progressive* and *New Republic,* for example, are considered on the liberal end of the spectrum, while *National Review* is considered conservative. Reading a variety of periodicals will ensure that you encounter many points of view on a topic.

To locate information on your topic in periodicals, begin with the subject guides in various indexes. Some indexes are "hard copy," that is, produced in booklet or bound form and constantly updated. Other indexes are "on-line" (on computer and accessed via telephone lines) or on CD-ROM (compact disk format run on readers connected to microcomputers). If your topic is current, check on-line and CD-ROM sources, which are often more current than hard copy sources.

Your first step is to determine the key words of the topic in your search. For example, key words for sex education in the high schools might be "sexuality," "education, secondary," and "pregnancy, teenage." In the index, you will find the authors, titles, and locations of articles on the subject. This information will enable you to select those articles that seem most relevant to your topic. Various indexes—popular as well as specialized—may need to be consulted. Here is a list of some of the most comprehensive indexes:

The Reader's Guide to Periodical Literature indexes U.S. periodicals of broad, general, and popular character and provides a well-balanced selection of approximately 200 popular, nontechnical magazines representing all the important scientific and humanistic subject areas. Because of its inclusiveness, the uniformity of its entries, and the consistency of its cataloging, this index is highly regarded. *However,* it indexes only popular periodicals. For more specialized, scholarly research, one must consult other indexes.

Infotrac (magazine index) indexes more titles (435) than the *Reader's Guide* and is often more current. *Infotrac* also indexes English language periodicals of general interest and includes short annotations for each article. It runs from 1980 to date.

Humanities Index covers scholarly articles in professional journals in fields such as archaeology, classical studies, folklore, history, language and literature, literary and political criticism, performing arts, philosophy, religion, and theology. There is a CD-ROM version of this index from 1984 to date.

Social Sciences Index indexes professional periodicals in fields such as anthropology, economics, geography, law and criminology, medical sciences, political science, psychology, public administration, and sociology. There is a CD-ROM version of this index from 1983 to date.

PAIS International in Print includes current information on government, legislation, economics, sociology, and political science. It includes periodicals as well as some government documents, pamphlets, reports, and books. It is international, including close to 1,400 journals and 6,000 other items.

If you wish to do in-depth research on a specific subject, you should consult the indexes for specialized fields that will refer you to scholarly research on a topic. There are indexes for all major fields, including *Psychological Abstracts, Sociological Abstracts, Education Index, Business Periodicals Index, Art Index,* etc. Many of the articles indexed in these publications will provide detailed analysis and information on a particular issue or aspect of your topic.

Newspapers

Newspapers are indispensable sources providing the most current information on major events, issues, and persons. Aside from their editorial pages, they provide mainly factual information, although certain newspapers, like certain magazines, may have an editorial slant that influences their news coverage. Newspapers are particularly useful when you need a rough chronology of facts and events related to a given topic. Newspapers are therefore valuable reference sources but are somewhat less convenient to use than magazines.

Most newspapers are on microfilm. Actual copies of the newspapers are kept for only a short time by libraries, then they are photographed and put on microfilm reels for compact storage. To consult them, you must locate a reel, load it on to a microfilm reader, and roll through the reel until you find the newspaper article you are seeking. This is time-consuming but only minimally problematic. You can use newspaper indexes to find out how long an article is, what its contents are, and how useful it will be to you. Then you can make an informed decision on whether microfilm consultation is worth your time. Consulting microfilm takes only a little more time than consulting the hard copy of the newspaper itself.

Most major metropolitan newspapers are indexed. These include *The New York Times, London Times, Chicago Tribune, Los Angeles Times, San Francisco Chronicle,* and *The Washington Post.* The major newspapers in your own state or locality are probably indexed. Check with your librarian for further information on this. In the United States, *The New York Times* has historically been and still is regarded as the national newspaper of record. Other highly regarded newspapers are the *Washington Post* and the *Los Angeles Times.* A brief description of the major newspaper indexes follows.

National Newspaper Index on CD-ROM includes *The New York Times, Washington Post, Wall Street Journal, Christian Science Monitor,* and the *Los Angeles Times.* It is a good source for topics of national interest and covers the last three years as well as the current year. (For earlier material, you must consult other newspaper indexes.) It is frequently updated and is therefore current.

Newsbank Electronic Index provides subject indexing of articles from a wide range of U.S. newspapers on current issues and events, business, people, film and television, fine arts, literature, and the performing arts. Articles are available on microfiche and date coverage varies.

The New York Times Index is a carefully made subject index giving exact reference to date, page, and column with many cross-references to names and related topics. It also includes brief synopses of articles that answer some questions without the need to refer to the article and, more important, that enable you to decide whether to consult the microfilm.

The Times Index is the index to the *London Times* and its supplements. It includes a detailed alphabetical listing referring to date, page, and column in which an article appeared. This index is particularly appropriate for international and British news.

General Reference Works

Some of the most comprehensive indexes for information, biographical facts, and statistical data are listed below.

1. *Encyclopedias.* If your topic is not particularly current and if you need basic information on it, then a college- and adult-level high-quality encyclopedia is an excellent place to begin your research. Articles on various subjects in such encyclopedias are generally written by experts whose initials follow the article. Somewhere in the encyclopedia—usually in the first volume or in the index—the qualifications of the authors are given and so are easy to locate. Such articles often include bibliographies and key words on your subject that will enable you to do further research.

Most respected encyclopedias have a continuous-revision policy used to keep information up to date. This means that, instead of publishing thoroughly revised numbered editions, the encyclopedias' editorial staffs are constantly surveying subjects and planning revisions. Articles on rapidly changing topics are brought up-to-date with each printing. The three encyclopedias listed below use this policy.

Encylopaedia Britannica is the most scholarly English language encyclopedia available and has undergone many changes. The revised 15th edition (1991) contains a micropaedia, a macropaedia, and an index. The micropaedia is an independent ready-reference source with short articles on a wide range of topics. The macropaedia contains monograph-length articles written by an expert on the subject. One should approach this work by way of the index, a valuable tool to using it to best advantage. (Note: The index is new to the 15th edition. Earlier editions incorporated the index in the micropaedia.)

Encyclopedia Americana is a good comprehensive encyclopedia for general use. It is particularly strong in information about Americans, American towns and cities, and other subjects particular to this country. The articles are generally short and on specific subjects, but many lengthy articles on broad topics are also included.

Collier's Encyclopedia is a usable, readable encyclopedia aimed at the high school and junior college levels. The style is popular, clear, and concise. Broad entries predominate, although there are also short, specific entries. *Collier's* has a good record for accuracy, objectivity, and relatively up-to-date coverage of topics.

2. *Biographical Dictionaries.* The purpose of biographical dictionaries is to give you information about people—the events in their lives, their positions and qualifications, and their achievements and publications. These dictionaries are very useful

if you wish to find out more information about one of your sources. They come in three types: general, national or regional, and professional or occupational. Each of these types can be retrospective (treating nonliving or historical persons) or contemporary (treating living persons). Most professions and occupations have specialized directories and biographical dictionaries containing information about the professional qualifications of individuals recognized for accomplishments in a given field. Two of the national general interest biographical dictionaries are described below.

Who's Who in America is the best known and generally most useful of current works of this type. It focuses on notable living men and women who are selected because of their accomplishments or positions. It contains biographical data, addresses, and lists of works. It is supplemented by regional *Who's Who*s for each area of the United States.

Dictionary of American Biography is published under the auspices of the American Council of Learned Societies. This scholarly dictionary includes signed articles and bibliographies for each entry. It is intended to include noteworthy persons of all periods who lived in the United States and does not include living persons.

3. *Fact Books and Compendiums.* Sometimes there are specific facts you need to know in order to prove a point or support a contention you want to make. On current events and conditions, there are books of facts and accounts of developments of general interest that may be useful to you. Sources in this category include periodical fact compilations and almanacs. Three of the most highly regarded sources of this nature are described here.

Facts on File is a world news digest with an index published in New York. It is very current and emphasizes news events in the United States. It gathers material from fifty major newspapers and magazines condensed into short, factual reports. It is published weekly and includes such headings as World Affairs, National Affairs, Foreign Affairs, Finance, Economy, Arts, Science, Education, Religion, Sports, and Obituaries.

World Almanac is the most comprehensive and useful of American almanacs of miscellaneous information. It contains statistics on social, industrial, political, financial, religious, educational, and other subjects. Current and generally reliable sources for many of the statistics are provided.

Kessing's Contemporary Archives covers primarily the United Kingdom, Europe, and the British Commonwealth. It is published in London as a weekly diary of important events worldwide and includes texts of speeches and documents, obituaries, statistics, etc., with the sources of the reports cited.

Government Documents

Government documents are rich and invaluable sources of information on almost any topic of interest to policymakers in Washington, D.C., and elsewhere. Many students are intimidated by the volume and complexity of the resources in government documents, yet they need not be. Librarians working with these collections generally recognize that the public needs assistance in getting acclimated to the use of these documents and are willing to help those seeking access to them.

There are approximately 1,400 government depository libraries in the United States. The Depository Library Program, established by Congress, is based on three principles: With certain exceptions, all government publications will be made available to depository libraries; depository libraries will be located in each state and congressional district in order to make government publications widely available; and these publications will be available for free use by the public.[20] You can interpret these principles to mean that there is a depository library near you, perhaps even in your own college library. You can ask your librarian where the nearest depository is located. Many of the most frequently used government publications are often available in nondepository libraries for public use.

There are numerous highly useful government publications. The government, after all, is the largest and most fully funded gatherer and disseminator of information in the United States. When you ignore government publications, you ignore a very rich source of information. Below are described just five of the many useful government publications.[21]

Monthly Catalog of United States Government Publications is the basic bibliography or catalog for U.S. documents. It consists of two basic parts: a bibliographic section that lists all the information necessary to locate a document; and six indexes (authors, titles, subjects, series report numbers, stock numbers, and title key words). This index appears monthly and is indexed cumulatively.

Congressional Information Service Index is a commercially published guide that provides abstracts and indexing information for congressional hearings, committee prints, reports, documents, Senate executive reports, and Senate treaty documents. Its abstracts of testimony before committee hearings are particularly useful.

Index to U.S. Government Periodicals is useful because government sources are generally not included in most periodical indexes. It provides author and subject access to over 170 government periodicals on a variety of subject matters. The coverage is eclectic and ranges from highly technical journals to nontechnical periodicals for special audiences.

Statistical Abstract of the United States is published annually. This invaluable compendium of statistics is complied by the Bureau of the Census. It has topically organized chapters on population, banking, finance, insurance, social welfare, environment, energy, agriculture, manufacturing, etc. It has a comprehensive and easy-to-use index. If you need to find a statistic, it's probably there!

Congressional Record prints the debates and proceedings of Congress on a daily basis. Speeches, articles read on the floor of either house, and voting records are all reported here. This source has a murky past because it has historically printed not only what was said, but also anything Congress members wanted inserted (from recipes to local newspaper articles). Although this situation has improved somewhat and there are now restrictions on what can be included, the *Record* is still not entirely accurate.

Other Sources of Information

Additional sources of valuable information include "fugitive materials"—pamphlets, brochures, leaflets, and unpublished manuscripts—as well as interviews and media broadcasts. We will close this section by making a few brief comments about these.

Sometimes valuable information on a topic is available from agencies and organizations that researched and compiled it. Information of this nature can be obtained by contacting such organizations. It can also be located in the "vertical file index" of many libraries. The vertical file index catalogs and files brochures, leaflets, and other printed materials. Materials of this type should be regarded with caution because they are often produced by special interest groups with a vested interest or bias in some aspect of the topic. The researcher must use personal judgment. Pamphlets or brochures produced by the League of Women Voters, the Brookings Institute, or the National Safety Council are likely to contain accurate information. Those produced by the John Birch Society, the National Tobacco Institute, or the National Rifle Association are suspect because these organizations have adopted ideological stands on issues.

Interviews are useful but cannot be used in a formal argument as opinion evidence because they are not in the public domain. The information you cite must be available for your audience or opponent to inspect independently. Otherwise, one would have to rely on your word alone for what was said and this is unsatisfactory. Nevertheless, interviews are very useful when you need to find out information that is not available elsewhere. For example, if you needed suggestions on sources to consult and were having difficulty locating them in your library, an expert or someone knowledgeable on the topic would probably be able to direct you to sources of which you would otherwise be unaware. Also, if private unpublished studies have been done or private agencies have collected information on a topic, a source you interview might be able to provide you with the information.

There are five guidelines to keep in mind when using interview sources.[22] First, start early. Many expert sources are very busy and hard to locate. You need to give them advance notice when trying to set up an appointment to see them, and you must see them at their convenience, not your own. Second, prepare for the interview. You should only take up people's time with interviews if you cannot find the information elsewhere. Otherwise they will feel you are wasting their valuable time. So it is necessary to determine through research that the information is unavailable elsewhere. Third, plan a schedule of your questions. The questions should generally be open-ended and cover all the major topics of concern to you. Fourth, record the interview carefully, either in writing or by means of a tape recorder (with the interviewee's permission). It is not uncommon for someone to discover after an interview that the recorder didn't work or that he or she cannot make out the notes taken in the interview and cannot remember what was said. An interview that is not carefully recorded and reviewed while the memory is still fresh is almost as bad as no interview at all. Fifth, express appreciation to the interviewee for the time devoted to giving you information both orally and in writing. It is important that the interviewee feels that the time has been well spent and not like a discarded information container.

Finally, media broadcasts can be cited. If the broadcast is particularly significant, you may want to send for the transcript. (There is usually a charge for duplication and mailing.) Information concerning where to write for the transcript is often given at the end of the program, or you can call the local station carrying the broadcast to find out where to write. Of course, you can also videotape the program if you have access to a video recorder. Extensive use of statements made during a broadcast would require permission from producers, but you can use a broadcast for general information if you cite it as a source. When citing a broadcast, you will need to give the name of the program and the date and network on which it was aired.

■ *Recording and Organizing Evidence*

Finding the evidence needed to support a value or policy argument is essential to constructing a persuasive case. Equally essential is the ability to record and organize the evidence to make it useful and easy to access. There are two major challenges the novice researcher must overcome in using evidence: knowing what material to collect and organizing the material as it is collected.

First, how can you know what evidence to select and record before you know how your case will be constructed? Doing research and constructing a case are *reciprocal* processes; they depend on each other. The more you read and research, the more confident you become about what evidence is important.

Eventually, when the researcher sits down to construct a case, he or she becomes aware that certain subclaims require evidence and support that may be lacking. Two strategies are helpful in dealing with this problem. The first is to carefully record in the early stages of research information that may be useful later so the predicament of "I read that somewhere but I can't remember where" is less likely to occur. The second strategy is to begin thinking about your outline and then to construct it as early as possible in the research process. Only then can you see what specific items of evidence may be needed. (Concrete suggestions for constructing theses, cases, and outlines on value and policy questions are provided in Chapters 9 and 10, along with examples and models that may be useful.) You cannot construct a case before reading and learning about the topic area, and you cannot systematically advocate a policy or value without a prepared outline and evidence to support your arguments. Researching and recording evidence is a process of balancing these two requirements.

The second challenge is simply that of organizing your materials so they can be used easily later on. After having spent hours doing research in the library, many students find themselves with stacks of photocopies (on which they have forgotten to record the source); disorganized notes; and facts, statistics, and quotations that seemed important initially but appear irrelevant or incomprehensible when they examine them later. A few simple procedures can help you avoid confusion, use research time efficiently, and produce evidence sufficient to support a well-argued case.

1. Begin by reading objective, accessible treatments of the topic. Two-sided discussions or articles containing many views on the subject are helpful. You should be careful about sources presenting biased or skewed treatments of the topic. Once you have gained a balanced understanding of the issues related to the topic, you can proceed to more specialized or partisan sources.

2. Know the requirements of the sort of argument you plan to make. What issues will need to be addressed? (Knowing case requirements such as those discussed in Chapters 9 and 10 is helpful here.)

3. For *every* source, *begin* by writing up a bibliography card noting author, article or book title, magazine, newspaper or publisher, and publication date. If the source contains information regarding the author's credentials, a note should be made of them on the bibliography card. General consensus holds that four-by-six-inch cards are best for recording this information. Further, *any* photocopied information should be clearly labeled with the source and date. (Note: Failure to record carefully all source information and to label notes and copies will send you back to the library and waste time.)

4. In copying or clipping out quotations and information for possible inclusion in your argument, limit yourself to *one* unit of evidence at a time. It is convenient to copy or cut and paste these "evidence units" to note cards. The cards can then be shuffled and rearranged easily as you prepare your speech or essay. This recommendation to limit yourself to a single unit of evidence per card is based on the principle that each of the principal claims and subclaims in your argument will require evidence for support. Having the cards recorded in this way allows you to shuffle and reshuffle them as you construct your argument. If many pieces of evidence are recorded on a single card, they can be shuffled in this way.

5. For *each* note card, make a note of the author, title, and year of publication. This will avoid the problem of having a succinct, highly useful citation for which the source is unknown or not cited.

6. Label note cards with a subject heading to make them easy to locate, use, and arrange. The labels should correspond to the issues that you plan to treat in your argument. For example, if you were planning a problem/solution analysis, you would have note cards on the causes of the problem, the problem's significance, possible solutions, and advantages and disadvantages of each solution.

7. It is better to take too many notes than too few. Therefore, if you are in doubt about whether information or a quotation should be recorded, you should record it. Nothing is more frustrating than knowing you have seen valuable information, but being unable to locate it.

■ *Summary*

It is vital to be aware of the absence or misuse of evidence in arguments we hear and read and of its importance in the arguments we make. As defined in Chapter 1, evidence includes objectively observable facts and conditions, generally accepted beliefs or premises, and previously established conclusions. The purposes of this chapter are to discuss the nature and types of evidence, to provide guidelines for using evidence, and to explain how to locate and organize evidence when doing research.

Evidence functions as such because it is accepted by recipients and can be used to support other statements. If participants in an argument dispute a statement, it cannot function as evidence because it is not agreed upon. Generally, evidence falls into two broad classifications—fact and opinion as to fact.

Factual evidence comes from our observations and experience. It includes reports and descriptions of events or phenomena, statistics, and artifacts that are actual objects used to support an argument. Factual evidence is expected to mirror physical reality.

Opinion evidence is someone's interpretation of the meaning of factual evidence. When an arguer uses opinion evidence, he or she uses the statement of someone else to support a claim. Opinion evidence from experts is useful when an arguer does not have a great deal of personal experience with the subject of the argument.

We should be aware of the quality of evidence so that we can judge the quality of support for our own and others' arguments. Evidence should come from reliable sources who have proven correct many times in the past. Sources for evidence should have expertise in the subject matter of the argument, and it is important that audiences be informed of sources' qualifications when evidence is given. Sources should be objective, offering an undistorted and fair view of the question or issue. Evidence should be consistent, both with itself and with evidence from other sources. It should also be of recent vintage, particularly on topics in which conditions change over time. Evidence offered to support a claim should be directly relevant to the claim as stated rather than tangential or irrelevant. People who testify about a situation should have had access to it and an opportunity to observe it firsthand. Otherwise, the evidence is hearsay and less reliable. Finally, arguers who cite the statements of others should be accurate. They should not violate the context or intended meaning behind a quotation by omitting crucial words, making secondary sources seem to be primary, or omitting information about the source's qualifications or where the information was found.

Like other forms of evidence, statistics are often subject to bias and human error as well as errors by the people who use them. There are certain problems unique to the discovery and use of evidence, however. First, we should be aware of pseudo-statistics, those that are applied to phenomena and situations in which it is difficult to imagine how they could have been compiled using good statistical methods. Second, we should be cautious about comparing noncomparable units that seem to be of the same class but that are actually different. Third, we should use a representative sample, one that includes all the important characteristics of the group from which it was drawn.

When conducting research and locating evidence, we should keep in mind the fact that all information sources are not equal in quality. Popular magazines and trade books may be an acceptable place to begin research, but you should move on to professional journals and scholarly books containing in-depth analysis and more extensive information on your topic. You should also aim for variety in the types of sources and viewpoints you research in order to obtain a broad range of viewpoints and information.

One source of information, of course, is books. The library card catalog may be a good place to begin research if the topic does not require very current information. Books take years to produce, and the information in them may be dated. When using a book, be sure of the author's qualifications and expertise on the topic.

Periodicals and newspapers provide very current information on most topics. Periodicals range in bias from the extreme left to the radical right. They also range from popular and trade magazines to scholarly journals. Researchers can avoid relying on slanted or inexpert information by being aware of the nature and editorial biases of the periodicals they use and by consulting a wide range of periodicals. Newspapers are very current and useful when you need a chronology of facts and events related to a certain topic. Most major metropolitan newspapers are indexed. *The New York Times* is the national newspaper of record, and *The Washington Post* and the *Los Angeles Times* are also highly regarded.

Other sources of information include encyclopedias, biographical dictionaries, pamphlets and brochures, interviews, and media broadcasts. The chapter suggests guidelines and lists specific indexes and catalogs for each of these forms of evidence. The type of information source selected depends on the arguer's purpose and the topic being treated. Since the support offered for arguments is an important factor in whether they are accepted, arguers should locate and use a large quantity of high-quality evidence.

Exercises

Exercise 1   The following passages help illustrate correct and incorrect uses of evidence. Identify the primary weakness of each passage by applying the following criteria as discussed in Chapter 4.

Reliability	Evidence should be drawn from sources that have proven to be correct many times in the past.
Expertise	Evidence should be drawn from sources that have a background of knowledge in relevant information.
Objectivity	Evidence should be taken from sources that hold fair and undistorted views on a question or issue.

(*continues*)

Consistency	Evidence should agree with other sources and should be consistent with itself.
Recency	Evidence should be based on the most current information available.
Relevance	Evidence should relate directly to the claim that is made.
Access	Evidence should be drawn from sources that have firsthand knowledge of the matter being disputed.
Accuracy	Quotations should be complete and the sources of evidence fully identified.

Now, here is the evidence to be evaluated.

✳ 1. Mr. Herbert Kause convincingly argued last month that pregnant women should restrict their intake of caffeine. According to studies he conducted over the last six years, he has found strong evidence that supports the conclusion that caffeine is dangerous to unborn children.

2. Recently, at the University of Wisconsin, a study was conducted on listening and study patterns of freshmen students in a Speech 101 course. This study found that students in this course exhibited a lack of concentration in their studies and note taking. Therefore, we can conclude that college students have poor study skills.

3. In a special advertisement on Zenith Data Systems, Enrico Pesatori, Zenith Data Systems president and chief executive officer, said, "We have taken many major steps over the past 18 months to respond to our customers' needs for innovative, aggressively priced products, and to adapt to the upheaval in the PC industry. The product lines we have developed will clearly distinguish Zenith Data Systems in the marketplace."

4. But, in actuality, almost 25,000 people are involved in fatal alcohol-related accidents per year. Of these 25,000 people, over 25 percent are under the age of twenty-one. This means we are losing over 6,000 young people per year because of alcohol. There are several reasons a nationwide drinking age should be enforced. Statistics show that raising the age would save over 750 young lives per year nationwide.

✳ 5. We should reinstitute the military draft in this country. After all, we should recall John F. Kennedy's famous words "Ask not what your country can do for you, ask what you can do for your country." Our country is currently in a military force crisis and a military draft is something we can do for our country.

6. As the National Rifle Association has argued, if handguns were made illegal, then only those people who abide by the law would be barred from obtaining handguns. The criminals and the smugglers and racketeers would still have them.

7. A nationwide survey of college freshmen by Alexander W. Astin in 1991 revealed that 85.5 percent of those polled agreed that the government is not doing enough to control pollution. Water and air pollution controls should definitely be increased.

8. According to the Environmental Policy Institute and the Health and Energy Institute, "The Food and Drug Administration allowed irradiation of canned bacon in 1963 based on Army research. Five years later the FDA rescinded the approval, saying that the tests had been improperly structured and sloppily conducted."

9. A cosmetic company conducted a study of prospective customers for a new skin lotion. They sent 10,000 questionnaires to these customers asking them to compare the new product with a variety of other products. Ninety percent of those responding favored the new skin lotion; therefore the cosmetic company should proceed with production of the new lotion.

✳ 10. Dr. Harvey Brenner concluded a study of unemployment in 1975. He argued that for each one percent increase in the unemployment rate, the death rate increases by 36,667 lives. Therefore, the federal government should take immediate action to decrease the levels of unemployment in this country.

Exercise 2   Here are a number of pieces of information that might be needed as evidence in an argumentative speech or essay. Using the description of reference works and other materials in Chapter 4, indicate library source materials in which the following information is most easily located.

✳ 1. Total federal expenditures for defense in 1992.

2. A particular Representative's voting record on education issues.

3. Current information on AIDS research studies.

4. Crime rates in major cities in 1991. Current crime rates in your city.

✳ 5. The life of Malcolm X.

6. Major events in the 1992 presidential campaign.

7. Opinions about the quality of a recently published book.

8. Japanese automobile production statistics in 1991.

9. Summaries of the Congressional hearings on alleged sexual harassment of Anita Hill.

✳ 10. Events in Franklin D. Roosevelt's life.

Exercise 3   The following persuasive speech was written by Nikki Poppen, a sophomore at Pacific Lutheran University. It was presented at the 1988 National Individual Events Tournament. Examine her arguments and describe how she uses evidence and evidence chains to prove her claims.

1. Read the speech and underline each example of evidence you can find.

2. On a separate piece of paper, make two columns: FACT and OPINION AS TO FACT. Place each piece of evidence under the appropriate column.

3. Based on the criteria for correct use of evidence given above, was each piece of evidence used properly? Why or why not?

Do You Know Where You're Going To?[23]

As I was sorting through my junk mail the other day, I came across the usual advertisement from Time-Life Books, Ed McMahon's envelope from Publisher's Clearinghouse, and one . . . postcard that offered me eight spectacular days and seven blissful nights in Paradise for only $289.00. All I had to do was pick up the phone and dial. I would have to be crazy to turn the offer down. Wouldn't you?

For . . . thousands of Americans, this offer of an inexpensive piece of Paradise has prevailed. While they may be all the wiser for the experience, they are certainly none the wealthier. These Americans are finding out a few hundred dollars down the road that they have become victims of the numerous travel scams that are sweeping the nation. Today, let's examine the extent of these scams, why they are so successful, and what we can do to take the wind out of their "sales"—literally.

Originally, most travel scams . . . operated out of Florida. But Jeanne Epping of the American Society of Travel Agents (ASTA) warns of a westward spread of these organizations. Travel scams have now branched out into Arizona, Illinois, Indiana, Iowa, Kansas, Minnesota, Nebraska, and Nevada. According to Iowa's attorney general, Tom Miller, "travel and vacation scams have become a new wave of consumer fraud that is sweeping the nation."

Certainly, there is merit to his words. Statistics reveal that over 200 travel scams were operating within the United States last year and the bargain-shopping consumer lost up to 300 million dollars to these scams in the last 12 months.

The scams operate on two levels. The first . . . involves a phone call and an offer you can't refuse, usually to London, Acapulco, or Tahiti. The sales person informs you that for around $139.00 you can join the travel club and receive a trip free of charge as a benefit. If you would like to give him or her your credit card number over the phone or send a check by private courier, he or she would be more than glad to sign you up right away. If you are lucky, the scam will end there and all you will have lost is your initial $139.00 investment.

However, most scams go on to a more elaborate second phase. After paying the membership fee, the consumer does receive brochures concerning the trip he or she has just purchased. Upon reading the material, however, the consumer should be dismayed by the number of stipulations and guidelines attached to the vacation. A quick call to the bogus agent soon placates the complaining consumer, who is informed that all he or she needs to do is pay an extra $49.00 to have the accommodations upgraded and then the trip can proceed as planned. But what follows are numerous overbookings, cancellations, and new vacation offers along with the payment of more money.

Peter and Lisa Naumann of New York found themselves victims of just such a caper. The Naumanns were contacted by Holiday Magic Travel Club and informed that for only $189.00 they could join the club, receive a free trip to Orlando, Florida and a discount on a Bahamas cruise. The Naumanns paid the membership fee. They even paid an extra $50.00 to have their accommodations upgraded in Florida. Upon their return from Orlando, they put down another $100.00 in the form of a nonrefundable deposit on the cruise. Needless to say, the Naumanns never saw the Bahamas or their money again.

But at least they can console themselves with having got part of the deal. Susan Kaplan of the American Society of Travel Agents revealed in an October interview with *Travel Age West* that 75% of the travel scam operators don't have the product to back up their promises and the 25% that do, don't have the product they advertised.

Ray Kelter found this out during his catastrophic hunting trip to Colorado. Kelter's brochure informed him that there would be one guide for every two hunters and that base camp would personify the complete outdoor experience. Upon arrival, however, it didn't take him long to notice that there were only two guides for 33 hunters and that the base camp was so accessible that one man had driven straight up to the cook tent in his Mercedes. To top off the less than perfect trip, the expedition's outfitter returned to town that evening under the pretext of purchasing more provisions and never came back.

Banks and credit card corporations are having to shoulder a financial burden due to these scams. Sergio Pinon, Southeast Regional Security Director for Mastercard, pointed out in a November 1, 1987 interview with Richard Burke of Knight-Ridder newspapers that consumers are refusing to pay charges run up by the operators on their credit cards. Pinon says that the problem is costing Mastercard millions of dollars and as of January the problem is "out of control."

Travel scams are flourishing, but why? Why are we so beguiled into believing in an offer that is clearly too good to be true? Well, the answer lies partly in airline deregulation and partly with the American psyche.

Since the deregulation of airlines, many legitimate travel bureaus have been able to offer us lower prices on airfare and vacation packages. We see ads for these on billboards and in newspapers. Why should the ads we receive over the phone or in the mail be treated with any more skepticism?

Reporter David Pauly wrote . . . that . . . "Americans simply want to believe the offer is true. 67-year-old victim, Ira McDonald, commented in retrospect that "they have the sale down pretty good, but I should have known by now that there is no such thing as a free lunch." Ira McDonald is not the only one who has been caught believing in a good deal. Ray Greenly, Director of Consumer Affairs for ASTA, reported in the July 2, 1987 edition of the *Fairfax Journal* that "we've been getting hundreds of calls a week. People actually still believe that they can go to Hawaii for 29 dollars."

These sultans of swindle gamble with our gullibility and win. Can they be stopped? Right now the answer is no. These organizations can pick up and leave town before prosecution can even get underway. According to Susan Henrichsen, spokesperson for the Attorney General's Office in California, . . . the biggest barrier in the way of preventing travel scams is that "it takes a very long time for the scams to surface." By the time the consumer discovers he or she has been ripped off, the operators have already left town.

Exacerbating the problem of preventing travel scams is the fact that victims are hesitant to report the incident. Donna Crocker of the Georges County Consumer Protection Commission in Virginia, reported that "some people may only be out $39-$49 and don't report it. They think, 'Well, they got me this time,' and let it go. That keeps us from getting to the people sooner."

Even the operators that are taken to court have been very hard to pin down on criminal charges. Eunice Barow, Assistant District Attorney in Miami, points out that operators evade charges of mail fraud because they don't use the U.S. Postal system. Instead, they use private couriers. The promises they make to the victims are made over the phone and the evidence is seldom admissible in court. The only evidence that is left to use for prosecution is the brochure that the operators print themselves and it is usually loaded with loopholes. A frustrated Eugene Dieringer of American Airlines Corporation comments that "they have so many guidelines and stipulations to hide behind, that prosecution is virtually impossible." Most of the verdicts rendered against travel scam operators usually only consist of "civil fines that are small in comparison to the profits they make."

While the law has been . . . unsuccessful in stemming the tide of travel scams, more and more attorney generals are filing suits against potential travel scam institutions. California has successfully cracked down on Resort Vacations of Canoga Park which had fraudulently advertised Mexican vacations. And Attorney General William Webster of Missouri filed suit against 25 travel companies last June.

But until the law finally gets travel scams under control, the best protection against the scam lies with us. As conscientious consumers, there are three steps we can take.

First, listen carefully to the sales pitch you are receiving. Does the salesperson push for an immediate commitment on your part, without allowing you time to think? Does the sales person offer an extra vacation as an incentive? And does he or she ask for your credit card number over the phone? If any of these three things occur, chances are, you are being had. Second, get all the specifics. Ask for the hotels you'll be staying in and the airlines you will be flying with, and then call them to verify that they are truly sponsoring that package. Finally, put in a quick call to the ASTA at (202) 965-7520. They can run a quick check on the people you plan to do business with and see if any complaints have been lodged against the institution.

These steps take just a few minutes of your time and have the potential to save you several hundred or thousand dollars in the long run. Each year millions of dollars are lost to travel scams, but this year there is no reason why those dollars have to be yours.

Vacations are fun to take and I, like the next person, find the thought of spending time in paradise very, very appealing. Even more appealing is the thought of paradise at an affordable price. But remember, no vacation is affordable unless you know where both you and your money are going.

Notes

1. Russel R. Windes and Arthur Hastings, *Argumentation and Advocacy* (New York: Random House, 1965), 95.

2. For an account of Nazi propaganda efforts, see Randall L. Bytwerk, *Julius Streicher* (New York: Stein & Day, 1983).

3. James C. McCroskey, "A Summary of Experimental Research on the Effects of Evidence in Persuasive Communication," *Quarterly Journal of Speech,* 55 (1969): 169–76.

4. A discussion of this division and the types of evidence is presented in George W. Ziegelmueller and Charles A. Dause, *Argumentation: Inquiry and Advocacy* (Englewood Cliffs, N.J.: Prentice-Hall, 1975), 49–82. See also a discussion of the types of evidence in J. Vernon Jensen, *Argumentation: Reasoning in Communication* (New York: Van Nostrand, 1981), 107–37; and Douglas Ehninger, *Influence, Belief, and Argument* (Glenview, IL: Scott Foresman, 1974), 51–66.

5. Ehninger, 52.

6. Joe Mooney, "Short Fuse to Insanity," *Seattle Post Intelligencer,* June 28, 1987, F1. Used by permission.

7. Shelby Gilje, "Some Want July Fourth Fireworks to Fizzle," *Seattle Times,* June 28, 1987, K1.

8. Mooney, F1. Used by permission.

9. Mark L. Knapp and Judith A. Hall, *Nonverbal Communication in Human Interaction*, 3d ed. (Fort Worth, Tex.: Holt, 1992), 22.

10. Mooney, F1. Used by permission.

11. Robert P. Newman and Dale R. Newman, *Evidence* (New York: Houghton Mifflin, 1969), 95–6.

12. This research is summarized in Robert N. Bostrom, *Persuasion* (Englewood Cliffs, N.J.: Prentice-Hall, 1983), 79–81.

13. Ehninger, 61.

14. *Seattle Post Intelligencer*, August 21, 1992, A13.

15. Newman and Newman, 75–6.

16. Newman and Newman, 223–24.

17. Newman and Newman, 206–07.

18. Newman and Newman, 211–13.

19. Much of the information about indexes and other reference works in this section was taken from William A. Katz, *Introduction to Reference Work* (2 vols.), 6th ed. (New York: McGraw-Hill, 1992); and *Guide to Reference Works*, 10th ed., ed. Eugene P. Sheehy (Chicago: American Library Association, 1986).

20. Peter Hernon, Charles R. McClure, and Gary R. Purcell, *GPO's Depository Library Program* (Norwood, N.J.: Ablex, 1985), 1, 18.

21. Three useful books about government documents and their uses are Edward Herman, *Locating United States Government Information* (Buffalo, N.Y.: William S. Han, 1983); Joe Morehead, *Introduction to United States Public Documents*, 3rd ed. (Littleton, Co.: Libraries Unlimited, 1983); and Leroy C. Schwarzkopf, *Guide to Popular U.S. Government Publications* (Littleton, Co.: Libraries Unlimited, 1986).

22. Useful material about constructing interview schedules and conducting information-gathering interviews can be found in Charles J. Stewart and William B. Cash's *Interviewing: Principles and Practices*, 5th ed. (Dubuque, Iowa: William C. Brown, 1988).

23. Nicki Poppen, "Do You Know Where You're Going To?", 1987 speech presented numerous times in intercollegiate competition as a member of Pacific Lutheran University Speech and Debate Team.

C H A P T E R 5

Reasoning: Making Inferences

■

CHAPTER OUTLINE

- **The Usefulness of Formal Logic**
- **Reasoning as Inference Making**
  Quasi-Logical Arguments
  Analogy
  Generalization and
  Argument from Example

Cause
Coexistential Arguments
Dissociation

- **Summary**
- **Exercises**

KEY CONCEPTS

inference
syllogism
categorical syllogism
enthymeme
disjunctive syllogism
quasi-logical arguments
analogy
literal analogy
figurative analogy
generalization

argument from example
cause
necessary condition
sufficient condition
correlation
argument from coexistence
person/act argument
argument from authority
dissociation argument
value hierarchy

This chapter will consider the reasoning process used in arguments. Reasoning, as you will recall from Chapter 1, is the process in which an arguer links evidence with claims. Reasoning can be expressed in an inference statement. *An inference is the step one makes when one links evidence with a claim.* When we reason, we help our recipients move from what is known and acceptable (the evidence) to the unknown or controversial (the claim). We do this in one of two ways. The first and most obvious is to state our inference explicitly. For instance, we say "Don't play in the street *because a car might hit you.*" A second way is to leave our reasoning implicit and expect our recipients to supply the connection between evidence and claims. For instance, we might simply say "Don't play in the street. You might get hurt." Here we have left the inference "because a car might hit you" unstated.

Often when a person makes an argument without stating the inference, it is important to determine what the unstated inference is. Consider the following examples, taken from Chapter 1:

In the discussion of women's inability to advance in the business world, one woman says:

> Look, we're our own worst enemies. We'd rather sit around complaining than do something about it.

The second woman responds:

> That's absolutely right. I'm a nurse and I tried to get the women I work with to stand up against management. None of them would.

Assume that the claim is "We are our own worst enemies," and the evidence is that a particular group of nurses would not stand up against management, even when urged to do so. What is the reasoning that links this evidence with this claim? Can you state it?

Or, consider Cindy's argument that Karen should not transfer to the main campus:

> I already looked into early transfer myself, and I decided against it. Have you checked out the main campus? The classes are *huge,* and they're so impersonal! You'd never get to know your teachers. And, besides that, it's more expensive. Tuition is higher, not to mention the living expenses.

If Cindy's claim is that Karen should not transfer to the main campus and her evidence is that Cindy discovered that the classes were huge and impersonal and that the tuition and living expenses were higher, what is Cindy's inference? If you can fill in the inferences these arguers themselves did not state, you are well on your way to understanding how reasoning works in arguments. In the first example, the reasoning was that this particular group of nurses is like most women. In the second example, the reasoning was that Karen's experience at the main campus would be like Cindy's if Cindy had transferred. Even if you could not supply these inferences, you should be able to do so after you have read this chapter.

It is important to recognize what inference is working in an argument because the inference is the key to the argument. Being able to *recognize how the inference works* in an argument will increase your ability to analyze and criticize your own and others' arguments. The purposes of this chapter are to explain six of the most commonly used types of inferences and to suggest tests or standards for judging each type.

When people use arguments, they employ various inference patterns that they themselves may not always be able to identify and explain. Sometimes you can "flush out" a person's reasoning by way of a challenge ("Wait a minute, how did you reach *that* conclusion, based on the information you just gave me?"). Often, the unstated inference is the weak point in the person's argument. If you can identify how the arguer connected the claim to the evidence, you will know what type of reasoning was employed. Each kind of reasoning suggests a set of tests or questions that function as standards to evaluate its quality. Knowing what type of reasoning was used and what tests to apply will improve your critical thinking skills as you become better able to analyze and critique others' arguments.

Knowing the various kinds of reasoning will not only make you a better argument critic, it will make you a better arguer yourself. If you know the various reasoning forms and the tests and standards for judging them, you will be better able to monitor the effectiveness and quality of your own reasoning which is another important critical thinking skill. Argument theorist Stephen Toulmin has observed that a "sound" argument is "one that will stand up to criticism."[1] Each of the inference types discussed in this chapter—quasi-logical, analogy, generalization, cause, coexistence, and dissociation—must meet certain standards to be judged to be sound.[2] Knowing these types and the tests applicable to them will enable you to foresee possible weaknesses in your arguments and anticipate objections others might raise to them.

■ *The Usefulness of Formal Logic*

Contemporary study of logic as expressed in inferences is rooted to two traditions. The first is formal logic which studies relationships between events or groups in certain formally prescribed ways. In formal logic, arguments are reduced to their basic elements and expressed in standardized forms for purposes of comparison and analysis. The second tradition, informal logic, studies naturally occurring arguments which rely on principles and rules particular to certain fields of argument.

For nearly two thousand years, the study of logic emphasized study of formal types of reasoning such as the syllogism. A syllogism is a set of highly structured statements about common nouns and their characteristics which lead to a conclusion. *A syllogism is defined by its form; it is made up of three statements, includes three terms associated in pairs throughout the statements, and draws a conclusion from a major premise and a minor premise.* The terms in the syllogism are connected in such a way that the associations made among them allow the arguer to draw a conclusion. An example of a syllogism is the following:

Major Premise:	Every mammal is warm-blooded.
Minor Premise:	Every whale is a mammal.
Conclusion:	Therefore, every whale is warm-blooded.

Symbolically, the statements in this syllogism could be represented as follows:

Major Premise:	Every A is B.
Minor Premise:	Every C is A.
Conclusion:	Therefore, every C is B.

Essentially, this syllogism works by means of classification. If the statements made in the major and minor premises are true and if the form of the syllogism is correct, then the conclusion necessarily follows. In this example, it is true that all mammals are warm-blooded and that all whales are mammals. By identifying what is called the "middle term"—mammal—with the other two terms, one can reliably connect the remaining terms together in a necessary relationship.

There are two forms of the syllogism often used by arguers seeking to draw probable and not necessary conclusions from premises.[3] The first type of syllogism providing a form of argument that can be used in practical reasoning is the categorical syllogism. *The categorical syllogism draws a necessary conclusion from two premises stated as simple propositions.* The categorical syllogism works from a principle of classification, that is, by putting objects or persons into groups and assigning characteristics to them, one is able to draw a conclusion. Here are some examples of categorical syllogisms:

All students at this institution must pay tuition.
Mary is a student at this institution.
So, she must pay tuition.

No men are amphibious.
Smith is a man.
Therefore, he is not amphibious.

In order for arguments of this kind to be sound, two conditions must be met. First, the initial statement must be true. That is, the predicate of the statement must apply to all the persons or things named in the subject. Second, the instance named in the second or minor premise must fall within the class with which it is associated.

As you will see in the next section, argument forms in everyday discourse are usually not as explicit as they are in the categorical syllogism. In his *Rhetoric,* Aristotle described a *rhetorical* form of the syllogism to be used in speeches and public discourse.[4] He called this form the enthymeme. *The enthymeme is a rhetorical syllogism that calls upon the audience's existing beliefs for one or both of its premises.* Aristotle said that in most forms of public speaking, one would not want explicitly to state all of one's premises, for that would belabor the point and bore the audience. To see how an enthymeme works, consider the following example:

Mario is an Italian, so he is probably Roman Catholic.

Here the major premise, "Most Italians are Roman Catholic," is implied because the arguer believes that most recipients already know and accept this fact. Another feature of this argument that distinguishes it from the other categorical syllogisms we have discussed is that it is not all inclusive or universally true. Instead, the inference in this argument moves from a statement about *most* members of a class and from what *usually* is the case to a conclusion about a particular instance that "probably" exhibits a certain characteristic or behaves in a certain way. As long as such claims are qualified so that their likelihood of being true is made clear, arguments based on the categorical syllogism can be very useful. For example, if 95 percent of all Italians are Roman Catholic, we could conclude that Mario almost certainly is too. But if only 60 percent of that country's population were Roman Catholic, then our conclusion about Mario would have to be more carefully qualified.

A second form of syllogism which provides a basis for practical reasoning is the disjunctive syllogism. Unlike the categorical syllogism in which we make a judgment about something based on its membership or inclusion in a class, a disjunctive syllogism uses a process of exclusion or elimination. *Disjunctive syllogisms set forth two alternatives in the major premise, deny one of them in the minor premise, and affirm the other in the conclusion.* For example,

That long-haired person over there is either a man or a woman.
It is not a woman.
Therefore, it is a man.

Jones said I would receive either an A or a B for the term, depending on how I did on the final exam.
I did not receive an A because I failed the exam.
Therefore, I must have received a B.

Symbolically, this reasoning form is expressed as follows:

Either *a* or *b*.
Not *a*.
Therefore, *b*.

Reasoning of this form works from two or more alternatives. One by one, each alternative is eliminated until the candidate that remains is selected in the conclusion. In order for this form of reasoning to be sound, two conditions must be met. First, all possible alternatives must be identified. If they are not, an unnoticed alternative which is not considered may turn out to be the best. During the gasoline shortages in the late 1970s, many people claimed that we must either ration gas or entirely deplete our oil reserves. As it turned out, the increased price of oil led to many energy-saving measures which made rationing unnecessary. Second, the alternatives given must be separate and distinct. Otherwise, they cannot be eliminated one by one. For example, suppose we assume that we could go either to the mountains or the seashore on vacation and that we made a choice based on that assumption. In some areas of the country, however, mountains and seashore are within a day's drive of each other, and both can be included in a single vacation, so use of disjunctive reasoning to choose between them might lead to a poor conclusion.

A complete discussion of the reasoning forms of formal logic would be quite lengthy and involved. Extensive explanations of this topic are available in other sources for those interested in studying the applications of syllogistic reasoning to everyday argument.[5] This discussion is intended merely as an introduction to the usefulness of categorical and disjunctive reasoning. The rest of the chapter will focus on applied or informal logic as used in arguments intended for a particular recipient or recipients. Our emphasis on informal logic is congruent with the rhetorical perspective on argument in this text. When people make arguments in speeches, conversations, essays, and task-oriented groups, they are very likely to depend upon the six types of inferences we will explain in the remainder of this chapter.

■ *Reasoning as Inference Making*

Scholars who have studied arguments have discovered various schemes or inference mechanisms that arguers use to move from their evidence to their claims. The syllogistic types of inferences we have just discussed represent the kinds of reasoning studied in formal logic. Formal logic studies arguments from a *logical* perspective that emphasizes the formal relationships between elements in an argument. Twentieth-century philosophers such as Stephen Toulmin and Chaim Perelman have noted that we need to study the more informal kinds of inferences used in everyday discourse. And Perelman, in particular, noted the importance of the *rhetorical* perspective in reasoning and argument. He believed that many inferences and forms of reasoning succeed because audiences recognize and accept them when an arguer uses them. *The New Rhetoric,* by Perelman and his coauthor, Lucie Olbrechts-Tyteca, considered how arguers make use of reasoning links recognized by their audiences so as to get their claims accepted.[6]

In this chapter, we will discuss six particular types of inferences described in *The New Rhetoric.*[7] The first five types—quasi-logic, analogy, generalization, cause, and coexistential—are *associative* schemes; they bring elements together and evaluate or organize them in terms of one another. The sixth is *dissociative;* it aims to disengage or disunite elements originally considered as a unity. Dissociation is unique from the other five types but equally important. Just as reasoning can bond evidence and claim, it can also separate, and this is the role of dissociation. While some of these inference types, such as analogy, cause, and argument from example, have traditionally been studied and examined, others, such as quasi-logical argument and dissociation, were only recently fully described by Chaim Perelman and Lucie Olbrechts-Tyteca in *The New Rhetoric,* first published in 1958.[8]

Quasi-logical Arguments

Quasi-logical arguments are labeled "quasi" because they appear *similar* to the syllogistic structures of formal logic. Their similarity to the formal reasoning of logic or mathematics gives quasi-logical arguments a compelling air, and people often find them persuasive because of their simplicity and clarity. *Quasi-logical arguments place two or three elements in a relation to one another so as to make the connections between them similar to the connections in formal logic.* It would be fair to say that quasi-logical arguments can be reduced to formulas because of their simplicity and clarity. For example, one could say: "If player A beats player B, and B beats C, it follows that player A would probably beat player C." This is simply stated and formulaic, but the statement is probable and not certain like the statements in formal logic. In the section that follows, we will emphasize three types of quasi-logical arguments that are quite common—transitivity arguments, incompatibilities, and arguments from reciprocity.

Transitivity arguments are structured like the categorical syllogism and function like enthymemes. They have three terms that are associated with each other through processes of classification, but the relations between the terms are probable and not certain. Nevertheless, the relations established between the terms by the arguer are so clear and simple that they seem compelling, just like formal logical relations. Consider the following example:

As a student at Big Time Private University, Mary is paying high tuition.

This could be reconstructed in the form of a categorical syllogism as:

Major Premise:	All students at Big Time Private University pay high tuition.
Minor Premise:	Mary is a student at Big Time Private University.
Conclusion:	So, Mary pays high tuition.

Notice that the middle term (students at Big Time Private University), appears in both the major and the minor premises. The middle term functions like an "equals" sign; it enables the arguer to associate the remaining two terms ("pay high tuition," and "Mary") in the conclusion of the argument.

Transitivity arguments have to meet certain tests in order to be considered cogent, and these tests generally are related to their form.[9] First, they must contain three and only three terms. If they have four or more terms, they do not have the simple infrastructure of the categorical syllogism and thus cannot be classified as transitivity arguments. Second, their premises must be true. Since the conclusion of a transitivity argument simply combines the substance of the two premises, those premises must be true or the conclusion will be just as false as the premise with which one starts! Third, all three of the statements must be stated (or restatable) as simple classifications. If the relations are too complex ("is greater than," "leads to," "is comparable to," "represents," and so forth), then the inference is not a simple categorical inference and the argument is not a transitivity argument. Fourth, the middle term must occur in both of the premises so it can fulfill its "equals" function and make it possible to connect the remaining two terms in the conclusion.

The next type of quasi-logical arguments are incompatibilities. Incompatibilities are similar to the contradiction in that they imply two alternatives between which a choice must be made. (That is, one must choose one *or* the other.) The problematic nature of the incompatibility results because both alternatives are stated at the same time. Since the two alternatives are opposite to each other and since they are being simultaneously stated, their combination is "incompatible" and implies a situation that should be resolved. Here are two examples:

> I hate all people who generalize.
>
> Wait a minute, if I want people to trust me, you're saying I have to deceive them into thinking I'm something I'm not!

Of course, the first person is making a generalization herself while at the same time claiming to hate everyone who generalizes. The second person observes that in order to obtain trust, he has to deceive others. Both are affirming mutually incompatible and conflicting ideas together. Incompatibilities, then, contain two alternatives that are incompatible and show a conceptual conflict or a conflict of interests.

Incompatibilities can be tested in much the same way as disjunctive syllogisms. First, the two terms must indeed be mutually exclusive; if they can be maintained together, then no contradiction exists. Second, they must be viewed as necessarily relevant to each other. If one of the terms can be defined as irrelevant, then the incompatibility can be resolved.

The third form of quasi-logical argument to be considered in this section is argument from reciprocity. Reciprocal relations are reflected in the if/then relation of the conditional syllogism:

Major premise:	If you expect your superiors to treat you well, then you should treat your own subordinates well.
Minor premise:	Your superiors do treat you well.
Conclusion:	So, you should treat your subordinates well.

Reciprocal relations assert a hypothetical relationship between two situations or conditions and imply a mutual dependence between them: "You should treat your own subordinates as you want your superiors to treat you." Reciprocity implies symmetry; the two parts of the argument are related to each other and their equivalence is emphasized.

Reciprocity is based on our belief that individuals and situations that can be put into the same category should be treated in the same way. It emphasizes the characteristics that make situations or persons equivalent to each other. How can supervisors who treat their employees badly complain when they are mistreated by their own bosses? Employees, supervisors, and their bosses are all workers in the same company; they all likewise deserve fair and equal treatment.

Reciprocity arguments may be stated in various ways:

If I were ever required to violate my conscience to keep the office of president, I would resign the office.

How can begging be a crime in this society when charity is viewed as a virtue?

What is honorable to learn is also honorable to teach.

In all of these examples, two actions or situations are treated as reciprocal. Violation of one's conscience in order to retain an office means that one should resign the office; begging and charity are viewed as symmetrical acts, as are teaching and learning. The first of these examples is stated as a conditional relation, the second as a question, and the third as a statement of equivalence.

Arguments from reciprocity generally should meet two tests. They should equate two situations, individuals, or phenomena with each other. If more than two are implied, then the argument falls into some other classification. Furthermore, the arguer should use the symmetry between the two to argue that they should be treated reciprocally. Since the claim of reciprocity arguments is that the two elements should be treated together and equivalently, the arguer must highlight the similarity between them.

Quasi-logical arguments occur frequently and are commonly used in ordinary speech. People using quasi-logical arguments generally attempt to simplify a situation by reducing it to a very limited number of component parts and then set those components into clear and unequivocal relations. The clarity and simplicity of these relations thereby give their arguments the same compelling nature that we find in formal logic and in mathematics.

Analogy

Like reciprocity, analogy emphasizes the similarity between two elements. *An analogy reasons that because two objects resemble each other in certain known respects, they will also resemble each other in respects that are unknown.* Analogy differs from reciprocity, however, because its purpose is different. A reciprocity argument claims that two situations should be treated alike; an analogy makes an attribution about something that is unknown. Most of our early learning occurs by means of analogy. The child who discovers that the flame of a candle is hot and can burn fingers will avoid other fires in the future. We come to expect that what has happened in the past will happen in the future, that similar situations will have similar outcomes, and that similar objects will exhibit the same characteristics. Such regularities give order and uniformity to our experience and interpretation of the world.

There are two forms of analogy. The first is the literal analogy and the second is figurative analogy. *A literal analogy compares two objects of the same class that share many characteristics and concludes that a known characteristic that one possesses is shared by the other.* The inference made in a literal analogy can be represented by Figure 5–1, and it can be stated as follows:

> Object X has attributes A, B, C, and D.
> Object Y has attributes A, B, and C.
> Therefore, Object Y will probably possess attribute D as well.

For example, if one were to argue that a ban on nonreturnable bottles and cans should be instituted in Washington state because a similar ban in Oregon worked to decrease container litter, the argument would be a literal analogy. The arguer would probably support the analogy by pointing out similarities between the two states and conclude that what worked in one state would work in the other.

> The state of Oregon has moderate beverage consumption, limited revenues for collecting and disposing of container waste, demographic characteristics similar to Washington state, and a ban on returnable bottles and cans that effectively reduced container waste.
>
> The state of Washington also has moderate beverage consumption, limited revenues for collecting and disposing of container waste, and demographics similar to Oregon's.
>
> Therefore, Washington state's proposed ban on nonreturnable beverage containers will reduce container waste.

In this analogy, the *evidence* consists of all the statements of similarity between the two states; the *claim* draws the conclusion that the ban (the unknown characteristic) will work; and the *inference* is that the two states resemble each other in all relevant respects.

Literal analogies are subject to tests of at least three different kinds. The first has to do with the *quality of the comparison*. To have probative value, literal analogies must compare two objects that belong to the same class. In the preceding example, Washington and Oregon are clearly in the same class: Not only are both states, but they are also similar in size and demographics and located in the same region of the United States. To the extent that the compared objects are not alike in respects relevant to the conclusion of the analogy, the comparison is undermined. Differences in the classes compared affect the cogency of an analogy, since they may lead to differences or discrepancies that could undermine the comparison.

Figure 5–1
Structure of the Analogy

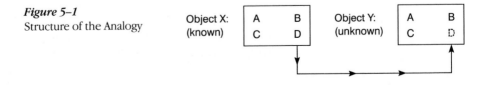

The objects compared do not have to be exactly in the same class, however. One could compare a program implemented citywide with one that is statewide; both are geographical areas although they differ in size, and the compared programs would differ in scope.

The similarities cited must also be relevant to the comparison and to the claim to which it leads. In the above example comparing Washington and Oregon, some aspects (patterns of beverage consumption, facilities for waste disposal, amount of litter) are relevant to the claim about whether a bottle bill will work. Other aspects, such as the climate and natural features of the two states, could be considered irrelevant.

A second test for the literal analogy has to do with *quantity;* is there a sufficient number of similarities to support the comparison? How many are enough? Obviously, there is no unequivocal answer to this question. The larger the number of relevant similarities, the more probable the conclusion. For example, if the support of the bottle bill could demonstrate that more bottles would be returned if purchasers had to pay a deposit than would be returned through increased recycling, the analogy would be strengthened. Or, if Washington and Oregon are virtually identical in all relevant demographic details, the comparison would be stronger.

The third test for a literal analogy is related to *opposition;* are there any significant dissimilarities that would undermine the comparison? For example, in Washington state at present, citizens generally recycle container litter. They are motivated to do so by the high cost of garbage disposal because recycling is free. Oregon does not have the same costs nor the same recycling program. Since so many containers are presently recycled in Washington, the benefit from a bottle bill might be minimal. This example illustrates the importance of considering possible significant differences when one advances a literal analogy or comparison to prove a claim.

The second type of analogy is the figurative analogy. From a logical point of view, figurative analogies do not have probative value but can be used to illustrate a point or to get listeners to see things in a different light. *The figurative analogy is a comparison between two objects of different classes in which a relation or quality within one is said to be similar to a relation or quality within the other.* Since the two objects in a figurative analogy are not truly similar, the comparison is metaphorical and illustrative rather than concrete and literal. Figurative analogies function primarily to make what is remote or poorly understood immediate and comprehensible. Speakers and public figures often use figurative analogies to focus the public's attention on the features of a situation that they want to emphasize.[10] President Reagan repeatedly referred to the Strategic Defense Initiative as a "shield," thereby causing the American public to see it as a passive barrier to be used only for defense. President Franklin Roosevelt compared the Lend Lease Act by which we supplied England with weapons and equipment to fight the Germans in World War II to the act of lending a garden hose to a neighbor to put out a house fire. Figurative analogies can be tested for their rhetorical effectiveness: Do they cause audiences to reshape their attitudes in the direction desired by the arguer? These analogies cannot be tested on logical grounds, however, since they compared items and objects from different classes.

Generalization and Argument from Example

In a generalization one reasons that what is true of certain members of a class will also be true of other members of the same class or of the class as a whole. As in the analogy, one begins with what is known or familiar (the examples that have been observed) and moves to what is less well known or less familiar. Furthermore, since reasoning is usually on the basis of characteristics that are known, the same type of inference is made in the generalization as is made in the analogy. The generalization, however, involves more than two instances and often makes claims about a whole class of objects.

Generalizations move from *some* to *all* members of a class. For example,

Because the rabbits I have seen have short tails, all rabbits must have short tails.

We've had a dry spell during July and August for the last three years, so there must be one every summer.

The characteristics (short tails, dry spell) that have been observed are generalized and applied to the class as a whole (rabbits, summer seasons). This sort of inference is illustrated in Figure 5–2.

Generalizations occur very frequently, and we use them to make conclusions about groups of people or experiences. We also see professionally produced generalizations in the form of Gallup polls, Nielsen ratings, market surveys, clinical experimentation, and other forms of statistical sampling where the population sampled is considered to represent the general population. Generalizations are also used when an arguer has been able to observe some but not all the members of a class and wishes to make a claim about the class in general. For example, Doris explains why she monitors her child's television viewing by referring to the programs she has seen:

DORIS: I never let Heather watch Saturday morning cartoons. I try to find something else to occupy her time.

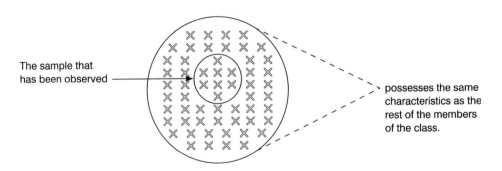

Figure 5–2
Structure of the Generalization

ANN:	Why? I surely do appreciate their babysitting potential.
DORIS:	Listen, have you ever watched that stuff? Crass commercialism and violence, that's all it is.
ANN:	Oh, come on. You're exaggerating.
DORIS:	No, I'm not. I watched "She-Ra" and "Hercules" and two other adventure cartoons one morning. Over one-third of the time was devoted to commercials for candy and toys. And I counted thirty-two violent acts in two hours of programming. I can think of better ways for my child to spend her time!

In her argument, Doris makes an inference about the programs she has not watched based on the programs she has watched. Her *evidence* is that one-third of the time was devoted to commercials and that she saw thirty-two violent acts. Her *claim* is that these programs display "crass commercialism and violence." Her *inference* is that "She-Ra," "Hercules," and two other programs are typical of all Saturday morning cartoons.

Another form of generalization is reasoning from example. Whereas a generalization will make a general statement based on observation of a *number* of examples, an argument from example will make a general statement based on observation of just *one* example. *Argument from example seeks acceptance for some general rule or principle by offering a concrete, particular case.* Suppose Doris had said, "In one of the programs I watched, there were eight fights in twenty minutes. The characters used swords, knives, and their fists to resolve every problem. Every disagreement led to a confrontation, and every confrontation led to a fight. This program shows how continuously violent these cartoons can be." As in the discussion between Doris and Ann, Doris is trying to establish a general trend. She does this by describing in detail a single program she has seen. The form of reasoning is illustrated in Figure 5–3.

Like the analogy, arguments from generalization and example are subject to tests of *quality, quantity,* and *general opposition.* First, the example or examples cited

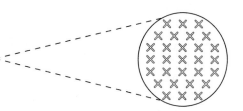

The one example
I have observed

represents the entire class
of which it is a member.

Figure 5–3
Structure of Reasoning from Example

must be *relevant* to the general claim. If the programs Doris cited were not cartoons, or if they were cartoons intended for older or adult viewers, her generalization would not be relevant to a claim about children's cartoons. Furthermore, the example or examples cited must be *typical* of the class in question. If no other Saturday cartoon has as many as eight acts of violence in a single showing, then the one Doris watched could not be considered representative of the rest of the cartoons, and her generalization would be open to question.

Second, the criterion of *quantity* (applicable only to the generalization) can be met only when Doris has cited a sufficient number of examples. There are nearly three dozen children's cartoons aired on commercial networks and cable channels on most Saturday mornings.[11] Are Doris's four examples enough to support her general claim? The cogency and persuasiveness of her claim will surely depend on the number of examples she can cite. This raises the question of how many examples are sufficient to support a generalization. There is no clear-cut answer because the requisite number of examples depends on the particular argument and the size of the available sample. There should be enough examples to satisfy the audience and to be weighed against possible counterexamples.

Third, the existence of counterexamples provides the test of *opposition* to both generalization and argument from example. Cartoons such as "Smurfs," "The Gummi Bears," and "Alvin and the Chipmunks" contain very few or no acts of violence and portray characters who cooperate peacefully with each other and have a good time. If Ann listed or described programs such as these, Doris would have to reconsider whether the characteristics of violence and commercialism really apply to *all* children's cartoons.

Cause

Arguments from cause claim that one condition or event contributes to or brings about another condition or event. Causal arguments are also arguments from succession; one event must happen before the other. But, further, the causal event must *produce* or *bring about* the effect.

There are two forms of causal argument. The first, or weaker form, is the necessary condition. *A necessary condition is one that must be present for the effect to occur.* To remain alive, people must consume both fluids and food. If either of these two necessary conditions is lacking, death from dehydration or starvation will result. In order to communicate, two people must speak the same language or at least understand the same nonverbal code. Reasoning from necessary condition is a relatively weak form because the effect is not guaranteed by the cause. For example, food does not *cause* life; it is simply *necessary* for life to continue.

The second form of causal argument is the sufficient condition. *A sufficient condition for an event or effect is a circumstance in whose presence the event or effect must occur.* In other words, the presence of a sufficient condition guarantees that the subsequent effect will occur. A broken fan belt on an automobile guarantees that the engine will overheat. If lightning strikes overdry timber, a fire will result. Further, a number of necessary conditions, taken together, may guarantee an effect. The presence of oxygen, combustible material, and temperatures in a certain range, taken together, constitute a sufficient condition for fire.

Causal influences are complex and frequently difficult to sort out and identify. The preceding examples of causes as necessary and sufficient were supported with examples of physical, natural, or mechanical phenomena in which causal sequences are clear and inevitable. In everyday affairs, however, causal sequences are often embedded in sets of necessary and sufficient conditions that mutually influence each other in complex relationships. Consider the following argument for increased state support of public education:

> We should increase our support for public education in our state. Rather than being a drain on our revenues, such an increase is actually a long-term investment. Increased funding will lead to a small class size, better facilities, and improved materials for use in the classroom. Students will complete their education with better skills than they now have and be more productive contributors to the work force. This, and the new industry which an improved educational system will attract to our state, will, in the long run, increase our tax base which will result in improved revenues for state government.

An arguer advancing such claims would have available data on the effects of increased state support on student/teacher ratios, capital improvements, and educational resources. These would serve as *evidence*. The arguer's *claim* would be "We should increase our support for public education in our state." The arguer's inferences are a series of causal claims: first, increased funding will lead to improved education; second, better-educated students will become more productive workers; third, increased productivity will improve the tax base and thus increase state revenues in the future. This network of causal claims is represented in Figure 5–4.

Like the other forms of reasoning, causal argument has tests to gauge its adequacy. The *quality* test deals with whether the cause is a necessary or sufficient con-

Figure 5–4
System of Causal Influence

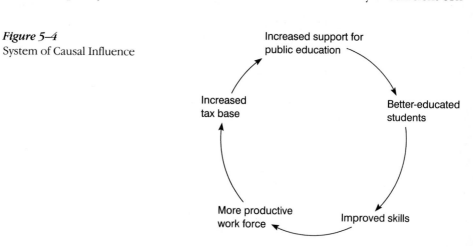

dition for the claimed effect. The fact that the necessary (as opposed to sufficient) condition does not *guarantee* the effect suggests weaknesses in the argument. Increased funding for education might be spent hiring more administrators and bureaucrats rather than on items that directly affect students; thus, education might not necessarily be improved. Furthermore, if a desired effect can be attained in the absence of the purported cause, that cause is not necessary. If the schools could be improved by being reorganized, or if teachers could be trained differently without spending more money, then increased funding could not be said to be a necessary cause.

The test of *quantity* is applied to a causal argument when one considers whether the cause is sufficient to produce the effect. If increased funding alone will not measurably improve the quality of education, then funding improvement alone is not enough. Other measures, such as improvement in teacher training programs and enhanced counseling to prevent student dropouts, may also be needed.

Finally, the test of *opposition* suggests that first, the effect may have been produced by some other cause; second, the effect may be the cumulative result of many causes working together; or third, there may be some other, unanticipated cause working counter to the cause the arguer has cited. For example, increased funding for schools may not lead to improved learning because of other forces in society, such as poverty and drug use, that undermine formal education. Factors such as broken families, child abuse, and racism might cause the failure of education even when large sums of money are spent to improve the schools.

Many times, although two events are related to each other, the relationship is neither necessary nor sufficient. For an argument to meet the tests for causal reasoning, it must be fairly rigorous. Because of the many causes that can contribute to a particular effect and because of the possibility that alternate causes can intervene and reduce or eliminate the expected effect, reasoning that relies only on linear, one-to-one cause/effect relationships is risky.

A method which has proved useful in discussing the relationships among phenomena is correlation. *A correlation claims that two events or phenomena vary together; an increase or decrease in one is accompanied by an increase or decrease in the other.* For example, if a market analyst observed that improvements in the economy would be bad for bond values (because higher interest rates devalue existing bonds carrying lower rates), the analyst would be correlating economic health, higher interest rates, and bond values with each other. The arguer who wishes to show a causal relationship among phenomena is often well advised to show that a variation in one will probably contribute to a variation in the other—an argument more modest than direct causal argument but also less risky because it acknowledges the possibility of alternate and counteracting causes.

Coexistential Argument

An argument from coexistence reasons from something that can be observed (a sign) to a condition or feature that cannot be observed. The sign or indication func-

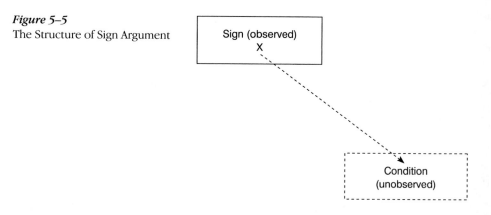

Figure 5–5
The Structure of Sign Argument

tions as the evidence; the existence of the condition or essence it indicates is the claim; and inferring from what we *can* observe something we *cannot* observe constitutes the inference. Coexistential reasoning is illustrated in Figure 5–5. As in analogy and generalization arguments, the inference moves from what is known (the sign) to what is unknown or less known (the condition or essence).

We frequently use signs that we can observe to infer conditions we cannot observe directly. A sore throat and runny nose are symptoms or signs of a cold. Buds on vegetation are a sign that spring is on the way. Or, consider the inference in the following conversation, for example:

JILL:	You need to put oil in your car before you drive it today.
JOHN:	Why? Is the oil low?
JILL:	Well, the oil light was on when I came home last night.

In this conversation, Jill's *evidence* is that the oil light came on. Her *claim* is that the oil is low. And her *inference* is that the light is a reliable indicator of the amount of oil in the car.

This example illustrates an important distinction between two forms of argument that are often confused—sign and cause. In a sign argument, the arguer intends to claim *that* a condition exists; in a causal argument, the arguer intends to explain *why* a condition exists or *how* it came about. Jill's intent is to claim that the oil is low in the car, not why or how it came to be that way. There could be an oil leak, the engine could be burning oil, or oil could have been consumed through normal wear and tear: If Jill had proposed one of these factors as leading to the low oil, she would have been making a causal argument.

Sometimes the distinction between coexistential and causal reasoning is subtle and depends on how the argument is worded. Consider the following examples:

The merchants downtown are beginning to close early and have installed iron grillwork on their windows. Crime must be becoming a serious problem in the community.

> Discrimination has existed in this country for a long time. This is shown by the Civil Rights Act, the Voting Rights Act, and the Equal Opportunity laws, all of which would have been unnecessary if discrimination did not exist.

Both of these are coexistential arguments that claim an unobserved condition—crime or discrimination—exists. In both of these examples, the arguer's intent was to show that certain underlying conditions existed, *not* to show their cause or how subsequent events came about. They could be viewed as causal arguments if the arguer had claimed that crime had *caused* the merchants to put up the grillwork or that discrimination *brought about* antidiscriminatory legislation, but then there would be a claim of a different type from the one in the above examples.

In coexistential arguments, both the sign and the condition it indicates *coexist,* or occur at the same time. Two varieties of coexistential argument are person/act argument and argument from authority. *Person/act argument reasons from a person's actions to his or her character or essence.* The act is taken as the sign; the person's character is taken as the essence.

> John turned in his last two papers late, hasn't washed his dishes in a week, and has a month's worth of dirty laundry piled up. He must be a procrastinator.

Unlike other forms of coexistential argument, person/act inferences often occur in the other direction; we reason that a person's essence or character will result in certain acts. ("Don't expect John to turn in his paper on time; he's a real procrastinator, and everybody knows it.")

Another variant of coexistential argument is argument from authority. *Argument from authority reasons that statements by someone presumed knowledgeable about a particular issue can be taken as evidence sufficient to justify a claim.* In argument from authority, the actual quote or statement functions as the evidence (sign); the claim is that whatever the quote attests is true (unobserved condition); and the reasoning is that the authority is qualified and accurate on the matter in question. Consider the following example:

> Dr. Daniel A. Lashof, senior scientist for the National Resources Defense Council, said in 1991 that "The United States cannot produce its way to energy security because it is responsible for 26 percent of the world oil consumption yet has only 3 percent of the world's oil reserves." From this we can conclude that efforts taken to increase production cannot alone solve our energy supply problems.[12]

Dr. Lashof's statement functions as the evidence in this argument; the claim is that production alone is an insufficient solution; and the inference is that a senior scientist for the National Resources Defense Council is a qualified authority to speak on this subject and that his statement should be taken as fact.

Like many other forms of reasoning, coexistential arguments must meet the tests of quality, quantity, and opposition. Sign, person/act, and authority arguments meet the test of *quality* when the relationship between the indication and the condition it indicates is constant and reciprocal. If the relation is only sporadic or intermittent, then the inference is unreliable. If a car's electrical system is shorting out, its oil light may come on even when the oil level is fine. One might see occasional grillwork on a building in an area because it is used for decoration, not protection. Making person/act ascriptions is usually a little risky because people do not invariably behave the same way all the time. (John might surprise you and actually get his paper written by the due date!) And authorities are often wrong on an issue, however compelling their credentials might be. The quality of authoritative arguments also depends on the quality of the source itself. Is the person cited truly an expert with current firsthand information relevant to the claim? The tests for authoritative opinion evidence, such as expertise, objectivity, consistency, and access, were discussed in Chapter 4.

The test of *quantity* is met when there are *enough* signs of the condition in question. We could be surer that crime was a problem in an area if there were further indications of it—a greater police presence and a higher incidence of arrests and convictions. We are more confident of claims based on authoritative statements when an arguer can cite *multiple* authorities with credible credentials on the issue.

Coexistential arguments meet the test of *opposition* when there are no countersigns that work against the arguer's claim. Frequently the presence of a condition might be disputed because there are as many signs indicating that it does not exist as there are that it does. A common example of this is speculation about the health of the economy. In a given fiscal quarter, durable goods orders and housing starts may increase, causing some economists to announce that the country is entering a period of economic growth. Meanwhile, unemployment may rise and productivity decline, causing other experts to point to these as countersigns that indicate economic decline. This same standard may, of course, be applied to arguments from authority; we are more likely to believe authoritative arguments when there are no other equally credible authorities testifying on the side of the issue opposite to the one in question.

Dissociation

The last type of inference to consider is dissociation. Unlike arguments from quasilogic, analogy, generalization and argument from example, cause, and coexistential reasons, which bring together or associate ideas, dissociation *disengages* or *differentiates between* two ideas. Furthermore, arguers using dissociation seek to assign a positive value to one of the ideas and a lesser or negative value to the other. *Dissociation arguments disengage one idea from another and seek a new evaluation of both ideas.* Most dissociations are based on the distinction between appearance and reality, with reality being what is valued. Consider the following dissociation used by Dr. Martin Luther King, Jr. in his speech "I Have a Dream":

> I have a dream that my four little children will one day live in a nation where they will be judged not by the color of their skin but by the content of their character.[13]

Here the external appearance—the color of one's skin—is dissociated from the internal substance—the content of one's character—and greater value is placed on the second concept. The claims in dissociative arguments are usually implied. Here, King's claim was that "people should not be judged by the color of their skin but by the content of their character." The success of King's argument is based on society's recognition that substance is more important and more to be valued than surface appearances. In a sense, this commonly recognized and accepted distinction functions as the basis or grounds for King's argument.

Dissociations are based on value hierarchies. *A value hierarchy places one value or values above another value or values.* There are many value hierarchies that are recognized and accepted in American society: The objective is valued over the subjective, the end over the means, the unique over what is common, and the permanent over the transitory.[14] Dissociative arguments make use of these hierarchies and especially of the appearance/reality hierarchy to dissociate concepts.

To clarify how value hierarchies are used in dissociation arguments, we will consider two more examples. In the first, a frustrated voter complains:

> I'm tired of all the rhetoric in this presidential campaign. I want to see the candidates engage in some substantive debate on the real issues.

This arguer dissociates "substantive debate" (real) from the candidates' "rhetoric" (appearance). Her use of "substantive" and "real" makes it clear that it is the second idea—engaging on the real issues—that she values. Or, consider another example from a discussion on corporate takeovers.

> I don't see a takeover plan here that's going to be beneficial to the corporation. It's a one-time hit, where we get a spike in the share price, and we cash out a corporation instead of operating it as a viable entity sometime into the future.

The value hierarchy behind this dissociation is the permanent as opposed to the transitory. The "beneficial" plan, the corporation as a "viable entity" (permanent), is dissociated from the "cash out," the "one-time hit" (transitory).

The tests for dissociation arguments are much more appropriately applied from the *rhetorical* rather than the *logical* perspective. Dissociation arguments rest upon hierarchies accepted by the arguer's audience. The *quality* of a dissociation depends upon the pervasiveness and strength of the value hierarchy used by the arguer. For example, during the 1992 presidential campaign, Vice President Dan Quayle repeatedly appealed to "family values" over other "life-style choices." He sought to dissociate family units made up of single parents and homosexual couples from the traditional two-parent family. His argument appealed to those audiences who believed the nuclear family unit should be valued over other kinds of families because the dissociations he sought to make depended on that hierarchy. A dissociation can meet the test of *opposition* when there are no hierarchies more pervasive and more accepted than the one the arguer is using. Quayle's dissociation was questioned by the segment of the American public that values freedom of choice over the more traditional life-style options.

■ *Summary*

This chapter defines and describes the types of reasoning used in arguments. The reasoning an arguer uses is expressed in an inference statement that links the argument's evidence with its claim. Often, arguers do not expressly state their reasoning in an inference statement. The ability to determine the nature of an unexpressed inference and its workings is an important critical thinking skill. Therefore, this chapter explains the various reasoning forms and the standards for judging them.

The first form of reasoning is quasi-logical which is based on formal logic and the syllogism. Quasi-logical arguments are comprised of a limited number of statements (three or less), and state relationships between a limited number of terms (three or less). The simplicity and clarity of quasi-logical arguments make them seem compelling and persuasive. This chapter describes three kinds of quasi-logical arguments—transitivity, incompatibilities, and reciprocity. Transitivity arguments are based on the categorical syllogism and link terms together through a middle term that functions like an "equals" sign. Incompatibilities are based on the disjunctive syllogism and state two incompatible alternatives at the same time, thus implying a contradiction. Reciprocity arguments state two mutually dependant alternatives and imply that they should be treated equivalently.

The second reasoning form is analogy. Analogies claim that because two objects resemble each other in certain known respects, they will also resemble each other in respects that are unknown. Literal analogies compare objects in the same class, whereas figurative analogies compare relations or qualities of objects in different classes. The probability or cogency of analogies depends on the number of similarities shared by the compared objects, the relevance of those similarities to the argument's claim, and the number of dissimilarities between the compared objects.

The third form of reasoning includes generalization and reasoning from example. A generalization attributes characteristics shared by certain members of a class to the class as a whole, while argument from example reasons from a concrete, particular case to a general tendency, rule, or principle. The strength of reasoning from generalization or example depends on how typical the example or examples are of the class, whether there are counterexamples, and, in the case of generalization, whether there are sufficient examples to represent the class as a whole.

Causal reasoning is the fourth reasoning form. Arguments from cause claim that one condition or event contributes to or brings about another condition or event. Causal relations take two forms: the necessary condition for an effect is one that must be present for the effect to occur, and the sufficient condition is a circumstance whose presence guarantees the effect will occur. The cogency of causal arguments depends on whether the cited cause is alone sufficient to guarantee the effect and whether there are countercauses working against the claimed cause/effect relationship. Furthermore, relations among phenomena are rarely as linear and rigorous as causal reasoning implies. For that reason, arguers wishing to show that variations are related often use correlation rather than causation.

Coexistential arguments are the fifth form of reasoning. An inference based on coexistence reasons from something that can be observed (a sign) to a condition or feature that cannot be observed. Two of the most common types of coexistential arguments are person/act inference and reasoning from authority. In order for coexistential arguments to be cogent, the relation between the sign and the condition it indicates must be reciprocal, the number of signs indicating the condition must be sufficient, and there should be no significant countersigns.

The sixth and last form of reasoning is dissociation. Dissociation distinguishes between ideas rather than bring them together as do other forms of reasoning. Dissociative arguments disengage one idea from another and seek a new evaluation of both ideas. Dissociations connect the first idea with what the audience most values ("reality") and the other idea with what is less valued ("appearance"). They thereby break the links between the ideas and cause the dissociated idea to be more valued. The tests for dissociation arguments depend on how strongly the audience actually holds the values relevant to the argument.

Exercises

For each of the following arguments:

1. Identify what type of argument it is—quasi-logical, analogy, generalization or example, cause, coexistential, or dissociation.
2. Identify the evidence, claim, and inference. (Remember that the inference is often implicit. If it is not explicitly stated, supply it.)
3. Provide two questions that you might use to test the argument.

Note: It is important to remember that sometimes an argument can fall into more than one classification. The nonreturnable bottle argument in this chapter, for example, was cause and analogy. *Note, too, that you will find some of these arguments quite controversial. They should be interpreted as sympathetically as possible, i.e., in line with what the author intended.*

The three steps described are demonstrated in regard to the following argument:

> About 35 years ago, the presidents of Harvard, Johns Hopkins, Stanford, Brown, and other colleges issued a manifesto warning against federal aid to education. Their point was that federal aid inevitably meant federal control, and of course they were correct. Federal aid now means that colleges . . . have to swear up and down that they do not discriminate against women. . . . And of course there is the whole business of affirmative action, and record-keeping that, one major college has complained, takes about $1 million worth of clerical time to complete.
>
> William F. Buckley, Jr., "The Feds and College Aid," *National Review*, August 1, 1986: 46.

A. This is an argument from *cause.*

B. *Evidence:*   Thirty-five years ago the presidents issued a warning. Colleges must swear they do not discriminate. One million dollars work of clerical time is spent in affirmative action record keeping.

Claim: Federal aid means federal control.

Inference: Federal aid and involvement causes the federal government to try to control education.

C. Might the effects of federal aid have desirable as well as undesirable consequences? Are the actions opposing discrimination the result of causes other than federal aid?

✳ 1. The listener should often be shown the conclusion contained in the principle. From this principle, as from the center, light shines on all parts of the work. In much the same way, a painter plans his painting so that light emanates naturally from a single source to each object. The whole work is unified and reduced to a single proposition enlightened in various ways.

> François Fénelon, *Letter to the French Academy,* Barbara Warnick, trans. (Lanham, Md.: University Press of America, 1984), 68.

2. Many of the stories depicting sexual harassment as a severe problem spring from "consultants" whose livelihoods depend upon exaggerating its extent. . . . Susan Webb, president of Pacific Resources Development Group, a Seattle consultant, says she spends 95 percent of her time advising on sexual harassment. Like most consultants, Miss Webb acts as an expert witness in harassment cases, conducts investigations for companies and municipalities, and teaches seminars. She charges clients $1,500 for her 35-minute sexual harassment video program and handbooks.

> Gretchen Margenson, "May I Have the Pleasure . . . ," *National Review,* November 18, 1991: 37.

3. It is said by those who have examined the matter closely that the largest number of divorces is now found in communities where the advocates of female suffrage are most numerous, and where the individuality of woman as related to her husband, which such a doctrine inculcates, is increased to the greatest extent. If this be true, it is a strong plea . . .against granting the petition of the advocates of woman suffrage.

> Joseph Emerson Brown, "Against the Woman Suffrage Amendment," in *American Forum,* Ernest J. Wrage and Barnet Baskerville, eds. (Seattle: University of Washington Press, 1960), 341.

4. Any Presidential candidate who would take a holiday on a remote Caribbean island with a woman to whom he is not married and with whom he plans to spend a non-working vacation is the biggest idiot who walked the face of the earth and for that reason alone is unqualified to be president of the United States.

> Adapted from a statement by Jeff Greenfield, "Politics, Privacy, and the Press" in *Ethics in America* television series (Corporation for Public Broadcasting, 1989).

5. [The following is said by the editor of a medical journal during a group discussion.] Our job is not to simply spread the bottom line in a few nifty, well-chosen paragraphs in the *Boston Globe*; our job and our responsibility is to review the data very carefully, to have experts in the field, recognized experts and statisticians, review it.

> Adapted from a statement by Arthur Relman, M.D., "The Human Experiment" in *Ethics in America* television series (Corporation for Public Broadcasting, 1989).

✳ 6. If we burn the forests of the Amazon, we are told, our planet's lungs will give out, and we will slowly asphyxiate. Surely we have better, more practical reasons for not burning them than to stave off universal catastrophe. I can easily imagine similar arguments that would have required the interior of North America to remain empty of cities—and yet I don't think this continent is a poorer place now than it was 20,000 years ago.

> Thomas Palmer, "The Case for Human Beings," *The Atlantic Monthly,* January 1992: 88.

7. We observe here today not a victory of party but a celebration of freedom—symbolizing an end, as well as a beginning—signifying renewal, as well as change.

> John Fitzgerald Kennedy, "Inaugural Address, 1961," *Speech Criticism: Methods and Materials,* William A. Linsley, ed. (Dubuque, Iowa: William C. Brown, 1968), 376.

8. Carla Kiiskila, a resident of a section of north Wallingford that seems pretty tranquil until you try to cross the street, wrote to the Engineering Department to complain about the hazards of N. 50th Street at Sunnyside Avenue. . . .Kiiskila complains that she has several times narrowly escaped being hit and had to run for the curb to get across 50th.

So the Engineering Department's van Gelder came out to examine the intersection. No doubt there's a danger and a problem there, he admits. [One citizen] got the Engineering folks to try crossing at the speed of an 85-year-old, and proved it was impossible. She unwittingly proved her point afterward, when she went to cross back (at normal speed) and very nearly got hit by a speeding car that spun broadside to avoid hitting her.

> Eric Scigliano, "How can a Citizen Cross the Road?" *The Weekly,* August 27–September 2, 1986: 22.

9. 1991 statistics from the Carnegie Foundation for the Advancement of Teaching show that SAT scores are directly proportional to family income. Students from families with incomes under $10,000 score an average of 768 (combined verbal and math scores) out of a possible total of 1,200. Students from families with incomes in the $30,000 to $40,000 range have scores averaging 884. Students from families with incomes over $70,000 have scores averaging 997. Since scholastic aptitude is related to a student's position on the wealth/poverty scale, which has a lot to do with where a family lives (affluent suburb or inner-city slum), alleviating poverty would be one way of improving scholastic aptitude.

> Edd Doerr, "Whither Public Education?" *The Humanist,* November/December 1991: 41.

10. If it were possible to conceive of a situation where after tonight no human heart would ever be raised again in gratitude to God and in appeal for forgiveness of sin and in petition for guidance, if never human heart again was open to divine suggestion . . .can you imagine the chaos that would follow?

> William Jennings Bryan, "Moses vs. Darwin," *Contemporary Forum: American Speeches on Twentieth-Century Issues,* Ernest J. Wrage and Barnet Baskerville, eds. (New York: Harper & Brothers, 1962), 109.

✳ 11. Let us not seek to satisfy our thirst for freedom by drinking from the cup of bitterness and hatred. We must forever conduct our struggle on the high plane of dignity and discipline. We must not allow our creative protest to degenerate into physical violence. Again and again we must rise to the majestic heights of meeting physical force with soul force.

> Martin Luther King, Jr., "I Have a Dream," in *Speech Criticism,* p. 381.

12. Solvents, refrigerants, methane, and oxides—all are among the pollutants that are increasingly gathering in the atmosphere. There they are dangerously altering the natural ozone layer that protects us against harmful radiation from the sun. . . .

> Michael H. Brown, "The Toxic Cloud," *Greenpeace,* October/December, 1987: 17.

13. The awesome power of government needs to be constantly checked by defense lawyers so that mere accusations don't inevitably turn into guilt. As Brandeis said, "In order to promote liberty, we need eternal vigilance."

> Adapted from a statement by Jack Litman, "To Defend a Killer" in *Ethics in America* television series (Corporation for Public Broadcasting, 1989).

14. But this man is innocent and your sources lied to you about him. The people who leaked to you leaked bad information. It seems to me the contract between a source and a reporter is honesty. I don't even understand what's on the other side.

> Adapted from a statement by Jeff Greenfield, "Public Trust, Private Interests" in *Ethics in America* television series (Corporation for Public Broadcasting, 1989).

15. Scandal has been part of the American system from the beginning. There were allegations of sexual misconduct during the Washington presidency. The Washington cabinet almost broke up over Hamilton and Jefferson fighting with each other. These are the problems that happen in a democratic government subject to public information.

> Adapted from a statement by Rudolph W. Giulani, "Public Trust, Private Interests" in *Ethics in America* television series (Corporation for Public Broadcasting, 1989).

16. On October 11, 1985, Alex Odeh, the 41-year-old regional director of the American-Arab Anti-Discrimination Committee in Southern California, was killed by a bomb trip-wired to the front door of the ADC office. . . . Alex Odeh was a victim of the new domestic terrorism against Arab-Americans. . . .

Shortly after major incidents in the Middle East, Arab-American students have been beaten in bars and on the streets—apparently because they looked Arab. After the announcement of the U.S. bombing in Libya, for example, ADC reports that five Arab students from Syracuse University were beaten up in a pub. A Saudi Arabian student in New Haven was assaulted outside a bar. And an Egyptian medical student required medical treatment after he was beaten in Royal Oak, Michigan. In each case, the assailants are reported to have made derogatory remarks about Arabs.

Steve Lerner, "Terror Against Arabs in America," *The New Republic,* July 28, 1986: 22–24. Reprinted by permission of *The New Republic,* copyright 1986, Washington, DC: The New Republic, Inc.

Notes

1. Stephen Toulmin, *The Uses of Argument* (Cambridge, Mass.: Cambridge University Press, 1958), 8.

2. Our typology of inferences is taken from Chaim Perelman, *The Realm of Rhetoric,* W. Kluback, trans. (Notre Dame, Ind.: University of Notre Dame Press, 1982), 53–137.

3. The treatment of syllogistic forms as used in practical reasoning is based on Douglas Ehninger, *Influence, Belief, and Argument* (Glenview, Ill.: Scott, Foresman, 1974), 73–76.

4. Aristotle *Rhetoric* 1357a and 1395b.

5. For excellent accounts of traditional syllogistic logic, see *The Encyclopedia of Philosophy,* s.v. "Logic, Traditional"; Edward P. J. Corbett, *Classical Rhetoric for the Modern Student,* 2nd ed. (New York: Oxford University Press, 1971), 50–81; Irving M. Copi, *Introduction to Logic,* 5th ed. (New York: Macmillan, 1978); and James D. Carney and Richard K. Scheer, *Fundamentals of Logic,* 2nd ed. (New York: Macmillan, 1974).

6. Here we draw upon our Chapter 1 distinction between the logical, dialectical, and rhetorical perspectives on argument taken from Joseph W. Wenzel, "Three Perspectives on Argument," in *Perspectives on Argumentation,* Robert Trapp and Janice Schuetz, eds. (Prospect Heights, Ill.: Waveland Press, 1990), 9–26.

7. Chaim Perelman and Lucie Olbrechts-Tyteca, *The New Rhetoric: A Treatise on Argumentation,* John Wilkinson and Purcell Weaver, trans. (Notre Dame, Ind.: Univ. of Notre Dame Press, 1969), 187–459.

8. In *The Realm of Rhetoric,* Perelman described four other inference types not discussed here. They are symbolic liaisons, double hierarchies, differences of degree and order, and model and antimodel. We have focused on the six we are discussing because they occur more frequently than the others. For a study of how frequently the various inference types are used, see Barbara Warnick and Susan L. Kline, "*The New Rhetoric*'s Argument Schemes: A Rhetorical View of Practical Reasoning," in *Argumentation and Advocacy,* 29 (1992): 1-15.

9. The tests for soundness of syllogistic reasoning are quite complicated and are beyond the scope of this chapter. For information on validity tests for syllogistic reasoning, see Corbett, *Classical Rhetoric for the Modern Student,* 50–81; *The Encyclopedia of Philosophy,* s.v. "Logic, Traditional"; and Copi, *Introduction to Logic*.

10. Perelman and Olbrechts-Tyteca, 385.

11. *TV Times* (supplement to *Seattle Times*), February 21, 1993.

12. Adapted from Daniel A. Lashof, "Should S.341, the National Energy Security Act, Be Approved?: Con," *Congressional Digest* (May 1991): 382.

13. Martin Luther King, Jr., "I Have a Dream," in William A. Lindsay, *Speech Criticism: Methods and Materials* (Dubuque, Iowa: William C. Brown, 1968), 382.

14. For a description of hierarchies accepted in Western society, see Gregg B. Walker and Malcolm O. Sillars, "Where is Argument? Perelman's Theory of Values," in *Perspectives on Argumentation,* 134–50.

Criticizing and Analyzing Arguments

■

CHAPTER 6

Fallacies: The Detection of Faulty Arguments

CHAPTER OUTLINE

- **The Nature of Fallacies**
- **Fallacies of Faulty Reasoning**
  - False Analogy
  - Hasty Generalization
  - False Cause
  - Slippery Slope
- **Fallacies of Grounding**
  - Begging the Question
  - *Non Sequitur*
- **Fallacies of Misdirection**
  - *Ad Hominem*
  - *Ad Populum*
  - Appeal to Tradition
  - Straw Arguments

- **Fallacies of Language Use**
  - Equivocation
  - Amphiboly
  - Emotive Language
- **Summary**
- **Exercises**

KEY CONCEPTS

fallacy
hasty generalization
single cause fallacy
non sequitur
slippery slope
ad populum
equivocation
emotive language

false analogy
post hoc ergo propter hoc
begging the question
straw arguments
ad hominem
appeal to tradition
amphiboly

Lawrence West's career has focused on developing nuclear weapons at the Lawrence Livermore National Laboratory. When he began, he expressed reservations about working on weapons of mass destruction and his role in their manufacture. Over time, however, he was able to dismiss his concerns and argued:

> Nowadays I would be quite willing to go and do full-time weapons work because I see the vast possibilities. . . . A tremendous amount of creativity is needed, and there are very few scientists willing to do it. Nuclear weapons can devastate the world. I recognize that. But we are making anti-weapons. My primary interest is not trying to find better ways to kill people, but better ways to kill arms. . . . I don't think I fall in that category of working on weapons of death. We're working on weapons of life, ones that will save people from the weapons of death.[1]

West's argument that building weapons of mass destruction saves lives is interesting because it juxtaposes two seemingly irreconcilable premises. On the one hand, a recipient is faced with the premise that nuclear weapons can destroy the world, and on the other hand, with West's conclusion that such weapons made by the United States are not weapons of death but are instead weapons of salvation. The argument is almost Orwellian in the sense that "War is peace" and "Weapons of mass destruction save lives."

This is an example of a flawed argument because the arguer uses the way it is expressed to convince the audience to simultaneously hold two mutually exclusive beliefs. While its surface meaning may seem apparent, closer examination of the argument reveals a flaw in the argument. The way it is expressed may seem reasonable, but its development is not.

West's argument reasons from dissociation as discussed in Chapter 5. It places opposite terms together in an attempt to justify building nuclear weapons. For example, West says that bad weapons are weapons of death which can result in world destruction. However, the weapons he helps build are weapons of life, weapon-killers, antiweapons, which preserve world peace. The problem with the argument is that it assumes the positive attributes through assertion without any justification for or evidence supporting his claims. Instead, West uses strong and emotion-laden language to focus attention away from his lack of evidence and support. The resulting argument is fallacious.

A fallacy is an argument that is flawed by irrelevant or inadequate evidence, erroneous reasoning, or improper expression. In other words, a fallacy is an incorrect argument. An argument can be fallacious because there is something wrong with its evidence, because the evidence does not support the claim, because its inference fails to meet standard tests of reasoning, or because the language in which it is expressed misleads the recipients. In other words, any time an advocate expresses an argument that either intentionally or unintentionally misleads or confuses a recipient, the argument is considered fallacious.

Arguers and critics of argument have long recognized that fallacies are a pervasive and persuasive part of argumentation. The first book on fallacies in the Western tradition was Aristotle's *De Sophisticis Elenchis (On Sophistical Refutations),* written in the fourth century B.C. In this book, Aristotle identified thirteen types of fallacies, and in the two thousand years since his book appeared, many more fallacies have been identified and classified.[2] Because there are so many ways that arguments can go wrong, some of the lists of fallacies are quite long, and the classification schemes vary widely. There are, however, certain common clusters of fallacies that are explained and exemplified in most studies of fallacies and that often recur in daily argument. These are the fallacies discussed in this chapter. These common forms of erroneous argument are frequently found in political speeches, advertisements, and other appeals to the public.

In Chapters 4 and 5 we discussed in depth the various tests of evidence and reasoning. As a general rule, if an argument's evidence or reasoning is somehow flawed because it fails one of these tests, the argument is most likely fallacious. Therefore, this chapter will not devote a great deal of time to repeating the various tests discussed earlier. We will emphasize again, however, that flawed evidence usually leads to a flawed argument. If a study cited in support of a claim is based on an unrepresentative or inadequate sample or weak methodology, its conclusions should be doubted and careful analysis may reveal one or more fallacies. If a source citation is inaccurate, secondhand, or taken out of context, it should be questioned. Arguments are only as good as the evidence on which they are based, and as recipients and critics of arguments, we should always examine evidence and reasoning carefully.

The fallacies in this chapter are divided into four groups: fallacies of faulty reasoning occur when the inferences drawn fail to meet one or more of the relevant tests of reasoning; fallacies of grounding stem from a lack of evidence or poor use of evidence; fallacies of misdirection focus the audience's attention away from relevant issues; and fallacies of language use occur when words and grammar are used by an arguer to mislead or confuse the recipients. This classification scheme reflects similar treatments of fallacies found elsewhere.[3] By the end of this chapter, you should be able to identify each of these standard fallacies when you encounter them, and you should also be able to explain why they are fallacious. Before turning to the specific types of fallacies, however, let us examine the general nature of fallacies as erroneous argument.

The Nature of Fallacies

Fallacies are the dark side of arguments. Too often they are unrecognized and receive little attention either by argument critics or by audiences. This chapter is devoted to a discussion of fallacies because they are both deceptive and persuasive. In fact, they are sometimes so persuasive that what an audience does not know can hurt it, or at least affect it in adverse ways.

The ability to recognize faulty arguments and to understand why they are faulty is a difficult skill to develop, yet it is an important skill. Faulty arguments are often hard to recognize because they are both appealing and deceptive. Faulty arguments are particularly important objects of study because they attempt to persuade an audience to alter ideas, values, beliefs, attitudes, or actions on the basis of misleading premises or faulty reasoning. Precisely because the purpose of argument is to persuade audiences to accept sound, well-supported claims, we should avoid practices which lead them to base decisions on erroneous inferences and assumptions.

While fallacies represent a misuse of argument, someone who commits a fallacy is not necessarily evil or ethically corrupt. Arguers may commit fallacies unintentionally as well as intentionally. Unintentional fallacies occur when an arguer is unaware of proper argument construction or use and commits a fallacy without realizing it. In this sense, fallacies are not only deceptive to audiences, but to speakers and writers as well.

Some arguers, however, may intentionally commit a fallacy so as to persuade a listener rather than search out appropriate support for argument positions. Intentional fallacies represent a deliberate attempt to mislead an audience into taking some action based on false information. For example, an arguer might use a biased source, omit part of a quotation thereby misrepresenting what a source said, or attribute a statement to an opponent that was never made. Such intentional fallacies carry important ethical implications as discussed in Chapter 2.

Theorists who study arguments agree almost unanimously that fallacies are deceptive and consequently dangerous.[4] Even Aristotle observed that honest speakers needed to prepare for spurious arguments and arguments that look genuine but are no more than shams.[5] All recipients of argument, therefore, need to develop a critical capacity to understand and assess the arguments directed at them.

The development of the capacity to recognize and diagnose the errors in fallacies depends upon skills this chapter is intended to help you develop. In order to recognize errors in inferences, you need to recognize what type of argument is being used and what tests of evidence or reasoning should be applied to it. To decide whether a premise adequately supports a claim you must determine whether the premise is relevant to the claim and at the same time independent of it. If an argument's language seems misleading, you need to identify the way in which its author is manipulating word meanings so as to deceive the audience. If an argument's central issue is evaded by the use of emotional appeals, you must be able to identify what the central issue is and how it is being avoided.

While many theorists have identified countless types and variations of fallacies, our focus here is to help make you aware of how fallacies can infiltrate arguments and unsuspecting audiences and deceive them. The treatment of specific fallacies in the remainder of this chapter will make you sensitive to the factors that make fallacies dangerous and enable you to identify and accurately criticize the fallacies you encounter. A final word of caution, however. Just because an argument is fallacious does not necessarily mean that the claim is incorrect. The claim may, in fact, be reasonable and valid, but not for the reasons and evidence expressed in the argument.

■ *Fallacies of Faulty Reasoning*

Often, erroneous conclusions are reached because arguers make errors in the inferences they draw. Such mistakes are fallacies because they fail to meet one or more of the tests of reasoning particular to the type of reasoning involved. In Chapter 5, we developed the various tests. In this section, however, we will focus on three types of faulty reasoning fallacies that commonly occur in arguments: false analogy, hasty generalization, false cause, and slippery slope.

False Analogy

You will recall that in Chapter 5 we defined a literal analogy as one which compares two objects of the same class that share many characteristics and concludes that a known characteristic that one object possesses is also shared by the other. Two of the tests for analogy are to ask whether the two objects being compared are sufficiently alike and whether there are any significant differences between them (in Chapter 5 we referred to these tests as quality of comparison and opposition). A false analogy fails to meet these tests. *A false analogy compares two things that are not alike in significant respects or have critical points of difference.*

People who use false analogies, then, overlook the possibility that the two objects they are comparing may be unlike each other in significant ways that affect the probability of their conclusion. Consider the following two examples:

> We should not teach socialism in the university any more than we should teach arson.

> The success of the 40-hour workweek in making corporate America efficient and productive suggests that we should use it on farms as well.

In each case the comparison is illegitimate because the objects being compared are not alike in significant respects. Arson is an illegal activity while socialism is an economic system which is neither legal nor illegal. Likewise, work in a corporate structure is regulated by the availability of resources, services, and personnel which are interdependent within an organization, whereas farm work is more independent and regulated by such factors as time of day, weather, and crop rotation.

As we observed in Chapter 5, figurative analogies compare two objects from different classes by means of a relationship that is more illustrative and metaphorical than literal. Such comparisons enliven arguments and bring their points home. The state has been compared to an organism, the kingdom of God to a mustard seed, and life to a theatrical play. When figurative analogies are used as if they were literal comparisons, however, and are the only form of support offered for a claim, they may be fallacious. Recipients of arguments based solely on figurative analogy should consider whether sufficient support has been offered for the similarity claimed in the argument's conclusion.

Hasty Generalization

In Chapter 5, we identified a generalization as an argument which reasons that what is true of certain members of a class will also be true of other members of the same class or of the class as a whole. Generalizations, then, extrapolate characteristics from *some* to *all* members of a class or may also attribute the characteristics of a class to its individual members. Two tests for a generalization are to ask whether enough members of the class have been observed and whether those members are truly typical—whether they possess the same characteristics as all other members of the class. A hasty generalization contains an error in sample selection. *A hasty generalization draws a conclusion about a class based on too few or atypical examples.*

Drawing general conclusions from too few examples is a common error of reasoning. For example, someone might say:

> I owned two MGs—a midget and an MGB—and they gave me nothing but trouble. The choke and the batteries froze up on the "B" and the clutches went out on both cars. They were always in the shop. MGs are poorly constructed and I think they should be avoided.

This generalization is unwarranted. The arguer's experience may have resulted from the way the two cars were driven and the care they received. Maybe the arguer rode the clutches and subjected the cars to excessively cold weather. We could only place confidence in the conclusion if we had performance and maintenance records for thousands of MGs and could compare them with other classes of cars comparable to the MG. Unwarranted generalizations of this type when applied to people are called stereotypes. Someone who believes that all Southerners are slow or that all Californians are easygoing based on an acquaintance with just a few members of either class is committing this fallacy.

Likewise, hasty generalizations can be based on observed samples that are not typical of the class about which the arguer's observation is made. Consider the following example:

> The growth and success of cottage industries in the Appalachian Mountains suggests that other impoverished areas can build small industries to raise their people out of debt.

This generalization is hasty because businesses in areas other than Appalachia are not like businesses there. The Appalachian Mountains are rural and remote, travel in portions of that area is difficult, and settled areas are widely dispersed and located some distance from shopping malls and convenience stores. These characteristics make patronage of cottage industries more likely. In other geographical areas, however, people might prefer accessible, inexpensive mass-produced goods, and cottage industries, which normally have a small profit margin, would fail.

Anyone to whom generalizations are addressed should ask the question, Are there other equally common examples that deny the conclusion? The key to discovering hasty generalizations is in discovering exceptions to the claim made. Stereotypes, for example, can always be undermined if one can cite instances of people who belong to the class in question but do not possess the characteristics attributed to the class.

False Cause

As we observed in Chapter 5, one reasons from cause when one concludes that one condition or event contributes to or brings about another condition or event. While critics may be able to expose many fallacious arguments by applying the tests of causal reasoning, there are two very common reasoning fallacies: *post hoc* and single cause. The former misidentifies a cause and the latter fails to go far enough in accounting for possible causes. Let us examine each of them.

Post hoc comes from the Latin *post hoc ergo propter hoc* which, literally translated, means "after this therefore because of this." *A post hoc fallacy mistakes temporal succession for causal sequence.* That is, one assumes that because two events are associated in time, one event must have caused the other. Consider four separate examples of *post hoc* reasoning:

> Serial killer Ted Bundy was found guilty of murder and executed in Florida. Before his sentence was carried out, he told an interviewer that he blamed pornography for causing his crime spree. Had it not been for pornography, he claimed, he would not have committed the crimes.

> A small university has been concerned with the increasing number of traffic accidents experienced by student drivers in university vehicles. In response to the problem, the university administration developed and administered a traffic safety program that consisted of a thirty-five-minute videotape on traffic safety and a five-question quiz on vehicle operation. To be a registered driver, the student needed to watch the video and pass the quiz. The Athletic Department registered drivers in a pilot program and then the program was extended to the entire university driving population. After one year, the program administrator wrote a memorandum to the campus community that argued the following: "Beginning with the appreciated assistance of the Athletic Department, the program, to date, has registered over 750 campus drivers and as a result, vehicle accidents have sharply decreased."

> John Hinckley shot President Reagan after seeing violent acts on TV. Therefore, violence on TV must have influenced his behavior.

> All people who have cancer drink milk. Therefore, drinking milk must cause cancer.

The arguer in each of these passages bases the claim on the assumption that some antecedent condition (pornography, driver registration, TV violence, or milk) resulted in some consequent condition (murder, decreased accidents, assassination attempt, or cancer). The connection between the antecedent and consequent, however, is temporal. In other words, the only apparent connection in each argument is that one condition followed the other, but in no argument does the advocate prove that there is a causal relationship that connects the antecedent with the consequent.

The sense in which antecedent and subsequent events in these examples are not causally connected can be clarified if one remembers the role of necessary and sufficient conditions we discussed in Chapter 5. If a subsequent event can and often does occur without the so-called "cause" preceding it, then the two events are not necessarily causally related. They may be, but the information provided in the argument does not provide sufficient warrant for the claim. Do all people who see pornography act violently? Even after participating in a traffic safety program, do accidents still occur? Do people who do not watch violent television programming commit violent acts? Do people who never drink milk have cancer? If so, then the antecedent conditions cited are neither necessary nor sufficient for the effects claimed. Just because two events occur one after another in a sequence does not mean that they are causally related; they might be, but then again they might not be.

Recipients of these arguments would need to seek out additional support to confirm or deny the reasoning. For instance, does TV violence cause violence or are violent people predisposed toward violent programming? In other words, is TV violence simply a symptom and not a cause of violence in society? Do all people who drink milk get cancer? Why are there exceptions? What the argument critic needs to look for is the regularity with which the time sequence of events holds true for the argument. If there are exceptions or other unexplained conditions which might account for the conclusion, then a fallacy has probably been committed.

The second causation fallacy is single cause. *Single cause fallacies occur when an advocate attributes only one cause to a complex problem.* As we observed in Chapter 5, there is almost never a single cause or explanation for any problem we face. Rather, most events in our complex society arise from a myriad of conditions and events. Yet advocates, hoping to simplify their arguments, attribute complex social problems to a single cause. This is misleading because it does not account for other, possibly important variables worth considering. Consider the following two examples:

> Low interest rates are the reason for increased housing purchases.
>
> Poor communication is the reason for the high American divorce rate.

In both cases only one cause is listed, but for an advocate to argue that there is only one cause for either housing purchases or the high divorce rate is naive at best. Increased housing purchases might be the result of a glut of houses on the market and higher individual incomes produced by a stronger economy. Financial problems and career choices may be alternative reasons for the high divorce rate. For any complex social, political, or economic problem we can think of, there is more than one cause and an arguer should take care not to oversimplify.

Slippery Slope

The slippery slope argument is often used by those who wish to argue against a new policy or proposal for change. *The slippery slope fallacy assumes, without evidence, that a given event is the first in a series of steps that will lead inevitably to some outcome.* Because the argument fails to provide evidence or support for the claim that some event will lead to disastrous consequences, it is a fallacy of evidence use.

This fallacy usually assumes some lockstep sequence of causal relations and argues that once we have instituted some particular measure, an uncontrollable series of events will happen. Damer describes the fallacious inference implied in this type of reasoning:

[The name of this fallacy suggests that] when we take one step over the edge of a slope . . .we often find ourselves slipping down the slope, with no place to dig in and stop the sliding, once we start the downward movement. While this image may be insightful for understanding the character of the fallacy, it represents a misunderstanding of the nature of causal relations between events. Every causal claim requires a separate argument.[6]

In other words, to conclude that event A leads to event B, we must have substantial evidence that one cannot occur without the other and that event B will always be produced by event A. This is what constitutes a sufficient condition and thus a causal claim. In most instances of the slippery slope, however, the relationship and predicted outcome is much less certain. Consider the following example of a conversation between James and his father, Jason:

JAMES:	I was really struggling with Biology 101 and I needed to drop it. I'm sorry because I know college is expensive, but I just wasn't getting it and I was concerned about my grade point average. I went in and I spoke to the prof. She seemed to think that dropping it was a good idea because I am so far behind.
JASON:	I don't care about the money as much as I care that you have dropped a class in your very first semester in college. It seems to me that once the going gets rough you're just going to quit. Is this going to be a pattern with you? Next time, will you drop the first class that is tough? I'm afraid that you might and if you keep this up you may never finish your degree.

Jason is concerned about his son's welfare. He wants him to succeed in college and he wants him to finish his degree. However, Jason commits a slippery slope fallacy. The implication here is that James will drop future classes if he is afraid of failure and that this one instance serves as a sign of a larger pattern of behavior. But Jason offers no *proof* for this claim. Instead, he discusses a particular event and reasons without evidence that it proves a larger pattern. The slippery slope is rarely accompanied by any evidence that the predicted series of events will in fact occur.

■ *Fallacies of Grounding*

Fallacies of grounding are the result of arguments that either use poor evidence or no evidence whatsoever. Instead, poorly grounded arguments tend to confuse reasoning or claims with evidence. When arguers commit this fallacy, they are asking recipients to draw conclusions from premises that are either missing or inappropriate to the claim. As you may recall from Chapter 4, there are many tests of evidence to help critics determine whether evidence is relevant, reliable, and valid. When arguers ground their arguments in evidence that fails the tests of evidence discussed in Chapter 4, then a fallacy of grounding occurs. While many such fallacies are possible, following are significant and prevalent forms of grounding problems.

Begging the Question

The fallacy of begging the question assumes as a premise or as evidence for an argument the very claim or point that is in question. Often, when arguers beg the question they are accused of circular reasoning because they use the argument's premises as their claims and reason that one supports the other when, in fact, there is little or no difference. Arguers who beg the question fail to seek external support for their claims so that they assume the point they are expected to prove. Consequently, as discussed in Chapter 4, the evidence for such claims is not externally valid and, in fact, cannot be validated through external sources.

You may recall that when we discussed the level of dispute in Chapter 1, we pointed out that in an argument one begins with evidence (statements which the audience accepts) and moves to prove a conclusion which is not yet accepted. Begging the question fallacies, however, are circular because they depend upon premises whose truth is assumed rather than established.

There are many ways to beg the question. Two of them are illustrated in the following examples.

The soul is immortal because it lives forever.

In this example, the arguer has simply stated the claim in two different ways. "Living forever" may be a definition of "immortal," but stipulating a definition does not constitute proof of immortality's existence. Put simply, the evidence in the argument cannot possibly be verified.

We must accept the traditions of men of old time who affirm themselves to be the offspring of the gods—that is what they say—and they must surely have known their own ancestors. How can we doubt the word of the children of the gods?[7]

The issue here is whether the ancestors' word can be trusted. To address the issue, the author commits an *ad verecundiam* (appeal to authority) fallacy to claim that we should trust their authority because their word on the matter is authoritative! This is a very clear example of the kind of circular reasoning often found in fallacies that beg the question.

When we suspect that a question-begging fallacy has been committed, we should determine whether premises independent of the claim have been offered to support it and, if they have, whether these premises are any more certain or acceptable than the claim itself. If the arguer has not offered accepted or proven evidence to support the claim, then he or she has begged the question.

Non Sequitur

This Latin phrase, literally translated, means "it does not follow." *The* non sequitur *fallacy contains a claim that is irrelevant to or unsupported by the evidence or premises purportedly supporting it.* In other words, the arguer grounds the argument in evidence that fails to support the claim advanced.

This fallacy, also known as "irrelevant reason," occurs very frequently. We are likely to be misled by it because the reasons or premises offered to support a conclusion somehow resemble the type of evidence which would be necessary to support it. People often present standards that *look* like evidence and connect them with claims in the same topic area, but actually the statements have no logical relation to each other. Consider the following two examples of *non sequitur* arguments:

> Plea bargaining affects many people. In the second quarter of 1993 in King County, there were 2,115 burglaries, 62 robberies, 109 rapes, and 2 murders.

In this argument, the first sentence is intended to be the claim and the second the evidence for it. But they are unrelated. The evidence does not tell us how many perpetrators of the listed crimes were arrested or charged, nor does it contain any information as to whether the charges were plea bargained. The only claim the evidence proves is there was crime in King County in 1993. The argument is clearly a *non sequitur.* The next one is more subtle.

> The United States is the only industrialized country in the world where teenage pregnancy is increasing. The Guttmachur study found that the U.S. pregnancy rate is twice that of Canada, England, or France, and seven times that of the Netherlands.

The first sentence is intended to be the claim and the second serves as evidence. Someone attending to this argument who is not aware of *non sequiturs* might easily be fooled. But notice that the evidence does not say that the pregnancy rate is *increasing,* only that it is higher than in other countries. To prove there's an increase, we would need comparable rates for different time periods showing that rates have increased in the recent past.

Non sequiturs are often subtle and yet seem obvious when they are pointed out. To detect them, we need constantly to ask, "What kind of evidence would be needed to support this claim?" and "Does this evidence qualify?"

■ *Fallacies of Misdirection*

When arguers present arguments to direct a recipient's attention away from the central argument and to some other irrelevant argument, then the advocate has committed a fallacy of misdirection. Most often, fallacies of this type are called *ad* fallacies. *Ad* is Latin for "to," and fallacies of misdirection are often called *Ad* fallacies because they appeal to the audience and not to the arguments. When an arguer shifts attention away from the argument and to the audience or something else, then the arguer has committed this fallacy.[8]

Such arguers may appeal to our stereotypes or prejudices about people, our tendency to go along with the crowd, our admiration for celebrities and famous people, or our respect for past practices. By appealing to such prejudices, which are often irrelevant to the claim made, arguments *ad* circumvent the substantive issues which should be considered in reaching a decision. Various forms of this category of fallacies include personal attacks on the arguer, appealing to audience emotions, and taking advantage of the audience's ignorance and gullibility to get a claim accepted.[9] In this section, we will discuss four of the most common fallacies in this category—*argumentum ad hominem, argumentum ad populum,* appeal to tradition, and straw arguments.

Ad Hominem

The issue an arguer raises and the meritoriousness of the arguer's claim are usually separate from the personal character, behavior, or characteristics of the arguer, yet the *ad hominem* fallacy diverts attention from the issue at hand and focuses instead on the personal character of the argument source. Translated literally as "to the person," *the* ad hominem *fallacy launches an irrelevant attack on the person or source originating an argument instead of responding to substantial issues raised in the argument.* For such an argument to qualify as a fallacy, the accusation must be irrelevant to the claim at issue and an effort to divert attention from it.

To illustrate this fallacy, let us consider two examples of it:

PARENT: I am really concerned about your grades this last semester. You were always such a good student in high school and now you have slipped to straight Cs. I think you need to study more and forget about seeing so much of your friends.

STUDENT: Why are you always on my back for not studying? *Your* grades in college were nothing to write home about!

In raising the issue of the student's grades, the parent makes three points—that the student had done well in the past, that his grades had slipped, and that he needed to cut back on his social life and study more. The student does not acknowledge or respond to any of these points but instead accuses the parent of being a slovenly student so as to put the parent on the defensive.

MARY: I think that 18-year-olds should serve a mandatory two years in the military. The United States should serve as a leader in the free world, and that requires a strong military to keep the peace. Often, however, our best people choose not to serve and avoid combat whenever they can. A mandatory service requirement would not be unreasonable.

GEORGE: The only reason you favor this is because you're a woman and women are not allowed to serve in combat zones. So, if your idea were instituted tomorrow, I would probably find myself fighting and in danger of losing my life while you would probably have some safe, cushy job here in the States.

In this case, Mary makes the argument that the United States might have a stronger leadership role and international presence by requiring all 18-year-olds to serve two-year terms. George, on the other hand, avoids the argument by attacking Mary's motivations and character instead of responding to the argument.

One way to detect *ad hominem* responses such as these is to be alert to instances in which an indictment of an argument seems intended to divert the discussion away from the central issues it raises so as not to respond to them. There are, however, many occasions in which the arguer's character is and should be a central issue. Assessment of the integrity of political candidates in election years may be an important part of determining whether they are fit to hold office. Questioning the qualifications of a source is also legitimate when one is responding to argument from authority in which the evidence offered is the statement of a source other than the arguer. An argument is *ad hominem* and fallacious only when it is used to circumvent and avoid a legitimate issue by arbitrarily attacking the person who raised it.

Ad Populum

Literally, *ad populum* means "to the people." *An* ad populum *fallacy occurs when the substance of an argument is avoided and the advocate appeals instead to popular opinion as a justification for the claim.* Consequently, the argument's claim is predicated on popular beliefs and opinions rather than on reason and evidence. Consider the following three examples:

> The President's approval rating has dropped to less than 35 percent. This is the first time during his term that his rating has dropped this low and proves, I think, that he is doing a very poor job.

> Most new parents buy Dr. Spock's *Baby and Child Care* book to learn about the care and feeding of newborn infants. So, it seems obvious that Dr. Spock has the best book available.

> Eighty-five percent of those polled believe fluoride in water causes cancer. Therefore, we should ban fluoride from our water supplies because of its consequences.

Each example presumes that if enough people believe something, it must be true. In fact, popular belief may even run counter to objective reality. Fluoridation does not cause cancer; at least there is no statistical validation for the popular conclusion. Appealing to popular beliefs, however, hides the reality of the argument and substitutes an extraneous issue.

As you can see in these three examples, just because many people agree about something does not necessarily mean it is true. The president's popular approval rating, taken alone, is not an absolutely reliable indicator of the quality of his work. Dr. Spock's book may contain no useful advice and still be a best-seller. And fluoride may actually prevent cancer, yet popular opinion might say otherwise. The point is that public opinion cannot control the factual nature of the world; public opinion only reflects the opinions and attitudes of a large group of people. If the claim of the argument does not involve the attitudes and opinions of people, arguments appealing to opinions commit *ad populum* fallacies.

We can think of many more examples to illustrate this point, and some have important social and economic consequences. Consider what happens when people stage a "run" on a bank or other financial institution. When this happens, depositors fear that the bank's financial situation is uncertain and a panic spreads throughout the depositors. When people begin withdrawing their money, others interpret this action as a sign of the bank's insolvency and begin to withdraw their money. The result is that the bank becomes insolvent because of popular opinion.

We are not suggesting here that arguments based on popular opinions are fallacious *per se*. Sometimes the argument seeks to focus on opinion. For instance,

> The latest Gallup Poll showed that the Superbowl is the most popular television event in history.

> Overwhelming popular support elected the president to office.

> The *Bill Cosby Show* was the most popular sitcom of all time.

In these cases, appeals to popular opinion are warranted because the crux of the argument is what the public thinks. The *ad populum* fallacy occurs only when the issues involved are not related to public opinion. Skillful argument critics should be able to discern the difference between arguments which depend on popular opinion and those which use popular opinion to avoid discussion of issues. Argument recipients who detect *ad populum* fallacies should attempt to redirect the arguments back to the issues at hand.

Appeal to Tradition

In Chapter 3, we discussed a convention of argument called *presumption*. Presumption is the assumption in favor of existing beliefs and states of affairs when proposals for change are made. Presumption exists as a convention of argument which reflects people's tendency to favor what is presently in practice until a good reason for changing it is offered.

Appeal to tradition attempts to convert that convention or practice into a right or a rationale for not making a change even when a good reason for doing so is offered. *The fallacy of appeal to tradition occurs when someone claims that we should continue to do things the way we have always done them simply because we have always done them that way.* Appeal to tradition takes advantage of people's reverence for past practice and attempts to avoid dealing with meritorious reasons for changing it.

Appeals to tradition are based on the often mistaken assumptions that what has worked in the past will work well in the future, that conditions have not changed, and that there is no better way of doing things. Consider the following true example (from a college curriculum committee meeting).

PROFESSOR SMITH: We should change the college grading scale to include plus and minus grading distinctions. A recent study by this committee indicates that there is a big difference between a B+ (94 out of 100 on most exam scales) and a B- (82 out of 100). Further defining the range of grades gives more precise information about a student's performance in the course.

PROFESSOR JONES: Why should we change? We've had simple letter grades without plus or minus distinctions in this college for over ten years and it's worked fine.

Professor Smith presented a good reason for changing the grading system—that the change will provide more precise information about student performance. Instead of responding to Smith's substantive argument, Jones merely appealed to tradition, saying that the way things have been done in the past should continue. When a cogent and meritorious argument for making a change occurs, then, the fallacy of appeal to tradition ignores the rationale given for change and assumes that traditional practice is the "best" way of doing things.

Straw Arguments

Straw arguments are often called "strawperson" or "strawman" arguments. They occur often in debates, discussions, and other situations where there is interactive argument. *The straw argument fallacy attacks a weakened form of an opponent's argument or an argument the opponent did not advance.* In committing this fallacy, arguers use as evidence an argument not advanced by their opponents but nonetheless an argument that bolsters their own position. It is very well described by Edward Damer in his book on fallacies:

> There are several different ways in which one may misrepresent an opponent's argument or position. First, one may state it in a perverted form by utilizing only a part of it, by paraphrasing it in carefully chosen misleading words, or by subtly including one's own evaluation or commentary in it. Second, one may oversimplify it. An opponent's complex argument can be made to look absurd when it is stated in a simplified form that leaves out important qualifications or subtle distinctions. Third, one may extend the argument beyond its original bounds by drawing inferences from it that are clearly unwarranted or unintended.[10]

As we will emphasize in Chapter 7 when we discuss the analysis and criticism of arguments, arguers should begin by grounding their arguments and criticisms on fair and reasonable representations of an opponent's argument. To do anything less is unethical. Consider the following examples of the straw argument fallacy:

MARY: I think it's time that this university begins to computerize its departments. Just think, if all the secretaries and all the professors were linked together by computer, access to student records would be more efficient, and students would save time and get better-quality advising.

DERRICK: Yeah, but if we computerized everything it would take forever to teach the secretaries and professors to use the system which would end up wasting more time than it saves.

Derrick took one aspect of Mary's proposal—the investment of time needed to get a computer network functioning—and discussed obvious problems with it. He did not, however, respond to the central issue she raised—the long-term gain in efficiency and quality of student service. By ignoring the major thrust of her argument, he created a straw argument. Here is another example:

GEORGE: With AIDS being the problem it is, I think this country is going to have to get tough. I think that within the next decade we're going to have to enforce some kind of mandatory AIDS testing for everyone.

HARRY: What a bad idea. This country would never have the ability to pay for testing. If we can't afford it, we shouldn't do it.

Here Harry selected an issue irrelevant to the thrust of George's argument and tried to divert the argument onto an entirely different track. If a large portion of the population is being infected and people are dying, then the major issue of public safety raised by George must be addressed. But Harry ignores it and instead attacks a strawperson—the cost of testing.

■ *Fallacies of Language Use*

Language is the medium in which arguments are communicated, and it has an inevitable impact on the way in which they are perceived and interpreted. In Chapter 11, we will examine the general influence of language on the composition and interpretation of arguments. In this section, however, we will be particularly concerned with instances in which the language in which an argument is expressed undermines the audience's ability to make a well-grounded decision about its acceptability. Most fallacies of language use are intentional. Arguers who use equivocation, amphiboly, or emotive language to get their claims accepted are deliberately trying to evade issues and avoid presenting solid evidence and reasoning in favor of what they advocate. How they succeed in these efforts will become clear as we examine the various stratagems employed in the fallacious use of language in making arguments.

Equivocation

Many words have more than one meaning, and occasionally arguers may exploit the ambiguity in language to make a fallacious claim. One way to do this is through equivocation. *The fallacy of equivocation exploits the fact that a word has more than one meaning so as to lead to a false conclusion.* For example, someone might say, "You shouldn't take that course in reasoning that is supposed to improve your ability to argue; you argue too much with your friends now!" Here the meaning of the term "argue" has shifted from "reasoning and correctly supporting claims" to "engaging in interpersonal squabbles." The arguer has made a false causal connection between the two based on the ambiguity of the meaning of the term "argue."

Equivocation is often used in deceptive advertising. For example, an advertisement that appeared in several national publications proclaimed that "Parents can receive a FREE college education" for their children. On its face, the bold letters across the top of the ad made a fairly spectacular promise that the average person might have a difficult time ignoring. For most people, the word "free" means without charge, cost, or obligation. But the word "free" means something very different to the producers of the ad. To them, "free" meant that parents needed to invest a substantial sum of money in their "tax-free open-end mutual funds and unit trusts" and pay for a variety of administrative "charges and expenses." The point was that if enough money was invested, then the interest produced should be sufficient to send a child to college. But placing money into a long-term investment is not "free" because there is an opportunity cost to having the money committed and there were administrative and other charges that were not "free". Words mean different things to different people and when word choice misdirects the audience's understanding of the argument, then an equivocation has taken place.

The question the recipient needs to ask is whether the argument contains any language that might be misconstrued by the arguer. If the answer is yes, then the recipient should ascertain what the words are intended to mean so that both recipient and arguer share a common understanding of the argument.

Amphiboly

Equivocation exploits ambiguities in word meanings, but *amphiboly exploits ambiguity in grammatical structure to lead to a false or questionable conclusion.* Just as there are many types of grammatical structure, there are many forms of amphiboly. For example, an advertisement might claim:

New, improved product X is unquestionably more effective.

Our product is new and improved.

More effective than what? New and improved compared to what? Here we have comparative adjectives used but no object provided for comparison. Perhaps product X is being compared with the "original" product, or perhaps with other brands of the product. We don't know.

Here is another example. An arguer claims that "When we compare the danger of spreading AIDS with the incursion of privacy involved in widespread AIDS testing, we must conclude that it is a risk we have to take." Is the antecedent of "it" the spread of AIDS or the incursion of privacy? Until we know what the arguer is referring to, the meaning of the claim is unclear.

An excellent example of the exploitation of amphiboly appeared in an article on the writing of recommendation letters. The article was in response to a number of defamation suits that had been filed against people who wrote unfavorable letters of recommendation. Faced with the problem of writing an honest letter without subjecting themselves to lawsuits, many letter-writers are puzzled about what to do. Robert J. Thornton, in his Lexicon of Inconspicuously Ambiguous Recommendations (LIAR, for short) recommends the circumspect use of amphiboly. Here are two examples:

> To describe a candidate who is woefully inept: "I most enthusiastically recommend this candidate with no qualifications whatsoever."

> To describe a candidate who is so unproductive that the position would be better left unfilled: "I can assure you that no person would be better for this job."[11]

Because of the ambiguity in the way the sentences are constructed, the reader of the first sentence assumes that the recommendation is unqualified (when it is actually the *candidate* who is unqualified). The reader of the second sentence may interpret it to mean that the candidate is the best alternative (when hiring *no one* would be the best alternative). Such examples remind us to be on the lookout for intentional and manipulative ambiguity. If we are confused about what the arguer meant by the wording of a claim, there may be a good reason for our confusion!

Emotive Language

The language used to express thoughts and ideas often is a potent force in influencing our opinions and actions. As one philosopher of argument observed, "An emotional appeal to us for some specific action may be so powerful as to inhibit our capacity to exercise critical judgment on the reasons offered in favor of the action urged."[12] *The fallacy of emotive language manipulates the connotative meaning of words to establish a claim without proof.* It attempts to persuade an audience by getting them to respond emotionally to images and associations evoked by the language used rather than by judging the quality of the arguer's evidence and reasoning.

Emotive language is often used by politicians, advertisers, and propagandists to get acceptance for ideas that cannot be effectively supported through reasoning and evidence. The idea behind the fallacy of emotive language is to set up associations in the audience's mind with either pleasant or favorable values and attitudes (in order to win acceptance for an idea) or with unpleasant experiences or disfavored values (to get an idea rejected). Language is therefore used suggestively and can have an unconscious influence.

President Harry Truman can serve as an interesting example. In 1962, a historian, Herbert Feis, contacted Truman with several questions about Truman's decision to use the atomic bomb on Hiroshima and Nagasaki during World War II. Truman had been the subject of much criticism on his decision and he responded with an emotionally laden letter that he never sent:

> My dear Mr. Feis:
> You write just like the usual egghead. The facts are before you but you'd like to garble them. The instruction of July 25th, 1945 was final. It was made by the Commander in Chief after Japan refused to surrender.
> Churchill, Stimson, Patterson, Eisenhower and all the rest agreed that it had to be done. It was. It ended the . . .War. That was the objective. Now if you can think of any other "if, as, and when" egghead contemplations, bring them out. . . .
> It is a great thing that you or any other contemplator "after the fact" didn't have to make the decision.
> Our boys would all be dead.[13]

While Truman's response may be understandable, it does not address the criticisms posed by others nor did it address Feis's request for information about the decision on whether to use the bomb to end the war. Instead, Truman used several emotionally charged words to place the researcher on the defensive. Terms such as "egghead", "contemplator 'after the fact'", and "dead" all help charge the letter.

Advertisements for many "self-improvement" cosmetics and health products often use emotive language to appeal to the prospective buyer's desire for a sudden and dramatic improvement in personal appearance. An advertisement for tan accelerator claims that

> Once in a generation there's a breakthrough so revolutionary it can change forever the way people tan.

Terms such as "breakthrough" and "revolutionary" are intended to convince consumers that the product's effects must be singular and a striking advance over other tanning methods. Or, consider this claim from a weight-loss ad:

> After years of research and testing, a scientist from Princeton University has finally developed a *miracle* weight loss formula which has clearly proven to be the *strongest fat-burning compound in the entire world!* [This product] is so *radically powerful* that it can actually make the *slim and shapely* figure of your *dreams a reality.* [Emphasis added]

Readers who are seeking a "radically powerful" "miracle" formula to make them "slim and shapely" may be persuaded by the emotive language of this advertisement. But the "Princeton scientist" is not identified, nor is the method used in the supposed study explained. Educated recipients of arguments should be skeptical of product claims that promise "revolutionary breakthroughs" and "miraculous results." Language such as this is often substituted for hard evidence and valid reasoning in order to make arguments and claims persuasive.

■ *Summary*

Arguments can go wrong in a number of ways, and a study of fallacies can alert us to the errors in reasoning. Fallacies are arguments flawed by irrelevant or inadequate evidence, erroneous reasoning, or improper expression. Although there are a large number of fallacies that have been identified by various authors, this chapter focuses on the most often used and frequently identified fallacies.

Although they are arguments that are incorrect, fallacies are also deceptive, persuasive, and hard to recognize. They are sometimes unintentional mistakes made by an arguer; at other times they are intentional efforts to mislead listeners or readers. In any case, detecting fallacies involves knowing what kinds of inference are correct and incorrect, knowing whether evidence is sufficient to support a claim, knowing when premises are relevant to claims, recognizing misleading language, and recognizing attempts to evade an issue through the use of emotional appeals.

The first group of fallacies—fallacies of faulty reasoning—occur when arguments fail to meet appropriate tests of reasoning. A false analogy, for example, compares two objects that are not sufficiently alike to justify the conclusion drawn from the comparison. An analogy is false when there are significant differences that undermine the claim or when the two objects do not share a sufficient number of characteristics to justify the conclusion. A hasty generalization draws a conclusion about members of a class based on too few or atypical examples. The arguer who makes a hasty generalization has either failed to take into account enough members of the class or has chosen members that are not representative. Two erroneous forms of causal reasoning include *post hoc* and single cause. A *post hoc* fallacy erroneously assumes that two events which are associated in time must be causally related as well. A single cause fallacy oversimplifies causal relationships by mistakenly assuming that for any effect there is one and only one cause. An arguer may argue about a "slippery slope" even if the evidence and reasoning does not support a trend.

The second group of fallacies occurs when arguments are misgrounded. Such fallacies confuse the roles of evidence and reasoning such that the evidence and reasoning do not sufficiently support the claim. Advocates may "beg the question" and equate the evidence with the conclusion it is intended to support. Or an arguer may commit a fallacy of *non sequitur* in which the evidence is irrelevant to the claim.

A third group of fallacies appeals to the audience's prejudices and predispositions to think in a certain way. These are fallacies of misdirection and, generally, fallacies of this type evade substantive issues by appealing to something irrelevant to them. *Ad hominem* fallacies attack the personal characteristics of the arguer who raises an issue instead of responding to the issue itself. *Ad populum* fallacies argue that a position should be accepted simply because the public supports it. Appeals to tradition argue that we should continue doing things the way we have always done them, even when good reasons for changing our attitudes or practices are offered. Similarly, arguers may use a "straw" argument which takes attention away from the issues under discussion.

The final group of fallacies results from deceptive or inappropriate use of language in arguments. Equivocation exploits the fact that a word has more than one meaning to lead to a false conclusion. Amphiboly exploits ambiguity in the grammatical structure of a sentence to deceive recipients of an argument. And the use of emotive language can manipulate the connotative meaning of words to establish a claim without proof. All three of these fallacies, then, substitute misleading use of language or sentence structure to gain support for arguments without adequate evidence and reasoning for the claims offered.

Fallacies may be intentional or unintentional and they come in many forms because there are many ways that arguments can go wrong. The list of fallacies provided in this chapter is not all-inclusive. We have provided an explanation of some of the most frequently identified and common fallacies. By noting how these work and why they are persuasive, you may more easily detect fallacies in general. Here is a list of questions helpful in diagnosing what is fallacious or wrong in poor arguments.

1. What type of inference is involved? What tests of reasoning must be met to legitimate the step from the evidence to the claim?

2. Is the evidence adequate to support the claim? (Refer to the tests of evidence in Chapter 4.)

3. Is the evidence relevant to the claim as stated?

4. Is the argument's language clear?

5. Does the arguer appeal to audience prejudices, emotions, or misconceptions so as to evade the issue?

This list of questions may assist you in identifying a problem in the argument. Regardless of whether you can label the fallacy, you will then know what is wrong with the argument and why it should be rejected. This will make you a better informed and more judicious recipient of the arguments you encounter.

Examining arguments to discover what evidence is needed to support the claims offered, what tests of reasoning are applicable, whether the evidence and claims are relevant to each other, whether the argument is expressed in clear and unequivocal language, and whether the arguer attempts to manipulate audience emotions can help us detect fallacies and identify the errors they contain. By providing methods to analyze the structure and function of arguments, Chapter 7 will also be of assistance in identifying erroneous reasoning. The discussion and classification of common fallacies in this chapter, however, should also be useful in argument criticism.

Exercises

Exercise 1 Does the following argument commit a fallacy? If yes, indicate what kind of fallacy was committed and rewrite the argument so that it is sound.

> Here in the United States we live without access to adequate health care. In fact, the lack of adequate funding is the single largest contributing factor to infant mortality in this country. This was illustrated recently by Mary H. Cooper ("Infant Mortality" *The CQ Researcher,* July 31, 1992, 646) when she wrote:
>
> > Indeed, for many women, a range of social and economic barriers block the way to a healthy pregnancy. The main obstacle is poverty, which is spreading. Today, more American children than ever—12 million under the age of 18, or one in five—are living in poverty.

Exercise 2   Fallacy Identification: Identify the fallacies stated in the following passages by placing the correct number of the fallacy next to each passage. Select from the following list:

1.	False Analogy	8.	*Ad Hominem*
2.	Hasty Generalization	9.	*Ad Populum*
3.	*post hoc*	10.	Appeal to Tradition
4.	Single Cause	11.	Straw arguments
5.	Slippery Slope	12.	Equivocation
6.	Begging the Question	13.	Amphiboly
7.	*Non Sequitur*	14.	Emotive Language

✳ 1. Women should not be allowed to join the Rotary Club because it's an all-male organization.

2. As we grow accustomed to thinking that unborn children are not really persons, is it not in fact easier to think of handicapped infants as somehow less human? Of the elderly and sick as "leaves that fall from a tree" to fulfill some "duty to die," as a prominent American governor has said?

3. We should have sex education in the public schools. A 1992 survey showed that 87 percent of the public supported public school instruction in marriage and family living.

4. 1993 Mercury Cougar. It moves the way it moves because it looks the way it looks.

✳ 5. If Dr. Mary Calderone (executive director of the Sex Information and Education Council of the United States) is the Joan of Arc of the school-sex revolution, Dr. Lester Kirkendall, professor of family life at Oregon State University and a member of the SIECUS board of directors, is its Pied Piper. Dr. Kirkendall, a prolific author of sex books and magazine articles about every conceivable sexual foible, will never be accused of being an old fuddy-duddy by even the hippest of the porno politicians.

6. Many sex education classes turn out to be only an exercise in destroying the conscience. Is it surprising that after hearing sexual intercourse discussed in class and shown in classroom movies, the reserves of young people are broken down and they are stimulated to experiment?

7. We should impose an income tax in the state to stabilize state government revenues.

8. If God had meant people to fly, He would have given them wings.

9. Interestingly enough, the Economic Opportunity Commission, which now processes all federal War on Poverty grants in the country, is completely controlled by Edward R. Becks, its acting executive director. Ed Becks is a member of the Communist Party.

✳ 10. Freedom has its enemies. Many are ensconced on university campuses, seeding receptive young minds with strains of noxious elitism and dreams of coercive utopias in which they would be the Castros, Khadafys, and Ortegas of tomorrow.

11. Are you in the used car market? Go to Smith's Autos for a better deal.

12. We have Pure Food and Drug laws. Why can't we have comparable laws to keep movie makers from giving us filth?

13. I wouldn't take that class from Professor Jones if I were you. I talked to three of my fraternity brothers who took courses from Jones last year and they all said his courses were really hard.

14. During the 1992 Republican National Convention, President George Bush declared that he had ended the Cold War with the former Soviet Union. I just don't understand how we didn't reelect the man responsible for ending this nation's longest and most dangerous war.

✳ *Exercise 3*   Answer these questions about the following argument:

1. Identify the fallacies in the argument.

2. What types of fallacies seem to occur most often?

3. How could the argument be rewritten to avoid the fallacies?

4. What effect do these fallacies have on the reader? Do different kinds of fallacies have different effects? Why?

In Support of Capital Punishment

People who oppose capital punishment should think about the consequences of abolishing it. They say it's wrong to take a human life. But they fail to consider the innocent victims slaughtered in their homes and communities by ruthless killers and heartless criminals.

We already give criminals too many protections. Because of the *Miranda* ruling, killers and felons get off scot-free all the time. Abolishing capital punishment is just one more step in letting criminals and murderers off when they should be punished. Pretty soon, we'll be handing out reduced sentences and letting them out on parole. What kind of deterrent is that?

Capital punishment works because of deterrence. You and I do not shoplift or drive while intoxicated because we are afraid of getting caught. Like us, the criminal contemplating murder will be less likely to do it if he thinks he will get the death penalty.

Deterrence is also shown by studies of the effects of capital punishment. An economist named Erlich concluded that for every execution, eight homicides were prevented. Also, when capital punishment was eliminated fifteen years ago in our own state, the number of homicides increased by 20 percent. This shows that when there is no death penalty, people are more likely to commit murder.

Capital punishment has been used since ancient times as a punishment for murder. That is what the Old Testament saying of "an eye for an eye, a tooth for a tooth" means. The Bible lists eighteen offenses punishable by death. Clearly, the ancient Hebrew tradition recognized the need for some form of capital punishment.

I believe we should keep the death penalty throughout the United States. Seventy-two percent of the American people favor it and therefore it must be the most justifiable and necessary measure in our fight against capital crimes.

Notes

1. *New York Times,* January 31, 1984, C5.

2. Aristotle *Sophistical Refutations,* Vol. 1 of *The Works of Aristotle,* W. D. Ross, ed. (New York: Harper & Row, 1928). W. Ward Fearnside and William B. Holther identify over fifty fallacies in their *Fallacy: The Counterfeit of Argument* (Englewood Cliffs, N.J.: Prentice-Hall, 1959); Howard Kahane discusses twenty-five fallacies in *Logic and Contemporary Rhetoric,* 4th ed. (Belmont, Cal.: Wadsworth, 1984): 47–122; and T. Edward Damer discusses over sixty in his *Attacking Faulty Reasoning,* 2nd ed. (Belmont, Cal.: Wadsworth, 1987).

3. We grouped together fallacies that fail to meet the tests of reasoning discussed in Chapter 5. Those treated separately in this chapter are false analogy, hasty generalization, and false cause. Although fallacies also occur in arguments from sign and authority, they do not appear separately in standard lists of fallacies and so are not included here. Fallacies of misdirection were identified as a group by C. L. Hamblin, *Fallacies* (London: Methuen, 1970): 135–76. Fallacies of language use are treated as a group by Hamblin, 283–303, Damer, 20–33, and Irving Copi, *Informal Logic* (New York: Macmillan, 1986): 69–97.

4. Copi, 114.

5. Aristotle *Rhetoric,* W. Rhys Roberts, trans. (New York: Modern Library, 1954): 160.

6. Damer, 94.

7. From Plato *Timaeus,* cited in Copi, 111.

8. Hamblin traces the origin of this group of argument to Francis Bacon's *Advancement of Learning* in the early 1600s. Bacon identified four types of "idols," or prejudicial habits of thought, that affect reasoning. Hamblin (p. 146) notes that after Bacon the study of fallacies included the study of the influence of psychological factors on human reasoning.

9. Hamblin (p. 41) lists the Latin names for the first two of these as *Ad Hominem* and *Ad Passiones.* Hamblin notes that there are many varieties of "arguments *ad*" and concludes that "We feel like adding: *Ad Nauseam*—but even that has been suggested before."

10. Damer, 128–29.

11. Robert J. Thornton, "Lexicon of Inconspicuously Ambiguous Recommendations," *Chronicle of Higher Education,* February 25, 1987: 42. Copyright 1987: *Chronicle of Higher Education*. Reprinted with permission of author.

12. Copi, 114.

13. Monte M. Poen, ed. *Strictly Personal and Confidential: The Letters Harry Truman Never Mailed* (Boston: Little, Brown, and Company, 1982): 34.

CHAPTER 7

Argument Analysis and Criticism

■

CHAPTER OUTLINE

- **Benefits of Argument Analysis**
- **A General Model for Argument Analysis**
  Analysis of Simple Arguments
  Analysis of Other Structural Patterns
  An Application
- **The Toulmin Model**
  The Nature and Background of the Toulmin Model
  Six Parts of the Model
  Difficulties in Applying the Model
  Argument Chains and the Toulmin Model
- **Comparison of the Two Models**
- **Summary**
- **Exercises**

KEY CONCEPTS

simple argument
complex argument
chain argument
compound argument
data

warrant
backing
qualifier
reservation

In our daily lives, we are constantly the target of persuasive appeals and in a position to judge the arguments of others. Campaign speeches, product advertising, editorials, business proposals, and even personal decisions require that we understand and evaluate arguments. In this process, it is useful to be able to tell a good argument from a bad one. In particular, judging others' arguments involves receptive critical thinking skills, such as understanding arguers' intended meanings, isolating their claims, deciding whether those claims are adequately supported by evidence, making unstated inferences explicit, knowing how those inferences work, pinpointing unstated assumptions, and detecting fallacies and erroneous reasoning.

In Chapters 1–6, we focused on the major parts of arguments and on the tests for evidence and reasoning. In this chapter, our purpose is to enable you to take an argument apart, consider how its parts are related and how the argument is structured, and then criticize and evaluate the argument using your critical thinking skills. This ability to dissect arguments and display their underlying structure is the key to judging their adequacy.

In Chapter 1, we introduced a simple model of argument. In that model, an individual argument was said to have three components—a claim (expressed opinion); evidence (facts, beliefs, or premises supporting the claim); and reasoning (the inference or link between the evidence and the claim). While arguments generally state or imply these three components, they often are more complicated, possessing many kinds of statements and a complex structure. In this chapter, we will extend and expand our Chapter 1 model by showing how to represent pictorially the workings of all kinds of arguments. These pictorial representations show how the parts of an argument are related to one another and are called argument diagrams.

These diagrams show how the statements comprising arguments support or reinforce each other. In this capacity they function like blueprints or wiring diagrams and have many of the same uses and advantages.[1] Many methods for constructing diagrams of arguments have been proposed by philosophers and argumentation theorists. This chapter will present two models for diagramming—a general model and the Toulmin model. Both models break arguments down into certain components and indicate how those components are to be arranged in diagrams. This chapter will outline these procedures; enable you to construct argument diagrams of your own; and thereby assist you in comprehending, criticizing, and refuting arguments.

▪ *Benefits of Argument Analysis*

Too often students (and other critics and recipients of arguments) attempt to refute arguments or to criticize them without having undertaken the necessary preparation. Criticism requires that one correctly understands an argument and carefully interprets it *before* attacking it or responding to it. One "correctly understands" an argument and interprets it accurately when one can provide an account of the argument that squares with its author's intended meaning and with the interpretations of other recipients of the argument. The need for systematic understanding and interpretation will become more apparent if we consider two of the principal benefits of argument diagrams.

One benefit of argument analysis is that it helps us better understand the arguments we encounter. Many arguments are not readily understandable when we first hear or read them. By diagramming and interpreting an argument, we come to a well-grounded comprehension of its language and structure. As an example, consider Daniel Webster's 1833 refutation of John C. Calhoun. Calhoun had earlier taken a strong "states rights" position, arguing that the federal Constitution was a compact between states, not an instrument of "we the people," and that each sovereign state should retain its power to judge the constitutionality of an act of Congress. Webster strongly objected to Calhoun's interpretation, claiming that it attributed too much power to the states, and he questioned Calhoun's wording as follows:

> The first resolution declares that the people of the several states *"acceded"* to the Constitution. . . . The natural converse of *accession* is *secession*; and, therefore, when it is stated that the people of the States acceded to the Union, it may be more plausibly argued that they may secede from it. . . . *Accession,* as a word applied to political associations, implies coming into a league, treaty, or confederacy, by one hitherto a stranger to it, and *secession* implies departing from such league or confederacy. The people of the United States have used no such form of expression in establishing the present government. They do not say they *accede* to a league, but they declare that they *ordain* and *establish* a Constitution.[2]

A thorough consideration of this argument would lead us to ask the following questions: What is Webster's major claim in this portion of his address? Is it implied or explicitly stated? What basic premises does he state for his argument? How are they tied together? Answering such questions leads us to an understanding of the basic thrust of Webster's argument and an identification of the statements and inferences pivotal in tying his premises to his claim. (We will answer these questions and show how Webster's argument is diagrammed later in this chapter.)

The second benefit to argument diagrams is that they enable the recipient to judge and evaluate the argument. They enable one to identify the premises and evidence, ascertain the reasoning used by the arguer, and consider how these two forms of support are linked to the claim. Diagramming is thereby an intermediate step to testing an argument's evidence and reasoning, as our critique of various arguments in this chapter will illustrate. Diagrams also isolate secondary claims on which the primary claim depends, show how the premises are linked to support the claim, and reveal statements that are tangential or irrelevant to the claim. One can therefore avoid wasting time attacking incidental remarks or unimportant premises and go to the heart of the argument—its central inference—by noting the roles of vital subsidiary claims and essential premises. We will now introduce diagramming by means of two models—the general model and the Toulmin model.

▧ *A General Model for Argument Analysis*

The general model for analyzing arguments discussed in this section has for a long time been used by philosophers to portray the structure of practical arguments. In a rudimentary form, this model was introduced by Monroe C. Beardsley in his book *Practical Logic* in 1950. Beardsley used his model to identify the skeleton of an argument—the pattern in which its premises and claims were related to each other.[3] Variations of this model have recently appeared in books by Michael Scriven and Irving Copi whose procedures we have adapted to a description of argument diagramming.[4]

Our variation of the general model divides arguments into four types or classifications. Arguments are classified according to the degree of complexity in their structure. By "complexity of structure," we mean how many statements there are in the argument and how they are linked together. This ranges from the simplest arguments (Type I), which are comprised of only one premise and one claim, to the most complicated (Type IV), which are comprised of many premises and many claims linked together in numerous ways. In addition, this section will explain five steps in analyzing arguments and constructing diagrams and illustrate them with examples.

Analysis of Simple Arguments

The best way to become acclimated to argument analysis is to begin with simple arguments. *A simple argument consists of one premise and a claim that follows from it.* The inference connecting the two may be stated or implied. The first task is to recognize a text as an argument and not some other kind of communication event. The definitions and descriptions offered in Chapter 1 are helpful here. Unlike other kinds of communication, arguments advance a claim, offer support for it, and are made in a context of disagreement.

It is important to note that statements function as premises and as claims *relative to each other*. No statement in isolation is either one or the other:

Because it's going to rain today, you should take your umbrella.

Because you are taking your umbrella, it's probably not going to rain today.

In both statements, the presence or absence of rain is claimed to be causally connected to the presence of an umbrella (although the second argument is facetious and an example of *post hoc* reasoning). However, the fact that either clause can function as premise or as claim in relation to the other illustrates the point. "Premise" and "claim" are relative terms like "employee" and "employer."[5] They function as they do only in context and in relation to each other.

The problem, therefore, is to be able to tell in any simple or complex argument which statements are premises and which are claims. There are two clues that can help one to do this. One is that the premises are generally *the most readily verifiable and least arguable statements in the argument.* In the first example above, the prediction that it's going to rain can probably be supported through reference to a weather report or conditions outside, and the arguer expects the arguee to agree that it will rain. In the second example, the arguee very likely has an umbrella in hand, a fact that can be observed by both parties. The most accepted statement, the one least likely to be questioned, then, serves as the premise of the argument.

The second kind of clue arises from the wording of the passage in which the argument occurs. Arguers often provide contextual cues called conclusion indicators and premise indicators to help recipients follow their arguments, and these can assist the analyst in structuring statements in the argument text. *Premise indicators* are words like "because," "since," "for," or phrases like "the fact that," "by considering," or "as shown by," and they indicate that what follows is to be relied upon as a base for drawing a claim. *Conclusion indicators* include "therefore," "so," "consequently," "it follows that," and so forth, and introduce statements by relating them to other, less-arguable statements. Such transitional words or signposts should be noted, for they indicate how the arguer intended that recipients relate statements within the argument to each other.

You may recall that in Chapters 5 and 6 we extensively discussed a third component of arguments—the reasoning linking the premises and the claim. This component is often implicit and not expressly stated in the argument. If it is stated, it is stated in the form of an inference. In the general model of argument being discussed here, an inference is not categorized as a separate or unique type of statement. Instead, it is simply treated as a linking statement or subsidiary claim to be placed between the premise and the final claim. How this occurs in diagrams will become clear when complex and compound arguments and argument chains are considered later in this chapter.

For now, let us apply the diagramming procedure to the simplest possible form—the argument with one premise and one claim. As our example, we will again use a passage from Webster's reply to Calhoun:

> Where sovereign communities are parties, there is no essential difference between a compact, a confederation, and a league. They all equally rest on the plighted faith of the sovereign party.[6]

We will now explain the five steps in argument analysis according to this general model and apply them to this simple argument. The five steps are ascertaining the meaning, numbering the statements in the argument, identifying the argument's final claim, constructing a diagram, and criticizing the argument.

The first step is to figure out what the arguer means. This step is important because many arguments hinge on definitions of terms and some arguments use technical or archaic language which is not readily understandable. The above argument, for example, is expressed somewhat archaically and relies upon a defining characteristic of agreements between governments. Reference to a dictionary reveals that "to plight" means "to pledge"; "faith" means "allegiance" or "duty"; and a "sovereign community" is an independent government of some kind.[7] So, restated in contemporary language, the argument would say:

> Where independent governments are parties [to an agreement], there is no essential difference between a compact, a confederation, and a league. They all equally rest on the pledged duty and allegiance of each government.

Checking on and verifying the meaning in this way helps the analyst to understand the argument and one to discover whether there was the kind of slippage in the use of terms or equivocal use of language that we discussed in Chapter 6.

When longer arguments are involved, the analyst should begin by reading the entire argument straight through once or twice to grasp its overall meaning, then look up any specialized, technical, or archaic words. There are two things to keep in mind about interpreting the language of the argument during this step. First, one should interpret the argument in a way that is fair to the arguer. For example, Webster in his argument is not claiming that compacts, confederations, and leagues are exactly alike, only that they share the characteristic of pledge of duty and allegiance. If the analyst interpreted the argument's claim to be that the three types of agreement were exactly alike, he or she would overstate Webster's claim (and thus make the argument easier to criticize). When interpreting an argument, one should define terms as the arguer intended them to be defined, make the strength of the claim proportionate to the author's intention, and otherwise give the argument a fair and sympathetic reading. To do otherwise would be unfair to the arguer. Second, one should not prematurely evaluate or criticize the argument but instead should seek to understand it. If one moves to evaluation and criticism too quickly, there is a danger that the argument and the arguer's intent will be misconstrued and that the evaluation will be concerned with a claim other than the one the arguer intended.

The second step in analysis is to number the statements in the argument. Numbers should be assigned consecutively in the order in which statements occur in the text of the argument, like this:

> ① Where sovereign communities are parties, there is no essential difference between a compact, a confederation, and a league. ② They all equally rest on the plighted faith of the sovereign party.

The question of what counts as a statement to be numbered and what does not will invariably arise during this step. Different analysts may number statements in a given argument in different ways, and such variations are not a problem as long as the diagrams are clear and useful in displaying the structure of the argument.

Two guidelines are useful in numbering statements because they lead to diagrams that display the thoughtline of the argument clearly and increase the effectiveness of subsequent analysis. First, one should assign numbers only to complete thought units, not to partial thoughts. A "complete thought unit," whether it is a sentence, an independent clause, a noun phrase, or a participial phrase, will be expressible as a complete and fully formed idea. In the example we have been using, the phrase "where sovereign communities are parties" is not a complete thought unit because it depends on the rest of the sentence for its meaning. Any statement that is not understandable when it stands alone is a thought fragment and not a complete thought unit. Therefore, it should not be numbered separately. However, some phrases occurring in sentences are capable of being expressed as complete ideas with only minor changes and should be separately numbered. This is illustrated in the following argument:

Despite the pessimism of the doomsayers, ① the economy will continue on the upswing this year. With ② low interest rates, ③ decreased energy prices, and ④ a booming stock market, ⑤ it's hard to visualize any cause for a slowdown.

The three noun phrases in the second sentence could easily be expressed as complete thoughts ("interest rates are low, energy prices are decreasing, the stock market is booming"). They should therefore be numbered separately.

The second guideline for numbering statements in arguments is also illustrated by the above argument. Rhetorical flourishes, editorial asides, repetitions, and other extraneous material should not be numbered. The phrase "despite the pessimism of the doomsayers" sets up the statement rhetorically but does not function as either premise or claim. It should not be included because it has no argumentative function and would detract from the clarity of the diagram. Any statement that is made merely to "set the stage," reinforce other statements, or digress from the main thoughtline of the argument should not be numbered because it is not a part of the central thoughtline of the argument taken as a whole.

The third step in analysis is to identify the argument's main claim. If there is more than one main claim, then there is more than one argument. The number of independent conclusions in a passage determines the number of arguments it contains.[8] This situation will be more fully discussed in the next section of this chapter. If there are conclusion indicators present, circling them may assist in diagramming the argument. In this third step, it is advisable to consider the possibility that the argument's primary claim has not been explicitly stated. If the preliminary interpretation of the argument in step one indicated that the arguer left the principal claim unstated, it should be supplied now. The analyst should explicitly state the claim and supply it with a number in parentheses (to show the claim is implicit) prior to diagramming.

The fourth step in the analysis is to diagram the argument. Circled numbers representing the thought units and statements in the argument can be used. Those representing basic premises are placed at the top, and the diagram flows downward to the final or main claim. When diagrammed, Webster's argument looks like this:

2

↓

1

The second statement in the argument was the premise, and the first was the claim. Webster's conclusion that there is no essential difference between a compact, a confederation, and a league rested on the premise that the three share a common characteristic—the "plighted faith" (pledged allegiance) of a "sovereign party" (independent government). Thus, the second statement is placed at the top of the diagram and the first statement at the bottom.

It should be noted that here we have placed starting points or premises at the *top* of the diagram and the claims at the *bottom*. The argument model we introduced in Chapter 1 placed evidence or premises to the left below the level of dispute, while the claim was on the right above the level of dispute. We are now asking that you rotate that model so that evidential statements are placed at the *top* of the diagram and the structure flows *downward* to the final claim. This keeps our presentation of the general model in line with its presentation by other authors. As you will see, in the second model presented in this chapter, the starting point of an argument is again placed on the left of the diagram instead of at the top. This should not present a problem as long as the analyst is consistent in the use of any given model.

The fifth and final step is to criticize the argument. Now that the argument's parts and their relation to one another have been identified, we are in a position to critique the argument's evidence and reasoning. In regard to the evidence, we can begin by observing that Webster cites no source for his observation that compacts, confederations, and leagues all rely on the pledged allegiance of the parties that agree to join them. Since Webster has cited no source other than what he thinks his audience already believes, some of the tests of evidence in Chapter 4 cannot appropriately be applied to his argument. It would not make sense to consider whether Webster's citation is accurate (since he worded it himself), or whether it is recent (since this historical citation was worded when Webster gave the speech). It would, however, make sense to ask whether this "fact"—that all three alliances rest on a voluntary agreement—is *relevant* to his argument about the Constitution. It would be very worthwhile, too, to consider whether Webster's observations about various forms of government are *consistent* with the observations of other political figures of his day and with scholarship on government and politics of that time. The tests of evidence applied to an argument, then, should be appropriate to the context and use of the evidence in that argument.

Criticism also involves testing the arguer's reasoning. Here Webster emphasizes the similarity between compacts, confederations, and leagues; all rely on the voluntary actions of their members. Further, he argues that there is "no essential difference between" the three. The tests of quality, quantity, and opposition described in Chapter 5 could be applied to Webster's comparison. Clearly, the three objects compared are all forms of consensual agreement and thus are in the same class, so Webster's argument meets the test of quality. But Webster cited only one similarity between the three forms of agreement; he could have cited more. Confederations, compacts, and leagues are formed voluntarily by parties of somewhat equal status who share a common purpose. Citing more similarities would certainly have strengthened Webster's argument and better met the test of quantity.

Diagramming and criticizing arguments using the general model for argument analysis therefore involves five steps. First, after identifying a statement as an argument with premises and claims, the analyst should carefully examine its terms and phrases to ascertain what the argument means. The resulting interpretation should be fair in recapturing its author's intended meaning and should refrain from evaluation and criticism. Second, the thought units in the argument should be assigned numbers in the order of their occurrence. Only sentences and phrases expressible as complete thoughts should be numbered, and tangential statements and digressions should not be assigned numbers. Third, the argument's main claim or primary conclusion should be identified. If implicit, it should be expressly stated and assigned a number in parentheses. Fourth, the argument's structure should be laid out in a diagram beginning with the most accepted or easily verifiable premises at the top and flow downward to the main claim. Fifth, the argument should be criticized and evaluated by using the tests of evidence and reasoning described in Chapters 4, 5, and 6 of this book.

Analysis of Other Structural Patterns

The foregoing illustration of argument analysis has made use of the simplest form of argument in which only one claim is stated and supported by a single premise. As might be expected, most arguments have a more complicated structure than this. Four categories or types of argument structure are illustrated in Figure 7–1. We have already explained Type I (simple) arguments. The remainder of this section will explain and illustrate the other three types.

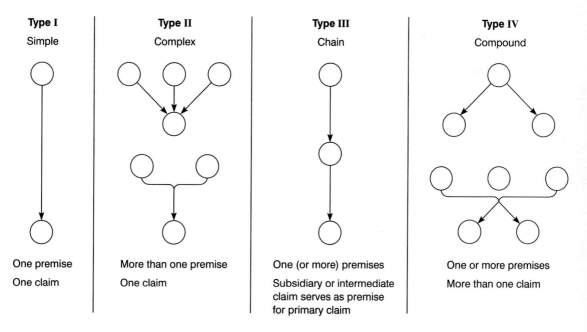

Type I	**Type II**	**Type III**	**Type IV**
Simple	Complex	Chain	Compound
One premise	More than one premise	One (or more) premises	One or more premises
One claim	One claim	Subsidiary or intermediate claim serves as premise for primary claim	More than one claim

Figure 7–1
Diagrams of Argument Structure

Type II (complex) arguments have two or more premises supporting a single claim. The following argument is a good example of this pattern:

① Constitutionality aside, setting the minimum [drinking] age at 21 has been a practical disaster.

Designed to attack drunken driving on the part of teenagers, ② it discriminates against a whole category of people, many of whom drink only moderately. ③ It penalizes female teenagers, whose DWI convictions are below the national average. ④ Furthermore, clandestine drinking has created mini-prohibition on college campuses.[9]

This argument makes a claim about the harmful practical effects of setting the drinking age at 21, and its premises describe three conditions resulting from the 21-year-old minimum. There are therefore three premises and one main claim, so the diagram would look like the one in Figure 7–2.

There are two characteristics to note about this argument. First, the phrase "designed to attack drunken driving on the part of teenagers" provides background information and does not support the argument's conclusion, so it should not be numbered. Second, each premise supports the conclusion *independently* of the others. If one or perhaps even two of the premises were removed, the remaining premise(s) would still be sufficient to support the claim.

A second variation of Type II arguments is one in which premises work *in combination* to support the claim. In this pattern, the premises are interrelated and cooperate with each other. The following argument illustrates this pattern:

① Skier attendance figures on a national level have reached all-time highs during the past five years. Unfortunately, ② Washington state has not enjoyed the increase in market share over the past 15 to 20 years that other Western states have. ③ During the late 1960s, Washington enjoyed 18 percent of all skier visits in the Western states. ④ This has declined steadily to a current 6 percent of that market.[10]

Here the author's premises are interconnected. He claims that overall skier attendance is up and simultaneously that the percentage of this market patronizing ski areas in Washington state has declined. The overall market has increased while Washington's share in it has decreased. If one disregards the information about the

Figure 7–2
Type II (Complex) Argument—
three premises independently
support one main claim

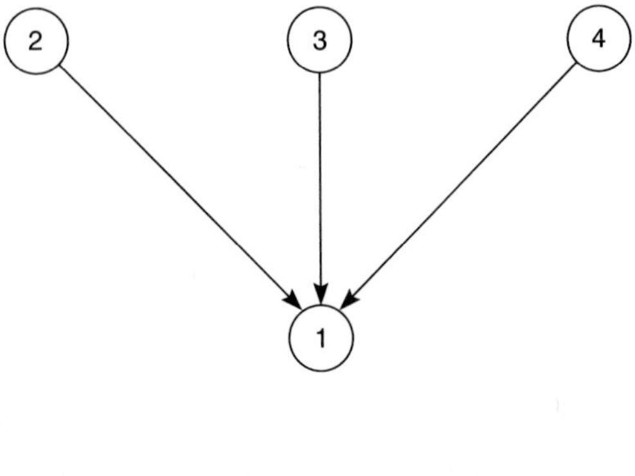

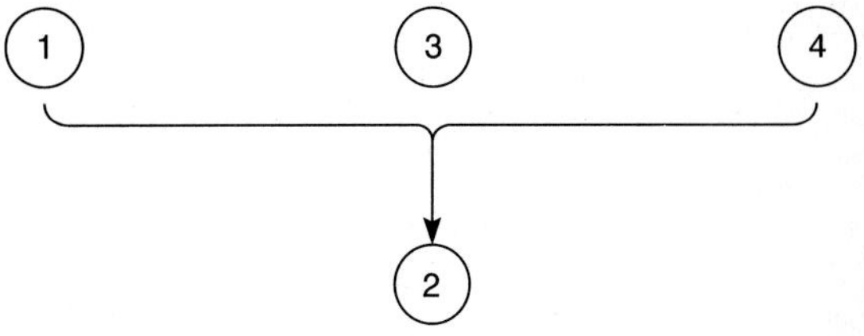

Figure 7–3
Type II (Complex) Argument—
three premises work in combination to support a claim

national increase *or* the premises stating Washington's decline in the share, the conclusion is inadequately supported. To indicate the interdependence of the premises
in the diagram, one can supply a brace or bracket to connect them as in Figure 7–3.

This clearly shows that the claim that Washington has not enjoyed an increase in
its share of the market is dependent on *both* a statement of the overall increase *and*
an indication that the individual state share has declined.

Type III arguments are also called argument chains. As we defined them in
Chapter 2, chains use proven claims as evidence for unproven claims. Initial
premises or evidence are used to support a claim which, once it is established and
falls below the level of dispute, can itself be used to support a further claim. A simple
example of an argument chain is the following:

① The weather's been warming up and ② there are buds coming out on my
shrubbery. ③ These are signs I'll have to start mowing the lawn soon, so ④ I'd
better get the lawn mower serviced.

When diagrammed, the argument's structure would look like that of Figure 7–4.

This is a simple chain because the first two premises independently support a
single intermediate claim that lawn mowing will soon be in order. Once supported,
the claim that the lawn needs to be mowed is moved below the level of dispute and

Figure 7–4
Type III (Chain) Argument—one
or more subsidiary claims support
the primary claim

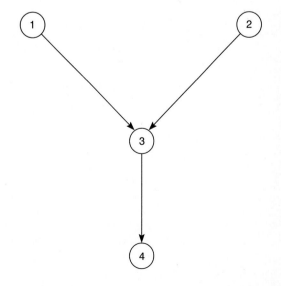

can in turn be used as a premise to support the main claim that the mower must be serviced. In Chapter 3, we called intermediate statements such as this subsidiary claims and noted their importance in linking together extended arguments. We will further discuss chains and subsidiary claims later in this chapter when we discuss another argument model. When chains and subsidiary claims play a role in the structures of arguments, the resulting diagrams take the form of tree diagrams. Tree diagrams display the linkages between thought units in the form of branching and intersecting lines flowing from the top to the bottom of the diagram. In the tree diagrams illustrated here, subsidiary or intermediate claims appear in the middle of the diagram between the basic premises and the main claim.

The most complicated argument structure is a Type IV or compound argument. *Compound arguments use one or more premises to support more than one conclusion.* Earlier in this chapter, we noted that the number of claims or conclusions in a text indicates the number of arguments present and that if there are, for example, two claims, there are therefore two arguments. This is *generally* true, but Type IV arguments are exceptions to this rule. (Type IV arguments occur infrequently, but as a class they occur often enough to be considered as an exception.)

In compound argument such as Type IV, one single premise leads to more than one claim or to a group of interdependent premises, which, taken together, lead to two or more further claims. Because the various premises cannot be isolated and assigned separately to individual claims, the argument must be considered as a whole. Here is an example of the simplest kind of Type IV argument:

> ① When asked on a recent survey what is most important to them on a job, teachers usually cite an opportunity to use their minds and abilities and a chance to work with young people. ② The vast majority of teachers are in their profession not for money but for all the reasons we hope they are. ③ Perhaps we should stop comparing teachers so quickly to high-priced professionals.[11]

The first statement, containing survey results about teacher attitudes, contains the evidence in this argument and states its premise—that teachers value aspects of their jobs other than salary. From this single premise, two conclusions are drawn— first, that teachers are not in their profession for money, and second, that they are not comparable to high-priced professionals. The argument when diagrammed, then, would look like Figure 7–5.

The second variation of a Type IV argument groups a number of premises together and uses them in concert to support multiple conclusions. Here is a simple example of this type of compound argument from the same article on teaching:

> As it stands now, ① teachers under nine-to-ten-month contracts who earn $25,000 have salaries slightly below the median for males with four or more years of college who are working full-time year-round. ② That $25,000 is in the top quarter of salaries paid to college-educated women working full-time year-round. ③ Teachers no longer fare so badly in the marketplace. ④ Their salaries and nine-to-ten-month teaching year make an attractive professional option.[12]

Figure 7–5
Type IV (Compound) Argument—
a single premise leads to more
than one claim

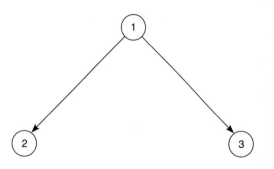

The first premise taken alone does not support either conclusion. Only when both of the first two statements as premises are combined does one get a complete picture of the situation for the entire teaching profession. Furthermore, teachers' status in the marketplace and the attractiveness of teaching as an option are two separate, although related, conclusions. This compound argument would therefore be diagrammed as in Figure 7–6.

Up to this point, this section of the chapter has described the general model for argument analysis, explained the steps to be followed in diagramming and criticizing simple arguments, and introduced three additional types of argument structures—the complex argument, the argument chain, and the compound argument. In order to bring the whole process together, let us consider the application of the five steps to an argument chain that includes complex arguments.

An Application

Because of its economy and flexibility, the procedure for argument analysis just outlined is useful in displaying and understanding the structure of long, complicated arguments. Let us return to Daniel Webster's lengthy argument cited at the begin-

Figure 7–6
Type IV (Compound) Argument—
multiple premises work in concert
to support multiple conclusions

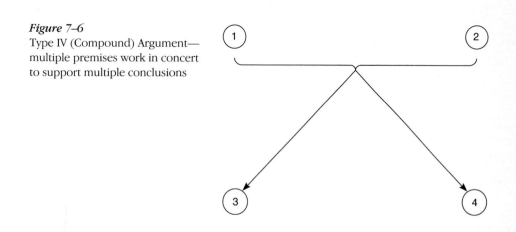

ning of this chapter to see whether argument analysis can assist us in understanding, interpreting, and criticizing it. Recall that the argument was stated as follows:

> The first resolution declares that the people of the several states *"acceded"* to the Constitution. . . . The natural converse of *accession* is *secession;* and, therefore, when it is stated that the people of the States acceded to the Union, it may be more plausibly argued that they may secede from it. . . . *Accession,* as a word applied to political associations, implies coming into a league, treaty, or confederacy, by one hitherto a stranger to it; and *secession* implies departing from such league or confederacy. The people of the United States have used no such form of expression in establishing the present government. They do not say they *accede* to a league, but they declare that they *ordain* and *establish* a Constitution.

The steps for analyzing this argument are as follows:

1. *Ascertain the meaning.* To ensure an accurate interpretation of Webster's argument, we could check its context and the definitions of any terms that might be unclear. If we did this, we would discover that Webster is refuting John C. Calhoun's interpretation of the Constitution as summarized in three resolutions being considered by the Senate. Webster seems most concerned by the use of the term "accede" in Calhoun's first resolution. His concern grows out of the implications for using this particular term. On the whole, Webster opposes the use of the term "accede" for two reasons: First, "to accede" means "to freely give consent to" and implies, by means of its opposite, that "to secede," parties which have "acceded" to an agreement can withdraw from it at will; and second, no such term was used when the Constitution was established, so Calhoun's interpretation cannot be historically justified.

2. *Number statements in the argument.* All of Webster's statements appear to be straightforward and relevant to his claim. The conclusion indicator, "therefore," in the second sentence should be circled, and all thought units stated in sentences or independent clauses should be numbered separately in the order in which they appear in the paragraph:

> ① The first resolution declares that the people of the several states *"acceded"* to the Constitution. . . .② The natural converse of *accession* is *secession;* and (therefore,) ③ when it is stated that the people of the States acceded to the Union, it may be more plausibly argued that they may secede from it. . . .④ *Accession,* as a word applied to political associations, implies coming into a league, treaty, or confederacy, by one hitherto a stranger to it; and ⑤ *secession* implies departing from such a league or confederacy. ⑥ The people of the United States have used no such form of expression in establishing the present government. ⑦ They do not say they *accede* to a league, but ⑧ they declare that they *ordain* and *establish* a Constitution.

3. *Identify the argument's primary claim.* A consideration of each of the statements in this paragraph reveals that none of them articulate a claim or thesis that ties all the ideas together, so the claim must be implied. From the context, we know that Webster is attempting to refute Calhoun's strong states rights position and his

use of the term "accede." Considering the thrust of Webster's statements in the paragraph, we are justified in supplying the following conclusion:

> The use of the term "accede" in Calhoun's first resolution should not be accepted.

The claim should be added and assigned the parenthetical number (9).

4. *Construct a diagram.* The first three statements in the argument can be grouped together because they are all related to the implications of the term "accede" and its opposite "secede." Furthermore, the first two statements are coupled together to support their conclusion which then in turn serves as a premise for the final (implied) claim. Statements ④ and ⑤ that respectively define the terms "accession" and "secession" should be taken together to support statement ② that one is the converse of the other. Statements ⑦ and ⑧ are again coupled together (the people do not say "accede" but instead say "ordain" and "establish") to support the subclaim that no such expression was used. Therefore, the overall argument should be diagrammed as in Figure 7–7.

This diagram illustrates many of the important features of Webster's argument. By examining it we know that the claim in the first complex argument (that, if

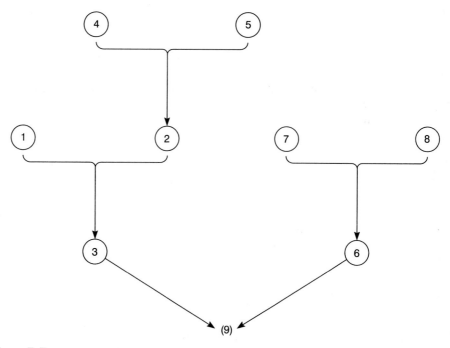

Figure 7–7
Type IV (Compound) Argument—premises join to support claims which chain to support a final (implied) claim

Calhoun's interpretation is accepted, people will find it easier to argue for secession) rests on two interdependent premises. Furthermore, we know that Webster's claim is implied, not stated, and that it rests on four more or less independent premises. Therefore, if a critic or opponent of Webster's argument successfully undermined only one of the premises, the argument as a whole would still hold up.

5. *Criticize the argument.* Webster's argument rests upon his definition of the terms "accede" and "secede" and on whether his interpretation of the intent of the authors of the Constitution is accurate. To test his evidence and premises, we might ask such questions as:

- Does Calhoun actually use the word "accede" in his first resolution?
- In the language of 1833, did the two terms "accede" and "secede" have the meanings Webster assigns to them?
- When the government was established, was any such term as "accede" used?
- Were "ordain" and "establish" the only words used in writing the Constitution?

Webster's reasoning in this argument is subtle but hinges on two unstated inferences: that use of a word implies its opposite, and that present interpretations of the Constitution should be governed by the intent of its authors. So, one might ask:

- *Does* the use of a word imply its opposite? What is the factual or cultural basis for this principle?
- How does Webster's argument about the intent of the authors differ from the fallacy of argument from tradition?
- Are the "people" referred to in statement ⑥ adequate authority on this matter?

Diagramming the argument has enabled us to identify the aspects that should be evaluated. For example, if the claim in statement ③ that use of a term implies its opposite can be undermined, then the argument as a whole is questionable. Does use of a term *always* imply its opposite? If someone retreats from a position, could he or she as easily advance upon it? If someone requires someone else to do something, could he or she as easily free that person from any obligation? Furthermore, by allowing us to identify the starting points of Webster's argument, the diagram reminds us that his account is an *interpretation* of the intent of the Constitution's authors and must be corroborated by considering all the language they used.

Tree diagrams are useful for discovering the pattern of claims and supporting statements in an argument. Tree diagrams help someone who wants to understand, criticize, or respond to an argument because they identify subarguments that relate to the conclusion and that link statements pivotal in supporting the claim. This approach is purely descriptive and analyzes the argument in terms of what is explicitly stated.

However, because it emphasizes only the premises that are stated explicitly, there is information this approach does *not* provide. As we observed in Chapter 1, inferences and vital assumptions are left unstated in arguments more often than not. The analyst using a purely descriptive approach has no occasion to look for statements left unsaid that may be essential to a complete understanding of the argument. The general model's usefulness will become clearer as we compare it with another model of argument analysis—the Toulmin model.

■ *The Toulmin Model*

Another method for diagramming arguments—the Toulmin model—requires the analyst to supply unstated inferences and the principles supporting them, and makes other contributions to argument comprehension as well.

The Nature and Background of the Toulmin Model

In Chapter 2, we introduced the notion of a field of argument taken from Stephen Toulmin's *Uses of Argument.*13 Following Toulmin, we noted that certain fields such as law, ethics, medicine, and science provide the various contexts for argument. Fields influence the forms of argument, the types of inferences used, the principles on which those inferences are based, the criteria applied to arguments, and the language in which they are expressed. Toulmin's model, which we are about to discuss, is based on the principle that the means for supporting and judging arguments are frequently an outgrowth of the fields in which they occur—they are field-dependent.

Toulmin believes that an argument is like an organism.14 Its individual parts each have a different function in relation to the claim. If an argument "works" (that is, is acceptable within the field it is used by those to whom it is addressed), it is because all its parts perform their functions and work together to form an organic whole. Toulmin's model identifies the ways in which each statement in an argument bears upon the claim and does justice to all the things an argument ought to do in order to be cogent. If important parts of the argument are implied or omitted, the Toulmin model directs the analyst to determine what they are and to supply them.

Six Parts of the Model

The Toulmin model contains six parts that are defined primarily by their function in an argument. The six parts are data, claim, warrant, backing, qualifier, and reservation.

The data function as the grounds for the claim and are synonymous with the evidence as we defined it in Chapter 1—"facts or conditions that are objectively observable, beliefs or premises accepted as true by the audience, or conclusions previously established." As has already been defined in Chapter 1, *the claim consists of the "expressed opinion or conclusion that the arguer wants accepted."*

The warrant expresses the reasoning used to link the data to the claim. According to Toulmin, if the data answer the question "What have you got to go on?", then the warrant answers the question "How did you get there?"[15] Warrants may take the form of rules, principles, or conventions particular to certain fields. Or they may be explicit statements of one of the patterns of reasoning identified in Chapter 5. In other words, warrants may state quasi-logical, analogical, generalized, causal, coexistential, dissociative, and other types of relationships. They function very much like inferences as we defined them in Chapter 5. In the general model explained earlier in this chapter, the warrant may be the linking or pivotal statement in the argument. (Such statements are not *always* warrants however; they may be intermediate claims in an argument chain.) What is important to remember about the warrant is that it expresses the reasoning that enables us to connect the data to the claim. If the warrant is not explicitly stated in an argument, it must be supplied when the argument is diagrammed using the Toulmin model.

Let us pause here to identify these first three parts of the model in an argument before going on to the other three parts. Consider the following argument:

> Twelve hours ago, the patient fell from a motor scooter and had a severe blow to the head accompanied by a deep scalp wound. He is pale, dizzy, lethargic, and has a low fever. The treatment strongly recommended includes flushing and stitching up the wound, administering antibiotics, and bed rest. Clinical experience has shown that without such treatment infection will set in within approximately 48 hours. Penicillin is most effective unless the patient is allergic to it.

What functions as data or evidence in this argument? Clearly, the circumstances of the accident and the patient's symptoms are readily knowable or observable facts and function as the starting point of the argument and the grounds for the claim. The claim—the conclusion or endpoint of the argument—is the specific recommended treatment. The warrant, or reasoned connection linking the data to the claim, is a causal prediction about what will happen to the patient if measures to prevent infection are not used. This predictive principle arises out of the field of medicine and is based on prior experience with patients in similar conditions and circumstances.

The Toulmin model is set out in a spatial pattern that is intended to show how the statements in the argument are linked to each other—what supports what and what leads to what. Generally, the first three parts are displayed as in Figure 7–8.

This arrangement indicates that the data lead to the claim and that the step which is made from one to the other is supported by the warrant. The data, warrant, and claim of the specific argument we've been considering would therefore be diagrammed as in Figure 7–9.

Figure 7–8
Toulmin model for data, claim, and warrant

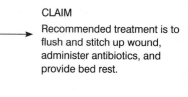

DATA

 – 12 hrs. ago, patient fell
   from scooter
 – had severe blow to head
 – has deep scalp wound
 – is pale, dizzy, lethargic
 – has low fever

CLAIM

Recommended treatment is to
flush and stitch up wound,
administer antibiotics, and
provide bed rest.

WARRANT

In the absence of preventive
measures, injuries of this
kind lead to infection.

Figure 7–9
Toulmin model applied for data, claim, and warrant

Figure 7–9 demonstrates how the Toulmin model is useful in identifying each statement's function in the argument. It indicates that the data serve as the argument's grounds and starting point; the claim as its endpoint; and the warrant as its rational support.

The remaining statements in this argument also each have a function in the Toulmin model. The statement that previous clinical experience has demonstrated that infection will set in is the backing. *The backing consists of further facts or reasoning used to support or legitimate the principle contained in the warrant.* Backing often consists of accepted principles or facts arising from the field in which the argument takes place. For example, the field of medicine universally accepts the principle that treatment regimens should be based on what has proven effective in prior clinical practice. This principle, as backing, supports the warrant in very much the same way that data support a claim.

Another portion of this argument to which the Toulmin model directs our attention is the qualifier. *The qualifier is a colloquial adverb or adverbial phrase that modifies the claim and indicates the rational strength the arguer attributes to it.*[16] When arguers make claims, they attribute greater or lesser degrees of strength to them. Some warrants authorize an unequivocal acceptance of the claim, whereas others may have much weaker force. The person making the diagnosis of the head wound recommends certain treatment "strongly." Other qualifiers frequently used to modify claims are "probably," "certainly," and "possibly." When they occur in arguments, qualifiers fulfill an important function because they indicate the degree of certainty that arguers feel regarding their claims.

Sometimes there are exceptions or limitations that invalidate the application of the warrant. Toulmin includes these in his model as the reservation. *The reservation states the circumstances or conditions which undermine the argument.* It is the "exception to the rule" expressed in the warrant. In the example argument, the arguer says that penicillin is recommended unless the patient is allergic to it. An allergic reaction, then, is a condition which would invalidate the recommendation that antibiotics be administered. In the Toulmin diagram, the qualifier and reserva-

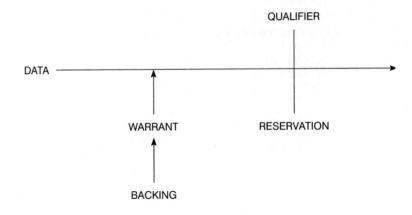

Figure 7–10
Toulmin model with all elements displayed: data, warrant, backing, qualifier, reservation, and claim

tion are linked because, to the extent that circumstances or conditions restricting the claim exist, the strength of the claim is limited.

Toulmin recommends that the six parts of the model should be set out so as to show their interrelationships as in Figure 7–10. When the additional three parts are added to the diagram, we can see more clearly how they function in the argument. The backing undergirds or supports the warrant. The qualifier modifies the claim by showing the strength the arguer attributes to it. And the qualifier is related to any reservations that express exceptions to the claim by stating conditions which undermine the force of the argument.

Applying the model to the example we have just discussed yields the diagram in Figure 7–11. The elegance and usefulness of the model becomes clear when we consider how the functions of the various statements in the argument are revealed through the diagram. As we have observed, the diagram reveals that the existence of previous clinical experience "backs up" the prediction made in the warrant. Furthermore, we can see that penicillin is recommended "strongly" but not "absolutely." The recommendation is tempered by the reservation "unless the patient is allergic to penicillin" and is thus functionally connected to the qualifier because it limits its strength.

This argument from the field of medicine was relatively straightforward and easily comprehended. To test the capacity and usefulness of the Toulmin model, let us consider this more complex argument from the field of law:

> On the thirteenth day of August, 1880, George R. Falls made his last will and testament in which he gave small legacies to his two daughters, Mrs. Smith and Mrs. Phillips, the plaintiffs in this case, and the remainder to his grandson, John E. Falls. The testator, at the date of his will, owned a farm and considerable personal property. He was a widower and thereafter, in June 1902, he was married to Mrs. Jones. At the date of the will, and subsequently to the death of the testator, his grandson lived with him as a member of his family.

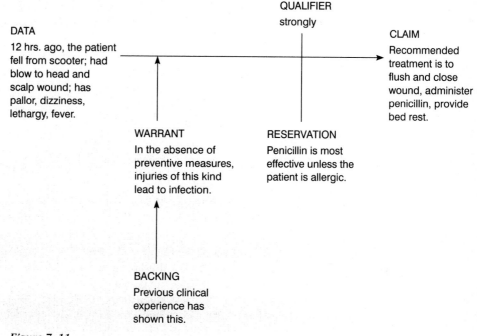

Figure 7–11
Toulmin model displays the six elements of an argument.

At the time of his grandfather's death, John was 16 years old. John knew of the provisions made in his favor in the will. To prevent his grandfather from revoking such provisions, which his grandfather had manifested some intention to do, and to obtain speedy possession of his grandfather's property, John murdered his grandfather by poisoning him. John now claims the property, and the sole question for our determination is, can he have it?

It is quite true that statutes regulating the making, proof, and effect of wills and the devolution of property, if literally construed, and if their force and effect can in no way and no circumstances be controlled or modified, give this property to the murderer. It was the intention of the lawmakers that the donees in a will should have the property given to them. But it never could have been their intention that a donee who murdered the testator to make the will operative should have any benefit under it. It is a familiar canon of construction that a thing which is within the intention of the makers of a statute is as much within the statute as if it were within the letter; and a thing which is within the letter of the statute is not within the statute unless it be within the intention of the makers.[17]

The *data* in this argument are stated by the judge before he states his decision. Briefly, they include the following: The deceased left small legacies to two daughters and the remainder of his estate to his grandson; he remarried; he was considering changing his will; he was poisoned by his grandson; the grandson now claims the estate. The *claim,* or endpoint of this argument, does not seem to be explicitly stated but clearly would take the form of the judge's decision in the case. Because

DATA

The testator left small legacies
to two daughters, left remainder
to grandson, remarried, was
considering changing his will,
was poisoned by his grandson.
The grandson now claims the
property.

CLAIM

The donee of this will shall not
have property.

Figure 7–12
Toulmin model, with implied claim indicated in dashed lines

the entire passage justifies denial of the property to the donee, we can safely assume
that the implied claim is "The donee in this case shall not have the property that has
been willed to him." In the Toulmin model, as in the tree diagram general model
introduced earlier, if the claim is not explicitly stated, the diagrammer should supply
it. To indicate that it's implicit, the diagrammer using the Toulmin model encloses
the implied claim in dashed lines, as indicated in Figure 7–12.

In seeking out the warrant linking the data and claim in this argument, we must
discover the reasoning that would link the data and the claim together. In this particular argument, the warrant is explicitly stated in the judge's opinion: "It never could
have been [the lawmakers'] intention that a donee who murdered a testator to make
the will operative should have any benefit under it." The judge believes this to be a
statement of principle inherent in the American legal tradition and, if there is a
precedent for it, he can thereby justify his decision that the property will be denied
to the murderer. It is important to note that this warrant, like the one in the medical
example given above, is *field-dependent*. It arises from the principle that legal
statutes should be applied in ways congruent with the intentions of the lawmakers
who proposed and approved them.

Only one remaining part of the Toulmin model is expressly stated in this argument. It is the *backing;* the principle which undergirds the warrant is expressly
stated in the decision ("A thing which is within the letter of the statute is not within
the statute unless it be within the intention of the makers"). The judge alludes to
this as a "familiar canon of construction" which would be common knowledge
among legal professionals. Because of its status as knowledge, this statement can
function as support for the warrant. The finished diagram—which contains four of
the Toulmin model's six parts—is shown in Figure 7–13.

Difficulties in Applying the Model

The Toulmin model's attention to the function that statements have within an argument makes it a complex model to apply to specific arguments. While most analysts
can readily identify the data and claim, they have more difficulty isolating and identifying the warrant and the backing that supports it. The following points may therefore be helpful in diagramming arguments using the Toulmin model.

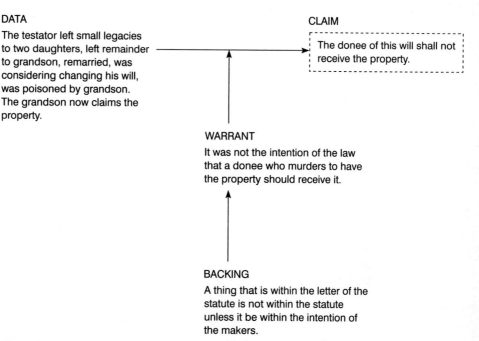

DATA

The testator left small legacies to two daughters, left remainder to grandson, remarried, was considering changing his will, was poisoned by grandson. The grandson now claims the property.

CLAIM

The donee of this will shall not receive the property.

WARRANT

It was not the intention of the law that a donee who murders to have the property should receive it.

BACKING

A thing that is within the letter of the statute is not within the statute unless it be within the intention of the makers.

Figure 7–13
Toulmin model displaying four of six possible elements of an argument

1. *Many arguments explicitly state only the data and claim, leaving the warrant implicit.* However, one must articulate the warrant in order to judge the reasoning contained in the argument. Therefore, every Toulmin diagram should include at least three parts—data, claim, and warrant. The warrant may be one of the reasoning forms explained in Chapter 5—quasi-logical, analogy, generalization, cause, coexistence, and/or dissociation. It may also be stated as a field-dependent rule, principle, law, custom, or accepted procedure. It is best to begin by attempting to locate a warrant in the argument as stated. If one is not stated, then the analyst should determine what kind of step links the data to the claim and express the warrant explicitly.

2. *The data and the warrant are often confused.* Most statements, taken in isolation, are not identifiable by their grammar or form as warrants. A warrant is a statement linking the data to the claim and functions as such within the context of the argument. Once the most readily verifiable statements—the data—and the endpoint of the argument—the claim—have been identified, the analyst should examine the remaining statements to see whether any of them expresses reasoning that connects the data-statements with the claim.

3. *The backing is frequently confused with the data.* This is understandable because they are often both stated in the form of verifiable facts. One way to distinguish between them is to realize that, while the data are almost always explicitly stated and function as the starting point or grounds for the argument as a whole, the

backing has a limited function. It is intended only to support the inference made in the warrant. In the court opinion cited above, the backing legitimized the legal principle applied in the judge's decision; in the medical diagnosis, the backing authorized the clinical prediction which justified treatment. Whereas backing is often stated only when the warrant is challenged, the data are nearly always explicitly stated in the argument.

4. *There is frequently more than one acceptable way to diagram an argument using the Toulmin model.* If the argument is very subtle or complex, different analysts may articulate the warrant differently or assign various warrants depending on how they interpret the data and the claim. (There are certain standards of correctness in analyzing arguments, however. The data and the claim are not interchangeable, and the warrant should not be confused with the data.)

Argument Chains and the Toulmin Model

The Toulmin model, like the general model of analysis, can be applied to argument chains. What serves as a claim for the initial data is then displayed as data for a further claim. If warrants are not explicitly articulated in the argument, they can be supplied, thereby providing information about the forms of reasoning used to link together the arguments in the chain. Adaptation of the Toulmin model to chains can be illustrated by using the same argument chains we used earlier to illustrate the general model.

A simple chain is evident in the following argument:

> The weather's been warming up and there are buds coming out on my shrubbery. These are signs I'll have to start mowing the lawn soon, so I'd better get the lawn mower serviced.

The data, of course, are the signs of spring readily observable in the physical environment. They are used to make a predictive claim in the second sentence that in turn becomes data for action that the arguer must take. No warrant is stated for the second inference, but the first subargument is from sign and the second is based on causal reasoning. (A serviced lawn mower will be a more effective solution for the growing grass than one which is not serviced.) So, supplying one implicit warrant would result in a Toulmin diagram of the chain that looks like Figure 7–14.

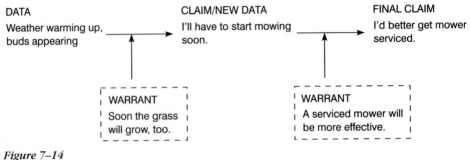

Figure 7–14
Toulmin model displaying five elements

A more complicated chain as contained in Webster's indictment of Calhoun cited earlier in this chapter is illustrated in Figure 7–15. The data, warrant, qualifier, and claim of Webster's first subargument are explicitly stated. But only the data and warrant of the second subargument are supplied. The analyst must fill in the claim of the second subargument, the final claim, and the warrant supporting the final claim.

■ *Comparison of the Two Models*

The Toulmin diagram of the chain in Webster's argument illustrates some of the advantages that Toulmin diagrams have over other argument models. First, the Toulmin model explicitly indicates the degree of cogency the arguer attributes to the claims made. By drawing attention to the qualifier in Webster's first subargument, the Toulmin diagram reminds us that Webster inferred that it was only "plausible" that people might secede as a result of Calhoun's interpretation. Evidently, Webster himself thought his argument was weak and did not attribute a high degree of cogency to it.

Second, the Toulmin model calls upon the analyst to supply unstated warrants. As a result, we see that the relationship of Webster's second subclaim to the final

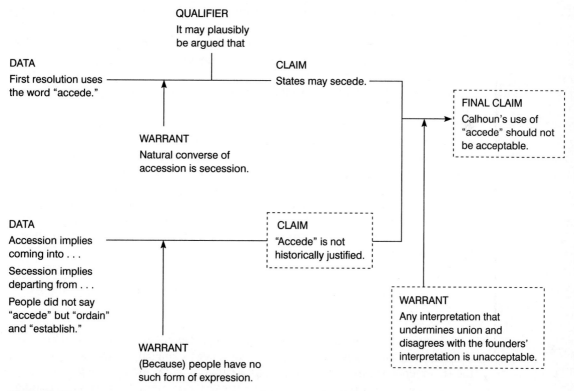

Figure 7–15
Toulmin model of argument with explicit and implied components of argument

claim depends on a warrant growing out of the principle, which Webster accepts, that interpretations of the Constitution should be based on the intent of those who wrote it.

Third, the Toulmin model emphasizes the roles and functions of each statement rather than merely shows how they relate to each other. Because a statement expressing the data in an argument should be assessed by different criteria from a statement expressing the warrant, one needs to know the difference between the two. People frequently acknowledge conditions and circumstances that limit the cogency of claims, and the Toulmin model, by way of the reservation, allows such statements to be diagrammed and expressly linked to the qualifier. This allowance for counterevidence and restrictions on the claim within the model recognizes the two-sided nature of most argument.

Fourth, as previously indicated, the Toulmin model recognizes the field-dependent nature of many forms of argument. Although many arguments are based on the field invariant categories of inferences discussed in Chapter 5 (quasi-logical, analogy, generalization, cause, coexistence, and dissociation), many are not. Arguments that occur in specific fields frequently rely upon conventions, principles, or rules particular to a specific field or area. The Toulmin model takes into account the role of such guidelines in generating the inferences upon which claims are based.

Fifth, the Toulmin model portrays any particular argument as an organic whole. In the model, data function as data only in relation to a claim; the degree of cogency expressed by the qualifier is limited by reservations which modify or restrict the warrant. In the Toulmin model, a diagram of an argument as an integrated unit displays that its persuasiveness depends upon how it functions as a whole rather than as a series of detachable statements.

The general model introduced at the beginning of the chapter also has its own advantages, however. Because the general model requires less to be supplied in order to construct a diagram, it is simpler to use. Because one can allow the diagram to conform to the structure of the argument rather than structure the argument to fit the diagram, the general model is more descriptive. The absence of a preset diagram format such as one has with the Toulmin model allows the analyst using the general model to work with the argument on its own terms. Finally, the general model shows *how* premises are related to each other—whether they work independently or together to support the claim. Working with *both* models to diagram a particular argument will often be beneficial because each model reveals different characteristics and aspects of an argument.

■ *Summary*

Argument analysis can be used to understand, evaluate, and refute the arguments one hears and reads. By interpreting an argument's language and discovering how the statements within it are related to each other, one can identify equivocation, isolate the argument's primary claim, articulate implicit inferences, locate secondary claims, disregard irrelevant statements, and perform other operations which lead to effective argument criticism and refutation.

Arguments can be categorized into four types. Simple arguments (Type I) consist of one premise and a claim that follows from it. Complex arguments (Type II) have two or more premises supporting a single claim. These premises can support the claim independently or in concert with one another. Argument chains (Type III) use one or more premises to support claims which, once proven, become premises for further claims. Compound arguments (Type IV) use one premise or two or more premises in concert to support more than one conclusion.

Having identified a statement as an argument, the analyst can use five steps to interpret and diagram it. These steps include determining what the argument means, assigning numbers to individual thought units in the argument, identifying the main or primary claim, displaying the argument's structure in a tree diagram, and evaluating the argument by using the tests of evidence and reasoning. During analysis, one should take into account the argument's context and the arguer's probable intent so as to render a fair interpretation of the argument.

Unlike the general model of argument discussed in the first half of the chapter, the Toulmin model assigns specific functions to each statement in the argument. The data function like evidence and premises on which the argument is based. The claim is the argument's endpoint or conclusion. The warrant states the reasoning used to move from the data to the claim and functions like an inference. The backing consists of facts or information used to support the inference made in the warrant. The qualifier modifies the claim and indicates the rational strength the arguer attributes to it. The reservation states circumstances or conditions in which the claim would not be true.

The Toulmin model often provides more information than the general model of argument analysis, and it is also more difficult to use. An analyst using the Toulmin model often encounters difficulties such as misidentifying unstated warrants, confusing the data and the warrant, confusing data and backing, and applying incorrect standards to diagrams of complex or subtle arguments.

The Toulmin model offers many advantages, however. It draws attention to how the arguer qualifies the argument, directs the analyst to stated implicit references, recognizes the field dependence of arguments, and emphasizes the functional nature of argument. The general model of analysis also has advantages. Because it does not have a preset structure to impose upon an argument, the general model is simpler to use and more accurately reflects the way premises and claims are related to each other.

Exercises

Diagram each of the following arguments using both the general model of argument and the Toulmin model of argument. (It might be helpful for you to review the steps described under "An Application" and the pointers for the Toulmin model under "Difficulties in Applying the Model" in this chapter before beginning.)

Then, criticize each argument by applying the tests for reasoning described in Chapter 5 and by making explicit the unstated assumptions in the argument that might be explicitly challenged. At times, the tests of evidence discussed in Chapter 4 might be useful as well. The arguments are arranged in order of difficulty, with the simplest at the beginning and the most complex at the end. For example:

> Capital punishment for murderers is widely supported by the general population. A Harris poll in 1975 reported 59 percent of the public in favor of capital punishment, and that proportion reportedly was increasing. Another poll in 1978 asked the question, "Are you in favor of the death penalty for persons convicted of murder?" The results showed 66 percent of the populace in favor of the death penalty.

General Model

1. Capital punishment for murderers is widely supported by the general population.
2. A 1975 poll reported 59 percent of the public in favor of capital punishment.
3. That proportion of people favoring capital punishment was increasing by 1975.
4. A 1978 poll asked if people favored the death penalty for convicted murderers.
5. Sixty-six percent favored the death penalty.

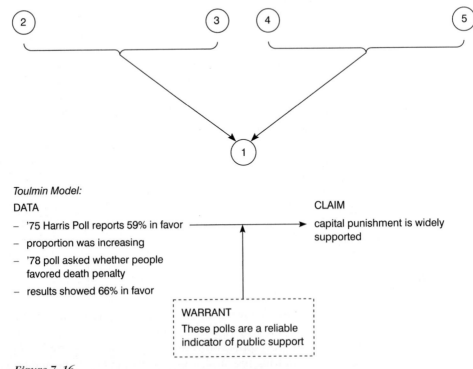

Toulmin Model:

Figure 7–16
Comparison of the General Model and the Toulmin Model

Criticism:

The polls are outdated. Perhaps pubic opinion has shifted since the 1970s. Besides, this is a form of *ad populum* argument that assumes that because the public supports something, it should be favored. Furthermore, the arguer does not report the source of the statistics or the method used to collect them. How large was the sample surveyed? Was the sample representative of the general population? Do other surveys and polls on this question (particularly those gathered since the mid-1970s) agree with the two polls cited here?

Arguments for Analysis and Criticism

* 1. It is the chemical firms that release the most troubling types of molecules into the environment. In Baton Rouge, according to company data, an Exxon chemical plant was leaking 560,000 pounds of benzene yearly, while just south of there, according to a survey by the Sierra Club, eighteen plants in and around St. Gabriel and Geismar dumped about 400 billion pounds of toxic chemicals into the air during the first nine months of 1986.

   Michael H. Brown, "The Toxic Cloud," *Greenpeace Magazine,* October–December 1987, 17.

2. But it was when Abbado had the orchestra to himself in the Tchaikovsky *Marche Slave* that the real magic showed. This hackneyed piece was treated with respect, and Abbado built it steadily to one final climax rather than playing each eruption as a show-stopping event.

3. Mountain goats were trucked into the Cascades by game wardens in the 1920s. After a few years the animals began to flourish, and now they're doing well. Too well, in fact. The park's mountain-goat population has nearly doubled in the past several years to 1,200 animals. Problem is, they're hard on the wilderness. They destroy the grass and other vegetation in fragile alpine meadows. They cause serious erosion by pawing and rolling in the dirt. They interfere with the park's natural ecosystem.

   "Problem in the Olympics," *The Seattle Times* editorial, August 31, 1986, A18. Used by permission.

4. Both public schools and colleges . . .face projected shortages of teachers in the 1990s and declining interest in teaching as the career choice of current students.

   Howard Bowen and Jack Schuster, the authors of "American Professors: A National Resource Imperiled," report that, over the past decade: "the quality of academic life has deteriorated"; the average professor's real earnings have declined further, since 1972, "than any other occupational group in America"; and, in the next 25 years, 500,000 of today's 700,000 American professors will retire, leaving a huge job vacuum.

   Adapted from Robert Marquand, "Concern for the Nation's Teachers Extends to the University Level," *The Christian Science Monitor,* vol. 78, April 28, 1986, 25. Reprinted by permission from *The Christian Science Monitor,* copyright 1986, The Christian Science Publishing Society. All rights reserved.

5. Is it not the great defect of our education today . . .that although we often succeed in teaching our pupils "subjects," we fail lamentably on the whole in teaching them how to think: they learn everything except the art of learning. It is as though we had taught a child mechanically and by rule of thumb, to play "The Harmonious

Blacksmith" upon the piano, but had never taught him the scale or how to read music; so that, having memorized "The Harmonious Blacksmith," he still had not the faintest notion how to proceed from that to tackle "The Last Rose of Summer."

> Dorothy L. Sayers, "The Lost Tools of Learning,"
> *National Review,* January 19, 1979, 91.

6. It's not too late. We can act. Today there are some 500 million women in the Third World who have told the World Fertility Survey that they want no more children. Most of them didn't want their last child, but they lacked the knowledge and the means to do something about it—whether it happens to be the three condoms for a penny that the United Nations Population Fund buys and distributes, or a cycle of oral contraceptives which the United Nations buys for 15 cents a cycle, or whether it's Norplant or vasectomy equipment.

> Werner Fornos, "The Environmental Crisis: A
> Humanist Call for Action," *The Humanist,*
> November/December 1991, 31.

7. The lunacy of modern city life lies first in the fact that most city dwellers who can do so try to live outside the city boundaries. The two-legged creatures have created suburbs, exurbs, and finally rururbs (rurbs to some). Disdaining rural life, they try to create simulations of it. No effort is spared to let city dwellers imagine they are living anywhere but in a city: patches of grass in the more modest suburbs, broader spreads in the richer ones further out; prim new trees planted along the streets; at the foot of the larger back yards, a pretense to bosky woodlands.

> Henry Fairlie, "Or the Cow's Revenge: The Idiocy
> of Urban Life," *The New Republic,* January 5 & 12,
> 1987, 21. Used by permission.

8. 1991 statistics from the Carnegie Foundation for the Advancement of Teaching show that SAT scores are directly proportional to family income. Students from families with incomes under $10,000 score an average of 768 (combined verbal and math scores) out of a possible total of 1,200. Students from families with incomes in the $30,000 to $40,000 range have scores averaging 884. Students from families with incomes over $70,000 have scores averaging 997. Since scholastic aptitude is related to a student's position on the wealth/poverty scale, which has a lot to do with where a family lives (affluent suburb or inner-city slum), alleviating poverty would be one way of improving scholastic aptitude.

> Edd Doerr, "Whither Public Education?" *The
> Humanist,* November/December 1991, 41.

9. Dieting is an urban obsession. Country dwellers eat what they please, and work it off in useful physical employments, and in the open air, cold or hot, rainy or sunny. Mailmen are the healthiest city workers. When was your mailman last ill for a day? If one reads the huge menus that formed a normal diet in the 19th century, you realize that even the city dwellers could dispatch these gargantuan repasts because they still shared many of the benefits of rural life. Homes were cold in the winter, except in the immediate vicinity of the hearth or stove. Cold has a way of eating up excess fat. No wonder dieting is necessary in a cosseted life in which the body is forced to do no natural heavy work.

> Henry Fairlie, "Or the Cow's Revenge: The Idiocy
> of Urban Life," *The New Republic,* January 5 & 12,
> 1987, 23. Used by permission.

✳ 10. Ladies make excellent teachers in public schools; many of them are every way the equals of their male competitors, and still they secure less wages than males. The reason is obvious. The number of ladies who offer themselves to teach is much larger than the number of males who are willing to teach. . . . The result is that the competition for positions of teachers to be filled by ladies is so great as to reduce the price; but as males can not be employed at that price, and are necessary in certain places in the schools, those seeking their services have to pay a higher rate for them.

> Joseph Emerson Brown, "Against the Woman Suffrage Amendment," in *American Forum* (Seattle, Wash: University of Washington Press, 1960), 339.

11. Why reports of hunger [in the United States]?

For two main reasons, specialists say. There are an estimated 4 million more poor people now than five years ago, due largely to job layoffs in troubled industries. And the federal government has lessened efforts to locate persons eligible for food stamps who do not apply for them, either because they don't know about it or are too embarrassed to apply.

> Robert P. Hay, "U.S. Hunger Grows; Programs Don't Keep Up," *The Christian Science Monitor,* vol. 78, May 20, 1986, 40.

12. For children uninstructed in the way television "frames reality," TV today is no longer simply a benign distraction—but something actually "hostile" to learning.

Neil Postman, who has researched the subject, observes that: "The great educators—from Cicero on down—have all taught that the purpose of education and schooling is to free children from the tyranny of the present, to help them see beyond the immediate. TV works just the other way."

Because TV reduces complex thoughts and ideas to mere images, because its sole operational criterion is "entertainment value"; because it demands no historical background as a key to understanding; and finally, because *it* does the thinking for passive viewers—TV is "by its very nature opposed to what education is all about."

> Adapted from Robert Marquand, "Teach Children How to See TV," *Christian Science Monitor,* December 26, 1986, 19. Reprinted by permission from *The Christian Science Monitor,* copyright 1986, The Christian Science Publishing Society. All rights reserved.

13. [For this dialogue, there are two arguments—Professor Smith's and Professor Jones's. The general model requires two separate diagrams, while the Toulmin model requires only one, because Professor Jones's objections can be included in the reservation.]

PROFESSOR SMITH: There is probably too much cheating going on in our department, and our faculty should do something about it.

PROFESSOR JONES: I haven't noticed any evidence of cheating in my classes. What makes you say it's widespread?

PROFESSOR SMITH: Well, I'm sure you remember that our colleague Adams found a lot of plagiarism on the course papers turned in to him last spring. Whole paragraphs were reproduced in more than one student paper. Then, of course, our graduate student proctors often have taken up crib sheets in the 100 course exam. And I've observed students during my own tests sharing information with each other. These are signs of a pervasive problem throughout the department. Every time our faculty, teaching assistants, and proctors look for wrongdoing, they seem to find it.

PROFESSOR JONES: I think you're exaggerating the extent of the problem; these are the behaviors of a small group of male students in their various courses who take pride in finding ways to "get around" the system.

14. So much of the male behavior that puts women at risk—multiple partners, bisexuality, reluctance or refusal to wear condoms—cannot be changed by women alone. And so many of the attitudes that pervade societies about women's worth and place and men's rights make effective prevention campaigns extremely difficult to achieve. . . . Even when informed of the risk, women too rarely have the power to protect themselves. In every society, women are subservient to men. Depending on the degree of pressure on her to be submissive in sexual and social matters, a woman who tries to use information to prevent infection may become the target of mockery, rejection, stigmatization, economic reprisal, violence, and death.

Marcia Ann Gillespie, "HIV: The Global Crisis," *MS. Magazine,* January/February, 1991, 17.

(The following two arguments are excerpted from a group discussion on the right to die. Assume that all the participants are working together to construct *one* argument and are pursuing a shared thoughtline.)

✳ 15. ANNE: Technology has affected every single part of the program.

CARRIE: Yes, technology is a big one.

ANNE: I don't really feel technology is just the mechanical aspect. It's chemical, biological, physical, everything. The advances in technology have gone so far that it can prolong life, yeah, but when you get in the position of an irreversibly comatose-type state, it's out of step with what man is. You know, should he be prolonged just to vegetate? Are they prolonging ill health or are they prolonging life? Technology has reached the outer limits where it's gone beyond what man is.

ANNE: It's gone beyond the purpose for which medical technology was originally intended. Its goal was to enhance human life, whereas now it just prolongs death, dying, and pain.

16. STEVE: The Hippocratic Oath, which states doctors must do everything within their power to keep the patient alive, is also a problem.

CARRIE: But the idea of the Hippocratic Oath is a problem. It says: "So far as power and discernment shall be mine, I will carry out the regimen for the benefit of the sick and will keep them from harm and wrong." Now the doctors or the law, . . .someone should explain the Hippocratic Oath to everyone, what exactly those words mean.

ANNE: But it's an archaic document. I mean, it talks about Greek gods. . . .

LEIGH: It's so ambiguous. It doesn't have to do with today's society.

STEVE: It's been outgrown by technology.

Notes

1. Irving M. Copi, *Informal Logic* (New York: Macmillan, 1986), 19.

2. Daniel Webster, "The Constitution Not a Compact between Sovereign States," in *American Forum: Speeches on Historic Issues, 1788–1900,* Ernest J. Wrage and Barnet Baskerville, eds. (Seattle: University of Washington Press, 1960), 136–37.

3. Monroe C. Beardsley, *Practical Logic* (New York: Prentice-Hall, 1950), 18–25.

4. See Michael Scriven, *Reasoning* (Point Reyes, CA: Edgepress, 1976). Copi's model is the simpler of the two and does not emphasize the interpretation and criticism of arguments as much as does Scriven's. To adjust our treatment of analysis to chapter length, we have eliminated steps Scriven recommends such as formulating unstated assumptions and considering related arguments. The reader interested in a more complete and extensive treatment of analysis should consult the works of both these authors.

5. Copi, 7.

6. *American Forum,* 139.

7. *Webster's New Collegiate Dictionary,* s.v. "plight," "faith," and "sovereign."

8. Copi, 20.

9. Adapted from "More Big-Brotherism," *National Review,* December 31, 1986, 18.

10. Adapted from a letter to the editor, "New Destination Ski Resorts Could Boost Clean Industry," *The Seattle Times,* December 21, 1986, by Mel Borgersen, A15. Used by permission of Mel Borgersen.

11. Adapted from Emily Feistritzer, "Balancing Act: Love and Money," *The Seattle Times,* August 31, 1986, A16.

12. Adapted from Feistritzer, A16.

13. Stephen Toulmin, *The Uses of Argument* (Cambridge, Mass.: University Press, 1969), 94–145.

14. Toulmin, 94.

15. Toulmin, 98.

16. Stephen Toulmin, Richard Rieke, and Allan Janik, *An Introduction to Reasoning,* 2nd ed. (New York: Macmillan, 1984), 86.

17. Adapted from *Riggs vs. Palmer,* 115 N.Y. 506 (1889), 22 N.E. 188.

Constructing Argumentative Cases

CHAPTER *8*

Principles of Case Construction

■

CHAPTER OUTLINE

- Values and Policies
- Constructing Argumentative Cases

- Refutation
- Summary
- Exercises

KEY CONCEPTS

case
prima facie case
refutation
burden of rejoinder

In the three chapters preceding this one, we have focused on the skills of constructing and analyzing individual arguments. Chapter 5 discussed types and tests of inferences; Chapter 6 explained how to detect errors in arguments; and Chapter 7 discussed analysis of individual arguments. While these are important critical thinking skills, they are only part of what you will need to know to become a competent arguer and thinker. Critical thinking researchers recently concluded that the skills of general advocacy and case construction are also highly important.[1] In fact, knowing how to analyze a problem and develop and defend a position on it are equally significant critical thinking skills. In this chapter and in Chapters 9 and 10, we will explain how to develop extended arguments supporting and opposing socially significant values and policies.

To develop an overall position on a topic, you must know how to identify a significant and controversial question or problem, seek out relevant information through research, select the issues that your audience will expect to see addressed, articulate your position, and defend your position against opposing views. You also will need to know how to select from a large number of potential arguments those that will be most effective with your audience. In completing all of these steps, you will be constructing a case. *A case is an extended argument supporting or opposing a proposition.* You may recall from Chapter 3 that a proposition is a "main claim" or the thesis statement of an extended argument. Examples would be the following:

> The federal government should significantly increase regulation of mass media advertising in the United States.
>
> Euthanasia for terminally ill patients is desirable.
>
> John Doe is innocent of murder in the first degree.
>
> The state of California should enact significant growth management legislation.

Cases favoring such propositions might take the form of a speech in support of some legislation, a case for the defense or prosecution in a criminal trial, or the affirmative or negative side in a debate. Cases are characterized by a network of claims and subclaims, each supported by further argument. (See Figure 3–1 in Chapter 3 for an example.)

Values and Policies

Advocates often construct cases supporting claims of value or of policy.[2] As we noted in Chapter 3, value claims assess the worth or merit of an idea, object, or practice according to an arguer's standards or criteria, whereas policy claims call for a course of action. Value claims and policy claims are not mutually exclusive; each implies the other. Policy claims are based on underlying values; we only decide on an action when we have determined that it is beneficial, and "benefit" is often measured by the value the action fulfills. Our staffed space program is an example of this:

Policy: We should engage in full-scale staffed exploration of space.

Benefits:	**Costs:**
Scientific knowledge	Lives lost—remember *Challenger*
Technological advances	Billions of dollars

Here the potential benefits are weighed against the costs, and the comparison is directly related to our value systems. After the *Challenger* disaster, many people argued that human life should always come first and scientific knowledge and technological advances should come second. In this case, the value of human life was so high that for some individuals the costs far outweighed the possible benefits.

On the other hand, values imply policies. If everyone could agree that certain forms of euthanasia were justified and desirable in certain circumstances, then lawmakers would enact legislation making those forms of euthanasia legal. The reason that there is so much variation in abortion laws in different states is that there is no value consensus between pro-choice and pro-life factions in various parts of the country.

Although values and policies are tied to each other, the types of claims and evidence used in policy and fact arguments are different from those in value arguments. In selecting policies, people make decisions about what action to take based on their assessment of the risks involved and the potential benefits to be obtained. Most people choose an action when the benefits are perceived to be greater than the costs or disadvantages of taking action. For example, a stockbroker might propose that his client invest heavily in the stock market. In support of this proposition, the stockbroker would cite market trends, projections of growth in the economy, and our competitiveness in foreign trade. These are all empirical economic facts, and in the end the broker places his faith in them and decides that the stock market *probably* will continue to rise. The broker's client weighs the broker's arguments and the facts and statistical projections he has cited and decides whether to invest. This process of risk analysis allows decision makers to decide in favor of policies and courses of action that appear to offer the greatest utility or benefit.[3]

Policy arguments therefore concern action to be taken in the future, and they are based on empirical facts and on trends and projections. Value arguments, on the other hand, are usually based in the present and rely on social agreement concerning values. In Chapter 3, we defined values as positive or negative attitudes toward certain end states of existence or broad modes of conduct. Examples of values are freedom, equality, self-respect, and family security. When we express our values, we express our own conceptions of the worth of objects or ideas. Values, then, regulate our orientations toward the objects and experiences in our lives.

Some people who believe that all decisions and choices should be made on the basis of "hard facts" also believe that we cannot argue about values. They will say "But how can you argue about values? What I think is important is my opinion and what others think is important is theirs. Values are a matter of personal choice, and no amount of argumentation is going to change them!" This view that values cannot be rationally argued is ill-founded. First, we commonly base decisions on other-than-factual considerations. In making these decisions, we use accepted value-related rules and norms to make choices. For example,

> It is wrong to harm someone else for no reason.
>
> One ought to keep one's promises.
>
> An accused person is innocent until proven guilty.
>
> When two of your friends meet for the first time, you should introduce them.

Although we cannot use such statements as evidence for our claims in the same way we would use empirical facts, we do feel comfortable using them as support in arguments. Second, value-based arguments are actually used all the time to make decisions in law, politics, and other fields. This is especially true when competing values force us to choose among alternatives. How should legislators weigh national defense against the needs of America's homeless and hungry? Should offensive pornography be openly sold because it is a form of freedom of speech, or should it be limited because it degrades people? Should economic development or environmental protection be the determining factor in approving new construction and public works projects? Even when all the factual information is in (and often it is not available or is contradictory), such decisions are based on values or argumentation about values.

Decision making is a complex process. It involves our value systems as well as our estimation of future costs and benefits. Any decision we make can involve many different systems that organize our thoughts and lives. We use the understanding of our value system, our political system, our economic system, and our social system to help make correct choices.

◼ *Constructing Argumentative Cases*

The process of decision making occurs in courtrooms, legislatures, board rooms, and voting booths. Ideally, decisions are reached because of argumentation by informed persons who support various positions on an issue. Argumentation and decision making are the processes we use in our society to reach reasonable consensus about the problems we face. To some extent, the nature of our problems and the issues we consider significant change with time. During the Persian Gulf War in 1991, for example, national defense and security were primary concerns of the American people. Just over a year later, the Soviet Union had ceased to exist, major arms reduction agreements were reached, and the level of concern about threats to our national security had greatly decreased.

Issues such as abortion, capital punishment, environmental protection, and crime control are continuing sources of disagreement and debate in our society. If you wish to become seriously involved in the discussion of topics such as these, you will need to know how to construct argumentative cases about them. Whether your case is oriented toward policy or values, there are certain recognized principles governing construction of cases in legal briefs, legislative proposals, speeches, and academic debates that you should know. Before we discuss the specific strategies for constructing and defending value and policy cases in Chapters 9 and 10, we will explain those principles here.

The first principle is that the person advocating a change in value or policy has the *burden of proof* and must overcome the *presumption* in favor of what presently exists or is accepted. As we explained in Chapter 3, the presumption "preoccupies the ground" of the controversy and will continue to do so until it is successfully challenged by some new value or proposal. The burden of proof is the requirement shared by all advocates of change to present an argument sufficient to overcome presumption. Presumption is the understanding that change involves risk and that the current state of affairs involves less risk than any change. Essentially, presumption can be understood using the aphorism "if it ain't broke, don't fix it" (because you may end up making it worse than when you began). Therefore, the function of the burden of proof for the advocate is to prove that the risks inherent in change can be overcome by the benefits of change.

On the topic of handgun control, for example, the present policy is that sale and possession of handguns is minimally restricted in most states. Anyone who can obtain a license and who can afford a gun can buy one. Those who supported passage in Congress of the Brady Bill (which requires a waiting period before a handgun could be purchased) had the burden of proof; they had to show that the benefits of enacting a waiting period outweighed the risks and costs of changing the present policy.

It is important to note that presumption is a convention of argument that grows out of a basic principle of audience psychology. Its description originated with Bishop Richard Whately, who noted that people are predisposed to favor what they presently believe and what exists.[4] In other words, people are by nature conservative when it comes to making decisions based on argument; they will only be persuaded to support a change if they come to believe it is a good idea. The convention of presumption in argument thus does not imply that the present system or value *should* be favored; it only implies that an arguer should recognize the necessity of overcoming this conservative predisposition if he or she expects to make an argument effectively.

There are times when it is unclear which side of an issue has the presumption and which side has the burden of proof, because policies and values may be inconsistent or not fully determined. On the topic of capital punishment, for example, present policies vary from state to state. Some states allow the death penalty for capital crimes, whereas others call for life in prison without parole. Public attitudes on capital punishment do not lie clearly on one side or the other of the issue. In the case of a topic such as this, the location of the presumption may be less important, and the convention of argument is that whoever asserts a position has the burden of proof.[5]

Sometimes presumption is assigned by mutual agreement of parties to an argument or by conventions of the field of argument. In criminal trials in the United

States, the accused is *presumed* innocent until *proven* guilty. The prosecution thus has the burden of proof. In enacting legislation, certain levels of government are presumed to control policy in certain areas. The federal government is responsible for national defense, for example, while the individual states primarily control public education. Consequently, when advocates propose policy changes of a certain kind, they must locate that change at the government level best suited to that policy area.

A second important principle of case construction is that the central claims advanced by an advocate should address the proposition's major *issues.* In Chapter 3, an issue was defined as a point of potential disagreement viewed as significant by parties to an argument. For example, if the main proposition of a policy dispute was whether "the federal government should significantly increase regulation of handguns in the United States," certain issues would likely come to mind (i.e., Do handguns cause significant harm? Is present regulation of handguns inadequate? Would increased regulation be beneficial?). These issues must be addressed because audiences would expect them to be addressed whenever a change in handgun policy is recommended. Because this claim is a policy claim, the issues concern the costs and benefits of present handgun policy vs. the costs and benefits of any new policy.

Assume the same topic is worded as a value claim: "Significant restriction on the use of handguns is desirable." A somewhat different set of issues is suggested. Are these "restrictions" to be total or partial? What standards should be used to determine whether restrictions are desirable? What values would be fulfilled or furthered by handgun restriction? How do present social values relate to a restriction on handguns? As we mentioned earlier, policy issues are potentially subject to empirical verification, whereas value issues refer to social consensus and reasonable opinion on a topic.

An arguer who initiates discussion on a topic by proposing a change must present what is called a *prima facie* case. *A prima facie case "on its face" presents good and sufficient reasons for adopting the viewpoint or action proposed by an advocate.* Cases are considered *prima facie* when their supporters satisfactorily address all of the major issues a reasonable audience would expect to see addressed. The issues that need to be addressed depend on the topic and on what the audience knows about it. For example, on the question of whether research funding should be granted for the investigation of AIDS, an advocate would probably not need to prove that there is a problem. If the arguer could prove that increased funding of a particular research application would dramatically reduce the incidence of AIDS, his or her case would be *prima facie.* Therefore, in the absence of opposition or significant questions regarding her proposal, it should be adopted.

Arguers should keep their audience's attitudes and expectations in mind when they construct cases. If there is a clear presumption in favor of existing policy or in favor of a certain value orientation on a topic, advocates must take that presumption into account as they construct a case. Furthermore, they should be familiar with the major issues related to a topic and make sure they address them. If the case is based on a reasonable proposal and if the major claims supporting that proposal are supported to the satisfaction of the audience, then the case will be *prima facie.* The general principles of case construction discussed in this chapter are based on reasonable audience expectation and the conventions of argument. Advocates who carefully take them into account will find that the cases they present will be persuasive and compelling to the audiences for which they are intended.

Refutation

Anyone who opposes a *prima facie* case, once presented, has the burden of rejoinder. *The burden of rejoinder is the requirement that those who oppose a proposal respond reasonably to the issues presented by the original advocate.* For example in a murder case, the state has the burden to prove beyond a reasonable doubt that the defendant committed the crime. The defense has a burden of rejoinder to refute the arguments presented by the state. And the defendant has the presumption of innocence until the burden of proof has been met by the state.

Meeting the burden of rejoinder means that the arguer must engage systematically in refutation of an opponent's case. *Refutation is the process of discrediting someone's argument by revealing weaknesses in it or by presenting a counterargument.* Refutation can be divided into kinds or types along two lines. First, refutation can be classified into case-level refutation (aimed at the opponent's whole case or extended argument) or specific refutation (aimed at individual arguments). Second, refutation can be classified as destructive (aimed at tearing down the opponent's arguments as presented) or constructive (aimed at providing counterarguments to be weighed against the opponent's).

Case-level refutation can be designed in three ways—direct refutation, counteradvocacy, or a combination of the two. Direct refutation moves down the opponent's case through his or her main claim, principle subclaims, and sub-subclaims; refutes each one; and then synthesizes these individual responses into a rationale for rejecting the opponent's proposal. In effect, this strategy shifts the burden of proof back to the original advocate. Counteradvocacy involves offering an alternative proposal of either policy or value to be weighed in comparison with the original proposal. Counteradvocacy more nearly reflects real-life decision making where various alternative proposals compete with each other than does direct refutation which assumes merely a "yes/no" decision. Refuting through counteradvocacy, however, means that the refuter, like the original advocate, assumes a burden of proof to support and defend the counterproposal. The most commonly used method of refutation is a combination of direct refutation and counteradvocacy in which the opponent attacks the arguments of the other person and at the same time offers an alternative proposal.

We will provide more specific suggestions for case-level refutation in Chapters 9 and 10 where we discuss propositions of value and policy. There we will indicate possible arguments that can be used by arguers seeking to refute value and policy proposals at the case level. It is important to remember that when you design case-level refutation, you must decide on an overall strategy, develop a response that is coherent, and communicate your overall approach or philosophy to the audience.

In the remainder of this chapter, we will discuss specific refutation which is directed at individual arguments within an opponent's case. The five strategies discussed here, taken together, constitute a repertoire of approaches that can be used to indict the arguments of an opponent and to defend your own position. Skilled arguers can use a variety of these strategies in combination to keep their opponents on the defensive. For purposes of illustration throughout this discussion, let us assume that the opponent has presented an argument for handgun control. The argument to be refuted asserts that in the past decade, over 200,000 people have been killed in handgun fire, that criminals and unstable people have legal access to handguns, and that a waiting period for handgun purchases will help to address these problems.

The first strategy for refutation is called "exploratory refutation." Use of this technique involves asking a number of questions or raising a number of objections designed to cause opponents to take a stand on issues an advocate hopes to refute. Exploratory refutation is analogous to drawing opponents out into the open so they can be fired upon. In response to the handgun argument, one might ask a number of questions: How many of the 200,000 handgun deaths were due to the lack of a waiting period? How long will the waiting period be? How will the mere existence of a waiting period ensure that criminals and unstable people cannot get guns? Exploratory refutation is especially effective when one's opponents have limited speaking time, because such questions often take a good deal of time to answer. Exploratory refutation is effective only when refuters pursue and critique claims made by their opponents in answer to their questions.

A second effective refutation strategy is to note contradictions or inconsistencies in the opponents' arguments or use of evidence. For example, assume that the supporters of handgun control stated that students shot in a high school had been wounded and killed by handguns. This argument could be refuted if one could show that a waiting period could not prevent such incidents because the handguns obtained in this incident were purchased legally by persons with no criminal record or history of mental instability. The advocates' original analysis of the problem could then be shown to be inconsistent with their call for a waiting period to screen out "undesirable" gun purchasers.

The third strategy is to apply the tests of evidence described in Chapter 4 to the opponents' evidence. Evidence may be biased, outdated, irrelevant, inexpert, inconsistent, unreliable, inaccurate, or inaccessible. Criticizing opponents' evidence is usually not as damaging as some of the other refutation strategies and should not be overused. However, when biased or inexpert evidence is used repeatedly, pointing out inadequacies in evidence can be very damaging. Opponents of gun control often cite the National Rifle Association for support, but this lobbying group is very biased on the topic.

The fourth refutation strategy is to attack opponents' reasoning by applying the tests of reasoning in Chapter 5 to their inferences, or by detecting fallacies as treated in Chapter 6 in their arguments. The refutation may charge that analogies were made between dissimilar phenomena; that generalizations were based on nonrepresentative samples; and/or that *post hoc* relationships were mistaken for causal relationships. The argument for a waiting period in obtaining handguns is based on a series of causal links: that the lack of a waiting period enables criminals and mentally unstable people to get guns, that these people substantially contribute to the number of handgun deaths, and that instituting a waiting period will therefore prevent the deaths. These causal links could be successfully refuted if it could be shown that most handgun deaths are accidents, suicides, or caused by people who know each other. The opponents of handgun control could show that merely instituting a waiting period will not substantially decrease gun deaths, because the presence or absence of a waiting period is neither a necessary nor sufficient condition causing handgun deaths.

Attacking opponents' evidence and reasoning and showing inconsistencies in their arguments are all forms of destructive refutation; they attempt to dismantle or undermine the arguments being refuted. The fifth refutation strategy is constructive. Here the opponent presents counterevidence and counterarguments to be weighed against the arguments being refuted. Opponents of a waiting period might argue that increased restrictions on the legal sale of handguns will not decrease those handgun deaths that are caused by "undesirable" handgun purchasers. The *real* cause, they might argue, is the ease of illegally obtaining guns through sources supported by organized crime. They might then refute the waiting period by arguing with evidence that handgun deaths and injuries are largely the result of illegal firearms and that a waiting period will not control illegal possession of firearms.

The experience of preparing refutations of other's arguments and of anticipating other's refutations of our own arguments can contribute substantially to the development of critical thinking ability. Our arguments often seem quite strong and airtight until they are attacked by people who are skeptical of our viewpoint. By carefully considering objections that might be raised against our arguments, we can improve our reasoning and become more discriminating in our use of evidence.

▓ *Summary*

This chapter concerns the principles for constructing cases, or extended arguments supporting or opposing a proposition. Most argumentative cases focus on policies or values. Policies and values are related to each other in that policies are based on underlying values, and values imply policies. The forms of analysis and support used to justify policies and those used to justify values are different from each other, however. Policy decisions are based largely on cost/benefit analysis and pertinent facts, whereas value selection relies on social agreement concerning values.

Advocates presenting a proposal for change in policies or values have the burden of proof to present good and sufficient reason for that change. Advocates for change must overcome the presumption that favors what presently exists or is accepted. Because change involves risk and because people are predisposed to favor present policy and value, they will only be persuaded to support a change if they come to believe it is a good idea. For this reason, advocates of change must satisfactorily address all the major issues on a topic that are viewed as significant by the audience.

Once advocates have fulfilled the burden of proof and presented a satisfactory case for change, their opponents have the burden of rejoinder to respond reasonably to the issues they have raised. In responding, the opponents engage in refutation. Refutation is the process of discrediting someone's argument by revealing weaknesses in it or by presenting a counterargument of one's own. Refutation can be divided into case-level (aimed at the opponent's case as a whole) or specific (aimed at individual arguments).

When refuting cases, opponents have three options. First, they can use direct refutation in which they tear down each of the arguments and the whole taken together. Second, they can employ counteradvocacy, by offering an alternative policy or value of their own. Third, they can employ a combination of direct refutation and counteradvocacy by attacking the advocates' arguments and at the same time offering alternatives of their own.

Specific refutation, which is directed at individual arguments, can be implemented through five strategies that can be used singly or in combination. First, refuters can use exploratory refutation; they can raise a number of questions and objections to draw out their opponents and make them take positions on issues on which their opponents might be vulnerable. Second, they can note contradictions and inconsistencies in their opponents' case. Third, they can indict their opponents' evidence, showing it to be biased, outdated, irrelevant, inexpert, or unreliable. Fourth, refuters can attack reasoning by revealing fallacies and mistakes in their opponents' inferences. Fifth, refuters can produce arguments and evidence of their own that can be weighed against the arguments their opponents have made. Knowing these strategies of refutation and anticipating objections and criticisms of one's arguments can contribute substantially to critical thinking ability and to the skills of advocacy.

Exercises

Exercise 1   For each of the following "main claims" or propositions for extended argument, identify at least three value issues and three policy issues that a general audience would expect to see addressed. Also, decide whether the proposition is one of policy (calling for action) or of value (advocating a particular value orientation on a topic). Finally, decide for each topic whether the presumption does or does not favor the "main claim" as stated.

Example:

Proposition	The federal government should enact significant restrictions on the sale of handguns in the United States.
(a) Value Issues	• Do all Americans have an intrinsic right to bear arms?
	• Is handgun control a form of invasion of privacy?
Policy Issues	• Are preservation of life and prevention of injury more important than the right to bear arms?
	• Are present minimal restrictions on handgun sales and purchases inadequate?
	• What proportion of gun deaths is caused by legally owned handguns?
	• Would state governments be better able to deal with gun control than the federal government?

(b)   This is a proposition of policy which calls for government action.

(c)   Because there are few national restrictions on the sale of handguns in the United States, this proposition does *not* have the presumption.

✳ 1. Membership in the United Nations is no longer beneficial to the United States.

   2. The United States government should significantly increase exploration of space beyond the earth's mesosphere.

   3. All United States military intervention into the internal affairs of any foreign nation in the Western Hemisphere should be prohibited.

   4. The method of conducting presidential elections in the United States is detrimental to democracy.

✳ 5. The American judicial system has overemphasized the rights of the accused.

   6. The United States is justified in aiding undemocratic governments.

   7. The federal government should guarantee an opportunity for higher education to all qualified high school graduates.

   8. The federal government should provide a program of comprehensive medical care for all U.S. citizens.

   9. Significantly stronger third-party participation in the United States presidential elections would benefit the political process.

  10. Environmental protection is a more important goal than the satisfaction of American energy needs.

Notes

1. Joanne G. Kurfiss, *Critical Thinking: Theory, Research, Practice, and Possibilities* (Washington, D.C.: Association for the Study of Higher Education, 1988), 2.

2. In this text, we emphasize extended argument in support of value and policy claims. Occasionally, fact claims are the subject of extensive argument, e.g., "Capital punishment deters capital crime," or "Marijuana is physically harmful." Claims of this sort are usually causal in nature. Should you wish to advocate a causal factual claim, you should follow the guidelines for causal argument discussed in Chapter 5.

3. Vincent Follert, "Risk Analysis: Its Application to Argumentation and Decision Making," *Journal of the American Forensic Association,* 18 (1981): 99–108.

4. Richard Whately, *Elements of Rhetoric,* ed. Douglas Ehninger (Carbondale, Ill.: Southern Illinois University Press, 1963), 112–113.

5. For further discussion of presumption in value and policy advocacy, see Gary Cronkhite, "The Locus of the Presumption," *Central States Speech Journal* 17 (1966): 276; and Barbara Warnick, "Arguing Value Propositions," *Journal of the American Forensic Association,* 18 (1981): 112–115. Permission to draw material from the latter article was granted by the American Forensic Association.

CHAPTER *9*

Arguing About Values

■

CHAPTER OUTLINE

- Values and Value
  Systems
- The Process of Value
  Change
- Values and
  Argumentation
- Stock Issues for Value
  Arguments
  Definition
  Field
  Criteria
  Application
  Hierarchies

- The Issues Brief
- Summary
- Exercises

KEY CONCEPTS

value system

instrumental values

value redistribution

value emphasis

value restandardization

value object

stock issues

issues brief

Two college roommates are discussing what to do over Thanksgiving break:

JANIE: Listen, John just called up to Whistler Ski Resort. They
                                have a 50-inch base and 10 inches of new snow. Seventy
                                percent of their runs are open. What a chance for a ski-
                                ing vacation!

SUE: But I told my parents I was coming home. They're
                                expecting me.

JANIE: Look, you're going home for three whole weeks at
                                Christmas. I'm sure your parents would understand if
                                you wanted to spend this weekend skiing. With a group
                                of us sharing a condo and cooking in, the only real
                                expense would be lift tickets. And we'll have such a
                                great time! We all need a break, especially you. You've
                                been studying so hard this term.

SUE: It will be more of a break and more restful for me to go
                                home. I can sleep in and enjoy Mom's cooking. Besides,
                                my brother's not coming home Christmas and I want to
                                see him. Thanks for the invite, Janie, but I'll take a rain
                                check!

On its face, this seems to be a discussion about what Janie and Sue will do during their break. But fundamentally, the difference in their viewpoint and priorities
arises from their different values. Janie tries to persuade Sue to join her by describing the skiing conditions, the ease and convenience of the trip, and the fun they will
have. Her arguments make little impact on Sue because she obviously values rest,
relaxation, and time with her family. In other words, the values held by the two
women are prioritized differently. One values excitement and a good time with
friends while the other values a quiet time with family. Many decisions about what to
do and what choice to make depend upon the values one holds and their relative
importance in one's overall value system.

The purpose of this chapter is to acquaint you with the basic dynamics of value
controversy. The first section will explain how choices are evaluated, how values are
prioritized by individuals, and how and why values change over time. The second
section will explain the relationship between values and argumentation and the
bases for value arguments. The third section will orient you to the basic kinds of
issues that arise in value argumentation, and the last section will describe specific
procedures for constructing cases supporting and opposing value propositions. The
formats suggested in this last section are particularly useful for essays, speeches, and
debates in which extended cases for or against value claims must be composed. But
value disputes also occur in conversations, discussions, and other argumentative situations. Because such disputes revolve around issues similar to the ones we discuss,
our strategies for constructing cases should be useful in other communication situations as well.

■ *Values and Value Systems*

Values are pervasive both in the life of society and the life of the individual. Milton Rokeach, who researched American values for the past three decades, made some important distinctions about the nature and types of values. He noted that each person has values organized into a value system. *A value system is an enduring organization of beliefs concerning preferable modes of conduct or end states of existence along a continuum of relative importance.*[1] By this, Rokeach meant that each of us have values that are organized into hierarchies. *A value hierarchy is an ordering of values such that some are ranked more highly than others.* In the conversation between Janie and Sue about skiing, Janie values pleasure, excitement, and a good time during vacation, while Sue values family security and comfort more than excitement and fun. The two women have different value systems or hierarchies, and they disagree about which values are more important.

A value is a particular kind of belief. Rather than being descriptive or capable of being true or false, a value is prescriptive; it helps us to judge whether an action or state of being is desirable or undesirable. Rokeach divided values into two main categories—instrumental and terminal. *Instrumental values concern modes of conduct or the means for fulfilling other values. Terminal values concern desirable end states of existence.*[2] We get an education (instrumental value) so that we can find a rewarding career (terminal value). We work hard (instrumental value) so that we can have a comfortable life (terminal value). Examples of instrumental values are educational opportunity, leisure time, and economic prosperity. Instrumental values have a means/end relationship with certain terminal values such as family security, an exciting life, a sense of accomplishment, and self-respect. Rokeach estimated that, whereas an individual possesses a limited number of terminal values—somewhere between one and two dozen—the total number of instrumental values may be several times that number because we use many avenues or instruments to reach our objectives or terminal value states.

Values can also be divided into personal and social values. Personal values such as self-esteem, salvation, and social recognition are self-centered and intrapersonal in nature, whereas social values such as world peace, family security and altruism are society-centered or socially centered.[3] Objects and actions are thus valuable because they fulfill our intellectual, biological, or spiritual needs at either the personal or social level.

From the 1960s through the 1980s, Rokeach conducted extensive studies of American value systems. Narrowing the list of terminal values to eighteen, he surveyed large samples of the American public to discover how these eighteen terminal values were ordered. Results from his studies in 1968 and 1981 are reported in Table 9–1. Three observations about this rank ordering of values are particularly noteworthy. First, American values appear to be quite stable across time. Although there are some changes, the same high- and low-ranked values in 1968 were ranked high and low in 1981. Concerning this stability, Rokeach and his coauthor noted that "such highly stable findings would seem to suggest that there is little, if any, value change

Rank Order of Terminal Values (1968)[1]			
Males (All races)	**Females (All races)**	**Blacks**	**1981 Survey**[4]
1. a world at peace	1. a world at peace	1. a world at peace	1. family security
2. family security	2. family security	2. equality	2. a world at peace
3. freedom	3. freedom	3. freedom	3. freedom
4. a comfortable life	4. salvation	4. family security	4. self-respect
5. happiness	5. happiness	5. a comfortable life	5. happiness
6. self-respect	6. self-respect	6. self-respect	6. wisdom
7. a sense of accomplishment	7. wisdom	7. happiness	7. a sense of accomplishment
8. wisdom	8. equality	8. wisdom	8. a comfortable life
9. equality	9. true friendship	9. salvation	9. salvation
10. national security	10. a sense of accomplishment	10. true friendship	10. true friendship
11. true friendship	11. national security	11. a sense of accomplishment	11. national security
12. salvation	12. inner harmony	12. inner harmony	12. equality
13. inner harmony	13. a comfortable life	13. national security	13. inner harmony
14. mature love	14. mature love	14. mature love	14. mature love
15. a world of beauty	15. a world of beauty	15. social recognition	15. an exciting life
16. social recognition	16. pleasure	16. a world of beauty	16. a world of beauty
17. pleasure	17. social recognition	17. pleasure	17. pleasure
18. an exciting life	18. an exciting life	18. an exciting life	18. social recognition

Table 9–1
Rank Order of Terminal Values, 1968 and 1981

occurring in American society, at least in the thirteen-year period under consideration. Many social scientists would probably interpret such findings as confirming the widely shared view that human values are deep-lying components of collective belief systems and are thus inherently resistant to change."[4]

Second, these value orderings are somewhat similar for men and women and for blacks and whites. In contrast to the stereotype that men value achievement and intellectual pursuits while women value love, affiliation, and the family, Rokeach found that these values were similarly ranked by Americans of both sexes. In regard to race, the rank orderings of blacks and whites were similar *with the exception of the value of equality* which was ranked second by blacks and twelfth by whites. Furthermore, when Rokeach matched blacks with the whites in his survey according to education and socioeconomic status, the differences between the two races in value rankings either disappeared or became minimal, again with the exception of the different rankings of equality.[5]

Third, this ranking of terminal values was specific to American culture. Rokeach gathered information on value rankings from Australians, Canadians, and Israelis and found sizable differences between cultures. Israelis ranked national security second, whereas it was never ranked higher than tenth by Americans. Canadians ranked happiness, mature love, and true friendship much more highly than Americans. Seymour Lipset, who has done extensive cross-cultural comparisons between Americans and Canadians, has noted that Americans are more religious, more patriotic, more populist and antielitist, and more socially egalitarian than Canadians and citizens of other developed countries. America is also more "antistatist" (distrustful of centralized government) than all other developed nations and thus is exceptional in the low level of support it provides for its poor in welfare, housing, and medical care. Lipset reports that among the developed nations, the United States has the highest proportion of its people living in poverty.[6] These studies of American values indicate that the orderings and priorities we place on various terminal values are culture-specific. As we noted in Chapter 2, people of different cultures and ethnicities will perceive and respond to value arguments in different ways. They will view as important those values that concern them most directly. The question of which values are ranked most highly by one's audience should always influence the design of one's value argumentation.

■ *The Process of Value Change*

In any society that is not experiencing violent domestic upheaval or social change, there will be many commonly accepted core values. As noted in Table 9–1, "a world at peace," "family security," and "freedom" are three central accepted and acknowledged values in American society. Nicholas Rescher, a scholar who has researched value-oriented reasoning, has observed that "there unquestionably exists (and will continue to exist) a prominent value consensus in America."[7] In our own society and in others, however, certain values are unstable and fluctuate in their importance and in the extent to which people adhere to them.[8] Because these fluctuations affect the hierarchies used in argumentation, advocates should be sensitive to them.

Values change in three different ways. One type of value change occurs when a value that was held by a minority becomes more widely disseminated and becomes a majority value. Rescher has labeled this *value redistribution, which is a process in which a value becomes more and more widely diffused throughout a society until virtually all its members adhere to it.* In the period of the Vietnam war protests, for example, peace activists staged marches, rallies, draft card burnings, sit-ins, and other forms of protest against the war. The existence of peace logos, signs, and symbols along with speeches and rallies gradually raised the consciousness of the general population about peace as a value so that it came to be more widely held. Ultimately, American sentiment against the war was a major factor influencing political figures to bring an end to our involvement in Vietnam.

Rescher observes that in the normal course of events, values come to be emphasized or deemphasized; that is, they come to be more or less important to the people who hold them. *In value emphasis, values move upward in a value hierarchy. In value deemphasis, they move downward.* This increase or decrease in the extent of our adherence to values can be brought about by new information or by changes in our social or economic environment. For example, new information about the causes of cancer, heart attack, and stroke has noticeably changed Americans' awareness of good health in prolonging life. This increased emphasis on good health has changed our attitudes and behavior regarding exercise, smoking, and salt and cholesterol intake. Changes in the economic environment in the early 1980s and the early 1990s led to a dramatic decrease in the number of professional jobs available to college graduates. As a result, college students came to value their education in terms of its "marketability" and sought degrees in business, engineering, and computer science in increasing numbers.

Rescher cites value restandardization as a third factor affecting the way in which values are applied within a society. *Value restandardization is a process in which standards used to measure whether a value is being met increase or decrease.* For example, the criteria to measure whether one has an adequate standard of living have changed over the years. In the late 1940s and early 1950s, costs and inflation were low; most families had only one car; and mortgages were well within the reach of middle-class income. Today in many areas even modest homes are expensive; cable television and telephones are considered basic utilities; life-styles require that most families have two cars; and many other costs have risen. Standards for an adequate income and life-style have changed dramatically over the last forty years.

In addition to cultural variations in value rankings, values vary in response to changing social conditions. As time passes, certain values may become more widely diffused in a society, may increase or decrease in importance, or be restandardized. Value advocates should consider what factors—new information, technological development, or economic fluctuation—might affect the values they are discussing. Also, when incompatible values conflict, advocates should determine what standards audiences are likely to use to choose between them. As we shall see in the remaining sections of this chapter, audience adherence plays a major role in establishing basic premises in a value argument.

■ *Values and Argumentation*

To support fact and policy claims, arguers can refer to truths and to facts that are verifiable and recognized by the audience. For example, if someone were to claim that "capital punishment deters crime," that person could use studies of the relationship between existence of the death penalty and the incidence of first-degree murder and other capital crimes. But if the claim was that "capital punishment is justified," a different strategy would be required. Here, the advocate would have to draw upon value hierarchies and the relationship between values recognized in society to provide justification for capital punishment.

This is why the research findings of Rokeach and others who have studied American values are so important to value argument. When people disagree about values, a choice must be made, and one criterion for deciding between competing values is their relative status in the larger society. Rokeach's findings reported in Table 9–1 tell us which terminal values are viewed as the most important by the American public, and his and others' studies provide resources that indicate which values should be favored.[9]

Another researcher who has studied values in Western society is Chaim Perelman. Perelman and his coauthor Olbrechts-Tyteca have identified particular value hierarchies that seem to be widely accepted in Western cultures and that are therefore used as a foundation for value claims.[10] First is the hierarchy of *quantity*—whatever produces the greatest good for the largest number of people at the least cost is to be preferred. This hierarchy, which values more over less and judges alternatives based on effects and outcomes, comes from utilitarianism. ("We should subsidize health care cooperatives to provide affordable health care for all citizens of the country.") Second is the hierarchy of *quality,* which values what is unique, irreparable, or original. Human life is often viewed from this perspective, as are great works of art. ("The Sistine Chapel is worth restoring, even at great cost, for the works of Michelangelo cannot be replaced.") Third is the hierarchy of *the existent,* which values the concrete over the possible. ("You should accept that job offer you have now rather than waiting for another one that might not materialize.") Fourth is the hierarchy of *essence,* which values what is at the core of a group or class rather than what is on the fringes. ("Free enterprise is central to what this country is all about, and we should do whatever we can to preserve free enterprise.") The fifth hierarchy, that of *the person,* values the dignity and autonomy of the person over all competing values.[11] ("Euthanasia allows a person death with dignity, and a dignified death is more important than life for a terminally ill person.") The hierarchies of quantity (more over less), quality (the unique over the common), the existent (the concrete over the merely possible), essence (the central over the peripheral), and the person (individual dignity and autonomy over all else) are very commonly accepted throughout society and can be used as a basis for value claims.

Perelman and Olbrechts-Tyteca remind us that "when a speaker wants to establish values or hierarchies or to intensify the adherence they gain, he may consolidate them by connecting them to other values or hierarchies."[12] In the examples above, such things as affordable health care, the restoration of the Sistine Chapel, free enterprise, and euthanasia were said to be preferable because of their association with the values higher in these five pervasive hierarchies. Each of these five hierarchies is common and used frequently in arguments.

The theorists whose work we have discussed, then, have suggested principles that can be quite useful in constructing arguments about values:

1. Generally, terminal values should be viewed as more significant and important than instrumental values.
2. When one is choosing between competing instrumental values (that is, choosing the most effective means to an end), the value that best meets the particular needs of the situation should be preferred.

3. In choosing one value over others, one should consider the hierarchies of quantity, quality, the existent, essence and the person if they are applicable to a particular choice or course of action.

4. The results of Rokeach's value survey of terminal values indicate a rather stable value system that is accepted by the American public and that can be used to support value preferences.

5. Values are not entirely fixed, however. Because values tend to change slowly, the advocate should consider the possibilities of value redistribution, value emphasis, and value restandardization as described by Rescher.

When a choice must be made between competing values, or when an arguer seeks to defend a particular value hierarchy, these five principles can provide the means for justifying a shift or change in values or for opposing value orderings proposed by other arguers.

■ *Stock Issues for Value Arguments*

As we observed in Chapter 3, propositions of value support a value orientation toward some value object. *A value object is an idea, practice, event, policy, or state of affairs that is to be judged by means of an evaluation.* In the proposition "euthanasia is desirable," euthanasia is the value object; in the proposition, "required sex education in the public schools is justified," required sex education is the value object. To argue successfully for a particular orientation to a value object, value advocates must address certain stock issues. *Stock issues are questions that must be asked and answered to construct a satisfactory case on a proposition.* Both policy and value propositions imply certain stock issues, and they are called "stock" issues because they are standard; they are the issues audiences expect to see addressed and resolved before they will accept a policy or value case. In Chapter 10, we will discuss the stock issues for policy cases; here we will discuss stock issues for supporting propositions of value.[13] These include definition, field, criteria, application of criteria, and hierarchies.

The role of stock issues will be illustrated through examples from supporting and opposing arguments on the topic "euthanasia is desirable." Euthanasia, generically defined as a means for producing a gentle and easy death, is a controversial topic in America today. The law holds that patients have the right to refuse medical treatment and that patients with living wills can be allowed to die without specific measures (hydration, feeding tubes, resuscitation) to preserve their lives. However, when a patient becomes comatose and has not expressed preferences regarding treatment, the course of action to be taken is much less clear. Furthermore, laws applying to doctor-assisted death (induced death) are also inconsistent, particularly in regard to penalties for assisted suicide. The public is aware of highly publicized cases in which an immediate family sued to have a relative removed from life-support mechanisms, or severely deformed infants were allowed to die, or spouses and other loved ones ended the lives of suffering patients. Euthanasia dramatizes the conflicts between our religious beliefs, our humanitarian instincts, our legal codes, and our medical practices. As such, it is a highly appropriate topic for value controversy.

Definition

The first issue on which advocates and opponents of value claims are likely to clash is that of definition. The value advocate must clearly define the value object, as well as any other controversial terms related to the topic. By defining terms, the arguer establishes his or her own views of the basic concepts on which controversy will turn. Some objects, practices, policies, and other phenomena may be readily understood, whereas others are more complex. With euthanasia as the value object, arguers supporting the claim that the practice is desirable might provide a definition that includes only passive euthanasia—the withholding or removal of life-sustaining treatment from patients who are dying and have no hope of recovery.[14] Their opponents might challenge this definition by arguing that it is insufficiently inclusive. "Euthanasia" is often said to include measures that bring about death ("mercy killing"). If opponents of euthanasia present an alternate definition, they must show why it is better than the original definition. One cannot just arbitrarily redefine the value object without showing the inadequacies of the original definition.

There are many methods that can be used to define terms. For example, one may provide actual examples of the value object with which the audience is familiar. (The removal of a feeding tube from the comatose Nancy Beth Cruzan is such an example.) The history of the status of the value object in society is another source for definitions. (One could cite a number of court cases and other situations where euthanasia has occurred.) The term's etymology or derivation is another source. ("Euthanasia" comes from the Greek *eu*=happy; *thanatos*=death.) The opinions of authorities and experts who have studied the topic may function as a useful source for definitions. Finally, ordinary usage based on dictionary definitions can serve as a basis for definitions.

Proponents of a value claim should avoid defining terms in ways that are incompatible with the values they are advocating. For example, those supporting passive euthanasia because it allows dying patients freedom of choice would not want to stipulate situations in which euthanasia must take place. This would deprive patients of freedom of choice by requiring actions mandated by the situation. The characteristics of the value object that are identified should be compatible with the field of analysis and the values that are applied within it.

Field

A second stock issue for value argument is the field within which the value object will be evaluated. In Chapter 2, we defined argument fields as contexts for argument commonly accepted by participants in a dispute. Fields such as law, medicine, physics, and economics suggest standards of proof and evidence useful in making evaluations. The priorities, practices, and conventions in certain fields determine what values are important and how judgments are to be made. If two fields are applied in evaluating the same value object, the standards and rules drawn from each of them may be in conflict. For example, at certain times in certain jurisdictions, the legal definition for death was "irreparable cessation of spontaneous cardiac and respiratory activity," while the medical definition was cessation of brain activity as indicated by a flat electroencephalograph. Furthermore, legal decisions are based on the letter of the law and precedent in similar court cases, while medical practice is based on medical ethics which obligate a physician not to do anything that makes the patient worse. Clearly, the fields of law and medicine have very different definitions, standards, and procedures for guiding decisions in euthanasia cases.

To argue successfully for the selection of a certain field for evaluation, advocates must select one that is appropriate to the topic and to the audience's values. For example, euthanasia probably cannot be successfully justified from an economic perspective. Although an increase in the frequency of euthanasia would save a great deal of money, most people in our society would find the idea of putting a financial value on human life repugnant. Given the attitudes and predispositions of Americans, selecting economics as the field of evaluation for euthanasia would be inappropriate.

Criteria

In addition to their definitions, value advocates should carefully select the criteria by which they will evaluate the value object. *Criteria are field-dependent standards to be used to decide whether the value object fulfills certain values.* Criteria are the measures, norms, or rules used to judge whatever is being evaluated. For example, if we say "this ice cream is good," we must have in mind certain criteria or standards (creaminess, good taste, natural ingredients) by which we will judge the ice cream. Here the value would probably be pleasure or enjoyment; if the value object meets or measures up to the standards, it fulfills the value in question; if not, then it must be judged negatively.

The standards advocates select should be taken from the field they have presented for evaluation. Advocates supporting the desirability of euthanasia could select individual ethics as their field and argue that the greater good of the individual is its purpose. Within this framework, they could defend the values of physical well-being, self-respect, and freedom of choice. Therefore, the standards these values suggest are that physical pain and suffering should be minimized or avoided, that those affected should be able to maintain dignity and avoid degradation, and that those affected should be able to make free choices concerning what happens to them. If the advocates can establish these three standards, they then only need to prove that euthanasia enables those standards to be met in order to establish their case.

Their opponents could argue for an alternate field and a different set of criteria. For example, they could argue that social ethics should be the field for evaluation rather than just what is good for the individual. On a social level, alternate standards might come into play. In opposition to the three criteria above, opponents might argue that the weak and the old should be protected, that life (the highest value) should be preserved, and that the medical profession should uphold its responsibility to preserve human life.

Both advocates and opponents of the desirability of euthanasia must validate their criteria through further argument, especially when those standards are questioned or challenged. Three strategies are available for establishing criteria. First, one can link them to more generally accepted and unquestioned standards and argue that because the more general standard is accepted, the audience should also accept the particular standard the advocate is supporting. For example, we put suffering animals out of their misery; why can we not allow a human being who is suffering to die? Or, we show compassion to strangers but refuse to allow our loved ones to end their own misery. Second, the standards can be justified by showing that no other standards take precedence over them. For example, in this country we believe that freedom of choice is more important than life itself. ("Live free or die" was a central motto of the colonial period, and Patrick Henry's "Give me liberty or give me death" is well known.) Third, advocates can show the logical consequences of failing to apply the standards they advocate. Advances in medical technology have made it possible to "keep alive" individuals who are brain dead by artificially stimulating respiration and heartbeat. Once the machines have been activated, doctors are afraid to discontinue them because they fear malpractice suits and even criminal charges. The logical consequences of a complete refusal to sanction euthanasia would be the continued existence of thousands of patients who could only be said to be "alive" in a technical sense.

Application

The fourth stock issue deals with the application of the criteria the advocates have established. That is, does the value object meet the standards for fulfilling the values in question? Here is where factual information and experience can be used for evidence. Supporters of euthanasia should be able to show that passive euthanasia enables patients to avoid suffering and to die with dignity. The extent to which the criteria apply and the number of patients affected by the criteria are significant here. How many patients are terminally ill and on life-support mechanisms? What proportion of these patients are likely to be affected by the euthanasia practices the advocates favor? If the proportion is small or the use of passive euthanasia likely to be infrequent, the advocates' argument may lack significance.

On the other hand, opponents of euthanasia would have at least two options open to them on this stock issue. First, they might argue that the supporters' criteria do not apply. If many terminally ill patients are not sustained by life-support mechanisms, then passive euthanasia would not diminish their suffering. Further, if most terminally ill patients are comatose and unable to express their wishes, then passive euthanasia would not provide death with dignity for those patients. Second, opponents might refer to the alternate criteria they have proposed and argue that applying those criteria better fulfills certain values. For example, if opponents of euthanasia established as a criterion that doctors should be able to uphold their responsibility to preserve life, then asking them to disconnect life-support mechanisms would work against that standard.

Hierarchies

In any extended value case, a certain value hierarchy is implied because in defending any value orientation, advocates implicitly favor one value or certain values over other values. The hierarchy applicable in any evaluation may become explicit only when that evaluation is challenged and contrasted to an alternate hierarchy. Therefore, explicit defense of a particular hierarchy may not be required when a value case is presented initially. Should the case be challenged by opponents with different values, however, opposing hierarchies will usually become a major issue in the controversy.

Supporters and opponents of euthanasia would quite naturally support different value hierarchies. Those supporting euthanasia would be likely to support freedom of choice and self-respect for the individual, whereas opponents might support the sanctity of human life and social responsibility. In defending their respective hierarchies, advocates of each position attempt to intensify their audience's adherence to and appreciation for the values at the top of their hierarchies. In other words, they attempt to persuade their listeners to rank order values in the same way that they do. In defending a certain hierarchy, the value advocates can make use of the resources provided in the last section: the distinction between terminal and instrumental values, the needs implied in the situation, Perelman's study of Western hierarchies, Rokeach's value survey, and Rescher's account of value change. In addition, advocates can seek out other studies of American values and value hierarchies.[15]

Opponents of a value proposition can also reorder the audience's hierarchies by showing that the evidence and arguments the supporters used to support their own hierarchies were questionable. If euthanasia supporters argued that their own values were highly ranked by Americans, their opponents could respond that this is merely a form of argument *ad populum*. You may recall from Chapter 6 that just because the majority of the people *believe* that something is right does not mean that it *is* right. Many Americans in the South favored school segregation at one time, but it was not morally "right." Perhaps the values presently ranked highly by most Americans reflect excessive self-interest and ought not to be the ones most valued. Euthanasia opponents could argue that the social welfare field they advocate is based on the idea that we should be more concerned with long-term consequences for the whole society than we are with the immediate interests of particular individuals.

Stock issues such as these therefore provide the points on which advocates on various sides of a topic clash or disagree with each other. If there is a debate, the advocates who present the most persuasive arguments for their views of the issues will win the debate. If the argument takes some form other than a debate, such as a discussion or an essay, most audiences will still expect value advocates to address the standard or "stock" issues satisfactorily in order to establish their value thesis and their position on the topic.

The Issues Brief

Writers on argument have recently pointed out that familiarity with multiple views on an issue improves one's own arguments as well as one's ability to anticipate and respond to others' views. As Josina Makau has observed, "the quality of deliberation on controversial issues depends, in large measure, on the arguers' ability to thoughtfully consider as many alternative perspectives as possible."[16] Many people who first approach a topic think they have their minds made up. As they conduct research on the topic and read the opinions of various authorities, they begin to see that the situation or the solution is not as readily apparent as they first thought. Often in the process of researching for a speech or debate, students will actually shift their opinions to the side opposite to the one they had favored in the beginning!

Researchers on critical thinking tell us this is a good thing. They have found that novice thinkers seek quick closure on a topic, neglect audience attitudes and possible objections, and fail to take into account obvious weaknesses in their own arguments. Experienced thinkers, on the other hand, withhold their opinions until they have gathered relevant information, begin by analyzing and interpreting the problem, study the attitudes of their potential audience, and develop a broad range of lines and types of arguments to support a claim.[17]

To assist you in becoming an "expert thinker" of the latter type, we recommend that you construct an "issues brief" on your topic. *An issues brief is a synthesis of opposing views on the stock issues of a controversial topic.* The weakness of the issues brief is that it appears to assume that there are only two polarized sides, one supporting the proposition and one opposing it. Of course, on many controversial topics people's attitudes are more complex than that. On the topic of euthanasia, for example, some people might feel that euthanasia is not justified under any condition, whereas others believe a terminal patient ought to have the final say in controlling the manner and timing of his or her death. There are also people who believe that some forms of euthanasia may be justified in some circumstances. In other words, they hold neither absolutely positive nor negative views on the topic but rather more complex ones that take circumstances into account.

Nevertheless, the issues brief allows the advocate to consider more than one viewpoint, and that is its value. What follows is a brief on the euthanasia topic that articulates arguments on all the stock issues discussed in that last section. Actually, the term "brief" is a misnomer, because a fully developed brief can be quite long. When examining this brief, you should realize that each of the arguments is a *claim* that would need to be supported by further arguments and/or evidence such as the opinions of authorities or facts or statistics. What is included in Figure 9–1 are the principal claim (the proposition), the major subclaims, and the sub-subclaims that constitute the two cases supporting and opposing the proposition.

Proposition: Euthanasia is desirable.

Issue 1: Definition. How should the value object and other terms important to the topic be defined?

I. Euthanasia will be defined as passive—withholding or removing life support systems from moribund patients.

    A. "Life-support systems" include equipment that provides basic life functions—respiration, heartbeat, etc.—through artificial means.

    B. "Moribund" patients are people with no possibility of recovery who will die in the normal course of events.

    C. This definition is supported by etymology and the opinion of experts.

I. This definition is overly restrictive and should include active euthanasia.

    A. Active euthanasia has traditionally been included in the term.

    B. Some "moribund" and comatose patients have, in fact, recovered consciousness.

    C. *Webster's Dictionary*, eighth edition, defines euthanasia as "the act of killing individuals who are hopelessly sick or injured."

Issue 2. Field. In what field or from what perspective should the value object be evaluated?

II. Euthanasia will be evaluated within the field of normative ethics.

    A. Normative ethics promotes the best quality of life possible for the individual.

    B. Normative ethics is appropriate because it overrides the letter of the law and the requirements of technology.

II. Euthanasia should be evaluated in the field of societal welfare.

    A. Societal welfare considers the moral fiber and well-being of society as a whole.

    B. Societal welfare is appropriate because it presumes that the quality of a society is measured by its ability to protect the weak and the old.

Issue 3. Criteria. What standards should be applied to determine whether the value object fulfills the desired values?

III. To be beneficial, euthanasia should meet certain standards.

    A. Euthanasia should allow free choice concerning the manner and timing of a person's death.

    B. Euthanasia should prevent needless suffering and futile prolongation of life.

    C. Euthanasia should prevent hardship for the families of terminally ill patients.

III. Other standards are more important.

    A. Treatment of the terminally ill should protect and preserve life.

    B. Treatment of the terminally ill should enhance the will to survive.

    C. Treatment should not undermine the general respect for life in our society.

Figure 9–1
Issues Brief with Definition, Field, Criteria, and Application

Issue 4. Application. Do the proposed standards in fact apply to the value object?

IV. Euthanasia is beneficial and desirable.

    A. It preserves freedom and dignity of the individual.

    B. It ends patients' suffering.

    C. It gives families a say in patients' treatment.

IV. Euthanasia is harmful to society.

    A. It puts pressure on terminally ill patients and undermines the will to survive.

    B. In the absence of active euthanasia, patients will continue to suffer anyway.

    C. Families can be distressed and torn apart by the responsibility to make these decisions.

    D. Society's attitudes toward the preservation of life will be negatively affected.

Issue 5. Hierarchies. What values and what rank ordering of values should apply to this value object?

V. Euthanasia preserves and promotes personal freedom, comfort, and self-respect.

    A. Freedom, comfort, and self-respect are three of the eight top-ranked values in Rokeach's value survey.

    B. Freedom of choice and dignity are the essence of what it means to be human.

V. Euthanasia undermines our respect for life which should be the highest value.

    A. If life is not preserved and protected, all other values are moot.

    B. Our Christian belief tells us that life is a gift, not ours to do with as we please.

    C. A human life is unique and irreplaceable.

    D. A society that does not value life becomes degraded and immoral.

Figure 9–1   *continued*

In his *Rhetoric* written over 2,000 years ago, Aristotle defended the art of speaking persuasively on issues. He wrote, "we must be able to employ persuasion, just as strict reasoning can be employed, on opposite sides of a question, not in order that we may in practice employ it in both ways (for we must not make people believe what is wrong), but in order that we may see clearly what the facts are, and that, if another man argues unfairly, we on our part may be able to confute him."[18] Aristotle recognized that matters that are subject to argument are never so straightforward and simple that they can be quickly resolved. (If they were, they would not be the subject of argumentation.) Rather, when we deliberate about policies or values, the issues we consider are difficult and nettlesome. An issues brief such as we have just presented can help the advocate weigh the various positions and arguments on an issue and produce a reasonable and considered argument in support of a proposition.

■ *Summary*

This chapter was intended to provide a systematic approach to value argument. Although some people have expressed the view that values are basically subjective and irrational, many contemporary theorists of argument have successfully provided the means for developing a rational approach to supporting value claims. They have recognized that many arguments in fields such as law and medicine are based on values and provide the grounds for making decisions and taking action. These theorists have explained how value arguments are structured, how they can be assessed, and how advocates can construct extended arguments supporting value claims.

Values are generally organized into value systems. A value system is an enduring organization of beliefs concerning preferable modes of conduct or end states of existence along a continuum of relative importance. Rokeach's surveys of American values have shown that Americans value family security, a world at peace, freedom, and self-respect over many other values and that these values are relatively stable and do not change dramatically over time. Surveys of value systems are important to the value advocate who must gauge his or her argument to suit the values and attitudes of an audience. Furthermore, when individuals or groups of people disagree about values, it is because their value systems are ordered differently. The values ranked as most important by one are ranked as less important by the other.

In any society, value hierarchies are subject to fluctuation and change. Values may become more widely held because a persistent minority successfully argues for their importance. Because of new information or changes in the social or economic environment, values may become more or less emphasized. The standards that are applied to determine whether a value has been met may become more or less stringent. Because audience adherence is a vital factor in establishing the basic premises in a value argument, advocates should be aware of factors that may bring about changes in the importance and pervasiveness of values in society.

An arguer supporting a particular value proposition must advocate some orientation toward a value object. A value object is an idea, practice, event, policy, or state of affairs that has to be measured in an evaluation. To successfully support a value proposition, the value advocate must address five stock issues. First is definition: How is the value object and terms important to the topic to be defined? Second is the field for evaluation: In what field or from what perspective should the value object be evaluated? Third is criteria: What standards should be applied to determine whether the value object fulfills the desired values? Fourth is application: Does the value object in fact meet the standards that have been proposed by the advocate? Fifth is the value hierarchy: What values and what rank ordering of values should be applied to this value object? The chapter concluded with an issues brief on the topic of euthanasia to illustrate how these five stock issues function in a value controversy.

Exercises

Exercise 1   The conversation that follows illustrates the fact that many of the value issues we've discussed in this chapter arise in interactive argument as well as in essays and public speeches. After reading the interchange, answer the following questions:

* 1. What is the value object being discussed?
* 2. What are the primary values of each discussant? How does the value hierarchy of each differ from that of the other?
* 3. What standards for judging the value object are relied upon by each person?
* 4. How do the arguments of each of the two discussants relate to the value hierarchies widely accepted in American society as reported in Table 9–1?
* 5. Which of the participants offers the better argument for her side of the question? Why?

Topic of discussion: Do mandatory seat belt laws violate our constitutional rights? Participants are Colleen Carney and Patty Pethick. The discussion took place on August 17, 1986.

COLLEEN:	Do you wear a seat belt?
PATTY:	Yes.
COLLEEN:	I just want to say I wear a seat belt for my own reasons. I think it's safer. Could you tell me, however, your thoughts on this statement: "Mandatory seat belt laws violate our constitutional rights."
PATTY:	I don't agree with it.
COLLEEN:	You don't? Why?
PATTY:	Because every society needs some laws to help protect its citizens, and this mandatory seat belt law is one of those laws. And because there's too many lives being lost. In our state alone, 350 people die.

COLLEEN: Is it not the intent of the Constitution to protect individuals' freedom of choice?

PATTY: Yes, but it also has the role to guide our society and help govern it. And this law to me falls under the category of having order instead of chaos in society. A lot of people have these nightmares about going through these checkpoints that have been set up. Well, that's not the way it's going to be. You have to be in violation of another law—like the speed limit. Then you're stopped and the police officer approaches your car and if he sees you without your seat belt then they can ticket you for that too.

COLLEEN: Yes. I talked with two different attorneys about this and what you just described is called "selective enforcement." And, like you said, you have to be breaking a law to get picked up. So, basically, that's discrimination, because I could be driving down the freeway going 55 mph and not wearing a seat belt, and the person next to me could be speeding and not wearing a seat belt, and that person's going to be picked up because he's breaking another law, and that's the only reason why he's going to be caught. And, since that's discrimination, that's unconstitutional, because it doesn't apply to everyone.

PATTY: The law applies to everyone.

COLLEEN: But it discriminates because, as I said, you actually have to be breaking another law, and so not everyone is going to get caught. It's really kind of an unenforceable law.

PATTY: OK. I see your point. I understand what you're saying about discrimination but I don't see how it's an unenforceable law when it has been enforced. Like I said, I'm from a state that does have the law, and I've seen it be enforced.

Exercise 2   What follows is an excerpt from an essay[19] by a biologist opposing "equal treatment" laws for public schools which would require them to teach creation science (the Biblical account of creation) as well as evolution in science classes. This essay appeared in a weekly newspaper directed primarily at members of the higher-education community—faculty, administrators, and graduate students. A number of values are explicitly stated or implied in this essay. To understand how and why this value argument might be persuasive, answer the following questions:

1. What forms of evidence (verification) does the author offer for his arguments?

2. What values does he hold?

3. What values does he think his audience holds?

4. Suppose the author was addressing readers who supported creation science? How would they respond to his argument? How might their values differ from higher-education readers?

5. What is the overall quality of the author's evidence and reasoning? (You might want to use Chapter 7 to diagram some of his arguments to discover how they are structured.)

Creationism cannot be divorced from the Bible without completely evaporating. There is no science in creation science. . . . Academic freedom does not require that all ideas be given equal weight. Most of us would agree that some ideas are well founded while others are not. For example, Copernicus and Galileo demonstrated that the sun is the center of the universe and that the earth revolves around it. The geocentric theory—that the earth is the center of the universe—has not been taught for centuries. Clearly, public school teachers do not and should not present both sides of this debate, except when referring to the history of science.

But perhaps the issue isn't quite clear to everyone. A number of vocal creationists insist that the geocentric theory is sound and demand that it be taught in public-school science classes. At the National Bible Science Conference in 1984, several speakers quoted Scripture to demonstrate that the sun does indeed revolve around the earth. Not one of the creation "scientists" present objected to this ridiculous view of astronomy. Perhaps even more absurd is the fact that this year the Arizona governor's chief aide for education testified before a legislative committee that classroom teachers should not impose their belief that the earth is round on students who have been brought up to believe that it is flat.

An equal-treatment law would require that geocentrism and perhaps flat-earthism, both of which long ago lost out in the free marketplace of ideas, be taught as alternative views in science classes. Likewise, the biblical theory of creation lost to the scientific theory of evolution in the 19th century. The creationists' appeal to academic freedom in support of their ideas is actually an appeal to artificially preserve outdated and disproved concepts. Vital scientific theories continue to stand on their own merits.

Exercise 3   Below are two arguments—one supporting required sex education in the public schools and another opposing it. Construct an issues brief of the two arguments using the value analysis format discussed in this chapter. Your issues brief should look like the one on euthanasia in this chapter, that is, organized according to the opposing positions on definition of the value object, selection of the field for evaluation, choice of criteria for judgment, application of criteria, and the respective opposing value hierarchies.

Argument supporting required sex education in public schools:

Sex education should be broadly defined as the study of human sexual behavior and development from birth to death. It includes more than just the study of anatomy; it includes examination of such issues as sexual abuse, gender roles, sexuality, and personal responsibility. To say that sex education should be "required" means that all pupils in grades K–12 *must* take it. Our definition is based on the opinions of educational experts Rex Roberts and William Clewar who support a separate sex education class.

We are evaluating sex education as a social benefit. Schools teach the values and responsibilities of citizenship, and they should likewise teach students the requirements of sexually responsible behavior. Sex education should be evaluated as a social benefit because it contributes to the terminal values of mature love and family security.

Furthermore, social benefit is an appropriate perspective from which to evaluate sex education. Any measure that promotes good health and self-respect is appropriately to be evaluated as socially beneficial. One of the main aims of the public schools is to promote the social welfare of society as a whole, and sex education will do that.

In fact sex education does promote these values. Studies have shown that sex education reduces teen pregnancies by over 10 percent. Furthermore, it has been shown to promote "safe sex" practices and to decrease the incidence of AIDS, gonorrhea, herpes, and other sexually transmitted diseases among the teen population.

Promoting family security, mature love, and self-respect are high priorities in American society. These three values are all ranked highly in surveys of American values. Furthermore, avoidance of pregnancy and sexually transmitted diseases is a part of freedom of choice, which is another highly ranked value in the American value hierarchy.

Argument opposing required sex education in the public schools:

The policy on sex education should be devised in accord with the major purpose of the public schools, which is to fulfill a need for basic education and knowledge, not to solve social problems. By "requiring" sex education for all pupils in all grades, our opponents will take time away from basic skills education and undermine the central purpose of public schools. Furthermore, their definition is inadequate because it does not include discussions of the emotions, personal responsibility, and respect for others that most experts feel should be included in sex education.

The appropriate perspective or field from which to evaluate sex education is education, not social benefit. This perspective is more appropriate because the schools are expected primarily *to educate* and not primarily to solve social problems. Furthermore, the only way to judge the adequacy of sex education is to judge its educational effectiveness.

The standards we propose for deciding on this issue are whether sex education contributes to or detracts from the overall education of the pupils. If it takes away from instruction in basic literacy and computational skills, then it detracts from the schools' primary purpose.

In fact, studies of sex education indicate that it erodes instructional time and resources in other areas. Furthermore, many of those who are employed to teach sex education are not adequately prepared or certified to teach in that area. In addition, sex education does not meet the standards advocated by its supporters. It reduces pregnancies only by 10 percent, and there is no hard evidence to show that it measurably decreases the incidence of sexually transmitted diseases.

An adequate education contributes to the values held most highly by the American public—namely, a comfortable life, self-respect, and a sense of accomplishment. Because the adequacy of education is undermined by required sex education, it should not be required in the public schools.

Notes

1. Reprinted with the permission of The Free Press, a Division of Macmillan, Inc. from *The Nature of Human Values* by Milton Rokeach. Copyright © 1973 by The Free Press.

2. Rokeach, 7–8.

3. Rokeach, 7–8. Another theorist who divided values along these lines is Donald Walhout who made a distinction between social values (political stability, equality, freedom, etc.) and individual values (social participation, friendship, proper self-love). See his *The Good and the Realm of Values* (Notre Dame, Ind.: University of Notre Dame Press, 1978), 45–46.

4. Milton Rokeach and Sandra J. Ball-Rokeach, "Stability and Change in American Value Priorities," *American Psychologist* 44 (1989): 777.

5. Rokeach, 57–59 and 66–72.

6. Seymour Lipset, *Continental Divide: The Values and Institutions of the United States and Canada* (New York: Routledge, 1990), 37–39.

7. Nicholas Rescher, *Introduction to Value Theory* (Englewood Cliffs, N.J.: Prentice-Hall, 1969), 115.

8. The account of value change in this section is drawn from Rescher, 111–118.

9. For other studies of American values, see Gail M. Inlow, *Values in Transition: A Handbook* (New York: John Wiley, 1972); and Ben J. Wattenberg, *The Good News Is the Bad News Is Wrong* (New York: Simon and Schuster, 1984). Many studies of contemporary American values are available.

10. Chaim Perelman and Lucie Olbrechts-Tyteca, *The New Rhetoric: A Treatise on Argumentation,* trans. John Wilkinson and Purcell Weaver (Notre Dame, Ind.: University of Notre Dame Press, 1969), 83–99. In addition to the hierarchies stated here, these authors noted the hierarchy of order—that the cause or that which comes first should be valued over that which comes later.

11. For further explanation of these hierarchies, see Gregg B. Walker and Malcolm O. Sillars, "Where is Argument? Perelman's Theory of Values," in *Perspectives on Argumentation,* ed. Robert Trapp and Janice Schuetz (Prospect Heights, Ill.: Waveland, 1990), 143–145.

12. Perelman and Olbrechts-Tyteca, 83.

13. The stock issues suggested here are taken from Paul W. Taylor, *Normative Discourse* (Englewood Cliffs, NJ: Prentice-Hall, 1961): 14–103. An earlier version of this explanation appeared in Barbara Warnick, "Arguing Value Propositions," *Journal of the American Forensic Association,* 18 (1981): 109–119. Many points in the euthanasia example appeared in Stainislaus J. Dundon, "Karen Quinlan and the Freedom of the Dying," *Journal of Value Inquiry,* 4 (1978): 280–291. This journal has many useful articles on value-oriented issues such as abortion, euthanasia, and human rights.

14. Richard Worshop, "Assisted Suicide," *CQ Researcher,* 2 (1992): 148.

15. Other studies of American values were cited in footnote 9.

16. Josina M. Makau, *Reasoning and Communication* (Belmont, Cal.: Wadsworth, 1990), 142.

17. Joanne G. Kurfiss, *Critical Thinking: Theory, Research, Practice, and Possibilities,* ASHE-ERIC Higher Education Report No. 2 (Washington, D.C.: Association for the Study of Higher Education, 1988), 25–34.

18. Aristotle *Rhetoric* 1355a.

19. From Michael Zimmerman, "The Creationists' Appeal for Freedom of Speech Diverts Attention from their Anti-Science Views," *Chronicle of Higher Education,* April 1, 1987, pp. 42–43. Used by permission.

C H A P T E R *10*

Arguing About Policies

◼

CHAPTER OUTLINE

- **Policy Arguments and Policy Systems**
- **Stock Issues in Policy Arguments**
    Ill
    Blame
    Cure
    Cost/Benefits
- **Issues Brief**
- **Alternative Formats for Arguing Policies**
    Comparative-Advantages Case
    Goals Case

- **Alternative Formats for Refuting Policy Arguments**
    Strategy of Defense of the Present Policy System
    Strategy of Defense of the Present Policy System with Minor Repairs
    Strategy of Counterproposals
- **Summary**
- **Exercises**

KEY CONCEPTS

systems perspective
qualitative significance
blame
structures
cure
agent
effects
benefits
direct refutation
goals argument
minor repairs

ill
quantitative significance
structural blame
attitudinal blame
plan of action
mandate
cost
needs-analysis case
comparative advantages
defense of the present policy system
counterproposal

We make policy decisions daily. We might decide to study instead of going to the movies or we might decide to live off-campus instead of in a dorm. Or, depending on our individual values and personal convictions, we might decide to buy shares in an oil company or support stronger environmental protection laws. Our daily decisions affect us personally, socially, economically, nationally, and internationally.

The decision to act or not to act involves a process of policy argumentation. For example, consider the following three claims:

> All U.S. citizens should be subjected to mandatory AIDS screening.
>
> I should study tonight.
>
> Politicians should be subjected to twelve-year term limitations.

These statements are policy propositions that focus arguments around specific choices and actions. Each asks the recipient to behave or cooperate in certain ways and, presumably, if the arguments supporting the claims are sufficient, then the recipient will fulfill the expected action.

This chapter examines how policy arguments work and how arguers construct and refute extended policy cases. When you have finished reading this chapter, you should be able to recognize, write, and respond to policy arguments and extended policy cases.

Policy arguments are different from the value arguments discussed in Chapter 9. If we argue that U.S. citizens should be tested for AIDS, we are advocating some future action. If we say that we should study tonight, we are also advocating future action. And if we support term limits, we promote a future action. Policy arguments are future-bound. Because historical policies and actions cannot be directly changed through argument alone, when we make policy proposals we focus on what *should* be done from this time forward. We could argue that we should have had AIDS testing, or we should have studied, or we should have had term limits, but because all of these fall into the past, arguing about them is more like speculation than advocacy because there is no opportunity to change what has happened. Policy propositions look toward what has not yet happened, but should. The "future action" nature of policy arguments is fundamentally different from value arguments because value arguments can examine and evaluate whether current and past values were justifiable or reasonable. In a value-oriented discussion, we can say:

> Testing all U.S. citizens for AIDS is justified.
>
> Studying would have been a good thing for me to do.
>
> Term limitations are justifiable.

Value propositions can study what presently is, what should have been in the past, or even what values we should hold in the future because the focus of such argumentation is evaluation—not action. We can evaluate the past and present to learn, but we cannot act differently in the past. Policy propositions are bound to future actions.

Because the future is uncertain, and no one can know precisely what will happen, policy arguments ask hearers to act based on a prediction of what will work or what will not work. We have only a tentative idea of what probably will *occur*.[1] Therefore, accepting a policy proposition commits a hearer to a future call to action. The decision to act, in turn, depends on the listener's assessment of how successful or reasonable an argument *probably* is.

■ *Policy Arguments and Policy Systems*

Policy arguments take a variety of forms. When Congress considers a bill, the hearings and debates about the bill take the form of policy argumentation. When the president argues in favor of a budget proposal, the argument is a policy argument. However, policy arguments are not reserved exclusively for passing legislation or for argumentation in formal or established forums. Often, extended policy arguments are developed without a large public audience and even without an explicitly stated proposition. Consider the following exchange between John and Jason:

JOHN:	I've had it with studying. My brain isn't working right anymore. I think we should take a break and go see a movie or something.
JASON:	Are you crazy? We both have finals in the morning, and I don't know about you, but I've put off studying way too long. As it is, I don't think I'll get any sleep tonight.
JOHN:	Well, even if we don't have a couple of hours to get out and see a movie, I think we should at least take a half-hour out to go up to the store and get some snacks.

In this discussion, John and Jason are arguing about a policy. Should they take a break from studying? Policy arguments often occur in personal and interpersonal contexts. We use policy arguments daily to help make decisions at many levels—personal, local, regional, national, and international. We often argue with our family, friends, and colleagues about decisions we want to make and actions we want to take. Such arguments may range from where to live, what job to take, whether to study or take a break, or whom to vote for in an upcoming election.

This section will examine how policy arguments function as part of a system. We take the position that extended policy arguments function systematically, which means that as we seek to change one part of the system through our arguments, we change the overall nature of the system. Such changes carry with them both benefits and cost that arguers should understand and consider.

It is not always clear how policy arguments affect our lives. Obviously, we make decisions about how our lives will be conducted, but we may not always be aware of the short- and long-term consequences and benefits of the actions we take. *A systems perspective recognizes that the world is a complex and interconnected set of relationships between and among component parts that compose a whole and that one change in any part of the system changes the other elements of the system.* This means, then, that a system is a set of parts that are interrelated with one another to form a whole unit.[2]

At its most basic level, a system has five defining characteristics.[3] First, systems possess objects or parts. When John and Jason argued about whether to study or take a break, both individuals and the subjects they studied served as objects or parts of the system. Each plays a role and performs a particular function: John and Jason studied together and studying is the focus of the discussion. Second, each object in the system has attributes. Attributes are the characteristics inherent in the objects or parts. John feels the need to take a break; Jason is concerned about how much time he has to prepare for finals. Third, the objects within a system are interrelated. This means that there is a relationship that binds John, Jason, and studying together. Their discussion would have been meaningless unless they both were studying. If their relationship changed or their tests had been completed, so too would the argument. Fourth, systems operate within an environment. This means that systems have a context that supports and gives meaning to the activity within the system. The environment for John and Jason consists of a campus community that has examinations and finals. Fifth, systems have boundaries. A boundary is a definitional line that separates the system from its environment. The only people involved in the decision to study or take a break are John and Jason. The ultimate decision rests with them. Boundaries enable us to define who or what constitutes the system and who or what does not.

Understanding the nature of systems enables arguers to appreciate the complexity and consequences of policy arguments. Consider the case of independent, unofficial presidential candidate, Ross Perot. In February 1992, Perot announced on a live news talk show that if voters in all fifty states placed his name on the ballot, he would run for the presidency. The outcry of support was staggering. Millions of people from across the country were unsatisfied with the two major party candidates. They believed that the American political system was in need of a major overhaul and that Perot, an outsider, could make the system work. State campaign headquarters for Perot sprung up all over the country as signatures were gathered and Perot's name was placed on the ballot in state after state. Then, without warning, in July, Perot announced he was dropping his campaign. He provided many arguments for his decision including his belief that if he ran, the election would be thrown into the House of Representatives. This, he argued, would result in chaos that would damage the country.

Perot functioned within a political system. The objects or parts of the system were the presidential candidates and the voters. Their attributes or characteristics included their party affiliation (or lack thereof), the relative disillusionment of voters with politics, the platforms of the candidates, voter motivation and dedication, among others. The environment was the United States in the election year 1992 and the boundary was the United States. Perot's decision affected more than him—it affected virtually every element of the American political system. As soon as he announced his decision to drop out of the race, his campaign offices staffed with thousands of volunteers were suddenly left without a leader. The result was anger, further disillusionment, depression, and in some cases the move to develop a new, third party. The presidential candidates of the two major parties attempted to take advantage of the opportunity to woo former Perot supporters. (Later Perot reentered the race.)

What affects one part of the system can be felt throughout the system. Any policy decision carries benefits and cost for the entire system. People act in contexts and the actions we take affect our contexts. Even something as simple as asking a question in a class affects all the members of the class, including the teacher as well as the question-asker.

When we take actions in a system, we may experience both benefits and cost. The benefits are all the associated advantages associated with the decision and the cost are all the associated disadvantages. For Perot, there were many costs associated with running for the presidency. Both he and his family came under intense media scrutiny. It became more and more apparent that he could not win in the popular vote and the result would have been an election thrown into the House of Representatives; this, he said, would cause chaos and confusion.

These costs can be weighed against the associated benefits of running for office. If he continued his campaign, his efforts would have been appreciated and applauded by his followers. He could direct some of the national issues agenda on the economy, foreign policy, and domestic issues. But when he examined the cost and the benefits together, the result was that the cost was greater and he dropped from the race.

When we evaluate whether we should engage in a particular action, we evaluate likelihood of the benefits as well as the likelihood of the cost throughout the system. Presumably, most people act when the net benefits are perceived to be greater than the net cost or disadvantages associated with an action. This process of decision making is called risk analysis and was introduced in Chapter 8.

■ *Stock Issues in Policy Arguments*

When a policy is proposed, it must address certain issues. These issues are the reasonable questions recipients have about the validity of any action and they were introduced in Chapter 9 as stock issues—questions that must be asked and answered to construct a satisfactory case on a proposition. Although many issues may serve as stock issues for policy analysis, we can generally group them into four categories: ill, blame, cure, and cost/benefits.[4] This section will develop each of these stock issues in detail, enabling you to identify and build arguments supporting each type. Imagine for a minute the following conversation between two roommates:

JULI: I think we should go to Alaska and work in a fish cannery. While that might sound like a strange idea, I've always heard that there is a lot of money to be made and they are always looking for people to work there.

NANCY:	Wait a minute! That's an awfully long way from home. Why don't we just find something around here for the summer instead of making such a long trip? I know of two or three fast food places that are hiring.
JULI:	I'm out of money and I need to find a good paying job for the summer. Otherwise I'm just not going to be able to stay in college. Besides, we've decided that we want to work together this summer, right?
NANCY:	Right. But still, can't we just stay around here—it would be more fun and we know people.
JULI:	We could, but I have a friend who said in her first summer up there she made more than $7,000 and that is much more than we could ever hope to make around here. Besides, it would be fun to get away for a summer.
NANCY:	Maybe, but I've heard jobs up there are difficult to get.
JULI:	Not unless you know someone, and I do. She said we could get hired without any problem.

The conversation between Juli and Nancy presents an extended policy argument the friends can either accept or reject. The proposition advanced by Juli is that the roommates should work in Alaska. In support of this, she said she has heard that a lot of money can be made there and that jobs are always available.

However, consider the order of the questions and answers. Juli began with a proposition for going to Alaska to work. It was phrased as a declarative sentence and Nancy did not need to respond—so why did she answer the sentence with a question? Her reason is the same as any listener's reason might be. People often do not accept propositional statements without asking for specific supporting arguments from the speaker. Nancy pointed out that they could find jobs nearby, so what made Juli think they needed to travel to Alaska? She also said that a few places were hiring. A correct answer to each question was important: If Juli had not thought her plan through sufficiently, or if her answers were unsatisfactory, Nancy would have rejected her idea because it would not have been *prima facie* (acceptable at first glance).

This conversation is typical of many policy arguments. The advocate needs to be aware of the stock issues and prove them reasonably before a recipient can be expected to take action.

Ill

When Nancy asked Juli what was wrong with their current plan for summer work, she was asking Juli to supply an argument proving the stock issue of ill. *An ill is a current wrong or harm the advocate is trying to resolve.* When Russian President Boris Yeltsin announced in June 1992 that Soviet authorities may have held as many as 2,800 American prisoners of war captured during the Cold War, the United States launched an immediate investigation of his claim including an inspection tour of Russian prison camps. If the Russians were holding American prisoners of war, then an ill existed. This is why American investigators looked for any evidence to support Yeltsin's claim to prove that in fact a wrong was present. If there must be a reason for people to act, this involves proving an argument of ill.

Before people are persuaded to act, they look for a significant ill. Most people do not act without some significant cause. For example, we might drive by litter scattered along a road. Although most of us agree that litter is a problem (an ill), we would probably not stop to pick it up and dispose of it properly; however, if the litter found its way into our front yard, we would be more inclined to do something. It is a question of significance. If the ill is seen as significant for us, we are more likely to act.

The difficult question to answer is whether an arguer is presenting an ill that is significant enough to warrant the type of action proposed. Significance can be either qualitative or quantitative. *Qualitative significance is related to the intensity of the effect; we assess something as significant to the extent that it strengthens or diminishes life.* Evaluating qualitative significance usually requires comparative consideration of values. An example of a value conflict of this type was shown during the hearings involving the Iran/contra arms deal during President Reagan's administration. Should Congress be systematically excluded from knowledge of covert operations in the interest of national security? Which is more important—the confidentiality and security of operations by the Central Intelligence Agency and the National Security Council, or public control (via Congress) of U.S. foreign policy? The significance of these two factors is qualitative and value-based; it cannot be reduced to quantitative terms.

Quantitative significance is related to the scope of the effects claimed; how many people will be affected and how frequently? Quantitative significance is often more easily evaluated than qualitative significance because it simply involves statistical comparison. As long as the evidence available is reliable and accessible, quantitative significance can usually be more easily weighed than qualitative significance. For example, if Juli argued that going to Alaska for two months would yield $10,000, the quantitative comparison of $10,000 to $3,000 at any other summer job is easier than evaluating the effect of such income on their life-styles.

Is it significant if one person's financial future is diminished? If one person becomes ill? If a hundred people become ill? The answer to these questions is difficult because a great deal depends on the context of the proposed policy. An ill is generally considered significant enough to warrant action if life or the quality of life is threatened. Of course, significance is a relative term and it depends on how we value life and quality-of-life issues. (A complete discussion of value and value hierarchies can be found in Chapter 9.) For example, preserving a right to free speech or association has value only to the extent that it helps or hurts people.[5] Or, when we express outrage against animal testing for cosmetics, we argue that it unnecessarily destroys the quality of animal life. But what happens in a case where animal experimentation is necessary for human survival? In 1992, for example, a baboon liver was transplanted into a human being to save the person's life. Is a human life worth more than a baboon's life? These qualitative issues can be difficult questions to answer, but generally, they involve the use of a value hierarchy. One of the ways of measuring the significance of an ill is by its impact on living beings.

Blame

We assume that most people in the world are relatively honest and caring and would not intentionally allow an ill to exist. If it is true, for instance, that prisoners of war exist in Russian prisons, we would assume that U.S. officials as well as Russian officials would try to bring these people home unless there was some compelling reason to leave them. But if there truly are POWs in foreign prison camps, why haven't the Russians returned them already? Although we may attempt to avoid ills and we may strive to overcome them, we continue to allow significant ills to exist. We allow people to starve in Ethiopia even though U.S. farmers produce a surplus of food each year. We have a tax system that is viewed by many to reward the wealthy at the expense of the middle class and indigent. We allow people to die for lack of adequate medical care.

The stock issue of blame helps explain why people are unable to resolve or diminish ills. Put simply, *blame is the attribution of an ill to causes within the present policy system.* Blame points to the person, people, or agencies responsible for the ill. For the ill to be corrected, the blame must be removed. If the blame for Juli's and Nancy's lack of money is lack of jobs, then they must find good summer jobs to provide them with income and to alleviate the ill. If Food and Drug Administration rules are written in such a way as to encourage animal testing, then they must be rewritten to overcome the ill. With the case of Juli and Nancy, once they take jobs in Alaska, they could make enough money to stay in school for the next year.

There are two types of blame that act as barriers to resolving ill: structural and attitudinal. *A structural blame is the result of a defect that is an integral part of the nature of the current policy system.*[6] Understanding a structural blame requires understanding a structure. *Structures are the fixed elements or features of a policy system.* Examples of structural elements of policy systems are laws, contracts, treaties, rules, and orders. Taken as a whole, structures reflect the formally accepted rules governing our society and political system. Such structures are "fixed" because they can be removed only by means of formal action taken to replace them with other structures. In 1973, Congress passed a law that lowered the maximum speed on U.S. highways from 65 mph to 55 mph. Then, again in 1990, Congress replaced the 55 mph speed limit law with a new and limited 65 mph speed limit law. When the U.S. Supreme Court prohibited a woman from using an abortion-inducing drug, RU-486, that had been prescribed to her while she was in Europe, a formal structure was introduced into the U.S. political and legal system that overrode the previous FDA rule that exempted such drugs from regulation provided they were for personal use. A formal action such as congressional legislation or a Supreme Court decision or other formalized rule requires a policy proposal for the removal or alteration of a structure.

In 1896, the issue of racial discrimination was before the Supreme Court, and it ruled in *Plessy v. Ferguson* that separate but equal facilities did not discriminate. Consequently, separate white and black lavatories, schools, and restaurants were seen as fair and just so long as the facilities were provided equally. In 1954, however, over the issue of equal educational opportunity, the case of *Brown v. Board of Education* was brought before the Supreme Court. This case charged that because of the "separate but equal" rule established in *Plessy,* an ill of educational discrimination existed and that black students were unfairly deprived of educational opportunities. The Supreme Court found for Brown on the ground that separate was inherently unequal.[7] The Court noted: "We conclude that in the field of public education the doctrine of 'separate but equal' has no place. Separate educational facilities are inherently unequal."[8] The blame for our inability to provide equal educational opportunity was attributed to a fixed structure—the Supreme Court decision in *Plessy v. Ferguson.* To correct the problem of discrimination, the decision had to be overturned—the structure had to be removed.

A second type of blame is attitudinal. *Attitudinal blame arises from peoples' beliefs and values rather than from a law or some other structure of the present system.* Typically, we assume that good people would not allow unnecessary evils to exist. We assume that if Juli and Nancy could, they would have enough money without traveling or working hard hours. We assume that if other countries hold American POWs, the soldiers will be returned. However, if an ill is allowed to exist because of prevailing beliefs or value hierarchies, then an attitudinal blame has been identified. Attitudinal problems may result in defective structures or failure to adequately support good structures within the system. For example, people smoke even though they know it will damage their health and eventually kill them. The blame does not rest in some law or structure forcing them to smoke, rather it rests in their attitudes toward smoking. Similarly, although the United States adopted civil rights legislation in 1964, attitudes continue to perpetuate *de facto* segregation in some regions.

With the *Brown* decision, the structural barrier preventing equal educational opportunity was removed. It seems reasonable, then, that once the structural blame was gone, educational equality could exist. However, apart from structural problems, resistance among administrators or influential community members may perpetuate the ill regardless of the presence or absence of a structure. The problem may not be in the structure at all, but could lie with the attitudes and value hierarchies of the people administering the system. In such cases, the structure is only a reflection of underlying attitudes that cause ills to exist.

Cure

Being able to isolate and attribute blame for a given ill is not particularly useful unless the advocate has some way of resolving the problem. This is the role of cure. Cure is the third stock issue for policy cases and is the one asked for by Nancy when she said she heard that jobs in Alaska were difficult to get. *Cure demonstrates that some course of action can work to solve the ill.* In other words, if Juli and Nancy go to Alaska, will they find jobs? If we send food to Ethiopia, does it cure starvation? How much of the ill does it cure—all, some, or none? If we mandate desegregation in the schools, do we alleviate discrimination?

Cures consist of two parts: a plan of action and its effect on the ill. *A plan of action is the specific program advocated in support of the proposition.* Examples include Juli's plan to work in Alaska and the government's plan to bus students to schools to overcome segregation. When advocates specify direct and definite courses of action, they are specifying plans of action.

Some plans of action are formal whereas others are much less so. Minimally, however, we expect anyone advocating change to offer a plan that describes both an agent and a mandate. *An agent is the person, group, or agency responsible for implementing the policy program.* For example, if Juli and Nancy decide to work in Alaska, they will have to contact Juli's friend and apply for jobs. *A mandate is the specific action the agent will undertake.* For example, school boards across the nation began developing plans for busing programs to ensure integration following the *Brown* decision. Such programs constituted a mandate for schools ("You will have busing programs") overseen by school boards.

Plans of action can be very detailed or very simple. Almost any legislation passed by Congress from the budget to foreign assistance programs involves extremely detailed plans of action that specify almost every action associated with the legislation. These plans can often take many volumes and thousands of pages to describe. On the other hand, Juli's plan for Nancy and her to work in Alaska is very simple and largely informal. Unlike Congress, her plan is not a law nor is it a contract; it is simply an informal agreement between two people to take a particular action to alleviate an ill.

Having a plan, however, does not mean it will work. Juli says working in Alaska will give her enough money to stay in school, but she needs to advance arguments to prove her claim that her plan will work. This is the role of effects. Effects is the argument that the plan of action can solve or cure the ill. In other words, what effect does the plan have on the ill? Too often, people assume that if a plan is designed to address an ill, it will automatically work. For example, busing was designed to alleviate the ill of school segregation, but it didn't entirely work. Aside from creating its own myriad problems, the plan did nothing to reduce segregated neighborhoods, differences in socioeconomic status, or any of the other variables that contribute to and perpetuate segregation. It addressed a symptom. *Effects is the argument presented about the relative effectiveness of a plan.* If the plan worked a little, is that preferable to nothing? The problem that remained beyond the structure of segregation was the attitude of segregation. If the plan of action cannot overcome prejudiced attitudes, then the ability of the plan to affect the ill is diminished because the social system will seek to undermine it.

Cost/Benefits

Recognizing that policies are adopted within a larger system is an important step in understanding cost. *The cost is the problems or disadvantages associated with taking a policy action.* The assumption is a simple one: For any action we take, we give up or pass by other actions or cause systematic changes that may not be beneficial. Therefore, the issue of cost asks, "What are the negative consequences of this action?" If Nancy and Juli decide to go to Alaska, their costs might be giving up social activities and friends at home or they may get homesick. If school boards are forced by the *Brown* decision to bus students, the cost is that schools now need to spend money on transportation concerns instead of classroom issues. Also, many students will need to be bussed to schools further from home, which means that students have the cost of time, that they are not in their community schools, and that their friends all live further away.

Benefits are the positive consequences of policy action. There are many examples of how enacting some policy will result in positive outcomes.[9] For example, busing will provide greater cultural diversity in the classroom. Students will have an educational opportunity that is superior on average because of a greater mix of teachers, students, and facilities. The worth of the benefits depends on the value structure—how much value do we place on the benefits and how much value do we place on the cost? If integrating the U.S. educational system is a highly placed value, then the benefits of busing probably outweigh the associated cost.

Cost and benefits are interrelated. When we make decisions, we examine both sides of the system and consider the cost and benefits of competing system alternatives. On the one hand, we look at the cost and benefits associated with the present system. On the other hand, we look at the cost and benefits associated with the proposed system. Whichever system has the greatest net benefits will, presumably, be the system we will support. Cost and benefits act as a fulcrum on which policy decisions are weighed. Arguers use this fulcrum to decide which system is most beneficial.

■ *Issues Brief*

As observed earlier, policy advocacy may occur in many settings—conversations, discussions, debates, editorials, etc. The advocate may have extended time for speaking and for presenting a case, or may have only intermittent speaking times and may have to develop a policy argument in several sections at different times. The situation may have an effect on how the policy argument is developed, structured, and presented. Regardless of situational constraints, policy advocates persuade their audiences that the benefits of their proposal outweigh its cost by showing the consequences of action and inaction through the development of extended arguments. This section will introduce and explain how a needs-based policy argument can be developed and refuted. While other approaches to arguing policies will be developed in the following section, the needs-based approach is the most commonly used means of advocating policy decisions. This section will introduce you to needs-based policy arguments and will illustrate how such arguments can be refuted.

On occasion, an advocate will find a problem that is caused by a defect in the current system that can be resolved. When such is the case, a needs case is appropriate. *A needs-analysis case claims that the ill existing in the current system cannot be corrected within the present system but can be cured by the advocate's policy proposal.*[10] Needs arguments are very common in persuasive speeches as well as more extended debates because the format and requirements for the argument are simple and straightforward. All that is required of an advocate is proof that a significant ill exists, that it is caused by some feature of the present system, and that it can be resolved through the proposed plan of action.

An extended needs argument is developed in two distinct clusters of arguments. The first establishes a significant ill and blame. The ill and blame are developed together to reveal that the present system suffers a significant problem that cannot be resolved for structural or attitudinal reasons. The second cluster presents a plan of action and proves that the proposed plan can cure the ill presented.

Often, needs-based cases will develop a third cluster of arguments that focus on the benefits of the plan. Although the plan achieves benefits by reducing the ill and overcoming the blame, it may also have additional benefits. For instance, busing students will have the effect of curing (at least in part) racially segregated schools. This functions as a benefit. However, there are additional benefits that are not related to the ill or the blame but occur as a natural consequence of changing the system. For instance, beyond integration, students will have the benefits of learning from a diverse group of teachers. These "spin-off" benefits add to the desirability of the plan of action, although they are not necessarily related to the ill as identified.

In response, an arguer who opposes the proposal may use the strategy of direct refutation. Although other refutational strategies will be discussed later, direct refutation is a common and effective means for an opponent to respond to proposals. *Direct refutation is an approach used by policy opponents that is designed to argue and disprove at least one of the stock issues in the proposal.* In using a direct refutation approach to a proposal, opponents attack it on one or more of the stock issues of ill, blame, cure, and cost/benefits. Because any policy proposal minimally must succeed in proving each of the stock issues, if an opponent can successfully defeat any one of the stock issues, the proposal is no longer *prima facie.* Direct refutation does not require the opponent to support any current or proposed policy system, only to argue against the one presented. Essentially, with direct refutation, the advocate takes the position "I am not going to defend any policy system but I will challenge everything my opponent has said and show the case to be insufficiently proven."

Fundamentally, arguers using this strategy take advantage of the issue of presumption. Because audiences are naturally predisposed to favor the current, known policy system, arguers using direct refutation simply must show that the policy proponents have failed to fulfill their burden of proof on one or more stock issues to show that the proposed plan should not be adopted.

Arguers using the strategy of direct refutation generally parallel the case they oppose in organization and argumentation. If the case presents significant ills, the advocate claims that these ills are caused by certain attitudes or structures, that a certain plan will correct the ills, and that it will produce certain benefits; then the person using direct refutation would attempt to show that the ills do not exist or are insignificant, that the causes for them have been misidentified, that the proposed plan is flawed and unworkable, that it will not correct the ill, and that the claimed benefits will not be produced. Figure 10–1 is an outline of how a needs case can be developed and opposed.

I. There is a need for a new system.	I. There is no need for a new system.
A. There are significant ills.	A. The ills are insignificant or do not exist.
B. The present system is to blame.	B. The present system is capable of handling any ills should they arise.
II. There is a plan that can solve the problem.	II. The plan should not be adopted.
A. This plan of action will resolve the ill.	A. This plan is unneeded or won't work.
1. What agent should act?	1. This agent is incapable or unqualified to act.
2. What mandate should be given to the agent?	2. This mandate won't work to cure the ill.
B. This plan will have the effect of curing the ill.	B. Even if this plan worked, it cannot cure the ill.
III. In addition to solving the ill, the following benefits will accrue (optional).	III. This plan will receive no benefits.
A. Benefit 1	A. Benefit 1 won't come true.
	1. The benefit is exaggerated.
	2. The plan of action does not get this benefit.
B. Benefit 2	B. Benefit 2 won't come true.
	IV. The case will accrue many costs.
	A. Cost 1
	B. Cost 2

Figure 10–1
Needs Case as Developed and Opposed

The emphasis with the needs-based organizational pattern is how well the plan of action can cure the ill. The stock issue of cost/benefits is not readily apparent in this format. Although the opposing side argues for specific costs, the benefits in the case are inherent in the plan's ability to cure the ill. This means that if the case is true, then the benefits will be realized when the plan works and the significance of the ill is diminished and a blame is removed.

Direct refutation presents a clear counterargument for each of the significant arguments developed in the case being opposed. Although the preceding example shows refutation against every case argument, a solid refutation may be conducted with less detail and breadth. Minimally, the advocate needs to disprove any one of the stock issues because in doing so one of the elements of a *prima facie* case is disproved. Notice too that beyond simply answering the case argument, an opponent would also offer the cost associated with a system change.

Consider an employee asking for a raise. The employee might begin by saying, "I am unhappy because my current pay is not enough to motivate me to do my best work. The problem is that the pay system does not recognize individual merit or responsibility and has not kept up with my abilities." Here the worker has isolated a problem ("I am unhappy") and placed the blame on the structure of the pay system. The next step is to present a plan ("I deserve another two dollars an hour"). And finally, the employee needs to offer the employer the effects of the plan ("If you give me the extra money, I will be happy and more productive; a happy employee is a good employee"). Beyond this, the employee may offer additional benefits ("I would be willing to work more overtime, take on additional responsibilities"). If the employee is successful and receives a raise, the original pay structure has been replaced with a new one because of a significant need.

The employer, on the other hand, could use a direct refutation strategy to counter the employee's case. For instance, the employer could say "I don't care if you are happy or not as long as you get the job done, and if you can't do your job there are many more people who would be more than happy to." This response mitigates the importance of the ill because, in essence, the employer is responding that the ill is unimportant. Similarly, the employer could point to cost ("If I give you a raise, I would have to give everyone a raise. This company cannot afford such an expenditure in recessionary times and we would go bankrupt. As much as you may deserve a raise, at least this way the company can remain solvent and in business."). The employer's argument in this case is that the cost, going out of business, outweighs the employee's harm of being unhappy.

There are many significant issues that require policy action that might use a needs-based approach. For example, consider the problem of hazardous waste exports. Currently, the United States ships upwards of a million tons of hazardous waste to less-developed countries each year. The reason the United States exports so much of its hazardous waste is that the disposal of such waste is highly regulated and expensive in the United States. Third World countries, on the other hand, receive from U.S. companies a tremendous amount of hard currency which serves to underwrite their economies. Undeveloped countries, however, have very few limitations or regulations governing disposal. The problem, obviously, is that as the practice continues, unregulated dumping of waste in Third World countries will eventually create an environmental nightmare. An issue brief of such an argument using needs and direct refutation might look like Figure 10–2.

This case argument in Figure 10–2 is fairly simple. A problem exists (waste exports) that has a clear and direct solution (a ban). The important feature of this argument is that the plan of action must cure the ill and the blame. If the ills cannot be cured, then the plan is irrelevant. While this might seem obvious, often advocates offer plans that will only partly solve a problem or only partly overcome the blame. In such cases, the need is only partially satisfied and the significance of the case is reduced.

I. The United States is destroying the environment in the Third World.

   A. Hazardous waste exports are destructive to the environment.

      1. Third World environments are irreparably damaged.

      2. Waste exports are increasing.

      3. This is becoming a worldwide problem.

   B. Regulations are insufficient to solve the problem. (blame)

      1. When we tighten waste disposal regulations in the United States, we provide an incentive to ship waste abroad. (attitudinal blame)

      2. Less-developed countries often have no regulations governing disposal. (structural blame)

      3. Current U.S. restrictions on waste exports are weak. (structural blame)

I. The United States is not destroying the environment in the Third World.

   A. Hazardous waste exports are not destructive to the Third World as long as they are managed appropriately.

      1. All the evidence supporting damage comes from environmentalists, not unbiased sources.

      2. Waste exports are decreasing and are less than 200,000 tons a year.

      3. There is little hard evidence to support any significant problem or long-term damage.

   B. Current regulations are adequate.

      1. We are passing regulations preventing exports.

      2. Third World governments provide adequate controls and safeguards.

      3. U.S. and world export restrictions are becoming much stronger.

Figure 10–2
Issues Brief with Needs and Direct Refutation

       The viability of a needs case rests on the advocate's ability to identify correctly an ill within the present system, to locate the features within the present system that cause the ill, and to remove the deficiencies in the present system through a plan of action that will work. In other words, the needs analysis rests on the premise that the present system has important defects that contribute to a significant ill. The needs approach offers a clear analysis of each stock issue and presents beneficial alternatives for the present policy system. The focus of a needs case is that the current system is unsatisfactory and the best solution is to adopt the advocate's course of action.

       Because the needs case seeks to replace the current structure, an arguer should use it when the ill is particularly significant and can clearly be cured through an alternative to the current system. Needs cases must overcome a greater presumption

II. The United States should ban the export of hazardous wastes. (cure)

    A. Plan of action: Congress (agent) should enact legislation that prohibits any export of hazardous waste. (mandate)

    B. Once a ban is in place, the level of waste exports will drop and the problem will diminish. (effect)

III. If we enacted a ban, the world would be healthier because all U.S. wastes would now be regulated. (benefit)

II. The United States should not ban the export of hazardous wastes now.

    A. The plan is unnecessary because all the necessary safeguards are in effect now.

    B. Because the waste exports are so low now, it is difficult to see how the effect of the proposed plan will diminish them further.

        1. How much will the ill be reduced?

        2. The current system is already moving to solve the problem.

III. Current regulations already guarantee that peoples' health is not at risk, so there is no benefit.

    A. Third World countries depend on U.S. money.

    B. Hazardous waste exports represent a significant portion of underdeveloped economies.

    C. Without U.S. hard currencies, these countries could be plunged into severe economic depression.

    D. Without economic support, the democratic governments in these counties are at risk from popular revolution.

Figure 10–2   continued

than other types of cases because they are a new system that seeks to replace the old system. Therefore, the evidence and reasoning supporting the cure (that the effect of the plan will be to cure the ill) is particularly important. This means that the role of the opponent is to cast as much doubt on the proposal as possible. Unless the benefits of the plan (through curing the ill as well as additional benefits) are sufficient to overcome the risk inherent in changing systems, the case will probably not be adopted by the audience.

■ *Alternative Formats for Arguing Policies*

In the previous section, you were introduced to a particular case format, the needs case. Needs arguments are based on the premise that the current system is a failure because it has been either unwilling or unable to redress a significant ill. On occasion, however, the present system is attempting to address a problem or is addressing a problem in a way that, in the advocate's view, is inappropriate. Such situations may require the use of alternative argument formats. This section will introduce and explain two alternate approaches to presenting and supporting policy propositions: comparative advantages and goal. While other approaches are possible, these two are commonly used and widely adaptable for many different situations. How they are used in policy argument will depend on the nature of the topic being discussed and the situation in which the argument is made.

Comparative-Advantages Case

Often, there are problems that have no clear-cut or easy solutions. Sometimes, the present system is already attempting to cure the ill and there is no obvious deficiency in the way the system is dealing with a problem. In such cases, an advocate may want to argue for a new system that is superior to the present system. The case argument that is developed compares the advantages and disadvantages of two competing system alternatives and, hence, is called a comparative-advantages case.

The comparative-advantages argument develops the position that in comparison with the current system, the proposed system has more benefits. Instead of isolating a problem and offering a cure (as with the needs case) the focus of a comparative-advantages argument is to argue that the advocate's proposal is comparatively stronger or more beneficial than the current system.

In a comparative-advantages argument, the ways stock issues are developed are different from a needs argument and the systems approach underlies the logic of the case. For instance, in a needs argument the ill was a harm that the current system could not cure. But if the present system has already identified the problem and is trying to cure it, then such an analysis would be redundant because both sides would agree that such an ill exists. For example, there is probably agreement that discrimination exists and that school segregation is bad. The present system is already attempting to solve the problem through mandatory busing and other programs designed to integrate education. An advocate wanting to cure discrimination would probably not have to prove that discrimination is bad because the current system already embraces that view. With a comparative-advantages case, however, the advocate would argue that there are more effective ways to reach a goal and address problems than those in the present system. With school busing, then, the advocate might claim that there are better ways to achieve equal educational opportunity than busing. In a comparative-advantages case, the ill is interpreted as inadequacies in existing plans and policies. The blame in such an argument rests on the way the current system seeks to cure the ill; the cure is the alternative.

Cost and benefits become an important argument in a comparative-advantages case. Whereas the needs case proved benefits by alleviating the ill, in a comparative-advantages case, the advocate makes the argument that there are many benefits associated with the proposed system and costs associated with the current system. Comparative-advantages cases seek to be accepted because they are better than the current system. This approach does not attempt to identify a single ill or set of ills or their causes; rather, it emphasizes the policy proposed and its effects in comparison to the present system.[11] This means that even if the proposal is not perfect and cannot entirely remove the blame or cure the ill, it is *comparatively* better than the present system.

An advocate using a comparative-advantages approach would cluster arguments in the following areas:

I.   Plan of Action

    A. Agent: Who should act?

    B. Mandate: What action should be taken?

II.   Benefit 1

    A. The scope and effectiveness of the present system is limited. (ill)

    B. The present system cannot remedy the ill. (blame)

    C. The proposed plan of action will solve the problem. (effect)

III.   Benefit 2

A comparative-advantages case fulfills its burden of proof by successfully arguing that the proposed plan is an improvement over the present system and can be favorably compared with other competing systems. To understand how this works, consider a conversation between two college roommates, Lucas and George.

LUCAS:	I think it is time to move off-campus. I hate living in the dorms and I hate eating cafeteria food. In general, I hate living on campus. So many freshmen, so much noise.
GEORGE:	Yes, but living on campus has many benefits. If we move into an apartment, who will cook our meals? Who will clean the bathrooms? Who will we socialize with? It seems to me that what we are doing now is the best alternative.
LUCAS:	You're wrong. Look at it this way—if we move off-campus, we will save a lot of money. In fact, I figure that our housing cost will drop by about a third. Besides, the freedom to come and go without worrying about dorm rules and regulations far outweigh any reason to stay in the dorms. Besides, I like the idea of just having time to get away from campus and relax.
GEORGE:	Well, I hadn't thought of it like that. I especially hadn't thought about the cost savings and I suspect that between you and me, we can cook better than the cafeteria. Let's move!

In this conversation, Lucas develops a comparative-advantages argument. Both Lucas and George want a comfortable place to live, they want to save money, and they want freedom. But Lucas points out that living off-campus will achieve these ends better than living in the dorm. Even though the present policy system, living in dorm rooms, was not bad *per se,* changing policy systems, living off-campus, produced more net benefits than net cost.

On a broader scale, consider the argument for reducing ozone depletion. During the 1980s and 1990s, ozone became an international concern. Ozone is the protective layer that shields the earth from the sun's ultraviolet rays. Without the ozone layer, people exposed to sunlight would develop much more severe sunburns and ultimately skin cancer. There is a great deal of consensus on this issue. Most researchers who have looked at the issue of ozone depletion have found that with a damaged ozone layer, the food chain in the oceans will be destroyed, that up to three million people will die of skin cancer by 2075, and that our forests will begin to die. In short, if the ozone goes away, so do most forms of life. Most also agree that human beings have contributed significantly to the problem with the use of CFCs (chlorofluorocarbons) which are found in refrigerators, air-conditioning systems, and aerosol cans, to name a few.

The question is, and remains, how can we deal with this problem? Many governments, including the United States, recognize the severity of ozone depletion and have begun to adopt programs to correct it. For instance, an international agreement, known as the Montreal Protocol on Substances that Deplete the Ozone Layer, has been continually strengthened and adopted by many nations. It includes a program to phase out dangerous CFCs and other substances that deplete ozone. At the same time, the United States has worked to phase out the use of CFCs and U.S. trade policies have placed restrictions on governments that fail to limit CFCs. In general, the United States recognizes a problem—as does most of the rest of the world—and is working to reduce the problem.

There is a problem that the current system recognizes should be addressed. Furthermore, there is a program that is designed to alleviate the ill imposed by the problem. Does this mean that an advocate has no ground on which to argue about CFCs or ozone depletion? Clearly a needs case wouldn't be appropriate here because the current system is not to blame—it is attempting to do something. There are programs designed to solve the problem. The broader question, however, is "Is there a better solution?" If there is a better alternative than the present system's, then a comparative-advantages approach is justified and might take the following form:

I.   The United States should ban CFCs now. (plan of action)

    A. Congress should enact a policy. (agent)

    B. The policy should eliminate the use and production of CFCs. (mandate)

II. This plan of action will help preserve the ozone layer. (benefits)

    A. Current efforts to diminish ozone depletion only postpone the end of life on earth. (ill)

    B. Present policies are too little too late. (blame)

        1. The Montreal Protocol is ineffective and unenforceable. (structural blame)

2. The U.S. policies have so many loopholes that they are ineffective. (structural blame)

C. A complete ban will preserve the ozone better than all of the current policies. (cure)

With this example, the case contrasts what is being done presently with what could be done—the comparison of alternative systems. The ill analysis in the benefits focuses on a deficiency in the current system. It would be inappropriate to argue that ozone depletion is bad because both sides would agree and the argument is simply a restatement of common ground. Instead, the ill focuses on the deficiency of the present system. The blame, then, becomes the reason why the present system is unable to remedy its own ill and the cure is the proof that the alternative will overcome the systemic defects identified in the ill and blame.

Goals Case

Extended policy arguments using a goals approach have a focus that is very different from either the needs or comparison approaches discussed earlier. *The goals argument presents a significant goal and the case revolves around a comparison of systems attempting to achieve the goal.*[12] This means that an advocate using a goals approach must identify and defend a specific goal that is or should be a focus in the current system. This goal is something that is or should be highly valued in the context of the policy system (see Chapter 9 for more detail on how values function). For example, a goal of the legal system is justice. A goal of the Supreme Court is to uphold the Constitution. A goal of families is to provide for one another a comfortable life. There are many different goals that operate from a social, and/or political, and/or economic level.

The goals approach functions on the premise that a particular goal is not being met because of a structure or attitude (blame) in the present system. Therefore, the proposal in a goals case seeks to eliminate factors that prevent the system from achieving the goal.

The goals case should prove that the present system cannot achieve the goal because of structural or attitudinal blames. The argument progresses by presenting a plan of action that overcomes the blame and better achieves the goal than the present system. This approach makes the assumption that eliminating inconsistencies between important goals and policies is a sufficient warrant for change.[13]

Generally, a goals argument develops in the following organizational pattern:

I. An important goal exists.

II. Flaws in the present system are to blame for its inability to achieve the goal.

III. There is a plan of action that will better achieve the goal.

IV. The proposed plan of action will better meet the goal.

With this format, the ill takes the form of an unmet goal. The case does not argue that the present system is bad *per se* but that it is missing an opportunity by failing to achieve an important objective. The blame argues that some feature or flaw in the present system prevents it from achieving the goal. The cure is a plan that removes the barrier to the goal and the benefits are the ability of the plan to better meet the goal. The case argument may also offer additional benefits from altering the present system.

Identifying the appropriate goal, however, can be difficult. The goal must either be accepted by the parties of the dispute or the advocate must argue that it should be an important goal. In our complex system of values and policies, it is not uncommon for different values to overlap and conflict. There are many instances in which individual rights conflict with social rights. Consequently, what has value and is an important goal for one person might be unimportant or a bad goal for another. It is important, therefore, to recognize that what is a reasonable goal for a given audience is largely dependent on the field used for the argument. (Refer to Chapters 2 and 9 for a description of fields and how they influence arguments.)

Different groups of people often have goals that conflict. For several years the goal of environmental protection has clashed with the goal of economic development and this has been a particularly heated issue with regard to the spotted owl controversy. The spotted owl is indigenous to the old-growth forests of the Pacific Northwest. It is an endangered species that does not appear to nest in newer forests. For it to survive, according to many environmentalists, we need to protect the ancient forests. On the other hand, people in the logging industry argue that placing the old-growth forests off-limits to harvesting could result in up to 700,000 jobs lost and will have the effect of destroying many small Washington, Oregon, Idaho, and Montana towns. Which value is more important? The protection of the spotted owl or the protection of jobs? This can be a difficult issue to resolve and President Bush, faced with deciding how to proceed, in 1991 called upon a group of investigators called the "God Squad" to determine whether logging should be allowed even at the expense of the owl. Logging won. In this case, the goal of protecting U.S. economic interests outweighed the goal of protecting species.

If we wanted to construct a goals argument, there are two ways we could proceed. First, we could argue that the goal of economy over species is an important goal but that the present system is unable to meet that goal because of some blame. In fact, this was the argument made by many loggers who claimed that the owl's status as a threatened species prevented the United States from achieving important economic goals. An alternative way of arguing this issue would be to prove that another goal is superior and should be supported. Such a case might be organized as follows:

I.   Protecting species should be our most important goal.

    A. Species diversity guarantees our own survival.

    B. We don't have the moral right to justify the extinction of a species.

II. The present system is allowing the spotted owl to die. (blame)

III. We should guarantee the right of owls and other protected species to live. Congress (agent) should eliminate the "God Squad" and place biodiversity as our highest priority. (mandate)

IV. Such a program has many advantages. (benefits)

A. The spotted owl will survive.

B. We set a much more reasonable precedent.

C. We help our economy become more diverse with less reliance on logging as the sole industry of many towns.

With the goals case, the present system's inability to meet the goal serves as the ill. The blame is the barrier that prevents the system from meeting the goal. The cure is the plan of action and its effects in guaranteeing better species diversity, and the benefits are the positive consequences associated with acting and better meeting the goal.

▪ *Alternative Formats for Refuting Policy Arguments*

As there are many approaches for supporting policy proposals, there are also many approaches for opposing them. As we noted in Chapter 8, listeners who choose to respond to the issues presented by the original advocate assume a burden of rejoinder. In other words, they must address the central stock issues as originally presented and provide a sufficiently strong reason for rejecting the case as originally presented. The central question guiding the response is, Why do we reject policy systems? You have already been introduced to one strategy called direct refutation which is based on the premise that the proposal is incoherent or inadequate in itself. It may have flaws or it may fail adequately to address all the stock issues.

Beyond direct refutation, an opponent may employ three other macrolevel strategies to counter an extended policy case. These strategies are defense of present policy, minor repairs, and counterproposals. The remainder of this section will describe each of these options and illustrate how each can be used to oppose policy cases.

Strategy of Defense of the Present Policy System

When advocates elect to defend the present policy system, they commit themselves to the argument that the present policy has greater systemic benefits than the proposal. *Defense of the present policy system rests on a comparison of the proposal and the present system and argues that the present system is superior.* Opponents of a proposal who use this strategy take the position that "compared with the proposed alternative, the present system is more beneficial." Arguers using this approach focus primarily on the issues of ill and blame and argue that present structures and attitudes are sufficient to cure the ill identified in the proposal.

Defense of present policies can be effective for any case approach. As with the strategy of direct refutation, it parallels the organization of the extended case and seeks to disprove at least one of the stock issues. The difference between this approach and direct refutation is that the utility and benefits of the current system become arguments against the proposal. In a sense, what is good about the present system is a reason not to replace it, such as the cost of the proposed system.

Respondents defending the current policy system will show that the present system is adequate and that any deficiencies have been erroneously identified or exaggerated by those advocating change. After all, any change involves risk and may result in disadvantages that outweigh the supposed benefits of correcting an ill or problem. As with those who use direct refutation, advocates of present policies take advantage of the presumption in their favor. It is advisable to assume that most audiences would prefer to stay with known policies than to assume the risk of adopting an untested policy unless the present policy is proven to be inadequate or problematic.

Recall the argument about exporting hazardous waste to underdeveloped countries. An arguer using defense of present policies would focus the refutation on the ability of current mechanisms and restrictions to cure the ill. Furthermore, the arguer would offer cost associated with changing systems that the present system does not accrue.

Defending current policies requires the arguer's commitment to support structures as they exist and presently function. When an arguer chooses to defend current policies, a commitment is made to adopt a consistent and systemic view of the argument. With direct refutation any responsive argument could be made; with support of present policies the answers should not contradict present policies. This approach should be used when the systemic benefits of the present system are greater than the benefits of the proposed system.

Strategy of Defense of Present Policies with Minor Repairs

Occasionally, people opposing policy proposals may recognize that the current policy, if left unaltered, cannot correct the ill or solve the problem. They believe, however, that if minor flaws such as inadequate funding, lack of information, or improper administration were corrected, the present policy could be made adequate. The premise of this strategy is that "the present system is basically fine, but it could be streamlined and improved with minor additions or changes that don't involve wholesale systemic changes." *The defense of present policies with minor repairs strategy offers small changes to existing policies to improve their effectiveness and efficiency in meeting the needs.*

Minor repairs are by definition minor. As such, they should not involve significant structural or attitudinal changes to the policies or their administration. To do so involves a fundamental change in the nature of the policy system and means that the arguer is no longer defending the present system but a new and different system. Advocates using this strategy should defend the integrity of the present system.

Offering minor repairs means that the essential characteristics of the present policy must remain intact.

For example, consider the case for preserving ozone. Perhaps the present system's failure lies in the cost of implementing programs and not in the programs themselves. An advocate using minor repairs might argue to reprioritize funding so that the current structures are allowed to work. The system is not changed, just its implementation.

The strategy of defending present policies with minor repairs focuses on the blame issue. If the respondent can prove that minor system changes can accomplish the same objective as the proposed case, there is no reason to act. The present system cannot be held accountable for shortcomings if it has the capacity to adapt to new challenges and ills. The minor repairs approach argues for a flexible system.

Defense of present policies with minor repairs is advisable when you believe that the blame has been exaggerated and that the change proposed by the opponents is greater than what is needed to correct the ill. Making minor modifications in an existing policy, it can be argued, is surely less risky than implementing an entirely new policy system.

Strategy of Counterproposals

If a respondent analyzes the proposition and the case presented and discovers that the opponent's indictments of the current policy system is justified, then a different strategy is needed because defending the present system is no longer an option. *A counterproposal is an alternative plan of action presented by the policy opponent that is different from both the present policy and the plan proposed by opponents.* An arguer presenting a counterproposal accepts that an ill exists and that the present system is unable to cure it. But the arguer maintains that the opponent's case is still invalid because either the case misunderstands the nature of the problems and a different solution is needed, or there is a better plan of action to solve the ill and blame as identified in the case.

The strategy of counterproposal argues that the alternative presented should supersede the proposed policy. Consequently, an arguer presenting a counterproposal develops an extended case independent of the original case argued. For example, with the case of hazardous waste exports, an arguer could argue that the wastes are bad but then so is a complete ban. Therefore, the advocate might offer a counterproposal of international regulation. Perhaps the United States and other industrialized nations should agree on international regulations such that underdeveloped countries can still reap the economic benefits of waste disposal but be protected by regulations and safeguards sanctioned by the international community.

The counterproposal does not disagree with the needs and blame analysis presented in the original proposal. Instead, the argument not only centers on the relative ability of the two systems to achieve the benefits but also diminishes the ill and blame. If the counterproposal is better able to cure the ill and overcome the blame than the original proposal, then it should be adopted instead.

When should a counterproposal be used? A counterproposal does not enjoy the same presumption of strategies using present policies because it offers a new plan of action. As with any new plan of action, there is risk involved with change. Therefore, when you put forward a counterproposal, you assume the burden of proof to demonstrate the proposed counterpolicy system can cure the ill and blame better than the originally proposed system.

In sum, the purpose of a counterproposal is to provide a competing policy system to compare with the advocated policy system. It should provide an argument for rejecting the proposition because it provides greater benefits with less cost than does the proposed system.

The three macrolevel argument strategies for refutation presented in this section are not mutually exclusive. Nor do any of these case-level arguments preclude using direct refutation. Depending on the respondent's analysis of the proposal, it may be appropriate to use two or more of the strategies in combination. Each offers different options for the arguer and each addresses different issues. The objective of the respondent is to provide an argument against adoption of the proposed policy system. As long as using multiple strategies does not lead the arguer to contradict his or her own arguments, a combination of approaches is useful.

◾ *Summary*

This chapter examined how to construct and refute extended policy arguments. It began by discussing the nature of extended policy arguments and important policy concepts.

Extended policy arguments are composed of subsidiary claims supporting a policy proposition and the reasoning and evidence that support them. Policy arguments, unlike other types of argument, ask audiences to make decisions about future actions based on their expectations of what is probable or likely to occur. When we decide between different policy alternatives, we base our decisions on our assessment of net benefits and net cost associated with a system.

Understanding systems is important because policy arguments seek to change the complex nature of our social, economic, and political systems. A systems approach to policy argumentation begins with the assumption that policies are interconnected and that changes in one part of a system have effects in other parts of the system. When we examine the relative merits of any particular policy system, we need to assess not only the policy but also the extended system of changes it represents and the system it is designed to replace. No action occurs in a vacuum and advocates as well as listeners need to be aware of the consequences of action or inaction.

Before listeners are likely to accept extended policy arguments, they expect certain issues to be addressed. Stock issues are issues that must be addressed adequately before a listener will accept a proposition. With policy propositions, we can discuss four categories of stock issues: ill, blame, cure, and cost/benefits. The ill is a current wrong or harm associated with the present system that the advocate is trying to resolve. The blame is the attribution of the ill to some deficiency in the present system, and blame may be both structural and attitudinal. The cure demonstrates that some course of action can work to solve the ill and consists of a plan of action and its effects. The cost is the problems or disadvantages associated with taking an action, and the benefits are the positive consequences of action.

When an advocate constructs an extended policy argument, all these issues must be addressed. However, depending on situational variables of audience and proposition, the advocate may choose to focus on different aspects of the proposition. This chapter discussed three different strategies for arguing in favor of policy propositions: needs, comparative advantages, and goals. A needs case maintains that the current system is unsatisfactory and the best solution is to adopt a new system to replace the defective one. The comparative-advantages approach argues that the proposed system can achieve greater advantages than the current system. The goals approach claims that the elimination of blame precluding the attainment of important goals is a warrant for change.

This chapter also discussed four possible strategies that can be used to oppose extended policy arguments: direct refutation, defense of present policies, defense of present policies with minor repairs, and counterproposals. The strategy to be chosen depends on the nature of the topic, the characteristics of the case to be opposed, and the beliefs and attitudes of the audience. The first strategy, direct refutation, does not involve defending any particular positions but instead tests each of the significant arguments presented in the opponent's case. Defense of present policies, however, defends existing structures and proves that such structures are of greater utility and benefits than the plan of action proposed in the case. When existing policies have minor flaws that prevent them from functioning correctly, a respondent may offer a defense of present policies with minor repairs. The minor repairs are intended as modifications designed to overcome minor problems in existing policies. Finally, advocates may use counterproposals. Counterproposals are an effective strategy if the opponent's case fails to understand the nature of the problem or if the respondent has a better proposal for curing the problem.

Taken as a whole, policy arguments are an important element in our daily lives. We decide whether or not to take action based on individual assessment of the cost and benefits derived from different extended policy arguments. This chapter was intended to help describe and systematize a process familiar to all of us and fundamental to the process of our decision making.

Exercises

Exercise 1   For each of the following propositions, outline a needs case, a comparative-advantages case, and a goals case using the formats discussed in this chapter:

A. Proposition: I should buy a new car.

B. Proposition:	I should live with my parents until I have established myself in a career.
C. Proposition:	The federal government should provide more student financial aid.
✳ D. Proposition:	I should attend a different school.

Exercise 2   Select two of the affirmative cases you constructed in Exercise 1. For each of them, construct a negative case. Use a different negative strategy for each of the propositions: direct refutation, defense of present policies, defense of present policies with minor repairs, and counterproposal. After you have completed your outlines, explain how each of them differs from the other. What are the advantages of each and in what type of situation would each be most appropriate?

✳ *Exercise 3*   Below is a set of scrambled claims supporting the proposition "The federal government should legalize the sale, possession, and use of marijuana." Some claims could be used to outline an extended argument using needs analysis, others could be selected to construct a comparative-advantages case, and still others could be used to make up a goals case. Organize the scrambled statements to make up a needs-analysis case, a comparative-advantages case, and a goals case. Note that some of the statements will be used in all three cases, others twice, and some only once.

1. A benefit of regulating marijuana will be to decrease the youth smoking problem.
2. A great deal of money is wasted enforcing present laws; hundreds of millions of dollars are spent and only 10 percent is confiscated.
3. Funds will no longer be spent needlessly enforcing an unenforceable law.
4. The plan will be financed by reallocating money presently spent for marijuana control.
5. There is a significant need to change marijuana laws in this country.
6. Legalization of marijuana will be beneficial.
7. A major goal of our society is to eliminate illegal drug use.
8. One-fourth of all marijuana users are under the age of 17.
9. By regulating marijuana, present laws divert law enforcement officials from pursuing and prosecuting hard drug traffickers, and thereby undermine our efforts to control hard drugs.
10. Marijuana sale and consumption will be regulated by the Food and Drug Administration.
11. Harmful substances such as paraquat will be eliminated, protecting consumers.
12. By focusing enforcement efforts on harder drugs, the proposed plan would enable us to better meet our goals of eliminating use of hard drugs.
13. The possession, sale, and use of marijuana will be legalized.

14. Experts estimate that marijuana regulation will prevent a significant percentage of the ten million underage smokers from trying marijuana.

15. These problems are caused by present marijuana laws that are vaguely worded and inconsistently enforced.

16. Monitoring and regulating of marijuana sales are the only ways to decrease youth consumption.

17. Some of the illegally sold marijuana contains paraquat, which causes physiological damage.

18. Young people will no longer be affected by marijuana and other harmful side effects.

19. The following plan of action should be adopted.

20. Decreasing usage has significant beneficial effects.

Exercise 4   Below are two sets of scrambled claims for cases opposing legalization of marijuana. The first is a direct refutation opposing the needs-analysis case included in Exercise 2. The second set of statements develops a counterproposal. Unscramble the claims in each case and construct an outline from them.

Direct Refutation

1. The plan to legalize marijuana won't work.

2. Two-thirds of high school seniors oppose marijuana use.

3. Reallocating present enforcement funds will not provide sufficient revenue to support the plan.

4. There is no need to change marijuana laws.

5. Young people who wish to experiment with marijuana will still be able to obtain it after it has been legalized.

6. Use among young people is decreasing.

7. Because marijuana is not physically or psychologically harmful or addictive, regulating its use will provide no benefits.

8. Funds spent on marijuana enforcement are insignificant; only four percent of drug arrests are for marijuana violations.

9. No benefits will result from the plan.

10. Paraquat is no longer used to destroy marijuana plants.

11. Personnel and funding to regulate and control marijuana distribution are unavailable.

Counterproposal

1. The counterproposal is a better proposal than legalization of marijuana.

2. It is true that there is a significant need to change marijuana laws.

3. Revenue collected from these fines will be given to law enforcement agencies for control of hard drugs.

4. Under decriminalization, we no longer need to use resources and time prosecuting people for a minor, victimless offense.

5. People found to possess marijuana in small amounts for personal use will be subject to minimal fines.

6. Decriminalization allows redirection of funds to areas in which enforcement is most needed.

7. Decriminalizing marijuana continues to indicate society's disapproval of substance abuse.

8. Instead of legalizing marijuana, we should decriminalize its use through the following proposal.

Notes

1. Jerome R. Corsi, "The Continuing Evolution of Policy System Debate: An Assessment and Look Ahead," *Journal of the American Forensic Association* 22 (1986): 158.

2. Ludwig Bertalanffy, "General System Theory—A Critical Review," *General Systems* 12 (1962): 1–20.

3. Steven W. Littlejohn, *Theories of Human Communication,* 3d ed. (Belmont, Cal.: Wadsworth, 1989), 46–48.

4. George W. Ziegelmueller and Charles A. Dause, *Argumentation: Inquiry and Advocacy* (Englewood Cliffs, N.J.: Prentice-Hall, 1975), 32–37.

5. William L. Benoit, Steve R. Wilson, and Vincent F. Follert, "Decision Rules for the Policy Metaphor," *Journal of the American Forensic Association* 22 (1986): 141.

6. Austin J. Freeley, *Argumentation and Debate: Critical Thinking for Reasoned Decision Making,* 6th ed. (Belmont, Cal.: Wadsworth Publishing Co., 1986), 167.

7. Richard Kluger, *Simple Justice: The History of* Brown v. Board of Education *and Black America's Struggle for Equality* (New York: Vintage Books, 1975), 781–82.

8. *Brown, et al. v. Board of Education of Topeka, Shawnee Co., Kansas,* 347 U.S. 483 (1954).

9. Many authorities have examined the nature of policy benefits and advantages. For more information see Russel R. Windes and Arthur Hastings, *Argumentation and Advocacy* (New York: Random House, 1965), 229.

10. Freeley, 184.

11. W. Scott Nobles, "Analyzing the Proposition," in Douglas Ehninger and Wayne Brockriede, *Decision by Debate,* 2d ed. (New York: Harper and Row, 1978), 169.

12. John D. Lewinski, Bruce R. Metzler, and Peter L. Settle, "The Goal Case Affirmative: An Alternative Approach to Academic Debate," *Journal of the American Forensic Association* 9 (Spring 1973): 458.

13. Lewinski, Metzler, and Settle, 458.

Communicating Arguments

■

CHAPTER *11*

Language and Argument

■

CHAPTER OUTLINE

- **The Nature of Language**
  Language and Meaning
  Language and Abstraction
  Connotations and
  Denotations
- **Language in Argument**
  Language, Thought, and
  Perception

  Functions of Language
  Using Language in
  Argument
- **Summary**
- **Exercises**

KEY CONCEPTS

language
denotative meaning
euphemism
emotive function
cognitive function
metalingual language
presence

abstraction
connotative meaning
terministic screen
phatic function
rhetorical function
poetic function

President Abraham Lincoln delivered the Gettysburg Address on November 19, 1863. It began:

> Four score and seven years ago our fathers brought forth on this continent a new nation, conceived in liberty, and dedicated to the proposition that all men are created equal.[1]

Is there any significance to the words used by Lincoln? The speech itself certainly carried with it an importance and elegance suitable not only for 1863 but for the twentieth century as well. But do the actual words used to convey the message carry with them any particular significance? Lincoln's opening could just as easily have begun:

> Eighty-seven years ago those who came before us established in this country a new system of government created in freedom and based on the idea that all people are created equal.

Is there a difference? The content has remained the same, but the words used to express the message are now simpler and perhaps more contemporary. But the change in language seems to change more than just the words; some of the force and spirit of the original version is gone.

The language Lincoln used to express his message was not chosen randomly—nor is the language used to express everyday arguments. Even if we are not aware of our language choices, we adhere to the rules of grammar and vocabulary inherent in our language. The stronger our command of language, the better able we are to select which words to use—but all of us make choices about how to phrase and develop the language of arguments. As you will see later in this chapter, the eloquent language Lincoln used contributed not only to the beauty of his address, but also to its persuasiveness. Harold Zyskind in his study of Lincoln's address noted that, although the occasion was ceremonial (dedication of the cemetery at Gettysburg), the address itself was argumentative and was designed by Lincoln to persuade members of his audience to rededicate themselves to the reunification and continuance of the federal government after the Civil War.[2] Gilbert Highet, writing of Lincoln's address, observed:

> No one thinks that when he was drafting the Gettysburg Address, Lincoln deliberately looked up these quotations and consciously chose these particular patterns of thought. No, he chose the theme. From its development and from the emotional tone of the entire occasion, all the rest followed, or grew—by the marvelous process of choice and rejection which is essential to artistic creation.[3]

In the course of devising and framing arguments, we select the words by which our claims and their support are expressed. These words have a profound impact on the use and interpretation of arguments because their significance lies not in the words themselves, but in what they come to mean for the people who use them. The effects of language depend upon the degree of concreteness and emotive significance of the words themselves. This chapter will examine the nature and functions of language in general and then make specific recommendations regarding its use in argument. By the end of this chapter, you should be able to explain how language works to influence arguers and recipients of argument. You should also be able to control how your arguments are received and understood by controlling your use of language when you make arguments.

■ *The Nature of Language*

There are over 3,000 languages in the world. Each one of them, including English, has a grammar and a vocabulary that control its use and structure. Throughout your primary and secondary education, you learned about the grammar and vocabulary of the English language. You learned grammar as a set of rules—for example, that each English sentence requires both a subject and a verb.

Language is the systematic coordination of grammar and vocabulary used to convey meaning. Grammar and vocabulary are the two components of language and the tools used to communicate meanings between people. This chapter does not focus on these components but rather on how language communicates meaning between people. How is language used to convey meaning? Specifically what are the implications for argument of the ways language works in communication?

Language and Meaning

Language is one of the most powerful tools humans have available to them. We use it daily to express feelings, arguments, fears, and excitement. Yet, we think it is a tool we have mastered, when in some senses it is a tool that has the ability to master us.

A few years ago, a TV program called "Candid Camera" illustrated this point well. The program's producers placed signs over two adjacent public telephones. One sign read "Men" and the other sign read "Women." Interestingly, even when one or the other phone was not being used, lines developed in front of the "Men" phone or the "Women" phone. The act of labeling a telephone as men's or women's changed the way people used them.

The "Candid Camera" example is a humorous illustration of the power words have over our actions and thoughts. Some words are considered taboo and we don't typically allow their use in public. Instead, we refer to the "four-letter words" or the "seven dirty words" that cannot be used on radio or television.

Nevertheless, words by themselves have no intrinsic meaning. They acquire meaning only insofar as people use them to describe their world. This is the point made by C. K. Ogden and I. A. Richards in their book *The Meaning of Meaning.*[4] Their argument was that humans are symbol users who develop symbols to stand for thoughts and ideas in their minds. The mental image, also known as a representation, is the result of direct experience or imagination. For example, if John Smith sees a green pine tree, he develops a representation of the tree through direct experience. John is also able to imagine a green pine tree that he has never seen—based on his past experience with pine trees.

Communication involves the process of transforming such representations into symbols. Therefore, the user's mental image of tree is translated into the word "tree" and the language provides the tool for sharing representations, or meanings, with other language users. Ogden and Richards' model is illustrated in Figure 11–1.

The referent is the actual material object referred to in language. The symbol is the word used to refer to the referent. The reference is the association the language user makes between the symbol "pine tree" and the material object that the user has experienced.

The major point this model makes is that the symbol is connected with the referent *only by way of* an association made by the language user. In other words, the meaning of the word rests in the people using the word. Therefore the connection is *indirect* and represented by a broken line in Figure 11–1. What is the implication of this for communication? Because there is no direct relation between symbol and referent, there is room for misunderstanding. Two language users could make the connection differently and therefore have two diverse understandings of what is meant by "pine tree." Language user 1 may think of a giant evergreen tree while language user 2 may think of a dwarf pine. It is not difficult to imagine the misunderstandings in language use that arise when symbols are ambiguous or when language users have widely discrepant experiences with some set of referents. Because of this, the level of abstraction and concreteness of words and symbols in the language system affects the precision and accuracy of communication.

Language and Abstraction

Because the relationship between the symbol and the referent is subject to variation, communication is not 100 percent efficient. For communication to be entirely effi-

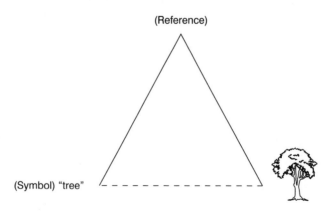

Figure 11–1
Symbol, Reference, and Referent

cient, the representation in the recipient's mind should be identical with the representation in the speaker's mind. In other words, if George says, "There is a tree outside my window," a hearer would have to be able to know exactly to which tree George is referring. This is not possible, because the symbol used is not the referent. It is only indirectly related to the referent through the user's mind.

Language serves as a vehicle for conveying meaning between a source and receiver. When we speak, we not only select words and gestures we think will effectively communicate our thoughts and intentions, but we also select those we think will have some meaning for the recipient. For example, this text could have been written for high school students. Although the language used would convey meaning for everyone reading the text, a college student would probably find it simple and boring. Similarly, the text could have been targeted toward a graduate-level course. It would convey meaning, but high school students would find it very difficult to understand.

The difference in each case is the knowledge and experience the recipient is able to use in understanding the language. If the recipient has a great deal of knowledge about argumentation, the text would not need to dwell on aspects of definition or concrete examples. Instead, the text could develop more abstract and theoretical discussions and the language used could be more complex. The complexity of the connection between the referent and the symbol is measured by the relative abstractness of the symbol. *Abstraction refers to the degree to which relevant characteristics are omitted in language.* As a recipient's knowledge of a subject increases, the language used to convey the subject can be more abstract. Consider the following:

| JOHN: | Would you go to my car and get my book? |
| JAMES: | Sure, but what book in what car? |

| JOHN: | Would you go to my car—the red '93 Prelude license WXI 401—and get my argumentation book? |
| JAMES: | Sure, no problem. |

In the first example, John assumed that James knew about his particular car and what book John wanted, so his language was vague and abstract. But James did not have sufficient information to accomplish the task. The second example provided James with the information he needed, based on his familiarity with the subject and the situation.

When we argue, we use language we assume the recipients can understand. We develop examples and speak with a level of abstraction and ambiguity that is appropriate for the given audience. It is important, however, to recognize that not all recipients have the necessary background and experience to understand abstract language. Based on the advocate's understanding of the particular recipients being addressed, relatively more or less ambiguous language and examples may be used to convey the argument.

S. I. Hayakawa was noted for his work in the area of language abstractness and the development of the abstraction ladder.[5] He argued that when we use language we choose to make it more or less abstract as the situation warrants. His abstraction ladder looks much like that in Figure 11–2.

The bottom of the ladder represents the most concrete—and least abstract—form of language. It uses symbols which represent the referent as specifically as possible. The top of the ladder, however, is the least specific. A manufactured item can be almost any human made product. A listener hearing more specific language would be better able to develop a mental representation of the referent than a listener hearing the more abstract language.

Abstract language is, by its nature, ambiguous. Arguers selecting ambiguous language run the risk of being misunderstood. Why, then, would a speaker choose to use abstract language? The answer can be found in the nature of the audience. For instance, most people have never seen John's car. If he refers to it and wants to persuade his listeners to buy it, they would be unable to create an accurate mental image if the language he uses is too specific for them to understand. Therefore, as a speaker he needs to orient the recipients with language they can understand by using more abstract, commonly understood language. He might say:

Figure 11–2
Hayakawa's Language Abstraction Ladder

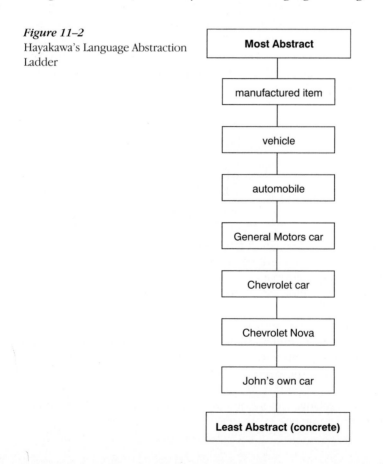

Come buy my car. It is a Chevrolet Nova built in one of the General Motors plants in California.

By blending the concrete with the abstract, an arguer is able to orient his or her recipients to the referent and then move to more concrete symbols. The significance of appropriately placing words on the ladder of abstraction when making arguments will be explored further in the last section of this chapter.

Connotations and Denotations

The triangle of meaning and abstraction has several important implications for arguers. If one recognizes that people may interpret words differently depending on the degree of abstraction, then an arguer should be able to consciously select words that affect people in the way the arguer intends.

The process to be used in selecting words can best be understood by considering the two poles of meaning in language use. Each word when used has a denotative meaning and also a connotative meaning. *The denotative meaning is the objective meaning held by language users in general.* A word's denotative meaning is usually found in dictionaries. Dictionaries record the meanings of words generally agreed upon and established in the culture as a whole. Denotative meanings are relatively stable, and are agreed upon by most language users at any given point in time. *Connotative meanings, however, are the subjective meanings a given individual holds of symbols used in a particular situation.* Connotative meanings have emotive significance and are unique for the individual. Words used by language users, therefore, have both denotative and connotative significance.

For example, consider the word "fag." *Webster's New Collegiate Dictionary* defines "fag" as "toil or drudgery."[6] Yet, if you were to call someone a "fag" referring to the nature of that person's work, odds are that person would respond impolitely. This is because the meaning of the word "fag" is found not in the word itself, but in the person to whom the word is addressed.

Examine the following list of words and write down the first word or phrase that comes to mind:

feminist

Miss America

Texan

construction worker

student

Take a look at your list. You will find that the words you most closely associate with each of these words are your own personal definitions—or connotations—for each of these symbols. The denotative definitions that are found in *Webster's Dictionary* are the objective, agreed-upon definitions for the list of words:

feminist: someone who believes the theory of the political, economic, and social equality of the sexes

Miss America:	young unmarried female who is representative of America
Texan:	someone from Texas
construction worker:	a person employed to build
student:	one who attends school

The odds are that your personal meanings are different than the denotative meanings for the same set of symbols. This holds some important ramifications for speakers of a given language. Whenever you construct a message or argument designed to persuade a listener, you must deal with not only the meaning of the language as you know it, but also with the meaning of the language the way the listener understands it.

Our language is full of words that have been replaced by other words carrying less negative or more positive connotations. This is the function of euphemisms. *Euphemism is a linguistic device for replacing words and phrases which carry a negative connotation with words and phrases which carry a positive connotation.* (Of course a speaker intending to convey a negative feeling might also substitute negative words for positive words.) For example,

Positive Term	Negative Term
daytime drama	soap opera
indiscretion	moral wrong
inappropriate	illegal
air support	bombing
terminated	fired
destabilize	overthrow
intelligence gathering	spying
sanitation engineer	garbage collector
correctional facility	prison
low-income	poor
freedom fighters	revolutionary guerrillas
passed away	died

There are many other possible examples, but in each case words with the same denotative meaning may be substituted for one another with the objective of changing the connotative meanings.

This section has illustrated three characteristics of language. First, the meaning of language depends on language users because symbols by themselves have no intrinsic meaning. Second, language can be abstract or concrete, and arguers must decide what degree of abstraction is appropriate for a given situation and audience. And third, because language allows room for variable interpretations of the meanings of symbols by both the speaker and the listener, meanings of symbols may vary. While denotative meanings are the objective meanings of words agreed upon by the language users, connotative meanings are the subjective interpretations of words that depend on the individual symbol user. Arguers should be sensitive to the fact that the words they use have both denotative and connotative meanings when they are interpreted.

■ *Language in Argument*

We have discussed the variability in the meanings of words from one context to another and from one language user to another. Not only does language affect the accuracy of understanding and interpretation of arguments, but it also influences our perception of our experience. This section will show how language shapes the way recipients think and therefore demonstrate its power in influencing human thought.

Language, Thought, and Perception

What is the relationship between language and thought? Simply stated, language molds and shapes our thoughts. It influences both our perception of the world and what we think about it. For example, imagine the implications of your instructor telling you that you will be comprehensively examined on the exact wording of each definition in this text—and nothing else. Immediately, the instructor's wording would begin to affect how you would think about studying the course material:

comprehensively examined

exact wording

each definition

nothing else

The use of this wording, then, would shape your perception of how to study the text and cause you to concentrate on argumentation terminology, perhaps much more than on argument analysis, construction of messages, and many other topics covered in this text.

Of all the means an advocate has for arguing, language is perhaps the most important. Through the skillful use of language, the arguer is able to help shape and change a recipient's perception of an issue and push the recipient toward a new action or way of thought. Although it is an integral facet of arguing, language is often overlooked in favor of understanding argument parts and tests of evidence and the like. But it serves a central and important function.

The words we use to communicate shape and focus the attention and thoughts of recipients. To demonstrate this, turn to the next page and circle every "the." When you have finished, the odds are that you can say how many instances of "the" appeared and even describe their physical placement. But you would probably not be able to recall the use or frequency of any other word on the page, the subjects discussed on the page, or any misspellings such as "teh." The reason is that the linguistic instruction focused your perception to isolate a particular symbol and this in turn focused your thoughts so that unrelated stimuli were systematically excluded.

In the mid 1950s, Edward Sapir, an anthropologist, and his student, Benjamin Whorf, advanced the hypothesis that people experience their world through language.[7] While they did not say that our thoughts are bound by language, they did argue that language and vocabulary influence our thought patterns.[8] Another noted intellectual, Kenneth Burke, introduced the notion of "terministic screens" to illustrate the role language plays in human perception.[9]

A terministic screen is a linguistic filter through which human beings perceive their world. In other words, our definition of the world, our environment, our relationships with others, and ourselves is created through the exchange of symbols. We know who and what we are because of the exchanges and interactions we have had with other people and our environment. Therefore, language—the tool we use to interact—serves to define our world. Language, according to Burke, allows us to see and understand our world and in essence affects how we experience it.

By way of illustration, Burke uses the example of a photograph. If you took three pictures of a house, each with a different color filter, each picture would be different—even though the subject remained the same. The filters give significance, substance, and contrast to different items in the picture. Likewise, language acts like a filter. The words we use to express ourselves lend different meanings to our world. Our linguistic filter shapes what we see. This is one reason an exact translation of English into French or Greek or any other language is impossible because the nature of the filters is different.

A dramatic example of the influence of language on thought and perception is provided in George Orwell's *1984.* The novel takes place in a totalitarian society. The novel's hero, Winston Smith, has long resisted the strong and pervasive force of the government to control thoughts, emotions, and actions. Part of the government's attempt to control thought is contained in the new language of the government called Newspeak. In the following passage, Syme, Smith's colleague, discusses the *Newspeak Dictionary* with him.

> "The Eleventh Edition is the definitive edition," he said. "We're getting the language into its final shape—the shape it's going to have when nobody speaks anything else. . . .You think, I dare say, that our chief job is inventing new words. But not a bit of it! We're destroying words—scores of them, hundreds of them, every day. We're cutting the language down to the bone. . . .
>
> "It's a beautiful thing, the destruction of words.
>
> "You haven't a real appreciation of Newspeak, Winston," he said almost sadly. "Even when you write it you're still thinking in Oldspeak. I've read some of those pieces that you write in the *Times* occasionally. They're good enough, but they're translations. In your heart you'd prefer to stick to Oldspeak, with all its vagueness and its useless shades of meaning. You don't grasp the beauty of the destruction of words. Do you know that Newspeak is the only language in the world whose vocabulary gets smaller every year?
>
> "Don't you see that the whole aim of Newspeak is to narrow the range of thought? In the end we shall make thoughtcrime literally impossible, because there will be no words in which to express it. Every concept that can ever be needed will be expressed in exactly *one* word, with its meaning rigidly defined and all its subsidiary meanings rubbed out and forgotten. . . .The Revolution will be complete when the language is perfect. . . ."[10]

This passage holds an important message for any language user. Although the English language contains more than 450,000 words, the average American speaking vocabulary is only about 3,000 words. Our tendency is to use highly abstract words so that by being vague we are able to discuss broad and complex subjects with very few symbols. We have begun to use words placed more highly in the abstraction ladder and let one word do the work of several. The shades of meaning are lost as the vocabulary contracts, and the arguer's intention is convoluted when the arguments are expressed in general or simple terms as opposed to the appropriately concrete and specific terms.

An arguer has the ability to change thought and perception through the use of language. But it is important that an advocate be aware of the influence words have on a recipient. Words restrict as well as enhance thought, and argument should develop opportunities for thought. The point here is that arguers should be conscientious users of language. Language should be used to its fullest extent to convey the arguer's intentions, and should be as clear as possible to the recipients to avoid unwanted and unnecessary ambiguity.

Functions of Language

The way in which language is used in argument to influence is affected not only by the available vocabulary and the terms used but also by the functions of language generally. In conveying our meanings to others, we express our thoughts in ways that enable us to reach our objectives in the communication situation. One observer has classified these functions used to express meaning into six categories—emotive, phatic, cognitive, rhetorical, metalingual, and poetic.[11] Let us consider these functions and then note which of them apply to language used argumentatively.

The emotive language function is used to express the feelings, attitudes, and emotions of the speaker. Language used emotively in argument is highly dependent on connotative meanings and the responses they evoke in the recipient. Sometimes this triggering of emotional responses becomes problematic when conviction and emotive expression are substituted for any form of proof. Consider the following statements about the Playboy Foundation:

> Although it calls itself a "foundation," it is actually an arm of Playboy Enterprises, a profit-making corporation that pollutes the moral environment and stands accused of victimizing women and children by portraying them as sex objects.[12]

The author here is making a veiled claim that the Playboy Foundation contributes to the moral degradation of society. His language, however, is heavily connotative and seems to function emotively to vent his own frustrations. Such words as "profit-making," "pollutes," and "victimizing" not only fulfill an emotive function for the author, but they may also influence readers to feel the same way he does. This is guilt by innuendo and association.

The phatic function of language is used socially to reinforce the relationship between parties to a communicative exchange. Language used phatically includes greetings, farewells, and "passing the time of day." The emphasis is not on the context of what is said but on the exchange of pleasantries as an expression of mutual good will. Since the phatic function is relevant to the relationship between arguers rather than to the topic in question, it may affect the rhetorical dimension of argument while having little influence on its logical content.

The cognitive function of language is used to inform. Unlike the emotive function, language used cognitively is primarily denotative and neutral. It is intended to inform recipients of something they do not know. It can also have the effect of alarming recipients or getting them concerned about a situation or problem of which they were unaware. Consider the following example:

Warning Signs of Suicide

Suicide is the second leading cause of death, following accidents, of adolescents between the ages of 15 and 19. Since 1950, the teen-age suicide rate has tripled.

Parents and friends should be aware of teen-ager's moods and actions. The warning signals for potential problems:

- unusual moodiness
- change in sleeping habits
- change in eating habits
- unusual belligerence
- apathy toward school, family
- decreased interest in outside activities
- feelings of desperation, despair
- reckless driving
- violent or rebellious behavior
- decline in the quality of schoolwork
- withdrawn behavior[13]

The primary function of this article is to inform readers of a little-known fact—that suicide is the second leading cause of teen death—and of measures to be taken about it. To the extent that the piece alarms readers and gets them to take precautions, however, it is relevant to argument.

The rhetorical function of language aims to direct or influence thoughts and behaviors. It is persuasive. This is generally the type of language use primarily associated with argumentation. The process of motivating hearers to accept a claim is rhetorical because it seeks to effect some substantive change in the listener's attitudes, values, or beliefs. The following excerpt, again from an article on teen suicide, exemplifies language used rhetorically:

Schools, churches, and civic groups are working overtime to communicate with youth, developing programs of counseling, altering those who could be of assistance—before it's too late. But the rest of the USA must not wait until there are hundreds of death clusters.

> And the media have a heavy responsibility to make sure that we do not wait.
>
> Read the symptoms [of suicide]. Think of youngsters you know. If you have any suspicions that they are troubled, find ways to smash through the barriers they have erected. The media must not ignore their duty to help you understand this problem.[14]

Unlike the earlier passage about suicide, this one makes an explicit attempt to influence the reader. It calls upon readers to take action and uses imperatives to address them directly. It also uses a greater number of connotative terms—"too late," "death clusters," "heavy responsibility," and "smash through"—than the informative piece. The rhetorical function of language can be effective in engaging and influencing recipients and thus persuading them.

Metalingual language comments upon language use itself rather than upon objects or ideas in the world. Its focus is on how language is used and why. Language is used metalingually in argument when arguers make claims about someone else's use of language for purposes of criticism or refutation. For example, if you were to attack an opponent's argument by showing that he or she had used one of the language fallacies identified in Chapter 6, you would be using a metalingual function of language to make an argument. Or, consider as an example Highet's appraisal of language use in the Gettysburg Address:

> It does not spoil such a work of art to analyze it as closely as we have done; it is altogether fitting and proper that we should do this: for it helps us to penetrate more deeply into the rich meaning of the Gettysburg Address, and it allows us the very rare privilege of watching the workings of a great man's mind.[15]

Highet here is commenting upon his own comments upon the language and composition of the Gettysburg Address. His own metalingual use of language is essential to his ability as a critic to assess and interpret the speech in a certain way. He thereby supports his own interpretation by making an argument.

The poetic function of language emphasizes the structure and artistry of expression in a message. Language used poetically is designed to be aesthetically appealing and distinctive. In it we look for creativity, uniqueness, figures of speech, rhythm, and melody. While the poetic function of language is not intended to persuade readers or listeners to action, it can affect arguments. Arguments that are finely and artistically expressed hold their listeners' or readers' attention, contribute to their enjoyment of discourse, and thereby increase the likelihood that recipients will accept the claims stated or implied by the discourse. Recall the original and "plain" versions of the opening words of the Gettysburg Address cited at the beginning of this chapter. Which version influenced you more? Most rhetorical critics would concur that it should be the first one, largely because of the artistry of its language.

As we have intimated, none of these six functions occur in a pure form in common speech. Depending on the arguer, the situation, or the recipients, any two or more of these six functions may combine in any instance of language use. The claim of an argument often functions rhetorically. The language used to make a claim is intended to effect some change in the listener. But the claim is based on evidence which emphasizes the cognitive function to make information or ideas available. The reasoning connecting the evidence to the claim may be rhetorical if it helps persuade the listener, or it may be cognitive if it provides backing for the claim, or it may even be metalingual if it highlights how the language was used in the evidence. Furthermore, the entire argument using the rhetorical, cognitive, and metalingual functions of language may be poetic if it is structured in an aesthetically pleasing manner.

Lincoln's address provides several examples of how the different uses of language can be blended into a single argument. The situation, in particular, helped provide the immediate impetus for Lincoln's selection of language. The address was intended to commemorate war dead as well as to serve as a turning point in the Civil War. Lincoln said:

> It is rather for us to be here dedicated to the great task remaining before us—that from these honored dead we take increased devotion to that cause for which they gave the last full measure of devotion—that we here highly resolve that these dead shall not have died in vain—that this nation, under God, shall have a new birth of freedom—and that government of the people, by the people, for the people, shall not perish from the earth.[16]

The closing of Lincoln's address illustrates several functions. First, it is cognitive. It asks us to think about and informs us of the war dead. Second, it is rhetorical because it asks us to rededicate ourselves—at least in attitude—to picking up where the dead concluded. And the structure is aesthetically appealing. For example, Lincoln uses parallel repetition to emphasize and provide richness to his argument:

government of the people
　　　by the people
　　　for the people

Such poetic use of language provides a richness, a rhythm, and a harmony to the speech.

Therefore, we can conclude that in any given argument, language can function in more than one way simultaneously. The functions of language in arguments should indicate to you the importance of language in determining an argument's persuasiveness and the likelihood that an audience will accept it. Having examined the role of language function, let us turn now to some specific guidelines for using language in the construction of arguments.

Using Language in Argument

Understanding the functions of argument can help you better construct effective arguments. That language is used referentially, artistically, and persuasively in arguments means that it must be understood, adhered to, and remembered to be effective. Certain strategies for the choice of language and phrasing in your arguments will make them clearer, more vivid, and more persuasive. In his essay "Politics and the English Language," George Orwell warned that if we allow our language to become imprecise and ambiguous, each one of us contributes to the decline of our society. To avoid such decline, he offered the following six guidelines that all communicators should use in the presentation of ideas:

(i) Never use a metaphor, simile or other figure of speech which you are used to seeing in print.

(ii) Never use a long word where a short one will do.

(iii) If it is possible to cut a word out, always cut it out.

(iv) Never use the passive where you can use the active.

(v) Never use a foreign phrase, a scientific word or a jargon word if you can think of an everyday English equivalent.

(vi) Break any of these rules sooner than say anything outright barbarous.[17]

Orwell's point was simply that we need to be vigilant when it comes to our communication skills and language use. Our ideas and argument should be clear. We should work to minimize confusion and maximize common understandings and shared meanings. What follows are general guidelines and principles for language use, not hard-and-fast rules. As you recall from previous sections, the use of language in argument depends as much on the situation and the listeners as it does on the argument itself; however, these guidelines will help to ensure that you make the best possible use of the resources language has to offer.

1. *Use clear language.* Clarity is comprised of two factors: selecting language at the appropriate level of abstraction for the recipient, and avoiding convoluted or ambiguous language. Matching the concreteness of the word choice to the experience of the arguee and expressing oneself simply and directly ensures that the argument will be understood as the arguer intended that it should be.

As we noted earlier in the chapter, the appropriate use of abstraction/concreteness depends on the relationship between the arguer and arguee. If the arguee does not know of or understand very concrete references made by the arguer, the language is too concrete. Likewise, if the arguer and arguee understand each other's personal references or the background to the argument, then more concrete terms can be used.

For example, consider someone trying to persuade a friend to take up a training program for running:

JOHN:	It isn't as difficult as you think to build speed and endurance.
JAMES:	Really?
JOHN:	Last summer I alternated sprints with long easy runs. On weekends I ran 10Ks—the St. Patrick's Day Dash, the Beat the Bridge, and the Symphony. By fall, I was able to run a seven-minute mile in a 10K run.
JAMES:	You're right! That sounds do-able!

John uses very specific concrete references—"sprints," "10Ks," and names of particular races—because he assumes that his friend James is familiar with the running scene. Because he has designed his argument to appeal appropriately to James's interests and knowledge, John's language choice is effective. If James were naive about running, then John would have to use terms at a higher level of abstraction—using "runs at alternating paces" for "sprints," "runs along a preset 6.2 mile course" for "10Ks," and the complete names and dates of the various races. Only by using more generalized references could John be sure that an inexperienced runner would understand and relate to his argument.

The second requirement of clarity is simplicity. Often when people have a choice, they will tend to use convoluted and ambiguous language to convey their argument when simpler language might be just as effective. In Chapter 6, we discussed the fallacy of equivocation wherein arguers actually exploit the vagueness in the meaning of a term in order to make a false claim. But such practices as circumlocution (using an unnecessarily large number of words to express an idea) and obfuscation (using words confusingly) do not have to be intentional. Their unintentional use often muddles up arguments and interferes with their effectiveness.

Because the objective of the arguer is to get the audience to understand the argument, the language used should be as simple and concise as possible:

> In my well-considered interpretation of the events preceding this encounter and considering what others have said to me as well as my own background, I think we should increase the expenditures for the bus fare by 10 cents.

A simpler way of conveying the same message is:

> I think we should raise the bus fare by 10 cents.

Generally, when an arguer has a choice, the words used should be as direct and simple as possible to get the message across. If the argument is not understood or if there is confusion about what the arguer actually is claiming, the argument will not be effective.

2. *Define terms when necessary.* If an arguer's argument hinges on a particular term and if there's a chance that an arguee might not understand the term in the way the arguer intended, then the term should be defined. By providing clear definitions, the arguer can help reduce unwanted connotations or ambiguities that might otherwise develop. For example:

> I think that regardless of the politics in any given country, we should provide the people with support—by support I don't mean military aid, I do mean economic and food assistance.

By defining "support," the arguer avoided possible pitfalls from a misinterpretation of what "support" is used to mean. Definition helps shed the connotation of military assistance and makes the claim more concrete.

Five ways of defining terms were explained in Chapter 9. They include giving examples of the term, describing the term's historical context, tracing the term's etymology, citing authoritative definitions, and describing ordinary usage. Any time an arguer's use of a term departs substantially from ordinary usage, the term should be defined and the new definition justified. Otherwise, the arguer can be nearly certain that arguees will understand and interpret the term differently than the arguer intended.

3. *Express arguments vividly.* An important dimension of an argument's persuasiveness is the vividness with which it is expressed. We can select words and modes of expression that depersonalize what we say and make it seem distant and remote from the audience. Using the passive voice, the antecedentless "it," and complex formal language makes what we say less vivid. Compare the following two arguments (which say essentially the same thing):

> Sometimes the debate over abortion asks the wrong question. What is truly at issue is not a balancing of the rights of one person against the rights of another. Rights are not zero sum, and they do not shrink when they are extended to someone else.[18]

> Sometimes the abortion controversy is directed at incorrect issues. It is believed that one person's prerogatives are counterbalanced against another's. Individuals' rights are not differentially assigned so that rights accorded to some individuals are removed from others.

The second passage uses the passive voice and such formal words as:

prerogatives

counterbalanced

differentially assigned

accorded

The original version uses active voice and everyday language. In addition, it employs colorful terms and metaphor to engage readers and enliven their interest, such as:

asks the wrong question

truly at issue

balancing . . .against

zero sum

shrink

When we make a problem or a description come alive for the arguee, we endow it with what one theorist calls "presence."[19] *Presence is a quality of argument which moves things near to us in space and time so they act directly on our sensibility.* This quality is best demonstrated by the following story:

> A king sees an ox on its way to sacrifice. He is moved to pity for it and orders that a sheep be used in its place. He confesses that he did so because he could see the ox, but not the sheep.[20]

We care much more about what is immediate to us than about that which is distant. Vivid language increases the immediacy of the arguer's subject and point of view.[21] By engaging his or her audience's care and concern, the arguer can use vividness to make arguments more effective.

4. *Avoid sexist and racist language.* Our discussion of the Sapir-Whorf principle, terministic screens, and the examples from *1984* earlier in this chapter made the point that language can limit and shape the way its users think and act. Women, minorities and other economically and culturally oppressed groups have become increasingly sensitive to language use that labels and disparages or devaluates them. Many language users are unaware of how their conscious forms of expression reflect unconscious assumptions about groups that may be a part of their audience. When those assumptions are negative and are negatively reflected in the claims an arguer makes, the argument's effectiveness is undermined.

Sexist use of language occurs in many of our habits. When we are referring to a group of mixed gender, we often use the masculine pronoun. The structure of our language typically gives men first priority.

> The men and women in this room . . .
>
> The men and women of this university . . .
>
> Mr. and Mrs. Smith

And women traditionally abandon part of their identity or definition upon marriage by giving up their "maiden" names.

Furthermore, women are often portrayed as children. The expression "women and children first" testifies to the linguistic equality women share with children. There are many terms used to define women as children or subhuman people. For instance, a woman may be called a "babe," "chick," "doll," or "fox."[22] Likewise, women are referred to as girls—even when they are 20, 30, 40, 50, and even 60 years of age ("The office girls got this for you").

In framing arguments, arguers often allow sexism to creep into their expression in very subtle ways. Can you detect it in the following paragraph?

> The standards of achievement in this profession are set by the men who have been most productive. The exceptional manager should recognize that his productivity depends upon his sales team and the women in his office staff.

A number of sexist uses of language are embedded in this passage. In the first sentence, "men" is used to refer generically to all practitioners of the profession (and they are *productive*). Again, in the second sentence, "the manager" is referred to by the masculine possessive pronoun "his." Furthermore, supervisors are characterized as male, while clericals ("the office staff") are assumed to be female. Slips such as these should be avoided.[23] Although nonsexist language rarely, if ever, alienates recipients, sexist language is almost certain to do so.

Unconscious racism in language use is also highly problematic. In the century following the Civil War, America became increasingly committed to equality among races and ethnic origins. In such Supreme Court cases as *Brown v. Board of Education* in 1954, in the Civil Rights Act of 1964, and in affirmative action measures, efforts have been systematically made to eliminate discrimination against minority groups.

These measures were important, but failed to provide for equality because, at least in part, they did nothing to override the attitudes of the people opposed to racial and ethnic equality. The laws changed, the language did not, and because language helps to shape a culture's reality, the attitudes were fostered by the language.

Civil rights leader Stokely Carmichael recognized the power of language as a barrier to racial equality when he spoke in 1967.

> The need of a free people is to be able to define their own terms and have those terms recognized by their oppressors. . .for white people to be allowed to define us by calling us Negroes, which means apathetic, lazy, stupid, and all those other things, is for us to accept those definitions. We must define what we are and move from our definitions and tell them to recognize what we are.[24]

Blacks and other minorities have objected to labels and terms of reference having negative connotations. The key terms to keep in mind when discussing minorities and minority issues are "respect" and "equality." Minorities should not be set apart unless there is good reason to do so, and if are, they should be referred to in nonoppressive ways. At one school, a discussion was held concerning salary differentials related to people's ethnic origin. Caucasians discussing the issue continually referred to themselves as "majority faculty." This self-reference reasserted their status within the system. When reminded that a term such as "nonminority faculty" might be more neutral, one officer responded that he was not about to make that concession. Evidently, he was well aware of the role language plays in reasserting power relations between Caucasians and minority groups in this country.

In framing arguments in language, arguers should make every possible effort to engage, befriend, and appeal to the recipient through the medium of their expression. Conversely, they should systematically avoid sexist and racist language along with obscenity or other inappropriate word choices. Nothing is to be gained by insulting or alienating recipients. It is in the arguer's best interest to word arguments with care, taste, and sensitivity for those to whom the argument is directed.

■ *Summary*

Language should not be used unconsciously or without concern; rather speakers should deliberately adapt language to their audience. Arguers, in particular, can enhance or inhibit their effectiveness through the uses they make of language. The purpose of this chapter is to enable arguers to understand, use, and criticize language as used in argument.

Language is the systematic coordination of grammar and vocabulary used to convey meaning. Although it is often thought of as a tool we use, language is also a tool that influences us. Words have meaning through the use and interpretations people make of them, but people's perceptions and experiences are also profoundly influenced by language itself. Since words and what they refer to are connected only by way of the thoughts of language users, there is room for misunderstanding in communication. By controlling the way they use language, arguers can prevent misunderstanding and enhance their own effectiveness in communication.

Words used to refer to objects or experiences have certain characteristics that influence their use in language. They are abstract—having general reference to broad classes of objects—or concrete—referring to specific or particular objects or experiences. They are also used denotatively as symbols with objective, generally agreed-upon meanings, or connotatively as symbols with subjective or emotive meaning for each individual. People manipulate words by replacing negative connotations with positive ones. These result in euphemisms such as "Peace Keeper" for first-strike nuclear missiles, "air support" for bombing, and "correctional facility" for prison.

In the 1950s anthropologists Edward Sapir and Benjamin Whorf proposed the theory that our system of language contributes greatly to how we think about and experience our social world and our physical reality. This can be demonstrated by such examples as George Orwell's *1984* in which a totalitarian government exercises thought control over its people by systematically altering the language which they speak.

The way language is used in argument is influenced by the six functions of language when it is used. Language is used emotively to express the feelings, attitudes, and emotions of people. Sometimes this results in fallacious argument when arguers intend to mislead recipients, or when recipients are unduly influenced by connotative language and the arguer's conviction rather than the facts of the matter under discussion. The phatic function of language, which is used socially to reinforce relationships between parties, seldom plays a role in argumentation. Used cognitively, language informs people about matters on which they are uninformed. It plays an argumentative role if providing the information alarms people and changes their attitude toward a problem or condition. Language used rhetorically is expressly intended to direct or influence thoughts and behaviors and plays a major role in argument. Language used metalingually comments upon the role of language itself and has an argumentative function when language is used to get a claim accepted or rejected. The poetic function of language emphasizes the structure or artistry of a message rather than its content, and plays a role in argument when the form of expression is used to hold recipients' attention and influence them to accept a claim. In any given argument, language may function in multiple ways simultaneously to enhance communication of the argument to the audience.

Understanding how language functions can assist arguers in getting their arguments understood, remembered, and adhered to by recipients. Four guidelines for using language can assist in this process. First, arguers should be clear. They should employ language that is sufficiently concrete to keep their messages interesting. They should also speak or write simply, avoiding convoluted or ambiguous language.

Second, arguers should define any terms that their recipients might misunderstand. This is particularly true when the terms have an important role in the argument and the arguers' usage of the terms departs from ordinary usage. Third, arguers should express their arguments vividly. Using active rather than passive voice, personalized constructions, and nonformal language along with colorful terms and metaphor will engage recipients and cause them to be more likely to accept an arguer's claim. Fourth, arguers should avoid sexist or racist language. Although few arguers intentionally try to offend recipients, many do so inadvertently by expressing their ideas in ways that set women and minorities apart as having less status in society than men and Caucasians. Concerted efforts to eliminate discriminatory forms of reference and ways of speaking will ensure that no recipients are inadvertently alienated by the way an argument is expressed.

Exercises

✳ **Exercise 1** In the chapter, we discussed Lincoln's Gettysburg Address. Following is a complete version of the speech. Read the speech and locate every use of language made by Lincoln. Next to each example, place

EM for emotive function of language

PH for phatic function of language

CO for cognitive function of language

RH for rhetorical function of language

ME for metalingual language

PO for poetic function of language

You may want to color-code each type of language using a felt marker for ease of identification. Once you have completed this task, tally each type of language used by Lincoln in the following space:

Language	Number of Times Used
Emotive	
Phatic	
Cognitive	
Rhetorical	
Metalingual	
Poetic	

What types of language were used most frequently? Least frequently? Why do you think Lincoln chose to use these types of language? Do they help or hurt the speech? How?

The Gettysburg Address

Four score and seven years ago our fathers brought forth on this continent a new nation, conceived in liberty, and dedicated to the proposition that all men are created equal.

Now we are engaged in a great civil war, testing whether that nation, or any nation so conceived and so dedicated, can long endure. We are met on a great battlefield of that war. We have come to dedicate a portion of that field, as a final resting place for those who here gave their lives, that that nation might live. It is altogether fitting and proper that we should do this.

But, in a larger sense, we cannot dedicate—we cannot consecrate—we cannot hallow—this ground. The brave men, living and dead, who struggled here have consecrated it, far above our poor power to add or detract. The world will little note, nor long remember what we say here, but it can never forget what they did here. It is for us the living, rather, to be dedicated here to the unfinished work which they who fought here have thus far so nobly advanced. It is rather for us to be here dedicated to the great task remaining before us—that from these honored dead we take increased devotion to that cause for which they gave the last full measure of devotion—that we here highly resolve that these dead shall not have died in vain—that this nation, under God, shall have a new birth of freedom—and that government of the people, by the people, for the people, shall not perish from the earth.

Exercise 2   Originally, S. I. Hayakawa proposed an abstraction ladder with Bessie the Cow as the most concrete symbol on the ladder. In the following space, draw an abstraction ladder that has you as the most concrete symbol.

Most Abstract

10.

 9.

 8.

 7.

 6.

 5.

 4.

 3.

 2.

 1.

Most Concrete

If you were introducing yourself to someone you had never met before, at what level would you begin?

Exercise 3   Each of the following words has a denotative and connotative meaning. Next to each word write the first definition that comes to mind and then look the word up. Is there a large difference? Why? Do you think your peers' answers would be closer to the connotative definitions you generated or the denotative definitions you looked up? Test it on five friends. What did your test show?

	Connotative	Denotative
school teacher		
Buick		
boss		
turkey		
sex		
trip		
work		
career		
education		
car		
emotional		

Notes

1. Abraham Lincoln, "Gettysburg Address," as cited in Philip B. Kunhardt, Jr., *A New Birth of Freedom* (Boston: Little, Brown and Co., 1983), 240.

2. Harold Zyskind, "A Rhetorical Analysis of the Gettysburg Address," *Journal of General Education* 4 (1950): 202–212. For other analyses of the rhetorical effects of this speech, see Ronald F. Reid, "Newspaper Response to the Gettysburg Address," *Quarterly Journal of Speech* 53 (1967): 50–60; and Barbara Warnick, "A Ricoeurian Approach to Rhetorical Criticism," *Western Journal of Speech Communication* 51 (1987): 227–244.

3. Gilbert Highet, "The Gettysburg Address," in *Readings in Speech*, 2d ed., ed. Haig A. Bosmajian (New York: Harper, 1971), 227.

4. C. K. Ogden and I. A. Richards, *The Meaning of Meaning* (London: Kegan, Paul Trench, Trubner, 1923).

5. S. I. Hayakawa, *Language in Thought and Action* (New York: Harcourt, Brace, 1964), 180.

6. *Webster's New Collegiate Dictionary*, s.v. "fag."

7. Benjamin L. Whorf, *Language, Thought, and Reality* (New York: John Wiley & Sons, 1956).

8. Whorf, 134.

9. Kenneth Burke, "Terministic Screens," in *Language as Symbolic Action* (Berkeley: University of California Press, 1966), 44–57.

10. George Orwell, *1984* (New York: Signet, 1977), 45–47.

11. Joseph DeVito, *The Psychology of Speech and Language: An Introduction to Psycholinguistics* (Washington, D.C.: Random House), 14–15.

12. Cliff Kincaid, "Playboy Hugh Hefner's Politics of Hedonism," *Conservative Digest* (August 1986): 16.

13. "Warning Signs of Suicide," *USA Today*, September 19, 1986, 10A. Copyright 1986, USA TODAY. Reprinted with permission.

14. "Media Can Help Prevent Teen Suicide," *USA Today,* September 19, 1986, p. 10A. Copyright 1986, USA TODAY. Reprinted with permission.

15. Highet, 227.

16. Kunhardt, 241.

17. George Orwell, "Politics and the English Language," in *Collected Essays,* (London: Mercury Books, 1961), 366–67.

18. Jack Kemp, "Why Abortion is a Human Rights Issue," *Conservative Digest* (August 1986): 40.

19. Chaim Perelman and Lucie Olbrechts-Tyteca, *The New Rhetoric: A Treatise on Argumentation,* trans. John Wilkinson and Purcell Weaver (Notre Dame, Ind.: University of Notre Dame Press, 1969), 116.

20. Vilfredo Pareto, *The Mind and Society* (New York: Harcourt, Brace, 1935), II, 1135, as cited in Perelman and Olbrechts-Tyteca, 116.

21. A wonderful little guide to making one's style more vivid is W. Strunk and E. B. White, *The Elements of Style,* 3d ed. (New York: Macmillan, 1979).

22. Haig A. Bosmajian, *The Language of Oppression* (Lanham, Md.: University Press of America, 1983), 118.

23. An excellent guide to how to avoid sexist and racist language is the American Psychological Association's *Publication Manual,* 3d ed. (Washington, D.C.: American Psychological Association, 1984), 43–49.

24. Stokely Carmichael, Address to students at Morgan State College, January 16, 1967, cited in Bosmajian, 45.

CHAPTER *12*

Arguers, Recipients, and Argumentation

■

CHAPTER OUTLINE

- **The Audience and Argumentation**
    Selecting the Starting Points
    Supporting Reasoning
    Using Evidence
    Organizing Arguments
    Additional Concerns about Audience
    Analyzing the Audience

- **The Arguer and Argumentation**
    Message Sources and their Influence
    Enhancing Credibility through Argument

- **Summary**

- **Exercises**

KEY CONCEPTS

strategies
source credibility
initial credibility
derived credibility
compliance

identification
internalization
trustworthiness
reluctant testimony

A student recently planned a speech to give to his argumentation class on piracy of computer software. Because the assignment required him to advocate a policy, he decided to try to convince his listeners that certain forms of software copying should be made legal. He gathered extensive information from the computer science and business libraries and publications of software manufacturers. In a technical but succinct analysis, he described how legalizing software duplication would provide economic and educational benefits for society. When he completed his presentation, he was certain that he had impressed and convinced his listeners with his complete information, thorough research, and carefully constructed reasoning. Can you imagine his surprise and disappointment when he discovered that his argumentation had failed?

The audience members said that they were bored and confused by his technical jargon, that he had not made the reasons for his position clear to them, and that they would need to know more before making a decision as to whether they favored his position. The few people in the class who did have some knowledge of the topic claimed he had cited only biased sources who stood to gain from indiscriminate software copying and had neglected the importance of copyright laws and protection. As you might imagine, this is an actual example rather than a hypothetical one. This student had somehow gone astray in planning and executing his speech. What had gone wrong?

Clearly, the student had done many things correctly. He had selected a topic on which he was well informed and in which he was interested. He had carefully researched the topic and had collected evidence to support his points. He had organized his speech logically and used sound reasoning. Unfortunately, he failed to consider some fundamental questions about his audience and their attitudes that were vital in getting his message accepted. These included: How much does the audience already know about the topic? What are the audience's present values and beliefs about software licensing? What sources are they likely to accept as credible? How should the speech be organized so that the arguments will have the greatest impact? How many arguments can be developed in the time available? What are the audience's attitudes toward the arguer and what can the arguer do to appear more believable to recipients?

This speaker had a good, well-substantiated, carefully reasoned argument, but he had forgotten his audience—its capacities, interests, and perceptions of him as a speaker. You may recall that in Chapter 1 we described three perspectives on argument—logical, dialectical, and rhetorical. The first perspective is concerned with the soundness of an arguer's premises and reasoning, the second with argument as a process of inquiry to uncover significant issues, and the third with argument in a social and political context and with the characteristics of audiences to whom arguments are directed. In the first nine chapters of this book, we were concerned primarily with the logical and dialectical dimensions of argument. In this chapter, we will emphasize its rhetorical dimensions—how arguments are designed and presented so as to influence specific audiences.

When arguments occur, the people for whom they are intended do not function as blank slates or logic machines responding only to the validity of an arguer's reasoning or evidence. Audiences are also invariably influenced by the rhetorical aspects of the message situation. These include the audience's own past experience, knowledge, and values; their inclination to believe what the arguer says; the language the arguer uses; and the way the argument is presented. This chapter will emphasize the ways in which such factors influence the persuasiveness of arguments. It will explain how audience members' knowledge, values and attitudes affect the use of premises, selection of evidence, and support for inferences. It will also consider how arguments can be organized to have the greatest impact on audiences and how arguers can enhance their own credibility so as to make their claims more persuasive.

Therefore, this chapter will focus on persuasive strategies. *Strategies are means used to adapt arguments and make them appealing to audiences.* The use of strategies does not require you to abandon your position or fundamentally alter your analysis. Rather, communicating strategically sometimes requires you to change the way a message is structured and presented. After all, arguments have a function and that function is to win acceptance for claims by getting audiences to attend to, understand, think about, and respond to a message. To elicit a favorable response, arguers should consider the issues raised in this chapter. Its purpose is to enable arguers to select evidence, state premises, organize their arguments, and present themselves in such a way as to enhance the acceptability and credibility of their arguments.

The Audience and Argumentation

At the beginning of this chapter, we described a student who prepared and presented an unsuccessful speech on software licensing. His speech failed to persuade his audience because he forgot a basic fact about persuasive arguments. Arguments are not prepared for the benefit of their author, nor are they meant to be written and filed away somewhere. Instead, they are intended for a particular set of audience members and must be adapted to be persuasive to that specific group.

These people—potential readers or listeners of an argumentative message—should influence the planning and preparation of an argument in at least four areas: selecting starting points for premises and evidence, finding backing or support for the arguer's reasoning, applying evidence in support of claims, and deciding what order to use in advancing various claims. One purpose of this section is to explain why and how audiences' values, knowledge, needs, and interests are relevant to these aspects of argument preparation. A second purpose of this section is to suggest some methods arguers can use to find out information about their audiences before they construct their arguments. Sometimes arguments are prepared before they are presented; at other times arguments must be adjusted and adapted as arguers proceed. In either case, audience analysis can make arguments more persuasive, and the last part of this section will suggest how this can be done.

Selecting the Starting Points

In Chapter 1, we observed that, in order to function as evidence in an argument, a statement must fall below the level of dispute—that is, audience members must agree with it. If a statement is uncontroversial and accepted by the people to whom the argument is made, then the arguers can get started "on the right track" and proceed to build an argument chain. Otherwise, the arguer will run into trouble and may be derailed. Consider the following two examples from sales interviews:

Car Salesperson:	This late model is a wonderful deal. The gas milage is exceptional and the car only has 30,000 miles on it. For $5,000 you can't beat it!
Car Buyer:	Oh, yes I can! I saw the same make, model, and year at Alternative Motors for $4,500, and it only had 20,000 miles on it!
ACME Representative:	As you know, the most important things to look for in copiers are versatility and the number of features they offer. Our new model reduces, enlarges, and sorts up to twenty copies and has seven print selections.
Client:	All these features are relatively unimportant to me. After my experience with your last copier, my concern is reliability. How many times will I have to call for repairs when it doesn't work?

In both cases, the arguers made incorrect assumptions about their arguees' values and priorities. The car salesperson assumed that the buyer would agree that no better deal was available and the copier representative assumed that the customer would value versatility over reliability, convenience, and other factors that might influence the client's purchasing decision. False starts such as these undermine arguers' credibility and make successful presentation of their claims especially difficult.

It is important, therefore, to have some knowledge of the audience's values and attitudes so as to be assured that premises will be accepted and not challenged or rejected. What are the recipients' needs and interests? What are their priorities? In the topic area in which the argument is made, what do they value? Finding out the answers to such questions will ensure that the process of making the argument goes smoothly.

Furthermore, arguers should be aware of their audience's level of understanding and knowledge of the topic. Premises and evidence that are not comprehended will not go far in getting recipients to accept arguments. Consider the following example:

Computer Salesperson:	The 486 machine has 2 MB of memory, a 32 KB cache, and special video enhancer.

CLIENT: Why is 2 MB of memory important? What's a cache? Why
                                        do I need a video enhancer?

In order to get her client interested in the product, this salesperson will have to
explain how the computer will meet the client's needs in terms that are meaningful
at her client's level of understanding.

To avoid unwarranted assumptions, confusion, and circular reasoning, then,
advocates must know their audiences well enough to estimate accurately their level
of knowledge and prior beliefs about the topic being discussed. It is important to
identify correctly the premises an audience will be likely to accept as a basis for one's
argument. One can then begin on a firm footing, avoid belaboring the point, and
move forward to establish a conclusion knowing that a foundation for one's argument has been laid in what the audience regards as "true." Methods for analyzing
audiences to discover such information will be described later in this section.

Supporting Reasoning

Arguers make arguments in various contexts—law, business, science, etc. When they
connect their claims to evidence by means of reasoning, they rely on certain principles, rules, or conventions that shore up or support the reasoning they use. In
Chapter 7 these were called *backing*—statements used to support or legitimate the
inferences or warrants expressing an argument's reasoning. If an arguer's reasoning
is challenged by an opponent or by members of the audience, the arguer will have to
produce something to further support his or her reasoning. That "something" will
usually consist of laws, principles, conventions, or value hierarchies the audience
accepts. The point to be made in this section is that knowing the audience well
enough to know what is accepted can greatly assist in making arguments effectively.

To review the ways in which principles and values function to support reasoning, consider two examples. In the first, a defense attorney attempts to persuade a
jury not to convict a defendant accused of murder based on circumstantial evidence.

DEFENSE ATTORNEY: Just because the defendant was seen leaving the victim's
                                        home the evening of the murder, owned a 22-caliber
                                        gun of the type used in the crime, and had recently
                                        quarreled with the victim, we cannot conclude he is
                                        guilty. His guilt must be proven beyond a reasonable
                                        doubt.

The attorney's *claim* is "you should not vote for a conviction." His *evidence* is that
the defendant was *only* seen leaving the home, owned a 22-caliber gun, and had
quarreled with the victim. The *warrant* or *inference* is unstated but is probably that
the signs shown in the evidence are insufficient to support a conviction. Why?
Because in our judicial system an accused person is assumed to be innocent until
proven guilty beyond a reasonable doubt. If challenged, the defense attorney would

further support his reasoning by stating this principle which he knows is recognized and accepted by the members of the jury.

As a second example, consider a student making a classroom speech opposing capital punishment. Here she attempts to refute an argument often put forward by supporters of capital punishment:

> Some people have argued that capital punishment saves taxpayers money because it costs society $35,000 per year to keep an inmate in prison. Over a lifetime that amounts to hundreds of thousands of dollars. I would argue that that does not mean we should put a person to death. How can we put a monetary value on human life, particularly when there is the chance that the accused may be proven innocent?

The *evidence* consists of the opposition's cost argument; her *claim* is that cost is an insufficient reason for putting a person to death; and her *reasoning* is that a monetary value cannot be placed on human life. To back up her reasoning, the arguer relies upon a value hierarchy she knows her audience to hold—that preservation of life is a supreme value in our society. You may recall from Chapter 9 that a value hierarchy is an ordering of values such that some are ranked more highly than others. The way audiences are known to prioritize values can be used by arguers to support their inferences and reasoning, but only if arguers know how values are ordered by the recipients of the argument.

Knowledge about the audience, therefore, can provide materials useful for supporting reasoning. Principles, conventions, rules, laws, value hierarchies, and other cultural artifacts act as resources arguers can call upon in constructing their arguments. Arguers preparing their arguments should ask questions about their audiences such as: What principles and laws are recognized by my audience? How do audience members order their values and priorities? What rules or conventions do they accept and follow? By determining the answers to such questions, an arguer can locate a foundation for the reasoning and inferences drawn in the argument as a whole.

Using Evidence

An arguer who knows how audiences are likely to respond to the use of evidence will generally be more effective than one who does not. A good deal of experimental research has been done on the use and effectiveness of evidence in speeches and arguments. The results of this research have at least three implications for the planning and presentation of arguments.

First, using evidence is generally more effective than not using it, other things being equal. Researchers who have compared the effectiveness of messages with evidence to those without it have found that messages that use evidence are more influential with their audiences.[1] In no case did the use of evidence *decrease* message effectiveness.[2] This is probably because most audiences are unwilling to take the arguer's word alone. They want to be reassured that the arguer's position is also supported by authorities whom they respect. Arguers, then, should use evidence to support claims the audience is likely to question. They have very little to lose and much to gain by doing so.

Second, arguers should be aware of authorities that the audience is likely to perceive as credible and unbiased on a given topic. Calling upon the statements and observations of individuals perceived as credible enhances one's own credibility. For example, the Rev. Jesse Jackson is generally considered to have had experience in the area of civil rights. Likewise, most people view Lee Iacocca as a leader in American business and as a role model of the values and ideals in his field; for this reason, he is considered credible when the condition of the American automobile industry is discussed.

Arguers should also be aware of the audience's perceptions of bias in authoritative statements. You may recall from Chapter 4 that a biased source is one who has personal, political, or economic reasons for supporting a particular point of view. A biased source has a "hidden agenda"—a vested interest in the outcome of the matter being discussed. Audiences are suspicious of biased sources and are likely to reject arguments based on their opinions.[3] Before an arguer cites the American Tobacco Institute's claims that there is no causal link between smoking and cancer or the National Rifle Association's arguments against gun control, the arguer should consider the effect of these authorities on the audience. Even if the facts or opinions of such authorities are well founded, what they say may be rejected by an audience because of its suspicion of their motives.

Third, arguers should introduce facts and information which is "news" to the audience rather than relying on information already well known to them. When people initially encounter evidence that shocks or disturbs them, they make an effort to reconcile or cope with it. Once the evidence has entered their cognitive systems and they have dealt with it, they are much less impressed or disturbed by it when they encounter it again. For this reason, research on the effects of evidence shows that people are more influenced by novel information than by information they have heard before.[4] The implication of this is that arguers should be aware of the nature of their audience's prior exposure to information on a topic. A fact which is well known and has been widely disseminated and discussed will not be as effective in supporting an arguer's claims as the kinds of facts and data gleaned from in-depth, specialized research on a topic. The latter is more likely to uncover information unknown to the public which dramatizes the nature and extent of a problem or a value discrepancy.

Therefore, research on the relationship between the use of evidence and audience reaction to an argument suggests three courses of action arguers should take: (1) They should use evidence to support any claim about which readers or listeners might be skeptical. (2) They should rely on authorities the audience is likely to respect and accept. (3) They should use information that is "news" to the audience rather than that which is familiar. As we observed in Chapter 4, evidence should also be expert, recent, relevant, accurate, and consistent with itself and with other sources. But knowing enough about the audience to select appropriate authorities and adjust information to the audience's level of experience and awareness of a topic will enhance the persuasiveness of most arguments.

Organizing Arguments

Students of argument frequently ponder the order in which to organize the arguments they have constructed. They often ask themselves such questions as: "Should I openly state my conclusion or thesis or leave it implicit?" "Where should I place my strongest arguments so they will have the greatest possible impact on the audience?" "Should I organize my argument around possible objections to my position?" "Should I use all my arguments, even the weaker ones?" and "Should I present both sides or one side of the question?" Arguers who ask such questions want to organize their arguments so that audiences will respond to them favorably. Although their decisions will probably be affected by the requirements of the topic being discussed and the nature of the situation, some information based on research about audience reaction to various patterns of organization may be helpful.

Should one openly state one's conclusion when making a controversial argument? Researchers have compared the use of explicit conclusions with conclusions which were implied or left unstated and have found that explicitly stated conclusions were generally more effective.[5] One researcher speculated that when claims are not explicitly stated, audiences fill in the gaps with claims and arguments of their own—ones that frequently go against what the arguer had intended.[6] The arguers in such cases can lose control of the argument. If the audience is intelligent and the argument very clearly organized, the audience may be favorably influenced even if the conclusion is not stated. Otherwise, arguers who fail to state their claim clearly may lose the concurrence of their audience.

Should one present both sides of an issue or only one side when making an extended argument? In answering this question, one should consider at least three factors besides the nature of the audience. The first is the nature of the topic itself. When two courses of action are obviously available and are recognized as such, for example, it is desirable to consider them both. A second concern is the time or space available for the argument. If time allows, a thorough analysis of all aspects of a topic is usually the best course of action. If time is limited, however, one must often develop thoroughly only the side one favors so that sufficient evidence and reasoning can be used to support one's claims. A third concern relates to the ethics of argumentation as we discussed it in Chapter 1. Arguers have an obligation, so far as is possible, to fully inform their recipients about available alternatives so that they can make informed choices about the best choice or course of action. For this reason, slighting or misrepresenting opposing points of view is undesirable.

Research into the characteristics of audiences has revealed a fourth concern affecting whether one- or two-sided messages are better. Certain audiences do respond more favorably to one-sided presentations.[7] These include audiences already favorably predisposed to the arguer's thesis and those who are poorly informed about the topic. Both types of audiences are evidently confused or disoriented by complex or discrepant information.

When the audience is well informed or disagrees with the arguer's position, however, the two-sided analysis is preferable. Audience members who favor the opposing position will tend to rehearse counterarguments or focus on silent refutation to a one-sided speech rather than concentrating on the advocate's message. When the arguer presents both sides of the question, he or she gives the impression of being fair and well informed, and thus the arguer's credibility is enhanced. Furthermore, hearing both sides of the question enables the audience to be more resistant to subsequent efforts to support the position the arguer opposes. One group of researchers referred to this resistance to counterpersuasion as the "inocula-tion effect" and concluded that "the refutation of arguments that are the same or similar to arguments to which a receiver will be exposed later . . .will reduce the impact of the counterpersuasion."[8] In many cases, then, a two-sided analysis will be more informative, fairer, more likely to have long-term influence on audiences than a one-sided message.

A two-sided analysis should not be confused with the sort of organizational for-mat that uses objections to the advocate's position as starting points around which the message is organized. A message organized in this way would begin with a pre-view like: "I will present three major objections to drug testing and show why they are untrue." This type of approach to a controversial issue is usually ineffective for two reasons. First, by merely *listing* objections to a proposal (without explaining the reasons behind them) and then extensively responding to them, one "stacks the deck" against the position one opposes and arouses audience suspicions about one's fairness and objectivity. Second, to begin with the objections to one's point of view gives the impression that one is on the defensive. Audiences are reminded of the opposing viewpoint and may focus on that rather than on the thesis the arguer is try-ing to uphold. Therefore, if a two-sided message is used, the arguer should give approximately equal time to both sides of the question.

Sometimes advocates wonder about how selective they should be about the arguments they use. Usually, they have a large number of potential arguments avail-able. Should they use them all? Or should they be selective, using only the best and most cogent in support of their thesis? Generally, selective application of only the strongest arguments is the better course of action. Ruth Anne Clark, a persuasion theorist, explains why:

> There is a major danger in this policy [of using weak arguments]. Members of the audi-ence who are predisposed to disagree with the advocate will look for some justification for discounting the validity of the entire message. Although it seems reasonable that such individuals would simply ignore arguments they do not agree with, often this is not the case. If an argument seems invalid or insignificant, they will concentrate on it, frequently ignoring all other arguments. A week later, if someone asks them what the message was about, they may recall only the argument they found invalid.[9]

Clark's observation reminds us of why we should not use weak arguments indiscrim-inately. Not only do they undermine our credibility, but they also give those who are opposed to our proposal a reason not to accept it.

The recognition that the arguments available for construction of a message have various degrees of strength implies another question about the relation between the audience and the organization of the message: Where should the stronger arguments be placed? People interested in this question have studied the cognitive processes and recall patterns people use when they respond to arguments. They have found that audiences are most likely to remember what comes at the beginning and end of messages.[10] This is called the primacy-recency effect. Whether placement of a strong argument at the beginning or at the end of a message is more effective depends on situational and other factors, but arguers are generally well advised to place their strongest arguments at either of the two positions.

Additional Concerns About Audience

The implications of an audience-centered orientation to argument construction that we have explored do not exhaust the ways in which a concern for audience affects argument success. Consistent awareness of the audience enhances the effectiveness of most arguments. Too often, arguers seem almost exclusively concerned with why they hold a view rather than with why their audiences ought to subscribe to it.[11] Considering the audience's orientations should affect the arguer's choices throughout composition of the message.

First, the arguer should consider whether the audience is as concerned about or interested in the topic as he or she is. Often the first challenge arguers must overcome is audience apathy or indifference. The more remote the topic from the daily lives or concerns of the audience, the harder the arguer will have to work to make it immediate and significant. Vivid examples of the nature and impact of the problem or situation, description of its effect on the daily lives of audience members, and carefully selected information regarding its scope and importance can help to overcome audience indifference. All this should come relatively early in the message.

Second, arguers should be sensitive to audience concerns when they select arguments for inclusion in their messages. In earlier chapters we have provided you with numerous types of arguments and with a variety of formats for making an extended argument. In deciding which of these to use or to emphasize, you should ask "What is the audience most concerned about?" For example, if it is likely that the moral and ethical dimensions of a topic will be of central concern to the audience, you should use a value analysis such as that described in Chapter 9 to discuss the topic. (Topics such as abortion, euthanasia, and capital punishment are prone to value-based analysis.) If the causes and existence of a problem are likely to be of most concern, then a problem/solution case might be most appropriate. If, on the other hand, the audience might agree that there's a problem but is primarily concerned with what to do about it, then comparative advantages analysis might be best. (Examples of the latter might be juvenile crime or drug and substance abuse.) Arguers often do not have unlimited time to discuss a topic. Their selection of arguments and their strategies for analysis should therefore be determined by what is of greatest concern to the audience for whom their message is intended.

Third, arguers should be aware of beliefs or reservations that might interfere with the audience's willingness to accept their thesis. What problems or facts likely to be known by the audience might undermine the arguer's analysis? For example, suppose someone wanted to argue that the drinking age should be lowered to 18 nationwide. Anyone defending such a proposal would have to address the problem of a rise in DWI arrests and alcohol-related auto accidents among young people. Or suppose an advocate argued that defense spending should be dramatically curtailed and the funds used for other purposes. The audience would need to be reassured that such a measure would not reduce our military preparedness and expose the nation to war or to military aggression. Although it is inadvisable to devote one's entire message to refuting possible objections, advocates should consider and deal with obvious objections that would readily occur to many or most audience members.

Analyzing the Audience

It is hoped that our description in this section of the many ways audience values and attitudes should affect how you plan and present your argument has convinced you that a knowledge of your audience is important to the success of your argument. But how is information about a particular arguee or audience to be obtained? In this section, we will briefly suggest some strategies for collecting such information.

First, it is important to remember that certain characteristics of audiences discovered by researchers are true of most audiences and most people as individuals. As we have explained, you can generally expect your recipients to want to hear or read evidence in support of your claims, to remember best those arguments which come at the beginning and end of your message, to discount authorities they consider biased, and to react negatively (and disproportionately) to weak or bogus arguments. You should keep these general tendencies in mind when making most arguments.

In addition, any recipients of any argument in a particular situation will have special needs, interests, values, and attitudes. How do you find these out? While most of the strategies for discovering them are commonsensical, they are often overlooked. For example, how often has a salesperson approached you in person or on the telephone and made a sales pitch without bothering to ask you any questions about your possible needs or interests concerning the product? If you are in a situation in which you can ask questions of an arguee or members of an audience so as to obtain information relevant to your topic, do so. Often arguments in an interview, conversation, or discussion can be made much more successfully if arguees are simply asked about their interests, concerns, needs, and values. Such questions as the following are helpful:

Could you please describe what you know about _____?

What are the sources of your information on _____?

What individuals or publications do you regard as authoritative on this topic?

What aspects or features of _____ concern you most?

What changes, if any, would you like to see in areas related to _____?

Of course, the answers to such questions will only be helpful if put to use to help you decide what premises to base your argument on, what information will be novel and interesting to the arguees, what authorities to use for evidence, what values to emphasize, and what alternatives to advocate.

Furthermore, if you will be speaking or writing for a larger group, it is important to obtain information about the group as a whole. If you know in advance that you will be making an argument to a specific group, you can talk with group members, read the group's publications, or attend prior meetings of the group. Obtaining information about the group will yield knowledge of the members' ages, political and religious affiliations, educational levels, economic status, ethnicity, and occupations. Since these factors often influence audience members' values and interests and indicate their level of intelligence and knowledge about the topic, obtaining such information will help you to make decisions about how to organize, explain, and present your claims. At best, the process of adjusting your argument to your audience will be a result of generalization and educated guessing, but information you obtain about your audience will nevertheless give you something to go on as you make choices in preparing and communicating your argument.

■ *The Arguer and Argumentation*

In the 1968 presidential campaign, opponents of Richard Nixon mass-produced a campaign button portraying a picture of a shifty-eyed Nixon and below it the question "Would you buy a used car from this man?" The button's producers were attempting to impugn Nixon's source credibility. *Source credibility refers to an arguer's ability to be believed and trusted by recipients.* The buttons functioned as an argument with an implied claim: "If you wouldn't trust this man enough to buy a used car from him, you should not elect him president." The buttonmakers counted on the public's recollection of charges that Nixon had illegally used campaign funds in 1952, that he had used questionable campaign tactics in the past, and that he had been an ill-humored bad sport after losing a campaign for governor of California in 1962. The button was intended to remind the public of all this and to cause them to question once again Nixon's trustworthiness and sense of integrity. Factors such as expertise, trustworthiness, and integrity cause people to accept claims because they have confidence in the character of the person making them. Such factors also contribute to an arguer's source credibility.

The importance of credibility as a factor in persuasion has been recognized at least since the time of Aristotle's *Rhetoric,* written over 2,000 years ago. Aristotle identified the personal character of the speaker as one of the three modes of persuasion and called it *ethos.* (The other two modes are *pathos,* the way the audience's emotions put them in a certain frame of mind, and *logos,* the rational proof offered within the message.) Of *ethos,* Aristotle said:

> Persuasion is achieved by the speaker's personal character where the speech is so spoken as to make us think him credible. We believe good men more fully and more readily than

others: this is true generally whatever the question is, and absolutely true where exact certainty is impossible and opinions are divided. This kind of persuasion, like the others, should be achieved by what the speaker says, not by what people think of his character before he begins to speak.[12]

Aristotle's statements about credibility bring out four points which should be kept in mind when we consider its relationship to argumentation. First, credibility is not a characteristic that the arguer possesses but one that is *attributed* to the arguer by the recipients. When Aristotle said that the "speech is spoken so as to make us think [the speaker] credible," he emphasized the fact that how the speaker appears and what he or she does lead recipients to form certain impressions and beliefs, both about the speaker and about the claims that are made. These impressions and beliefs then influence the recipients so as to cause them to accept or reject the speaker's message.

A second and related point is that credibility is a field- and context-dependent phenomenon. If credibility results from what recipients perceive about the arguer rather than from intrinsic characteristics of the arguer, then it will vary from one time and situation to another, depending on what an arguer does or says. For example, once elected, Nixon found his credibility rising after foreign policy successes such as his trips to China and Russia and the settlement of the Vietnam war, and dropping sharply once the revelations about Watergate became known to the public.[13] Even within a speech or during reception of a message, the credibility of an arguer may increase or decrease depending on how recipients perceive and react to the points made by the arguer.[14]

The third point Aristotle made is that we value credibility most "where certainty is impossible and opinions are divided." If we ourselves cannot check out facts to find out whether a claim is true or if the claim is value-based rather than fact-based, we will rely upon credibility heavily as a source of our belief. Four decades of research in social psychology and communication have confirmed the importance of credibility.[15] Having reviewed this research, R. Glen Hass concluded, "Few areas of research . . . have produced results as consistent as the findings that sources high in expertise and/or trustworthiness are more persuasive than those low in these qualities."[16] The implications of this for argument, of course, are that one should design one's arguments so as to enhance the audience's perceptions of one's expertise and trustworthiness. The last section of this chapter will suggest means of enhancing credibility so as to make arguments more persuasive.

The fourth point Aristotle made is a distinction between the credibility "achieved by what the speaker says" and that attributed to the speaker based on prior reputation. This latter form is called initial credibility. *Initial credibility is based on an arguer's credentials, status, and reputation as known to recipients before they hear or read the message.* Although initial credibility is an important factor in persuasion, its role is based largely on noncognitive factors in the recipients' response to the arguer—the extent to which they feel attracted to the arguer or attribute prestige to him or her. *Derived credibility results from what is said in the message—the quality of the claims and evidence used and the ways arguers employ their own expertise to get their claims accepted.* Compared with initial credibility, derived credibility depends much more on the recipients' cognitive responses—what they think about the arguer's claims, the extent to which they produce counterarguments, and their assessment of the quality of an arguer's evidence.

Because this is a book on argumentation and because we focus upon the rational dimensions of a message, we will emphasize derived credibility. Specifically, the remainder of this section will consider how credibility works generally to enhance the persuasiveness of arguments. After a brief explanation of the noncognitive factors in the persuasiveness of a message source, we will focus on cognitive factors—how the expertise and trustworthiness of an argument source influence acceptance of its claims. Having explained this process, we will offer specific recommendations for structuring arguments so as to enhance the recipients' impressions of an arguer's expertise and trustworthiness.

Message Sources and Their Influence

Social psychologists who have studied persuasion and compliance gaining have identified three major ways that people get others to comply or agree with their requests or claims. They are compliance, identification, and internalization.[17] The first two depend heavily on nonlogical responses to messages and are independent of many of the reasoning processes described in this book. The third, however, is closely related to the quality of argument in a message and will be carefully considered later in this section.

Compliance is the use of rewards and punishments by a powerful source to get recipients to believe or act in a certain manner. A very familiar example is shown in the way students undertake an academic assignment. They recognize that the teacher possesses the means to reward for the work in the form of a favorable grade, so they carefully structure their work to conform to the teacher's expectations. In order for a person to get acceptance of a position through rewards and punishments, other people must believe that person has the resources to reward or punish them and cares whether or not they comply.[18] Argumentation, however, is not a necessary condition for compliance. A teacher *may* attempt to justify an assignment; a supervisor *may* explain a work order. But such actions are not required in order for the outcome they desire to be produced. The power they possess by itself causes others to do as they say. This form of influence is therefore relatively unimportant for our own purposes.

Identification is influence that occurs because people find a source attractive and wish to enhance their own self-concepts by establishing a relationship with the source. People identify with other people whom they like and admire. People often want to be like someone else who possesses traits similar or complementary to their own. This identification plays a prominent role in advertising. Because we want to be attractive and sexy like the models in their ads, we buy Jordache jeans. Because we admire the athletic prowess of Larry Bird or Ken Griffey, Jr., we are persuaded to buy the athletic shoes and products that they endorse. Ray Charles's musical ads for

Pepsi appeal to a wide range of the American public, whereas Ed McMahon's endorsement of Publisher's Clearinghouse gives that operation credibility for some audiences.

Hass has observed that attitudes changed through identification "are not incorporated into the individual's system of beliefs and values; nor are they maintained independent of the message source."[19] In other words, people's acceptance of an argument because of identification is not related to message content but instead to the identity of its source. If the source loses his or her attractiveness or changes the claim in the message, then the recipients will change their own positions as well. This was demonstrated in a rather amusing experiment that showed the influence of attractiveness. Experimenters designed a questionnaire, and a female confederate volunteered to assist by contributing to the group discussions the experimenters would lead. She would make the same responses in both discussions, and the same people would participate in both groups. For one discussion, she was made up to look very attractive with a stylish hairdo, chic clothing, and becoming makeup. In the other condition, she appeared repulsive with ugly clothing, messy hair, and the trace of a moustache on her upper lip. The results showed that in the attractive form she was much more effective in influencing the group.[20] The group's reactions were based solely on her attractiveness and not on cognitive processes. They had not thought about her message or about its quality.

Unlike compliance and identification, internalization is based on the thought recipients give to the content of a message. *Internalization is a process in which people accept an argument by thinking about it and by integrating it into their cognitive systems.* While attitudes and beliefs acquired because of compliance or identification often fade or disappear when the message source loses power or attractiveness, attitudes and beliefs that are internalized often persist and are maintained.

Before continuing our discussion of internalization and the form of source credibility connected with it, we should pause to stress here that, like all category schemes, this three-part division of source influence by means of compliance, identification, and internalization is somewhat oversimplified. Power, attractiveness, and content-related credibility often are closely related in any given argumentative situation. If a confident, attractive, highly respected supervisor explains a new marketing plan to subordinates and details a strategy for implementing the plan, that supervisor has clearly influenced the subordinates in all three ways simultaneously. Furthermore, one study of attractiveness revealed that attractive persuaders also tended to be perceived as better communicators, more highly educated, and better informed.[21] In many situations, then, it would be very difficult, if not impossible, to separate any one of these three forms from the other two.

Nevertheless, researchers have linked internalization most closely to what is actually said in the message. People who believe an argument because of its content are most affected by two aspects of the arguer's credibility—expertise and trustworthiness. Expertise was defined in Chapter 4 as the quality of having background knowledge and information on a subject. It depends on whether people believe an arguer knows the correct position on a topic. *Trustworthiness depends on whether people believe the arguer is motivated to tell them the truth.*[22] Although expertise and trustworthiness are often established partly by initial credibility (the arguer's reputation for being knowledgeable, sincere, and honest), what the arguer actually says and does while presenting the argument is even more vital.

There are five situational factors that determine the importance of expertise and trustworthiness in judging an arguer's credibility. First, expertise and trustworthiness are especially influential when the question being discussed appears to have a "right" and "wrong" answer. For example, if the question is whether violence on television causes violent behavior in children, we are more likely to accept the claims of a media scholar who has studied the relationship than we are the claims of the "average" parent. However, if the question relates to values and preferences, such as what television programs are most enjoyable and entertaining, we may be heavily influenced by persons we find attractive.[23]

Second, the less involved people are in a message and the less knowledge they have of the topic, the more influenced they will be by the credibility of the source. Presumably, people with low levels of knowledge and interest are not prepared or inclined to think about the content of arguments or to weigh the merit of claims and evidence advanced in their support. Arguers with low credibility who must address uninformed and disinterested recipients must therefore cope with a greater challenge than arguers with high credibility.

Third, people who hear and read arguments from arguers with varying degrees of credibility will tend to forget who made the argument and remember only its content. So people who are initially influenced by an arguer's credibility will later forget the source and remember only the arguments made. Researchers call this the "sleeper effect." While research experiments showing this phenomenon have been somewhat inconsistent, they do indicate that often people forget the identity of a message source and remember only what was said.[24]

Fourth, expertise seems particularly important when recipients disagree strongly with the position an arguer favors. In a situation in which the position advanced is very controversial and in basic disagreement with the recipients' position, a highly credible source will be more persuasive than one who has less credibility. In one experiment reported by Richard E. Petty and John T. Cacioppo, the argument concerned how many hours of sleep per night were necessary. It was attributed either to a Nobel Prize-winning physiologist or to a YMCA director. The highly credible source influenced recipients even when he advocated extreme positions (such as two or three hours of sleep per night). When the less-expert source advocated the same extreme position, however, recipients were much less likely to believe it.[25] The researchers in this study concluded that the more extreme the discrepancy between an arguer and his or her audience, the more pronounced will be the influence of credibility in producing attitude change.

Fifth, as we emphasize in the last section of this chapter, it is vital that recipients perceive a source as being free of bias and vested interest and concerned primarily with their welfare. Researchers have found that subjects were more influenced by a message when they thought arguers were unaware they were being overheard and thus did not intend to persuade them.[26] Research has also shown that when arguers are expected to have a personal interest in one side of an issue and actually favor the other side, they have high credibility. This indicates, for example, that a union officer who opposes a strike will be more likely to be believed than one who advocates a strike simply because he would be expected to do the latter. These results and others indicate that recipients' perception of arguers' objectivity, fairness, sincerity, and disinterestedness all contribute to their trustworthiness and thus to their credibility.

Enhancing Credibility through Argument

A moderate- to low-credibility arguer such as a student or entry level professional worker faces a challenge every time he or she produces a persuasive message. That challenge is to enhance credibility through and by means of the message itself. As we explained earlier, this is derived credibility which results from the qualities of the message content and the arguer's effort to have recipients believe that the arguer has their best interests in mind. When prior reputation and qualifications are not a major factor in audience perception, most arguers will have to implement the strategies for credibility enhancement described in this section. Let us examine some of these strategies and how they work in practice.

Arguers have three goals related to credibility—first, to have their recipients form a favorable initial impression of them; second, to get attention focused on the content of their message; and third, to develop audience perception of their expertise and trustworthiness. The first two are preliminary but necessary conditions for the development of the third. Initial impressions are based on the source's attractiveness and self-presentation. Although impressions formed on this basis are superficial, they are important. Arguers who cause negative perceptions because of careless appearance or an offhand or grating manner create a deficit against which they must work in order to get their message fairly considered. If the argument is orally presented, such matters as appearance, delivery, and vocal mannerisms will be significant. If it is in written form, poor style, misspellings, and other visual cues will affect the reader.

If a communicator has made a favorable initial impression through an attractive (or at least not unattractive) presentation, the next task is to win a favorable consideration of claims and evidence by holding the listeners' or readers' attention and keeping them engaged in the argument. This is essential to the process of internalization by which audiences integrate new beliefs and attitudes into their cognitive systems through active consideration of the arguer's claims. Many strategies for accomplishing this aim have been suggested throughout this book. They include use of examples close to the recipients' experiences, concrete information, good style, personal narrative, novel and unknown facts, and other materials contributing to the immediacy of the message. As we noted in the last section, people who have low involvement in the arguer's topic and little prior knowledge of it will attend more to the credibility of the source than to the content of the message. The low- to moderate-credibility arguer, therefore, should expend effort in getting recipients to actively attend to and consider the message.

The next item an arguer should have on the agenda is to enhance recipients' perceptions of his or her expertise and trustworthiness. Expertise is enhanced by showing that the position advocated is well supported and thus "correct." Trustworthiness is developed when arguers show that they have no biases or vested interests that they are trying to hide from their recipients. Seven specific strategies for accomplishing these ends will be described here. The first four relate to expertise and the last three to trustworthiness.

1. *Show that you or the sources you use have experience with the topic.* Before they will seriously consider your position on a topic, audiences must be reassured that you have studied the matter. Obvious as this might sound, the frequent use of unqualified and inexperienced sources to support claims shows that it's a practice often neglected. When the executive director of the Attorney General's Commission on Pornography was interviewed for a magazine article, he wasted no time in attempting to establish the credibility of its chair.

> Mr. Hudson is the new U.S. Attorney for the Eastern District of Virginia. He previously served for a number of years as the commonwealth attorney for Arlington County, Virginia. *The Washington Post* and other critics of Mr. Hudson have repeatedly noted that Arlington County is completely free of illegal obscene material.[27]

Clearly, this author expected to establish the commission's credibility by showing the extent to which its chair had direct experience cleaning up pornographic materials in an area where he served as U.S. Attorney.

2. *Use as many qualified sources as possible.* Qualified and respected sources have a "halo effect." They endow those who cite them with their own credibility. If a well-intentioned and earnest but inexperienced and unqualified arguer assures us of something, we may be equally likely to believe as not to believe her. But if the same speaker cites a number of respected authorities in support of her claim, the claim gains cogency. The impact of many authorities in support of a position seems to be well recognized by the author of a letter to a newsweekly who opposes using chimpanzees instead of humans in AIDS research.

> Even Dr. Anthony Fauci, head of the National Institute of Allergy and Infectious Diseases, says that the initial phase of a genetically engineered vaccine could be tested in human volunteers before chimpanzee experiments are finished. Other strong proponents of early human tests are Dr. Robert Pollack of Columbia University and Dr. Donald Francis, a virologist at the Centers for Disease Control who recently changed his mind regarding the necessity of testing first on chimpanzees.[28]

This author's use of authorities illustrates the effectiveness of using sources with a variety of backgrounds who have independently reached the same conclusion.

3. *Use sources the recipients are likely to respect.* Sources that one audience might perceive as highly respectable may not be respected by another audience. For example, a labor union officer might be highly credible with union members but

have very low credibility with management on the subject of working conditions and employee benefits. In arguing against federal aid to higher education in a popular conservative magazine, William F. Buckley, Jr., readily selected individuals whom his reading audience would accept as authorities on higher education.

> About 35 years ago, the presidents of Harvard, Johns Hopkins, Stanford, Brown, and other colleges issued a manifesto warning against federal aid to education. Their point was that such aid inevitably meant federal control, and of course they were correct.[29]

4. *Use sound reasoning and avoid fallacies.* Recipients who are involved in an arguer's message and who are being persuaded through the process of internalization will often detect weaknesses in the inferences an advocate makes and will think of counterarguments. Well-educated or intelligent recipients often have native reasoning skills and can criticize the arguments of others. As we observed earlier in this chapter, a weak and easily rejected argument will often do more harm to one's case than no argument at all because it will raise doubts in recipients' minds about the arguer's credibility on all the other issues in the message.

5. *Demonstrate fairness.* As we observed earlier in this chapter, audiences often become suspicious when they believe an arguer is presenting a one-sided or biased treatment of an issue. Directing *ad hominem* attacks at opponents, ignoring or superficially citing their points of view, twisting or misconstruing their position, or engaging in other similar practices are not only unethical but also have a "boomerang effect" because they cause audiences to suspect an arguer of unfairness and to distrust his or her overall trustworthiness. Notice how the arguer in the following example, who is attempting to persuade her friend that mandatory seat belt laws are unconstitutional, makes an overt attempt to establish her fairness:

COLLEEN:	Do you wear a seat belt?
PATTY:	Yes.
COLLEEN:	I just want to say that I wear a seat belt for my own reasons. I think it's safer to wear a seat belt. I just think the question here is: Is this law constitutional or not?

By showing that she was not opposed to seat belts *per se* but concerned only about the constitutionality of laws requiring them, Colleen showed that she was reasonable and wanted to be fair about the argument she was making.

6. *Use reluctant testimony. Reluctant testimony is testimony made by sources who speak against their own vested interest.* Anyone who furnishes evidence against his or her own interests or prejudices is likely to be highly credible to most audiences. After reviewing research on this effect, Petty and Cacioppo concluded that "the source who violates our expectations by being trustworthy when we expected untrustworthiness is especially effective."[30] The student who argues that tuition should be increased to maintain quality in education, the teacher who maintains that

competency tests for teachers are necessary, and the lawyer who supports no-fault divorce laws are all likely to be believed. That is because they are all advocating positions opposite to the ones they would be expected to advocate.

7. *Avoid inconsistency.* People who take a strong position on an issue and then reverse it lose considerable credibility in the eyes of the public. Sudden reversals in position give people the impression that one does not think through one's position very well and lacks a sense of principle. In 1972, George McGovern accepted the Democratic Party's nomination for president and selected Thomas F. Eagleton as his running mate. Shortly thereafter, it became known that Eagleton had received electro-shock treatments for depression. Many sectors of the public apparently became concerned about Eagleton's mental stability. Undaunted, McGovern insisted that he would not drop Eagleton from the ticket and that he backed him "1,000 percent." Less than two weeks later, however, Eagleton did in fact withdraw, probably at McGovern's request. Not only did McGovern have great difficulty finding another running mate, but he also lost the election. Among other things, this inconsistency damaged his credibility with the public, as the drop in his approval rating in polls taken immediately after the incident indicated.

■ *Summary*

This chapter emphasizes a *rhetorical* perspective on argument—a concern with adapting arguments to specific audiences and with building up the arguer's credibility through arguments as they are made. How are arguments designed and constructed so as to be suited to the particular audiences for whom they are intended? How do arguers ensure that they will receive a favorable hearing or reading because they are perceived as well informed and trustworthy? This chapter is directed at answering these two questions and at providing recommendations for audience analysis and for developing one's own credibility.

Arguments have a particular purpose—to influence another person, a group, or a gathering of individuals. The interests of recipients should be taken into account in many dimensions of argument construction. First, the premises used should be statements audience members can safely be expected to agree with. If recipients reject an arguer's starting point, the arguer will not get far. For this reason, the arguer must have some knowledge of preexisting audience beliefs and predispositions.

Second, the principles and values held by recipients can be called upon to support the inferences made by an arguer. Most reasoning is based upon assumptions, principles, and value hierarchies that can be called into play if the reasoning is questioned. In Chapter 7, we called such materials backing. Awareness of audience predispositions and assumptions can provide important materials for backing inferences.

Third, understanding audience orientations should influence the process of selecting evidence. Research on the use of evidence has shown that recipients are more likely to accept arguments supported by evidence than those which are not, that they are highly suspicious of authorities they regard as biased, and that they are much more influenced by information that is novel than that which is "old hat." Again, only an awareness of audience knowledge and beliefs can ensure that an advocate will select his or her evidence with these factors in mind.

Fourth, audience influence also affects the way messages should be organized. Research on various audiences has shown many behaviors that are generally true of most audiences and of which arguers should be aware. First, explicitly stated conclusions are more effective than unstated conclusions. Second, whether one should present one or both sides of a question depends on whether audiences are well or ill informed on a topic and whether they agree with the arguer's position. Third, weak arguments should not be used because they are often the only ones recipients remember and fourth, the arguer's strongest arguments should be placed at either the beginning or end of the message because such placement will make a greater impression and will be more easily remembered.

A concern for audience orientation should also affect other aspects of the argument. How difficult will it be to get and hold the audience's attention? What issues are foremost in the audience's mind and what form of analysis best might deal with them? What reservations and objections does the audience have and how might they best be dealt with? Sensitivity to such questions will cause the arguer to construct an argument effectively and appropriately tailored to the audience for which it was intended.

Incorporating audience beliefs, values, and attitudes into the planning of argument requires one to know something about the recipients. Such information can be gathered in a number of ways. First, one can inform oneself about the general tendencies of most people when they attend to persuasive messages. Second, one can strategically question arguers to find out about their interests, concerns, needs, and values before making one's argument. And third, if one is speaking or writing for a large group, one can read its publications, talk with its members, and attend its meetings. Doing so will provide information about members' knowledge, education, occupations, ages, and economic status that may be useful in adapting the argument to the audience.

Another audience-related factor in the persuasiveness of arguments is the recipients' perception of the arguer's source credibility. Source credibility refers to an arguer's ability to be believed and trusted by recipients. Credibility is not an inherent characteristic of the arguer but varies according to the situation and what the arguer says and does. There are two kinds of credibility—initial credibility, which arises from the arguer's preexisting credentials, status, and reputation; and derived credibility, which results from what is said in the message. Argumentation is more closely related to derived than to initial credibility.

Social psychologists have identified three major ways that people get others to comply with their requests. The first is *compliance,* or the use of rewards and punishments to compel action. The second is *identification,* or influence which occurs because recipients find a source attractive and want to emulate him or her. And the third is *internalization,* in which recipients adopt a new attitude or belief by integrating new information into their cognitive systems. Only internalization, which results from the thought audiences give to the content of an argument—the quality of its claims and evidence—is directly related to the processes we have described in this book.

Internalization occurs when a source is perceived to possess expertise and trustworthiness. Expertise depends on whether an arguer is viewed as knowing the correct position on a topic. Trustworthiness is the extent to which recipients believe the arguer is willing to communicate that position for their benefit. Expertise and trustworthiness are most important when the topic is fact-based and susceptible of a correct answer, when the positions of arguer and recipient are widely discrepant, and when the source appears to be free of bias and vested interest. Other research findings indicate that over time people tend to remember the content of a message more than the source from which it came. Also, people who are disinterested and uninformed about a topic will rely more on whether its source appears credible than on what they think of the message content.

Arguers should be aware that, in order to win favorable consideration of their messages, they must make a good initial impression on recipients and gain and hold their attention. Credibility plays a role in this entire process. Arguers who have moderate or low credibility with audiences initially must develop their derived credibility through construction and presentation of the message. Seven strategies for doing this are described in this chapter.

Arguers should demonstrate their own and their sources' experience with the topic. They should use a large number of diverse, qualified sources and depend upon sources their recipients are likely to respect. They should avoid weak or easily rejected arguments that might cause doubt in recipients' minds about their overall credibility on other issues in the message. They should demonstrate their fairness by providing a balanced treatment of the topic, avoiding inconsistency, and citing sources likely to be perceived as trustworthy by the audience. The effectiveness of an argument is often highly dependent on the recipients' perceptions of the arguer's credibility; awareness of this influence will assist arguers in getting their claims believed and accepted.

Exercises

Exercise 1   Select a situation in which you have recently made or will soon make an argument to a particular recipient or group of recipients.

A. Think of at least three strategies you could use to find out information about your audience's values and attitudes.

B. How could you incorporate the information you would gather into the planning of your message? Specifically, what changes or adjustments could you make in your argument to design it for this particular audience?

C. What strategies could you use to appear credible to this audience? How could you enhance the credibility of your arguments so they would be accepted?

Exercise 2 This chapter provided a number of strategies arguers could use to relate their arguments to the orientations of their audiences and to enhance their own credibility. These included:

A. Use premises the audience accepts.

B. Use audience values and principles for backing.

C. Cite authorities the audience is likely to respect.

D. Use novel evidence.

E. Keep the audience interested and involved in the argument.

F. Focus on issues about which the audience is likely to be concerned.

G. Be aware of possible audience objections and reservations.

H. Appear attractive and emphasize similarities you share with the audience.

I. Emphasize your own and your source's experience with the topic.

J. Use unbiased and reluctant testimony.

K. Avoid inconsistency.

Examine each of the arguments below in which the speaker or writer adheres to or violates one or more of these strategies. Decide whether the audience would respond more or less favorably to the argument because of what is said. Also, decide which of the strategies the arguer uses or violates. Some information about the audience is provided.

✳ 1. From Martha D. Lamkin, manager of the Indianapolis Office for the U.S. Department of Housing and Urban Development. "Power: How to Get It, Keep It, and Use it Wisely," a speech delivered to Women in Communications, Inc., Indianapolis, Ind., October 24, 1986. Reprinted in *Vital Speeches of the Day* 53 (1986): 153.

I mentioned at the outset that Machiavelli's essay, "The Prince," gave power a bad name. Perhaps it's up to a woman, Rosabeth Moss Kanter, to reverse this perception. Her book, entitled *The Changemasters,* makes the point that organizational genius is 10 percent inspiration and 90 percent acquisition—acquisition of power (that is information, resources, and support) to move beyond the formal job charter to influence others to accomplish organizational objectives.

2. From Zane G. Todd, chairman of the board, Indianapolis Power and Light Company, "Electric Power: A Look Back, a Look Ahead," a speech delivered at Franklin College, Franklin, Ind., October 21, 1986. Reprinted in *Vital Speeches of the Day* 53 (1986): 149.

We are all for a clean environment. None of us wants dirty air or polluted water. But the environmental standards set by our Federal Government were set far above the danger levels. In a word, they were 'harsh.' While we in our industry complained that these restrictions would inflict punitive costs on our customers, the Government was adamant. They reasoned that these high costs were justified because, in addition to protecting the environment, they would impose energy conservation. As a result, about 20 percent to 25 percent of your electric bill goes to pay for environmental improvements.

3. From "Marginalia," a column in *The Chronicle of Higher Education* (June 3, 1987): 2.

A reader found this ad on a bulletin board at the University of Delaware and sent a copy to us:

ONE DAY RESUME PRINTING SERVICE

A resume which produce exceptional results is one that is *clean* and *distinctive in appearance*. Your resume must be *attention getter*, more *readable*, and *attractive* with a *visual impact* then competitive resumes. . . .

We'll do our own, thanks.

4. From Anton J. Campanella, president of New Jersey Bell, "Public Education is Turning the Corner," a speech delivered to the New Jersey Council of Education, Bridgewater, N.J., October 3, 1986. Reprinted in *Vital Speeches of the Day* 53 (1986): 81.

But the quality of our state's public education system is of vital concern to me. I'm concerned as a parent, as a citizen, and as a business leader.

My wife was a teacher.

Our three sons attended public schools.

I've served on my local school board and two college boards of trustees.

But my status as president of one of New Jersey's largest private employers ensures that education is far more than a passing interest to me. My company, like many others, looks to our public education system for the human resources—the people—we need.

✳ 5. From Glenna M. Crooks, director of the policy division of the American Pharmaceutical Association, "How to Make a Difference: Shaping Public Policy," a speech delivered to the First Annual National Conference on Women's Health, Washington, DC, June 18, 1986. Reprinted in *Vital Speeches of the Day* 52 (1986): 756.

When I first began to work on this topic I was a government official assigned to attend an international meeting of policymakers, theologians, philosophers and scientists to discuss the ways in which the religious values and cultural ethics of a nation affected the ways in which health policy was made. . . .

They assigned me a title, "Policymaking in America," and I set out to explore how I made my living in the public policy arena. My social science perspective shifted into high gear. I read the Declaration of Independence and the Constitution and observed the actions of my contemporaries in government, associations and as individuals in a new light. My observations impressed and awed me. I saw a process that I have come to passionately believe in and promote; one that in my opinion truly capitalizes on the great strengths of the nation.

Some of my friends and colleagues here today know that I have just returned from the Soviet Union where I led a group of health professionals in an international professional exchange. As a result of that experience and my observations of such an oppressive society, my views about the strengths and value of our consensus-building passions as Americans are even stronger. It is one of our greatest national treasures.

6. R. L. Crandall, chair and president, American Airlines, Inc., "The Volatile Airline Industry," a speech before the Economic Club of Detroit, February 23, 1987. Reprinted in *Vital Speeches of the Day* 53 (1987): 468.

It's a pleasure to address such a distinguished audience as the Economic Club of Detroit, for two reasons: First, because I suspect many of you are frequent flyers on American, and I always like to be among our best customers. Second, because, for a long time, the name Detroit has been synonymous with transportation—admittedly, of the four-wheeled, rather than the airborne kind, but transportation nonetheless.

7. And, from another section of Crandall's speech (p. 469):

[Bankruptcies and other moves following deregulation of the airline industry] created vast differences in the costs that different carriers incur to provide the same transportation. Continental and American, for example, provide a comparable product—transportation from point A to point B. But our labor cost per available seat mile . . .is 2.6 cents and theirs is 1.4 cents. Multiplied by the number of available seat miles we provide each year, that amounts to a $600 million labor cost difference. If American had had Continental's labor costs in 1986, our operating earnings would have risen from $392 million to over $900 million on approximately $5.9 billion of revenue.

8. From Margarita Papandreou, president, Women's Union of Greece, "Women in Politics: Human Rights a Dominant Force," a speech delivered at the National Organization for Women in Denver, Colo., June 13–15, 1986. Reprinted in *Vital Speeches of the Day* 52 (1986): 744.

Perhaps [during the early stages of the contemporary women's movement], we didn't pay enough attention during our struggle for equal rights to that heavy sack, that sandbag, we carried on our backs . . .the responsibility for the house, the children, the oldsters. So, when the doors were finally opened to us . . .for education, for entry into so-called male jobs and professions, for political participation, etc., there we were, standing at the door, a man next to us, we—our bag—a staggering weight as we moved forward to take advantage of our new opportunities.

9. Ronald Reagan, president of the United States, "President's Response to the Tower Commission Report: Iranian Affair," a speech delivered to the American people in Washington, D.C., March 4, 1987. Reprinted in *Vital Speeches of the Day* 53 (1987): 323.

Let's start with the part that is most controversial. A few months ago I told the American people I did not trade arms for hostages. My heart and my best intentions still tell me that is true, but the facts and evidence tell me it is not.

　As the Tower board reported, what began as a strategic opening to Iran deteriorated in its implementation into trading arms for hostages. This runs counter to my own beliefs, to Administration policy, and to the original strategy we had in mind. There are reasons why it happened but no excuses. It was a mistake.

Notes

1. These studies are summarized in James C. McCroskey, "A Summary of Experimental Research on the Effects of Evidence in Persuasive Communication," *Quarterly Journal of Speech* 55 (1969): 169–70.

2. Thomas B. Harte, "The Effects of Evidence in Persuasive Communication," *Central States Speech Journal* 27 (1976): 42–60. In this study, it was shown that sources extremely low in credibility may produce evidence which has negative immediate effects, but the results were not statistically significant.

3. McCroskey, 172.

4. McCroskey, 174–75.

5. Stewart L. Tubbs, "Explicit versus Implicit Conclusions and Audience Commitment," *Speech Monographs*, 35 (1968): 14–95.

6. Tubbs, 18.

7. This research is effectively summarized in Bert E. Bradley, *Fundamentals of Speech Communication,* 4th ed. (Dubuque, Iowa: William C. Brown, 1984), 346–48.

8. James C. McCroskey, Thomas J. Young, and Michael D. Scott, "The Effects of Message Sidedness on Inoculation Against Counterpersuasion in Small Group Communication," *Speech Monographs*, 39 (1972): 205.

9. Ruth Anne Clark, *Persuasive Messages* (New York: Harper & Row, 1984), 28.

10. This research is summarized by Robert N. Bostrom in his *Persuasion* (Englewood Cliffs, N.J.: Prentice-Hall, 1983), 178.

11. Clark, 17.

12. Aristotle, *Rhetoric,* 1356a.

13. Bradley, 66.

14. R. Brooks and T. Scheidel, "Speech as Process: A Case Study," *Speech Monographs*, 35 (1968): 1–7.

15. See, for example, R. Glen Hass, "Effects of Source Characteristics on Cognitive Responses and Persuasion," in *Cognitive Responses in Persuasion,* ed. Richard E. Petty, Thomas M. Ostrom, and Timothy C. Brock (Hillsdale, N.J.: Lawrence Erlbaum Associates, 1981), 141–72; Bostrom, 63–87; Gary Cronkhite and Jo Liska, "A Critique of Factor Analytic Approaches to the Study of Credibility," *Communication Monographs* 43 (1976): 91–107; Jesse G. Delia, "A Constructivist Analysis of the Concept of Credibility," *Quarterly Journal of Speech,* 62 (1976): 361–75; and James C. McCroskey and Thomas J. Young, "Ethos and Credibility: The Construct and its Measurement after Three Decades," *Central States Speech Journal*, 32 (1981): 24–34.

16. Hass, 154.

17. Hass, 142–51. Hass's account is based on H. Kelman, "Compliance, Identification, and Internalization: Three Processes of Attitude Change," *Journal of Conflict Resolution,* 2 (1958): 51–60.

18. Hass, 149.

19. Hass, 144.

20. J. Mills and E. Aronson, "Opinion Change as a Function of the Communicator's Attractiveness and Desire to Influence," *Journal of Personality and Social Psychology*, 1 (1965): 173–77.

21. S. Chaiken, "Communicator Physical Attractiveness and Persuasion," *Journal of Personality and Social Psychology,* 37 (1979): 1387–397.

22. Hass, 143.

23. Hass, 153.

24. Richard E. Petty and John T. Cacioppo, *Attitudes and Persuasion: Classic and Contemporary Approaches* (Dubuque, Iowa: William C. Brown, 1981), 89–94.

25. Petty and Cacioppo, 64, report a study by S. Bochner and C. A. Insko, "Communicator Discrepancy, Source Credibility, and Opinion Change," *Journal of Personality and Social Psychology,* 4 (1966): 614–21.

26. Hass, 159.

27. Connaught Marshner, "Inside Look at Pornography and the Commission," *Conservative Digest* (August 1986): 29. This is an interview with Alan Sears.

28. From a letter to the editor by Murray J. Cohen, M.D., in *The Chronicle of Higher Education* (April 1, 1987): 44.

29. William F. Buckley, Jr., "On the Right," *National Review* (August 1, 1986): 46.

30. Petty and Cacioppo, 64.

A P P E N D I X *A*

Basic Debate Theory and Practice

■

APPENDIX OUTLINE

- **The Nature of Debate**
- **The Debate Proposition**
- **Analyzing the Debate Proposition**
  Topicality
  Jurisdiction
  Generalization

- **Debate Pragmatics**
  Taking Notes
  Debate Formats
- **Conclusion**

KEY CONCEPTS

debate
cross-examination
flow sheet

extension
parameter
debate format

One of the most enjoyable and challenging forums for practicing argumentation is debate. Debate brings together many of the ideas and activities discussed in this book. For instance, debate includes gathering and using evidence, analyzing topics, constructing cases, presenting persuasive argumentation, and criticizing others' arguments. In addition, debate offers speakers an opportunity to refute, challenge, and respond to the arguments of others.

Debate can be a highly competitive and motivating activity. It hones an individual's analytic and speaking abilities and many classes using this book may have one or more classroom debates as assignments in the course. This appendix is intended to assist instructors and students in planning and carrying out such debates.

Many topics that would be germane to such an assignment have been discussed elsewhere in this text, and they will not be repeated here. These include conducting research (Chapter 4); using reasoning (Chapter 5); detecting flaws in opponents' arguments (Chapter 6); and constructing and refuting cases on topics of value and policy (Chapters 8, 9, and 10). This appendix will focus on the following topics: the nature of debate, types of debate, and pragmatic considerations in debating. This appendix, taken together with material in other chapters, should provide all the basic knowledge necessary to engage successfully in a debate.

The Nature of Debate

In Chapter 1, we defined argumentation as the process of making arguments intended to justify beliefs, attitudes, and values so as to influence others. We observed that argumentation occurs in many forms—speeches, essays, and conversations, for example. *Debate is a specialized form of argumentation in which two or more people advocate competing positions in a topic area.* Although informal debates occur frequently among friends and acquaintances who disagree with each other, we will be concerned here with formal debates conducted according to established and agreed-upon rules and procedures. Formal debates are structured situations in which advocates speak in opposition to each other on a particular proposition.

Typically, formal debates in general, and academic debates in particular, involve a third party who serves as judge. Just as in a court of law, the judge or jury has the power to decide the merits of arguments presented by lawyers, in academic debates and other formal debates, third parties ultimately decide which side won. This means that in a formal debate, advocates do not speak to or try to convince each other but instead address a third party, or judge, who is expected to render a decision about who won the debate or who did the best job of debating. The presence of the third party distinguishes formal debates from informal debates and other types of speaking situations. Debate has historically been defended as worthwhile because, through the efforts of advocates wholeheartedly defending their respective positions, all the issues on a controversial topic emerge to be examined and considered. The final decision is then left to the judge who, having been apprised of all the relevant information and reasoning on a question, is prepared to make a fully informed and well-grounded decision. Debate thus can be viewed as a form of inquiry and a means of discovering truth. The advocacy model used in the courts is based on the idea of debate and the third party as judge.

There are other characteristics that differentiate debate from other forms of argumentation. In a debate, advocates typically speak for a preset amount of time and then yield the floor to an opposing debater who, in turn, argues an opposing position. In most formal debates, each speaker speaks more than once so as to be able to respond to the attacks and criticisms of opponents of his or her argument. *The process whereby a debater refutes an opposing argument and then reinforces and develops the original argument is called extension.* Debaters continually attempt to respond to the opposition and extend their original arguments. Sometimes, participants in formal debates pose questions and respond to questions about issues being discussed. *Cross-examination occurs when the debate format allows for time in which the participants can question one another.* In any case, debate is interactive argumentation in that most arguments are made in the expectation that they will be criticized or responded to in some way.

Debate occurs frequently in American society. Most of us are familiar with political debates in which various candidates for the presidency or other political offices speak in opposition to each other on governmental policies. These debates are aired by the media and, although there is no single judge rendering a decision about them, media commentators and the electorate respond by means of criticisms and voting behavior. In Congress and state legislatures, floor debates occur between senators and representatives on issues prior to voting. As we have already noted, the patterns of prosecution and defense speaking in court trials are based on a debate model. Finally, educational debates are used in schools and colleges to train students in advocacy skills and reasoning.

Debate has been used to teach the skills of analysis and reasoning in educational forums since ancient times. In Greece, debate was conducted in the academies. In medieval and Renaissance universities, it was used to teach disputation. And in modern England and the United States, debate has been a major form of interscholastic rivalry. In the United States, intercollegiate debating began in the late nineteenth century, and in 1947 the U.S. Military Academy began the National Debate Tournament (NDT) at West Point. NDT-style debate concentrates on propositions of policy. Each year, during the summer, a proposition is announced and all member schools debate the proposition at tournaments across the country. Participating schools often accumulate thousands of pieces of evidence and hundreds of prepared briefs that are used in tournament rounds. At the end of the school year, two-person debate teams may qualify to participate in the National Debate Tournament which is held annually.

In 1971, the Cross Examination Debate Association (CEDA) was established on the West Coast to provide an alternative to NDT-style debating. CEDA debate, in contrast to NDT debate, was originally designed to be audience-centered and communicative as opposed to evidence-centered and dialectic. The CEDA organization announces a national topic for fall and one for winter/spring each year and hosts a national tournament for its members. Although CEDA debate has used policy propositions, the majority of propositions used by CEDA have been fact and value propositions.

Both NDT and CEDA debate focus on two-person debate teams and these are the dominant forms of debate in college. Many high schools across the country also participate in interscholastic debate and they typically engage in one of two types. The first type of high school debate is policy debate which focuses, much like NDT-style, on two-person teams and policy propositions. In addition, many high schools engage in Lincoln-Douglas–style debate which focuses on individual competitors as opposed to two-person teams and value-oriented propositions.

Whether or not you have an opportunity to engage in interscholastic debate, you will find that in-class debating can be stimulating and exciting. It will give you an opportunity to sharpen your argumentation skills as you expose weaknesses in the reasoning of your opponents, to speak extemporaneously as you adjust your refutation and organization to the available time and the nature of your opponents' case, and to analyze and criticize a large number of arguments in a short period of time. To prepare you for the experience of debating, this appendix will briefly discuss major debate concepts and practices.

■ *The Debate Proposition*

The first requirement of a high-quality debate is a well-worded proposition for debate, often called a resolution or a topic. The debate proposition usually states a general course of action or a general value orientation that the affirmative will defend and the negative will oppose. For example, here are some appropriate propositions on policy and nonpolicy topics:

Policy

Resolved: That the United States federal government should significantly increase exploration and/or development of space beyond the Earth's mesosphere.

Resolved: That the United States should significantly increase its foreign military commitments.

Nonpolicy

Resolved: That American television has sacrificed quality for entertainment.

Resolved: That the United States is justified in aiding undemocratic governments.

In the same way that a thesis statement sets the general theme for an essay, the debate resolution sets out the general topic for debate. It must meet the criteria for propositions explained in Chapter 3 and should focus attention on some significant social, economic, or political issue. If it does not, the debate will be muddled because the respective teams will not have a clear understanding of the issues to be discussed and the matters relevant to the topic. A brief review of the criteria for wording a proposition is therefore necessary.

The four criteria for wording propositions described in Chapter 3 are also applicable to debate resolutions. A proposition for debate must be controversial so that both sides of the relevant issues can be developed and supported by each team. For example, if the proposition were "Freedom of speech is important in a democracy," where would the negative team find evidence and information to oppose freedom of speech? This proposition states an idea so entrenched in our society as to be non-controversial and universally accepted.

The proposition must also be clearly stated. If two ideas are combined in one proposition, or if misleading terms are used, the two teams may be very likely to discuss two different topics and to fail to come to grips with each others' cases. If they were debating whether "Washington state should stabilize revenues by imposing an income tax," one team might favor an income tax whereas the other might oppose the desirability of stabilizing revenues. This is because two topics would have been combined into one proposition. The difficulties arising from question-begging propositions were discussed at length in Chapter 3.

It is most important that the proposition for debate be balanced and neutrally stated so that both the affirmative and the negative are comfortable with it. If the proposition is worded in a lopsided fashion, the deck is stacked against one team or the other at the very outset. Imagine a debate on the proposition that "Ruthless and unprincipled repeat offenders should be put away for life." In accepting such a proposition for debate, the negative tacitly agrees that all offenders are ruthless and unprincipled, thus granting a major point in favor of the affirmative. All propositions for debate should be stated objectively.

The fourth criterion described in Chapter 3 was that the proposition must challenge present policies or values. In a debate, the affirmative must reject the present system whereas the negative may defend it. In other words, the affirmative has the burden of proof to present a good and sufficient reason for change; the negative enjoys the presumption favoring existing values and policies. By presenting a case systematically supporting change, the affirmative fulfills the burden of proof. The negative, however, has the presumption only as long as it elects to defend existing policies and values. If the negative chooses to oppose the affirmative by putting forward a counterproposal, it loses its presumptive advantage and, as with the affirmative, assumes a burden of proof.

Incidentally, it is worth noting that both teams have the burden of proving any contention or claim they advance by means of reasoning and evidence. Furthermore, as the debate progresses, both teams have a burden of refutation. The burden of refutation is the obligation to respond to claims and objections advanced by one's opponent. For example, the affirmative may begin the debate by presenting a sufficient case proposing a change. The negative is then obligated to respond, to defend successfully the present system as indicated by the affirmative, or to broach a counterproposal. If the negative is successful in showing that the affirmative has exaggerated or misdirected their indictment of the present system, then the affirmative has the burden of refutation to respond to the negative's responses. And so it goes as the burden of response and refutation shifts back and forth between the two teams throughout the debate. The team that has the greatest net argumentative advantage at the end of the debate should be the team that wins the debate. Should both teams be even on all issues when the debate ends, the negative should be given the decision because it had the presumption at the outset.

A fifth and final requirement for the debate resolution arises from its role as the overarching theme to be developed by both teams. The debate resolution should indicate both the nature and direction of the change to be advocated by the affirmative. In other words, the resolution should be so stated that the negative team can correctly anticipate the general nature of the affirmative's case and prepare to respond to it. The two propositions that follow are so vaguely stated that the negative would have no idea of the direction the affirmative could be expected to take in defending them.

> Resolved: That our national health care system should be substantially changed.
> Resolved: That the Social Security system should be restructured.

In both cases, the affirmative might support or oppose expansion or near elimination of either program. The negative team, consequently, would not know for which side of the issue to prepare. Because high-quality debating requires advance research, analysis, and preparation by both teams, each team should have advance knowledge of the side of the topic it will be expected to defend.

■ *Analyzing Debate Propositions*

Once the teams have agreed upon the proposition for debate, they can begin their analysis of the topic. Analysis begins when the advocate determines the major issues to be addressed. As defined in Chapter 3, issues are specific points of disagreement between parties in a dispute. Chapters 9 and 10 address the specific stock issues associated with a proposition that an affirmative advocate should prove in presenting a case.

Generally, the affirmative case is supposed to meet the criteria implied by these issues, whereas the negative attempts to show that the affirmative has failed to meet one or more issues. If the negative can show compellingly that the affirmative case has failed to meet any single issue, the negative team should win, since the affirmative has the burden of proof in the debate. Beyond these proposition-specific stock issues that have been addressed earlier, there is a second set of stock issues called resolutional issues. *Whereas proposition-specific stock issues address how well the particular case argument addresses minimum standards of proof, resolutional issues address whether the case has sufficiently warranted the entire proposition.* These issues include topicality, justification, and generalization.

Topicality

The wording of a debate proposition creates a boundary that defines what is considered "topical" and what is considered "nontopical." In other words, any given proposition defines what is a relevant issue for discussion and what is an irrelevant issue. For example, if we were discussing the proposition "Resolved: That euthanasia should be legal," the topic would include issues of right to die, death with dignity, patients with terminal illnesses, and whether doctors should knowingly allow people to die. Yet, the topic also excludes issues such as foreign policy, whether Democrats are better that Republicans, or any other irrelevant issue.

The dividing line between what is relevant and irrelevant is called a parameter. *A parameter is the boundary or barrier that defines what is included in the relevant set of issues so that advocates can understand what issues are relevant and what issues are irrelevant for a given proposition.* For example, consider the following proposition.

Resolved: That the United States should adopt a national health care program.

The wording of this topic creates an area of issues. In other words, we know that the status of health care in the United States is an issue. We know that the insurance industry and fee-for-service medical care are all issues. And we know that a lack of health insurance is an issue. All of these issues fall within the parameter of the topic—these are issues that the resolutional area contains.

At the same time, we know that there are some issues that are irrelevant for this proposition. The term "United States" for example constrains us to proposing a program that is in the United States and not some other country. We are also constrained by the term "health care" which excludes issues such as life or car insurance, military expenditures, and the like. And we are constrained by the term "national" which means that whatever the affirmative case proposes, the plan of action must have a national scope. If affirmative advocates argue for positions or plans of action that fall outside the topic, they are considered nontopical and irrelevant to the discussion. Consequently, a nontopical case does not support the resolution (because it falls outside the parameter of the topic) and an advocate arguing for a nontopical case should lose the debate.

Although the proposition indicates the general nature and direction of the affirmative's position on the topic, the case offers a specific interpretation of how the proposition should be enacted. For example, the proposition might call for a significant increase in federal government support for health care, whereas an affirmative case would identify specific problems with the health care delivery system in the United States and present a plan for solving the problems—through support of health maintenance organizations, subsidies to private health insurance companies, or some other means. Similarly, a value proposition states a general value orientation, but an affirmative team's case on the proposition will specify what value hierarchies to apply as well as the criteria to be used to make the evaluation.

Topicality deals with whether the affirmative's specific case is a legitimate application of the general proposition for debate. The affirmative case should adhere to the letter and spirit of the meaning implied in the proposition. Affirmative teams, because they lose sight of the central issue of the proposition or because they wish to surprise their opponents, often (but by no means always) offer cases that depart from the proposition in some way. When this happens, the negative should demonstrate that the case is not propositional through reasoning and explanation.

Jurisdiction

Just as a judge in a court of law must have the jurisdiction to decide a legal case, so a debate judge must have jurisdiction to decide a debate. For example, if in a court of law a prosecutor wanted to try a defendant in Portland, Maine, for a crime committed in Los Angeles, California, the court in Portland would not have the right to decide the case because it does not fall within its jurisdiction (unless the appropriate procedures for change of venue or extradition were followed).

Similarly, in a debate, the judge must either vote affirmative in favor of the resolution or negative against the resolution. This means that if the affirmative case fails to adequately address all of the resolution or defends a resolution that is different than the one agreed on by the participants, then the affirmative has not justified the resolution and the judge has no jurisdiction to vote for it.

Consider, for instance, the following proposition:

Resolved: That the welfare system has exacerbated the problems of the urban poor in the United States.

If an affirmative argued that the welfare system adversely affects the lives of poor people in the United States, the affirmative's argument would ignore the term "urban"; although the case may fall within the parameter of the resolution and be topical, by ignoring or minimizing the significance of one of the defining terms of the proposition, the affirmative would not have justified the topic as it was written. Instead, the affirmative has justified a different proposition, that the welfare system has exacerbated the problems of the poor in the United States.

Affirmative cases are limited by the proposition. They must prove the proposition and present a reasonable and *prima facie* argument in support of it. If the affirmative omits relevant terms or substantively alters the proposition, then the affirmative has not justified the initial proposition that both teams came prepared to debate.

Generalization

When deciding how to approach the analysis of a debate topic, affirmative speakers are faced with a decision. Can the affirmative adequately argue all of the proposition or must the affirmative focus on a case that represents a subset or example of the proposition? This decision is an important one and depends on the nature of the proposition.

Consider the following proposition:

Resolved: That the tuition at our school should be increased 6 percent for next year.

In this example, the resolution is focused and narrow, which means that an arguer is tightly constrained with regard to how the topic can be interpreted. The plan of action is a simple one: raise tuition.

On the other hand, consider this proposition:

Resolved: That the United States should significantly increase its foreign military commitments.

Contrast this proposition with the previous one and the difference becomes apparent. While the first proposition specified a singular and concrete plan of action, the second proposition allowed an affirmative advocate to examine many different plans of action. In fact, it is difficult to imagine any one plan of action that would address all of the topic's subject matter. Increased military commitments could involve hundreds of different plans. Since time limits and research ability prevents a team from addressing all of this proposition (because of its breadth), the affirmative case may select a single, representative example that proves the resolution. For example, the United States could increase its aid to Somalia, Russia, or China. The United States could send troops to Europe or sell aircraft to Saudi Arabia. There are many possible plans of action.

Because many possible plans are available, the advocate, when dealing with a broad proposition, will typically select a subset of the topic—an example—and argue that the example (perhaps placing nuclear missiles abroad) is typical of the entire proposition and therefore warrants the entire proposition. If, however, the affirmative example is not typical because the case is a hasty generalization or the sample is not representative of other important military concerns, then the negative would argue that the affirmative's case represented an invalid generalization.

■ *Debate Pragmatics*

Successfully conducting a debate involves handling practical matters such as note taking, speaker order, and time limits. Methods for dealing with such matters have evolved in tournament debating and are usually carried over into educational debate in the classroom. They will be discussed briefly in this section. Further information on these subjects is available in a number of texts on debate theory and practice.[1]

Taking Notes

Skill in refutation requires you to keep track of the arguments introduced and developed by both sides in a debate. Most people have learned to take notes in a linear format. For instance, in classroom lectures, we learn to begin at the top of the page and work our way to the bottom. Such a system does not work well in debate because the arguments do not remain static—they are dynamic. In debate, arguments are introduced, refuted, extended, refuted again, and summarized. Keeping track of arguments as they develop over time, then, can be challenging and requires the use of two-dimensional note taking which is called "flowing." *A flow sheet is a two-dimensional representation of all the arguments presented in a debate by both teams.* It is similar to a balance statement of a business's financial status in that it provides an overall picture of the status of arguments in a debate.

Debaters use flow sheets to keep track of arguments. Each speech is summarized in a separate column on the flow sheet, and responses to specific arguments are connected horizontally across the page. The flow sheet for the first four speeches in a debate on limiting firearms in the United States is represented in Figure A–1. As you read vertically in each column, you will see how each speech developed and what its contents were. As you read horizontally across the page, you will see what responses each speaker made to the arguments of the preceding speaker. For example, under blame, an issues raised by the first negative speaker, you will see that she argued that people will not comply with gun control because they do not believe in it. The second affirmative speaker responded that most people favor gun control as shown in public opinion polls conducted since 1963. The second negative speaker attempted to contradict this evidence by presenting her own poll that showed overwhelming opposition to gun control. This is an example of horizontal tracking of a particular argument across the flow sheet.

Developing note-taking skills in flow sheet form requires practice. You must listen closely and take rapid, accurate notes. Debaters often develop a system of abbreviations to facilitate this task, such as ↑ for "increase," ↓ for "decrease," # for "number," "hi" for "high," etc. A clear, orderly flow sheet enables a debater to see at a glance the status of important arguments in the debate. The debater can note which arguments were granted, ignored, and dropped in the round so as to remind the judge that his or her own position on them is unchallenged. When there is a response from the other team, the flow sheet enables a speaker to see quickly what the response was and to plan his or her own responses before speaking.

Debate Formats

In political and parliamentary debates, many types of formats are used. *A debate format is a statement of the order in which participants in a debate will speak and the length of speaking time allocated to each speech or question/answer period.* Debate formats are prearranged before the debate—either because of agreement by participants or because of conventions or rules governing the practice of debate in a particular forum. For example, the League of Women Voters sets the format for many presidential debates, whereas parliamentary debates are governed by the rules of parliamentary practice.

RESOLVED: That the federal government should initiate and enforce a program that would significantly limit the use of firearms in the United States

1st Affirm, Constructive	1st Negative Constructive	2nd Affirm, Constructive	2nd Negative Constructive
III			
— There are 55 mil. handguns in circ.	— Not quantitatively significant	— Is significant	— Auto deaths kill 10× more people
— ↑ by 2 mil. per yr.	— 26,000 people killed in drunk driving accidents	— since '63, more Ams. killed by handguns than died in WWII	— Aff. plan will channel funds away from drunk driving
— 10,000 people killed per yr.	— 24,000 killed in falls, drowning, fires	— 10,000 per year is signif.	
— 250,000 people wounded per yr.		— 77% killed by family member or acquaintance	
Blame			
— 1986 Gun Control Act last legislation enacted			
— Patchwork quilt of 25,000 state/local laws re. guns	*Topicality*		
— No formal screening process	1. 21 day waiting period not a "signif" change		DROPPED
— Of 2,000 people who applied, 187 were felons	2. Proposition calls for fed'l enforcement, not state	Like 55 mph speed limit which is state enforced	
	— Courts will not enforce stiffer penalties		
	— Jail terms do not deter; prisons overcrowded		
Plan			
1. National gun regis. prog.			
2. 1 yr. jail term + $500 fine for noncompliance	How much will this cost?		
3. Nonsporting handguns banned	How will you provide financing?	1. ↑ in lic. fee to $500	
4. Dealer lic. fees ↑ to $500		2. gun regis. fee of $50	
5. 21 day waiting period bet. applying & obtaining gun		3. Fines for nonenforcement by states	
6. Admin. by Fed'l Bureau of Alcohol and Firearms			
7. Enforced by states			

Figure A–1
Sample Flow Sheet

1ST AFFIRM, CONSTRUCTIVE	1ST NEGATIVE CONSTRUCTIVE	2ND AFFIRM, CONSTRUCTIVE	2ND NEGATIVE CONSTRUCTIVE

	Blame
	Many people do not believe in gun control.
	Many people believe they have a "right to bear arms"
	Criminals will circumvent plan through smuggling, etc.
		— 2/3 of American public have favored greater controls since '63	How will checks be run on firearm purchasers during waiting period?
			How many dealers will be deterred by increase in fee?
			How many violators will be sent to jail?
			
			— Poll showed
			  — 337,000 against
			    7,000 favor

Cure '82 pilot study in DC — guns banned in '77 — in '74 there were 174 killings — in '78 there were 112 killings	— Poor study with flawed methodology — Overall DC crime actually ↑ during this period	— W. Germany & other countries do show rel'ship bet. guns & gun deaths — crime went up generally during this period	
Benefits 1. # of dealers ↓ because dealer fees ↑	How can you guarantee this result? Increase can easily be made up through lucrative sales		
# of guns & gun deaths ↓	— No correlation between # of guns and # of homicides — 6 states with strictest laws have highest homicide rates	— These 6 states had "unusually high" homicide rates before gun laws enacted — Gun laws not the causal factor	
2. ↓ # of felons with guns because of waiting period	— Present system already has waiting period	— Present system allowed example of John Hinckley — He had been arrested before — He had psychiatric problems — Yet he bought a gun from a pawn shop and shot the president	— How does your waiting period ensure such people won't get guns? — How can psychiatric disorders be detected in your plan? *Cost* 1. When handguns unavail., people resort to long guns—more deadly 2. Enforcement means violation of civil liberties to locate gun 3. Plan too financially burdensome

Figure A–1
continued

In educational debate, certain formats are standard. Generally, each speaker in a debate speaks twice, and the sides (affirmative and negative) alternate in speaking turns. Initial (or "constructive") speeches are longer than refutation (or "rebuttal") speeches. The standard format for an educational debate is as shown in Figure A–2.

Affirmative speakers begin the debate because they present the initial case for a change that gets the debate under way. Because they have the burden of proof, the affirmative is also allowed to speak last. Although being first and last speaker may seem advantageous for the affirmative, it does have a disadvantage. That is the uninterrupted negative speaking block of thirteen minutes in the middle of the debate. During this time, the second negative constructive speaker ordinarily presents broad arguments against the case such as disadvantages (cost) or objections to the affirmative value. The first negative rebuttalist responds to the second affirmative constructive speaker's attacks on his or her first speech. In any case, the first affirmative rebuttalist obviously has the challenging task of responding to two negative speeches in only five minutes. If question/answer periods or cross-examination are used in an educational debate, they are usually interspersed with the earlier speeches in which affirmative and negative cases are initially presented.[2]

An alternative to the traditional two-person team debate format is Lincoln-Douglas–style debate. LD debate takes its name from the famous senatorial debates between Abraham Lincoln and Stephen Douglas, and instead of involving two people on each side of the proposition, it uses only one person on each side. Lincoln-Douglas debates typically take the format shown in Figure A–3.

To fit classroom debates into available time, your instructor may use some variation of these formats. Occasionally time is allowed to both teams for between-speech

First affirmative constructive	8 minutes
Second negative cross-examination of the first affirmative speaker	3 minutes
First negative constructive	8 minutes
First affirmative cross-examination of the first negative speaker	3 minutes
Second affirmative constructive	8 minutes
First negative cross-examination of the second affirmative speaker	3 minutes
Second negative constructive	8 minutes
Second affirmative cross-examination of the second negative speaker	3 minutes
First negative rebuttal	5 minutes
First affirmative rebuttal	5 minutes
Second negative rebuttal	5 minutes
Second affirmative rebuttal	5 minutes

Figure A–2
Speaker Order and Time Limits in Educational Debate

Affirmative constructive	6 minutes
Negative cross-examination of affirmative speaker	3 minutes
Negative constructive	7 minutes
Affirmative cross-examination of negative speaker	3 minutes
Affirmative rebuttal	4 minutes
Negative rebuttal	6 minutes
Affirmative rebuttal	3 minutes

Figure A–3
Speaker Order and Time Limits in Lincoln-Douglas–Style Debates

preparation and consultation for rebuttals. Whatever the format for a debate may be, it is necessarily adjusted to the circumstances and conditions under which the debate is presented.

■ *Conclusion*

This appendix was designed to provide you with basic information needed to participate in a classroom debate. As noted earlier, debate provides a challenging and stimulating forum for practicing the argumentation skills discussed in this book. Although novices often find their first debate assignment intimidating and frustrating, they also quickly recognize the fact that debating develops many valuable and essential skills—critical listening, analytical thinking, proficiency in reasoning, research, use of evidence, and, as one author noted, courage![3] Should a debate assignment be a part of your argumentation course, we hope that knowledge of debate stock issues and formats will assist you as you speak in competition with other members of your class.

Notes

1. See Austin J. Freeley, *Argumentation and Debate,* 6th ed. (Belmont, Cal.: Wadsworth, 1986), 16–18; Douglas Ehninger and Wayne Brockreide, *Decision by Debate,* 2d ed. (New York: Harper, 1978), 110–16; James Edward Sayer, *Argumentation and Debate: Principles and Applications* (Sherman Oaks, Cal.: Alfred, 1980), 341–42 and 307–17; Carolyn Keefe, Thomas B. Harte, and Laurence E. Norton, *Introduction to Debate* (New York: Macmillan, 1982), 41–59; J. W. Patterson and David Zarefsky, *Contemporary Debate* (Boston: Houghton Mifflin, 1983), 94–97 and 222–26; and Russell T. Church and Charles Wilbanks, *Values and Policies in Controversy* (Scottsdale, Ariz.: Gorsuch Scarisbrick, 1986), 4–6 and 338–44.

2. Space limitations preclude a discussion of cross-examination strategies in this appendix. Should you engage in cross-examination in a debate, you should consult the explanations of question/answer strategies in Freeley, 294–99; Sayer, 345–53; Patterson and Zarefsky, 256–81; and Church and Wilbanks, 217–29.

3. Freeley, 25–26.

APPENDIX *B*

Answers to Selected Exercises

CHAPTER 1

Exercise 2

1. This is clearly an argument. Its claim is that [Monday's unanimous Supreme Court ruling] "should be recognized as yet another in a series of reasoned, constitutionally anchored defenses of the basic, precious right of free speech." The support is contained within the claim statement: the decision was carefully reasoned and anchored in the constitution. That the author expects many in his audience to disagree with him is made clear by the first sentence.

5. Deciding whether or not this is an argument is complicated because three people are together constructing a procedure for giving raises. But Dan's proposal to "start out with what the staff ought to receive and concern ourselves with what's available later on" could be considered a claim. His support is that a reserve fund is available to cover excesses over a minimum across-the-board raise.

Exercise 3

Please help me save lives. Add your voice to mine. Help stop random gun violence.	*Claim*
I know firsthand the daily pain of a gunshot wound. And I'm one of the lucky ones. I survived a bullet to the head. Since I was shot eleven years ago, more than 220,000 men, women and children have been killed in handgun fire. Each night's news seems to bring a more horrible story. Shots fired in a classroom. Two students killed in a high school hallway. Woman shot in the head while driving on a freeway.	*Evidence*
America's epidemic of random gun violence rages on.	*Subclaim*
I'm calling on Congress to enact a common sense law—the Brady Bill—requiring a "cooling-off" period before the purchase of handgun so police can run a thorough background check on the buyer.	*Claim as request*
Time to cool off a hot temper. Time to screen out illegal purchasers.	*Reasoning*
Every major police group in America supports this public safety measure.	*Evidence*
So why hasn't Congress passed the Brady Bill? Because too many Members of Congress are either afraid of the hard-core gun lobby or pocket the gun lobby's PAC money.	*Reasoning*

Like Senator Phil Gramm (R-TX) who has received more than $349,000 in campaign support from the NRA since 1984.	*Evidence*
Right now, the Brady Bill is being blocked from final passage by Senator Gramm and a few others controlled by the gun lobby.	*Evidence*
We need to send these politicians a message. It's time to put public safety ahead of politics.	*Claim*
If our legislators really care about saving lives, they will pass the Brady Bill.	*Reasoning*
Let your Senators know you want action on the Brady Bill now—before you or someone you love becomes a victim.	*Claim as Request*

CHAPTER 2

Exercise 2

How does educational discourse operate to influence lectures or other persuasive speeches?

We have certain expectations about teachers and the material they present. Students, as well as teachers, come to expect that for any given course there will be certain types of content presented, there will be a particular style, and there will be an evaluation process. With regard to fields, we use our expectations as ground for evaluating any given lecture or teachers. The traditional forms (styles, organizational patterns, etc.) for lectures and discussions guide our understanding and interpretations of them. And, our understanding of the field implies certain rules of appropriate or inappropriate classroom behavior. For example, while it may be appropriate for an instructor to use personal examples and poke fun at himself or herself, it would be inappropriate for the instructor to use the lecture forum to denigrate students.

What forms of grounding are implied?

Grounding focuses on the assumptions and evidence that the field recognizes as valid and appropriate for building arguments. In education, presumably, different subjects (such as history, philosophy, speech, etc.) will ground their arguments differently. However, any educator will ground arguments on certain assumptions such as: What will help the students learn? What issues or ideas are intellectually or personally stimulating? Can my arguments be supported based on the literature in the discipline? Are the students achieving a better understanding of themselves and their world? In other words, the implied grounding of an educationally based argument should focus on whether the students learn and improve themselves.

What are the audience expectations in this field?

Generally, the audience consists of students who expect to be: educated, challenged, and tested. Furthermore, they expect that these objectives will be achieved through: lectures, discussions, reading, writing papers, and other forms of homework.

What are some conventions or rules for giving lectures or other persuasive speeches?

Educational speeches should be organized, coherent, grounded in the literature of the field, clear and understandable, focused, full of examples and other illustrations, and applicable to students' lives and understanding of their world.

CHAPTER 3

Exercise 1

1. Noncontroversial. This is a factually true statement.

5. Double-barreled. Whether a practice is "desirable" and whether it is "necessary" are two different issues. Here they've been combined in one claim.

12. Does not challenge the present system in which abortions are already legal and generally available.

Exercise 2

1. Past fact

5. Value

10. Value ("inefficient")

CHAPTER 4

Exercise 1

1. *Expertise*: Is Kause an expert? What are his credentials? Neither his title nor his position is cited.

   Recency: Since no date is cited in the evidence, we do not know the period covered by "the last six years."

   Accuracy: What studies did Kause conduct? Where can they be found? What constitutes "strong evidence?"

5. *Relevance* and *Accuracy of citation*: Is Kennedy's quotation relevant to the military draft? In what context was it made? The crucial part of this argument—that the country is in a military force crisis—is not supported by any evidence.

10. *Expertise*: Who is Dr. Harvey Brenner? His credentials aren't given.

    Recency: This study was conducted in 1975. It is questionable as to whether it applies to current conditions.

    Relevance: The argument assumes a causal connection between unemployment and death, but the evidence does not state a causal relation, only a correlation.

Exercise 2

1. *U. S. Statistical Abstract for 1992*

   Congressional Information Service index to the U.S.

   Budget for 1992.

4. *U.S. Statistical Abstract for 1991*

   Your city's police department would have up-to-date local crime statistics. You might also check the index to your local newspaper, if it is indexed.

10. An article on Franklin D. Roosevelt in an American encyclopedia (*Encyclopedia Americana* or *Collier's*), or Dictionary of American Biography

---

CHAPTER 5

Exercise 1

Analogy

Evidence: A painter paints his painting so that light shines on all parts of the work.

Claim: The listener should . . .be shown the conclusion contained in the principle.

Inference: (implied) [The speaker's task is like the painter's.]

Questions: Is writing a composition or giving a speech like painting a picture in this sense? How is aesthetics like composition?

Exercise 6

Analogy

Evidence: North America did not remain empty of cities; the continent is not a poorer place now than 20,000 years ago.

Claim: We have more practical reasons for not burning Amazon forests than to stave off natural catastrophe.

Inference: (implied) [The forests of the Amazon are like the natural state of the North American continent 20,000 years ago.]

Questions: Were the original North American forests as essential to environmental preservation as Amazon forests?

Have conditions changed in 20,000 years such that destruction of Amazon forests would have more impact now?

Exercise 11

Dissociation

Evidence: We could act through bitterness and hatred; we could allow our protest to degenerate into violence.

Claim: We must struggle on the high plane of dignity and discipline; we must meet physical force with soul force.

Inference: (implied) [Effective response to oppression need not be violent; it can be dignified yet forceful.]

Questions: Should not oppression, which is a form of violence itself, be responded to by violence?

Are not bitterness, hatred, and violence justified in such circumstances?

CHAPTER 6

Exercise 2

1. Begging the question, or appeal to tradition
5. *Ad hominem,* or emotive language
10. Emotive language

Exercise 3

1st paragraph: *Emotive language* ("innocent victims," "ruthless killers," "heartless criminals")

2nd paragraph: *Single cause* ("because of the *Miranda* ruling") Slippery slope ("just one more step")

3rd paragraph: *False analogy*—fear of getting caught is not the only factor motivating law-abiding citizens not to break the law, and fear of punishment is not the only factor on a criminal's mind when he or she commits a murder

4th paragraph: *Post hoc*—there are other factors besides deterrence that could have caused these results. The events reported may be only chronologically related.

5th paragraph: *Argument from tradition* ("since ancient times")—The Old Testament is not in itself an adequate authority on this topic, because "an eye for an eye" conflicts with teachings of New Testament and other religions.

6th paragraph: *Ad populum*

Note: This entire passage is very weakly argued. The unsophisticated reader might be persuaded by these arguments, but now that you know about fallacies, you shouldn't be!

CHAPTER 7

Note: *There is often more than one correct way to diagram an argument using either model. Because there may be individual variations in the ways different analysts number and connect statements in the general model and supply principles as warrants in the Toulmin model, there are often two or three correct ways to diagram an argument. There are, however, incorrect diagrams. The claim should not be mistaken for data, for example. The following diagrams are therefore suggestive. Further refinements should be made through class discussion and consultation with your instructor.*

1. ①It is the chemical firms that release the most troubling types of molecules into the environment. ②In Baton Rouge, according to company data, an Exxon chemical plant was leaking 560,000 pounds of benzene yearly, while just south of there, ③according to a survey by the Sierra Club, eighteen plants in and around St. Gabriel and Geismar dumped about 400 billion pounds of toxic chemicals into the air during the first nine months of 1986.

General Model:

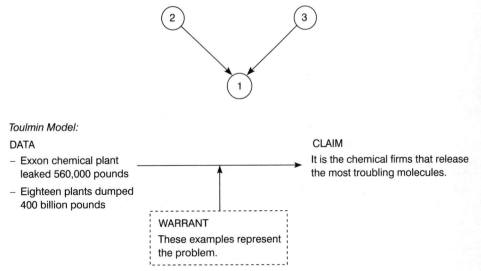

Toulmin Model:

DATA

– Exxon chemical plant leaked 560,000 pounds

– Eighteen plants dumped 400 billion pounds

WARRANT
These examples represent the problem.

CLAIM
It is the chemical firms that release the most troubling molecules.

Criticism:

The argument seems too ready to indict chemical plants as the main source of the problem. The evidence focuses on only two examples, and one of those is water and the other air pollution. What other sources of pollution (such as nonpoint pollution) might there be? Have the various possible sources been compared as to their impact?

10. ①Ladies make excellent teachers in public schools; many of them are every way the equals of their male competitors, and still they secure less wages

than males. ②The reason is obvious. ③The number of ladies who offer themselves to teach is much larger than the number of males who are willing to
teach. . . . ④The result is that the competition for positions of teachers to be
filled by ladies is so great as to reduce the price; but ⑤as males cannot be
employed at that price, and ⑥are necessary in certain places in the schools,
⑦those seeking their services have to pay a higher rate for them.

General Model:

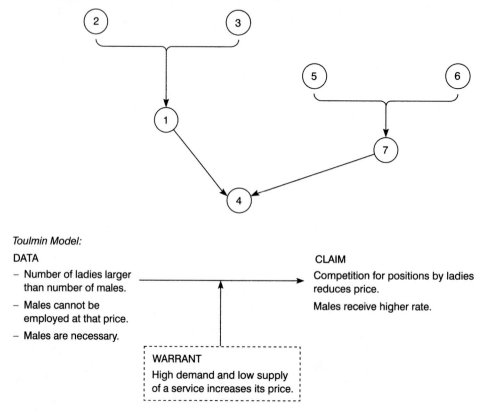

Toulmin Model:

DATA

– Number of ladies larger
  than number of males.

– Males cannot be
  employed at that price.

– Males are necessary.

CLAIM

Competition for positions by ladies
reduces price.

Males receive higher rate.

WARRANT

High demand and low supply
of a service increases its price.

Criticism:

The argument rests on a "supply/demand" relationship: that a larger supply of a
commodity (in this case, female teachers) decreases its value. First, for the argument
to hold up, the assumptions made by its author must all be true: Male teachers must
be "necessary" in certain places, and there must be a much larger supply of females
competing for positions than there are males. Second, other causes (rather than sup-
ply/demand) are not considered. For example, females might simply be willing to
accept lower pay than males, or the pay differential might be the result of systematic
discrimination.

15. ANNE: ①Technology has affected every single part of the program.

CARRIE: Yes, technology is a big one.

ANNE: ②I don't really feel technology is just the mechanical aspect. ③It's chemical, biological, physical, everything. ④The advances in technology have gone so far that it can prolong life, yeah, but when you get in the position of an irreversibly comatose-type state, it's out of step with what man is. ⑤You know, should he be prolonged just to vegetate? ⑥Are they prolonging ill health or are they prolonging life? ⑦Technology has reached the outer limits where it's gone beyond what man is.

ANNE: ⑧It's gone beyond the purpose for which medical technology was originally intended. ⑨Its goal was to enhance human life, whereas now it just prolongs death, dying and pain.

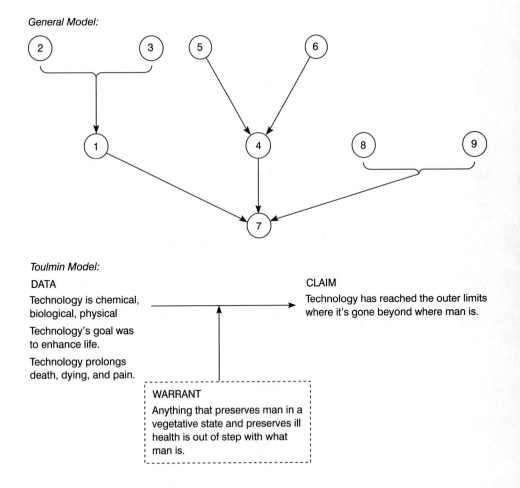

General Model:

Toulmin Model:

DATA

Technology is chemical, biological, physical

Technology's goal was to enhance life.

Technology prolongs death, dying, and pain.

CLAIM

Technology has reached the outer limits where it's gone beyond where man is.

WARRANT

Anything that preserves man in a vegetative state and preserves ill health is out of step with what man is.

Criticism:

Part of the evidence here is that technology's original goal was to enhance human life. That may or may not be the case, but is technology intended to "enhance life" in the immediate situation, or to enable research and conditions that would enhance life in the long run? Furthermore, the group is applying its own conception of what "life" is (not vegetative, but something to be enhanced and enjoyed). This conception should perhaps be questioned and not merely assumed and accepted.

CHAPTER 8

Exercise 1 (a) Value issues Is isolationism preferable to participation in the global community?

Does the United Nations preserve peace in the world?

Does the United States as a world leader have a responsibility to participate?

Policy issues Did the United Nations act effectively in the Persian Gulf War?

Does the United States benefit economically from participation in the United Nations?

What would happen if we withdrew from the United Nations?

(b) This is a value proposition because of the term "beneficial" in its wording and because it does not call for action.

(c) Because the United States is presently a member of the United Nations, the proposition does not have the presumption.

Exercise 5 (a) Value issues Are the rights of the accused more important than protection of society?

What are the primary responsibilities of the judicial system?

Do the *Miranda* rule and other protections constitute "overemphasis?"

Policy issues Do dangerous criminals go free because of these protections?

Does protection of accused rights impair the effectiveness of law enforcement?

Would effects of removing protections be seriously harmful?

(b) Because no action is called for, this is not a policy but a value proposition.

(c) The presumption does not favor the proposition which explicitly challenges the present judicial system.

CHAPTER 9

Exercise 1

1. Mandatory seat belt laws

2. *Colleen* favors freedom of choice, fairness, and safety. (She makes it clear that she does value safety but that it's not her primary value.)

   Patty favors safety, protection, and order in society. She believes it's the government's responsibility to protect its citizens.

3. *Colleen*: That the law should be enforceable. That it should not violate personal rights and freedom of choice. That it should not discriminate arbitrarily and inconsistently between various groups.

   Patty: That lives should be saved whenever possible. That the law should be enforceable.

4. *Colleen* clearly favors freedom of choice and equality in enforcing laws, and freedom and equality are both highly ranked in Rokeach's system. *Patty* favors protection and preservation of life and safety; because neither of these values are highly ranked in Rokeach's system, Patty would have to locate value consensus in other sources to support her views.

5. *Colleen*'s conclusion that people who are breaking the law should not be treated differently than those who are abiding by it may be open to question. In any case, *Patty*'s claim that the law can be enforced because it already has been elsewhere seems like a sound analogy.

CHAPTER 10

Exercise 1

First proposition: I should attend a different school.

Needs Case

I. My personal situation is such that I should transfer to another college.

   A. Northeast Exclusive College no longer meets my needs.

      1. It does not offer a program in my chosen major.

      2. The high tuition is causing me to go into debt.

   B. The prospects of getting the education I want here are dim.

      1. No curriculum changes in my interest area are planned.

      2. The high tuition will force me to drop out of school.

II. Transferring to another college seems the best plan.

   A. My parents and I will discuss my options during spring break.

   B. Next fall I will probably transfer to State University.

        C. This action will allow me to stay in school in my chosen major.

  III. A transfer to another college will be beneficial.

        A. It will save thousands of dollars in tuition.

        B. It will broaden my educational experience.

        C. It will allow me to enroll in a major department which is highly ranked nationally.

Comparative-Advantages Case

  I. Transferring to another college next year is my plan.

        A. I will consult my parents about the decision.

        B. I will transfer to State University next year.

  II. The transfer will be economically beneficial.

        A. I will save $4,000 in tuition next year alone.

        B. Neither my parents nor I will have to go into debt to finance my last two years of college.

        C. Four thousand dollars is a significant proportion of my family's annual income.

        D. Only a transfer will avoid indebtedness because I do not qualify for financial aid or scholarships.

  III. The transfer will be educationally beneficial.

        A. State University offers the major program I've selected.

        B. This major is exciting to me and offers excellent career opportunities.

        C. Northeast Exclusive College does not offer this major and has no plans to do so.

Goals Case

  I. My goal is to obtain a bachelor's degree in dental hygiene in a quality program at reasonable cost.

  II. Northeast Exclusive College does not offer this program and its tuition is very high.

  III. Transfer to State University seems advisable.

        A. I will discuss this with my parents during spring break.

        B. I will transfer into the hygiene program at State University next fall.

  IV. In two years, I will receive a degree in a field with good career opportunities.

Exercise 3

Needs Case

  I. (5)

    A. (2)
    B. (8)
    C. (15)
    D. (17)
II. (19)
    A. (4)
    B. (10)
    C. (13)
III. (6)
    A. (1)
    B. (3)
    C. (11)

Comparative-Advantages Case

I. (19)
    A. (4)
    B. (10)
    C. (13)
II. (6)
    A. (3)
    B. (11)
III. (1)
    A. (14)
    B. (16)
    C. (18)
    D. (20)

Goals Case

I. (7)
II. (19)
    A. (4)
    B. (10)
    C. (13)
III. (9)
IV. (12)

CHAPTER 11

Exercise 1

PO	Four score and seven years ago
RH	our fathers brought forth on this continent a new nation, conceived in liberty, and dedicated to the proposition that all men are created equal.
CO & RH	Now we are engaged in a great civil war, testing whether nation, or any nation so conceived and so dedicated, can long endure.
PH	We are met on a great battlefield of that war. We have come to dedicate a portion of that field, as a final resting place for those who here gave their lives, that that nation might live. It is altogether fitting and proper that we should do this.
PO & RH	But, in a larger sense, we cannot dedicate—we cannot consecrate—we cannot hallow—this ground. The brave men, living and dead, who struggled here have consecrated it, far above our poor power to add or detract.
ME	The world will little note, nor long remember what we say here,
RH	but it can never forget what they did here. It is for us the living, rather, to be dedicated here to the unfinished work which they who fought here have thus far so nobly advanced.
PO & RH & EM	It is rather for us to be here dedicated to the great task remaining before us—that from these honored dead we take increased devotion to that cause for which they gave the last full measure of devotion—that we here highly resolve that these dead shall not have died in vain—that this nation, under God, shall have a new birth of freedom—and that government of the people, by the people, for the people, shall not perish from the earth.

Lincoln relied most frequently on the poetic and rhetorical language functions. Rather than emphasizing his own feelings through the emotive function or informing his audience through the use of cognitive language, he wished to eulogize the fallen troops and urge the country to rededicate itself to preservation of the union, freedom, and democracy. Lincoln's poetic and rhetorical uses of language have been widely admired and praised by his contemporaries and successors. The Gettysburg Address is considered a classic of English prose style and rhetorical effectiveness.

CHAPTER 12

Exercise 2

1. Lamkin cited the author Rosabeth Moss Kanter to give credibility to her own claim that women must work to gain organizational power.

By focusing on the specific sources and methods of gaining power, Lamkin kept her audience interested in her topic.

She emphasized a feminist perspective by citing a female authority when addressing an all-female audience.

Because of her reliance on a respected source, similarity in attitudes with the audience, and focus on a topic in which the audience was probably interested, Lamkin was probably able to hold audience attention and win acceptance for her ideas.

5. First and foremost, Ms. Crooks stressed her long and intensive experience with the topic.

She stressed the American value of consensus building through open exchange—a value her audience shared.

One problem with this treatment is that the author's purpose was vague. Her audience may have wondered what her point was and have lost interest in what she had to say.

References

Anderson, Ray Lynn, and C. David Mortenson. "Logic and Marketplace Argumentation." *Quarterly Journal of Speech* 53 (1967): 143–51.

Aristotle. *The Rhetoric of Aristotle.* Translated by Lane Cooper. New York: Prentice-Hall, 1932.

—. *Rhetoric.* Translated by W. Rhys Roberts. New York: Modern Library, 1954.

—. *Sophistical Refutations.* Vol. 1 of *The Works of Aristotle.* Edited by W. D. Ross. New York: Harper & Row, 1928.

Bem, Daryl J. *Beliefs, Attitudes, and Human Affairs.* Belmont, Cal.: Brooks/Cole, 1970.

Benoit, William L., Steve R. Wilson, and Vincent F. Follert. "Decision Rules for the Policy Metaphor." *Journal of the American Forensic Association* 22 (1986): 135–46.

Bitzer, Lloyd F. "The Rhetorical Situation." *Philosophy and Rhetoric* 1 (1968): 1–15.

Booth, Wayne C. *Modern Dogma and the Rhetoric of Assent.* Chicago: University of Chicago Press, 1974.

Bosmajian, Haig A. *The Language of Oppression.* Lanham, Md.: University Press of America, 1983.

Bostrom, Robert N. *Persuasion.* Englewood Cliffs, N.J.: Prentice-Hall, 1983.

Bradley, Bert E. *Fundamentals of Speech Communication.* 4th ed. Dubuque, Iowa: William C. Brown, 1984.

Brockreide, Wayne. "Arguers as Lovers." *Philosophy and Rhetoric* 5 (1972): 1–11.

Brooks, R. and T. Scheidel. "Speech as Process: A Case Study." *Speech Monographs* 35 (1968): 1–7.

Burke, Kenneth. *Language as Symbolic Action.* Berkeley: University of California Press, 1966.

Carney, James D., and Richard K. Scheer. *Fundamentals of Logic.* 2d ed. New York: Macmillan, 1974.

Chaiken, S. "Communicator Physical Attractiveness and Persuasion." *Journal of Personality and Social Psychology* 37 (1979): 1387–97.

Church, Russell T., and Charles Wilbanks. *Values and Policies in Controversy.* Scottsdale, Ariz.: Gorsuch Scarisbrick, 1986.

Clark, Ruth Anne. *Persuasive Messages.* New York: Harper & Row, 1984.

Copi, Irving. *Informal Logic.* New York: Macmillan, 1986.

—. *Introduction to Logic.* 5th ed. New York: Macmillan, 1978.

Corbett, Edward P. J. *Classical Rhetoric for the Modern Student.* 2d ed. New York: Oxford University Press, 1971.

Corsi, Jerome R. "The Continuing Evolution of Policy System Debate: An Assessment and Look Ahead." *Journal of the American Forensic Association* 22 (1986): 158–63.

Cox, Robert J., and Charles Arthur Willard, eds. *Advances in Argumentation Theory and Research.* Carbondale, Ill.: Southern Illinois University Press, 1982.

Cronkhite, Gary. "The Locus of Presumption." *Central States Speech Journal* 17 (1966): 270–76.

Cronkhite, Gary, and Jo Liska. "A Critique of Factor Analytic Approaches to the Study of Credibility." *Communication Monographs* 43 (1976): 91–107.

Delia, Jesse G. "A Constructivist Analysis of the Concept of Credibility." *Quarterly Journal of Speech* 62 (1976): 361–75.

Damer, T. Edward. *Attacking Faulty Reasoning.* 2d ed. Belmont, Cal.: Wadsworth, 1987.

DeVito, Joseph. *The Psychology of Speech and Language: An Introduction to Psycholinguistics.* Washington, D.C.: Random House.

Diggs, B. J. "Persuasion and Ethics." *Quarterly Journal of Speech* 50 (1964): 359–73.

Eemeren, Frans H. van, and Rob Grootendorst. *Speech Acts in Argumentative Discussions.* Dordrecht, Netherlands: Foris Publications, 1984.

Eemeren, Frans H. van, Rob Grootendorst, and T. Kruiger. *The Study of Argumentation.* New York: Irvington, 1984.

Ehninger, Douglas. "Argument as Method: Its Nature, Its Limitations, and Its Uses." *Speech Monographs* 37 (1970): 101–10.

—. *Influence, Belief, and Argument: An Introduction to Responsible Persuasion.* Glenview, Ill.: Scott, Foresman, & Co., 1974.

—. "Validity as Moral Obligation." *Southern Speech Journal* 33 (1968): 215–22.

Ehninger, Douglas, and Wayne Brockreide. *Decision by Debate.* New York: Dodd, Mead, and Co., 1963.

Fearnside, W. Ward, and William B. Holther. *Fallacy: The Counterfeit of Argument.* Englewood Cliffs, N.J.: Prentice-Hall, 1959.

Flaningam, Carl D. "Value-Centered Argument and the Development of Decision Rules." *Journal of the American Forensic Association* 19 (1982): 107–11.

Follert, Vincent. "Risk Analysis: Its Application to Argumentation and Decision Making." *Journal of the American Forensic Association* 18 (1981): 99–108.

Freeley, Austin J. *Argumentation and Debate: Critical Thinking for Reasoned Decision Making.* 6th ed. Belmont, Cal.: Wadsworth, 1986.

Hagan, Michael R. "A Missing Chapter in Argumentation Texts." *Journal of the American Forensic Association* 9 (1972): 274–78.

Haiman, Franklyn S. "Democratic Ethics and the Hidden Persuaders." *Quarterly Journal of Speech* 44 (1958): 385–92.

Hamblin, C. L. *Fallacies.* London: Methuen, 1970.

Harte, Thomas B. "The Effects of Evidence in Persuasive Communication." *Central States Speech Journal* 27 (1976): 42–46.

Hayakawa, S. I. *Language in Thought and Action.* New York: Harcourt, Brace, 1964.

Herman, Edward. *Locating United States Government Information.* Buffalo, NY: William S. Han, 1983.

Jackson, Sally, and Scott Jacobs. "Structure of Conversational Argument: Pragmatic Bases for the Enthymeme." *Quarterly Journal of Speech* 66 (1980): 251–65.

Jensen, J. Vernon. *Argumentation: Reasoning in Communication.* New York: Van Nostrand, 1981.

Johannesen, Richard L. *Ethics in Human Communication.* Prospect Heights, Ill.: Waveland, 1981.

Kahane, Howard. *Logic and Contemporary Rhetoric.* 4th ed. Belmont, Cal.: Wadsworth, 1984.

Klumpp, James F., Bernard L. Brock, James W. Chesebro, and John F. Cragan. "Implications of a Systems Model of Analysis to Argumentation Theory." *Journal of the American Forensic Association* 11 (1974): 1–7.

Kurfiss, Joanne G. *Critical Thinking: Theory, Research, Practice, and Possibilities.* Washington, D.C.: Association for the Study of Higher Education, 1988.

Lewinski, John D., Bruce K. Metzler, and Peter L. Settle. "The Goal Case Affirmative: An Alternative Approach to Academic Debate." *Journal of the American Forensic Association* 9 (1973): 458–63.

Littlejohn, Steven W. *Theories of Human Communication.* 3d ed. Belmont, Cal.: Wadsworth, 1989.

Lichtman, Allan J., and Daniel M. Rohrer. "General Theory of the Counterplan." *Journal of the American Forensic Association* 12 (1975): 70–79.

McKeon, Richard. "Communication, Truth, and Society." *Ethics* 47 (1957): 89–99.

McCroskey, James C. "A Summary of Experimental Research on the Effects of Evidence in Persuasive Communication." *Quarterly Journal of Speech* 55 (1969): 169–76.

McCroskey, James C., and Thomas J. Young. "Ethos and Credibility: The Construct and its Measurement after Three Decades." *Central States Speech Journal* 32 (1981): 24–34.

McCroskey, James C., Thomas J. Young, and Michael D. Scott. "The Effects of Message Sidedness on Inoculation against Counterpersuasion in Small Group Communication." *Speech Monographs* 39 (1972): 205–12.

McMillan, James H. "Enhancing College Students' Critical Thinking: Review of Studies." *Research in Higher Education* 26 (1987): 3–29.

Makau, Josina. *Reasoning and Communication.* Belmont, Cal.: Wadsworth, 1990.

Mills, Glen E., and Hugh G. Petrie. "The Role of Logic in Rhetoric." *Quarterly Journal of Speech* 54 (1968): 260–67.

Mills, J., and E. Aronson. "Opinion Change as a Function of the Communicator's Attractiveness and Desire to Influence." *Journal of Personality and Social Psychology* 1 (1965): 173–77.

Morehead, Joe. *Introduction to United States Public Documents.* 3d ed. Littleton, Colo.: Libraries Unlimited, 1983.

Newman, Robert P., and Dale R. Newman. *Evidence.* New York: Houghton Mifflin, 1969.

Nilsen, Thomas R. *Ethics of Speech Communication.* Indianapolis: Bobbs-Merrill, 1974.

Nosich, Gerald M. *Reasons and Arguments.* Belmont, Cal.: Wadsworth, 1982.

Ogden, C. K., and I. A. Richards. *The Meaning of Meaning.* London: Kegan, Paul Trench, Trubner, 1923.

O'Keefe, Daniel J. "Two Concepts of Argument." *Journal of the American Forensic Association* 13 (1977): 121–28.

Perelman, Chaim. *The Realm of Rhetoric.* Translated by W. Kluback. Notre Dame, Ind.: University of Notre Dame Press, 1982.

Perelman, Chaim, and Lucie Olbrechts-Tyteca. *The New Rhetoric: Treatise on Argumentation.* Translated by John Wilkinson and Purcell Weaver. Notre Dame, Ind.: University of Notre Dame Press, 1969.

Petrie, Hugh G. "Does Logic Have Any Relevance to Argumentation?" *Journal of the American Forensic Association* 6 (1969): 55–60.

Petty, Richard E., and John T. Cacioppo. *Attitudes and Persuasion: Classic and Contemporary Approaches.* Dubuque, Iowa: William C. Brown, 1981.

Petty, Richard E., Thomas M. Ostrom, and Timothy C. Brock, eds. *Cognitive Responses in Persuasion.* Hillsdale, N.J.: Lawrence Erlbaum Associates, 1981.

Rescher, Nicholas. *Introduction to Value Theory.* Englewood Cliffs, N.J.: Prentice-Hall, 1969.

Rhodes, Jack, and Sara Newell, eds. *Proceedings of the Summer Conference on Argumentation.* Annandale, Va.: Speech Communication Association/American Forensic Association, 1980.

Rieke, Richard D., and Malcolm O. Sillars. *Argumentation and the Decision-Making Process.* 2d ed. Glenview, Ill.: Scott Foresman, 1984.

Rokeach, Milton. *Beliefs, Attitudes, and Values.* San Francisco: Jossey Bass, 1968.

—. *The Nature of Human Values.* New York: The Free Press, 1973.

Rowland, Robert C. "The Influence of Purpose on Fields of Argument." *Journal of the American Forensic Association* 18 (1982): 228–45.

Rybacki, Karen C., and Donald J. Rybacki. *Advocacy and Opposition: An Introduction to Argumentation.* Englewood Cliffs, N.J.: Prentice-Hall, 1986.

Sartre, Jean Paul. *Being and Nothingness.* Translated by Hazel E. Barnes. New York: Philosophical Library, 1956.

Scheidel, Thomas M. *Persuasive Speaking.* Glenview, Ill.: Scott Foresman, 1967.

Schwarzkopf, Leroy C. *Guide to Popular U.S. Government Publications.* Littleton, Colo.: Libraries Unlimited, 1986.

Scriven, Michael. *Reasoning.* Point Reyes, Cal.: Edgepress, 1976.

Sheehy, Eugene P., ed. *Guide to Reference Works.* 10th ed. Chicago: American Library Association, 1986.

Simons, Herbert W. "Persuasion in Social Conflicts: Critique of Prevailing Conceptions and a Framework for Future Research." *Speech Monographs* 39 (1972): 227–47.

Skyrms, Brian. *Choice and Chance.* Belmont, Cal.: Dickenson, 1966.

Sproule, Michael J. *Argument: Language and Its Influence.* New York: McGraw Hill, 1980.

Stewart, Charles J., and William B. Cash. *Interviewing: Principles and Practices.* Dubuque, Iowa: William C. Brown, 1985.

Strange, Kenneth M. "An Advocacy Paradigm of Debate." Paper presented at the annual meeting of the Speech Communication Association, Anaheim, Cal., November 1981.

Strunk, W., and E. B. White. *The Elements of Style.* 3d ed. New York: Macmillan, 1979.

Taylor, Paul W. *Normative Discourse.* Englewood Cliffs, N.J.: Prentice-Hall, 1961.

Thomas, David. *Advanced Debate: Readings in Theory, Practice and Teaching.* Skokie, Ill.: National Textbook, 1981.

Toulmin, Stephen E. *The Uses of Argument.* Cambridge: University Press, 1969.

Toulmin, Stephen E., Richard Rieke, and Allan Janik. *An Introduction to Reasoning.* 2d ed. New York: Macmillan, 1984.

Trapp, Robert, and Janice Schuetz, eds. *Perspectives on Argumentation.* Prospect Heights, Ill.: Waveland, 1990.

Tubbs, Stewart L. "Explicit versus Implicit Conclusions and Audience Commitment." *Speech Monographs* 35 (1968): 14–19.

Warnick, Barbara. "Arguing Value Propositions." *Journal of the American Forensic Association* 18 (1981): 109–19.

Warnick, Barbara, and Susan L. Kline. "*The New Rhetoric*'s Argument Schemes: Rhetorical View of Practical Reasoning." *Argumentation and Advocacy.* In press.

Watzlawick, Paul, Janet Beavin, and Don Jackson. *Pragmatics of Human Communication.* New York: Norton, 1967.

Wenzel, Joseph W. "On Fields of Argument as Propositional Systems." *Journal of the American Forensic Association* 18 (1982): 204–13.

—. "Toward a Rationale for Value-Centered Argument." *Journal of the American Forensic Association* 13 (1977): 150–58.

Whately, Richard. *Elements of Rhetoric.* Edited by Douglas Ehninger. Carbondale, Ill.: Southern Illinois University Press, 1963.

Whorf, Benjamin L. *Language, Thought, and Reality.* New York: John Wiley & Sons, 1956.

Windes, Russel R., and Arthur Hastings. *Argumentation and Advocacy.* New York: Random House, 1965.

Woods, John, and Douglas Walton. *Argument: The Illogic of the Fallacies.* Toronto: McGraw Hill, 1982.

Zarefsky, David. "Persistent Questions in the Theory of Argument Fields." *Journal of the American Forensic Association* 18 (1982): 191–203.

Zarefsky, David, Malcolm O. Sillars, and Jack Rhodes, eds. *Argument in Transition.* Annandale, Va.: Speech Communication Association/ American Forensic Association, 1983.

Ziegelmueller, George W., Jack Kay, and Charles A. Dause. *Argumentation: Inquiry and Advocacy.* Englewood Cliffs, N.J.: Prentice-Hall, 1990.

Ziegelmueller, George W., and Jack Rhodes, eds. *Dimensions of Argument.* Annandale, Va.: Speech Communication Association/ American Forensic Association, 1981.

Index

Abstraction, in language use, 269–70
Accessibility, as criterion for evidence, 82–83
Ad hominem, fallacy of, 148–49
Ad populum, fallacy of, 149–50, 222
Ad verecundium, fallacy of, 146
Agent, in plans on policy propositions, 244
Amphiboly, fallacy of, 153–54
Analogy
  false, 141
  as form of reasoning, 115–17
  tests for, 116–17
Appeal to tradition, fallacy of, 150–51
Application, stock issue of, 221–22
Arguer, intentions, 140, 147–52. *See also* Source credibility
Argument
  analysis of, 166–79
  audience adaptation and, 17
  cases, 20
  chains, 19, 75, 171, 173, 186
  contexts, 28–29
  definition of, 6
  ethical context, 28, 29–42
  fields, 28, 35–37
  functions, 9–10
  locus, 28
  model, 15–20
  occasion, 37–38
  strength of, 297–98
  type of interaction, 6–8. *See also* Criticism, of arguments; Field
Argumentation
  and critical thinking, 10–11
  conventions of, 10–12
  definition of, 6
  perspectives, 12–15
Aristotle
  De Sophisticis Elenchis, 138–39
  Rhetoric, 224, 300–301
Artifacts
  definition of, 78
  as evidence, 78

Attention gaining, strategies for, 305–8
Attitudes, of audience, 299–300
Attitudinal blame, in policy analysis, 243, 249, 254
Attractiveness of sources, and persuasiveness, 302–4
Audience
  analysis of, 298–300
  attitudes of, 9–10, 296–98
  evidence and, 75, 306–7
  expectations of, 239–40
  indifference to argument, 298, 303
  level of dispute and, 17–20
Authority
  as form of reasoning, 124–25
  tests of, 124–25

Backing
  as support for reasoning, 293–94
  in Toulmin model, 181, 185–86
Balance, as criterion for proposition, 61–62
Beardsley, Monroe C.: *Practical Logic*, 166
Begging the question, fallacy of, 146
Beliefs, 213. *See also* Value
Benefits, in policy argument, 245
Biographical dictionaries, 92–93
Bitzer, Lloyd F., on the rhetorical situation, 37
Blame
  definition of, 242
  stock issue of, 242–43
Book reviews, 89
Books, as evidence, 88–89
Brockriede, Wayne, on ethics, 41
Burden of proof, 63, 203
Burden of rejoinder, 205
Burke, Kenneth, on language and terministic screens, 274

Cacioppo, John T., on expertise, 304
Case
  definition of, 200
  prima facie, 204, 246–48. *See also* Policy argument, Value hierarchy

Case level refutation, 205
Categorical syllogism, 110
Causal argument
    false, 142–44
    as a form of reasoning, 120–22
    and relational and predictive claims, 64–65
    in slippery slope fallacy, 144–45
    tests of, 121–22
Challenge, as criterion for proposition, 62–63
Claim
    in analogy, 116
    in argument chains, 19, 74–75
    as argument part, 15–20, 169, 176–77
    characteristics of, 52–57
    definition of, 7–8
    double-barreled, 60–61
    and evidence, 82, 146–47, 166
    explicit vs. implicit, 296
    implicit, 169–70, 177–78
    networks of, 55–56
    placement in argument, 54–55
    and proposition, 52–57
    in Toulmin model, 179–80
    types of, 63–67
Clarity
    as criterion for proposition, 58–62
    in language use, 278–82
Coexistential argument, as form of reasoning, 122–25
Cognitive language, function of, 276
Cognitive processing
    and persuasion, 302–3
    versus noncognitive factors, 302
Comparative advantage argument, 251–52
Compendiums, 93
Complex (Type II) argument, 171–72
Compliance, 302
Compound (Type IV) argument, 171, 174
Conclusion. See Claim
Conclusion indicators, 167
Concrete language, 269–70, 278–79
Congressional Information Service Index, 94
Congressional Record, 94
Connotative meaning, 271
Consistency, and credibility, 308
Consistency, internal and external, 80–81
Contexts for argument, 28–43
Contradictions, as means of refutation, 206
Controversiality, as criterion for proposition, 58
Copi, Irving, 166
Correlation, 122

Cost, in policy argument, 244
Cost/Benefits, stock issue of, 244–45
Counteradvocacy, 205
Counterproposal, strategy of, 258
Credibility. See Source Credibility
Criteria
    definition of, 220
    stock issue of, 220–21
Critical thinking, 11
Criticism, of arguments, 170–71, 178
Cross examination, 319
Cross Examination Debate Association, 319
Culture
    characteristics of, 29–34
    mythology in, 30
    rituals in, 30
    subcultures in, 31–33
Cure, as stock issue, 243–44

Damer, Edward, on fallacies, 151–52
Data, in Toulmin model, 179
Dause, Charles, on claims, 61
Debate
    definition of, 318
    educational, 318–20
    extensions in, 319
    formats for, 326
    propositions in, 320–22
Defense of present policies, strategy of, 256
Defense of present policies with minor repairs, strategy of, 257
Definition, stock issue of, 219
Definition of terms
    for clarity, 280–81
    for criticism, 167
    in value debate, 219
Demographics of audiences, 300
Denotative meaning, 271
Derived credibility, 301–2
Descriptions, as evidence, 77
Diagrams
    of argument, 164–89
    of argument model, 15–20
    of argument structure, 171
Dialectical perspective, 12–14
Direct refutation, strategy of, 205, 246
Disjunctive syllogism, 111
Dissociation, as form of reasoning, 125–26
Double-barreled claims, 60. See also Begging the
        Question fallacy

Effects of plans in policy proposals, 244
Ehninger, Douglas, on evidence consistency, 80–81
Emotive language
    fallacy of, 154–55
    function of, 275
Encyclopedias, as source for evidence, 92
Enthymeme, 110
Equivocation, fallacy of, 153
Ethics
    and accuracy of citation, 83–85
    content and relational levels, 40–41
    as context element, 39–42
    definition of, 39
    fallacies and, 140
    and misdirection, 147–48
    and organization of arguments, 296–97
Ethos, 300
Euphemism, definition of, 272
Evidence
    accuracy of citation, 83–85
    as argument part, 15–20
    characteristics of, 75
    consistency, 80
    credibility of, 306–8
    definition of, 8, 74
    ethical requirements for, 85
    evaluating statistics, 85–88
    evaluation of, 78–85
    expertise, 79
    external consistency, 80
    fact, 77
    fallacies of faulty, 145–47
    internal consistency, 81
    and level of dispute, 18, 75
    locating, 88–96
    objectivity, 80
    opinion, 78
    organization of, 96–97
    primary source, 84
    recency, 81–82
    recording, 96–97
    relevance, 82
    reliability, 79
    secondary source, 84
    tests of, 78–85
    types of, 76–78
Examples
    in argument from generalization, 118–20
    as form of reasoning, 118–20
Exigence, 37–38

Expertise
    in argument from authority, 124–25
    as criterion for evidence, 79–80
    and source credibility, 300–1
    strategies for enhancing, 301–2
Extended arguments, 55
Extraneous material, in argument diagrams, 169

Fact, claims of, 64
Fact books, 93
Fallacy
    definition of, 138
    ethics of, 140
False cause, fallacy of, 142–44
Field dependence, 36
Field invariance, 36
Fields
    characteristics of, 35–36
    definition of, 35
    and evaluating arguments, 36
    stock issue of, 219–20
Figurative analogy, 117
Flow sheet, in debate, 326
Formal logic, 109–12
Formats, for debate, 326

General model
    for argument analysis, 166–79
    Toulmin model, compared to, 187–88
General reference works, as evidence, 92–93
Generalization
    in debate, 324–25
    as form of reasoning, 118–20
    reasoning from examples, 119–20
    tests of, 119–20
Goals argument
    definition of, 254
    format for, 254–56
    identification of, 255
Government documents, as evidence, 93–94

Harm. *See* Ill.
Hass, R. Glen, on expertise, 301
Hastings, Arthur, on evidence, 74
Hasty generalization, fallacy of, 141–42
Hayakawa, S.I., on abstraction, 270
Hierarchies, stock issue of 222–23
Historical claims, 65
Humanities Index, 90

Identification, and source credibility, 302–3
Ill
    in counterproposal strategy, 258
    issue in policy refutation, 249–50
    in policy cases, 247, 251, 255
    stock issue of, 240–42
Incompatibilities, as form of reasoning, 114
Index to U.S. Government Periodicals, 94
Inference
    analogical, 115–17
    in argument from authority, 124–25
    in causal argument, 120–22
    and claims of fact, 64
    definition of, 8–9, 108
    in generalization, 119–20
    in sign argument, 123
    as statement of reasoning, 112
Informal logic, inferences in, 112
Information: novel and persuasiveness, 295
Infotrac, 90
Initial credibility, 301
Inoculation effect, 296–98
Instrumental values, 213
Internalization, and source credibility, 303
Interpretation, and language fallacies, 152–56
Interviews
    and audience analysis, 303
    as evidence, 95–96
Invention, in argument, 11
Issues
    avoidance of, in fallacies, 147–52
    definition of, 52, 204
    relation to proposition, 204
    stock in policy arguments, 239–45
    stock in value arguments, 219–23
Issues brief, definition, 223

Johannesen, Richard L., on ethics, 40
Jurisdiction, as argument in debate, 324

Language
    ambiguity in, 153, 269–70, 278–82
    connotative, 271
    definition of, 267
    denotative, 271
    fallacies of, 152–56
    functions of, 275–78
    influence on perception, 273–75
    presence in, 281
    racist, 282

    sexist, 282
Level of dispute
    and argument chains, 173
    and claims, 55
    definition of, 17
    in fallacy of begging the question, 146
    and the proposition, 20
    role in argumentation, 17–19
Literal analogy, 115–16
Logic, formal, 109–12
Logical perspective, 12–13
Logos, 300

Macro arguments, 20
Magazines, as source of evidence, 89–91
Mandate, in policy plans, 244
Meaning, in language, 267–68
Metalingual, language function, 277
Metaphor, and figurative analogy, 117
Minnick, Wayne, 40
Minor repairs, strategy of, 257
Misunderstanding, of language, 267–68
Model of argument, 15–20. *See also* Diagrams,
        General Model
*Monthly Catalog of United States Government
        Publications*, 94

National Debate Tournament, 319
National Newspaper Index, 91
Necessary condition, reasoning from, 120
Need. *See* Ill
Needs analysis case, 245–46
New York Times Index, 91–92
Newman, Dale R.
    on accessibility of evidence, 83
    on reliability, 79
    on using statistics, 85
Newman, Robert P.
    on accessibility of evidence, 83
    on reliability, 79
    on using statistics, 85
Newsbank Electronic Index, 91
Newspapers, as sources for evidence, 91–92
Non sequitur, fallacy of, 146–47

Objections, responding to, 297–98
Objectivity
    as criterion for evidence, 80
    and language use, 271–72
    and source credibility, 300

Ogden, C. K.: *The Meaning of Meaning*, 267
Olbrechts-Tyteca, L.
    on inference making, 112
    on value hierarchies, 217
One-sided analysis, 297
Opinion
    as argument from authority, 124–25
    as evidence, 78
Order effects, 296–98
Organization of arguments, 296–98
Orwell, George, on language use, 278–79

PAIS International in Print, 90
Parameter, 323
Pathos, 300
Perelman, Chaim
    on inference making, 112
    on value hierarchies, 217
Periodicals, as source of evidence, 89–91
Persuasion, and language use, 271–72, 276–77
Persuasiveness
    and argumentation strategies, 291–95
    and credibility of sources, 301–2
    and organization of arguments, 296–98
Petty, Richard E., on expertise, 304
Phatic language, function of, 275
Plan of action
    effects of, 244
    in policy arguments, 244
Poetic language, function of, 277
Policy argument
    comparative advantage format, 251–52
    future orientation, 236
    goals format, 254–56
    needs format, 245–46
    probability and, 237
Policy claims
    definition of, 66
    in extended arguments, 66–67
    relation to other claims, 67
Post hoc ergo propter hoc, fallacy of, 143
Predictive claims, 65
Premise, major vs. minor, 109
Premise indicators, 167
Premises
    relation to claim, 172, 174
    as starting points for argument, 75, 166
Presence, language use in argument, 281
Presentation of message, and source credibility, 305–6

Presumption
    and appeal to tradition, 150–51
    and burden of proof, 203
    definition of, 63
Primacy-recency effect, 298
Proposition
    boundary, 53
    and claim, 52–53
    definition of, 52
    emergence, 55
    in extended arguments, 7
    and field of argument, 55
    formulating, 57
    irrelevant issues, 53
    relevant issues, 53

Qualifier, in Toulmin model, 181
Qualitative significance, 241
Quasi-logical, as form of reasoning, 113–15

Racist language, 282
Reader's Guide to Periodical Literature, 90
Reasoning
    in argument model, 19
    definition of, 8–9
    person/act, 124
Recency, as criterion for evidence, 81–82
Recipients. *See also* Audience
    and emotive language, 154–55
    as evaluators of evidence, 139–40, 292–93
    framework for opposition, 294
    predisposition of, 222
Reciprocity, as form of reasoning, 114–15
Refutation
    definition of, 205
    exploratory, 206
    tests of evidence, 206
Relational claims, 64–65
Reliability, as criterion for evidence evaluation, 79
Reluctant testimony, 307
Reports, as evidence, 77
Rescher, Nicholas, on values, 215–16
Research, conducting, 88–96
Reservation, in Toulmin model, 181
Resolutional issues, in debate, 322
Rhetorical language, function of, 276
Rhetorical perspective, 12–14
Rhetorical situation, definition of, 37
Richards, I. A.: *The Meaning of Meaning*, 267
Rokeach, Milton, on values, 213, 216–17

Sample, representative vs. unrepresentative, 86–87, 141–42
Sapir, Edward, on language, 274
Scriven, Michael, on argument analysis, 166
Sexist language, 282
Sign, as form of reasoning, 123
Simple argument, definition of, 166, 171
Simplicity, in language use, 279–80
Single cause, fallacy of, 144
Slippery slope, fallacy of, 144
Social Sciences Index, 90
Source credibility, 300
Sources
    citation of, 83–85
    objectivity of, 80
    primary, 84
    qualifications of, 79
    secondary, 84
Statistical Abstract of the United States, 94
Statistics
    collection of, 77
    evaluation of, 85–88
    as evidence, 77
    poor method, 87
    pseudo, 86
    representative sample, 87
    unrepresentative sample, 86–87
Stock issues
    definition of, 218
    in policy arguments, 239–45
    in value arguments, 219–23
Strategies, for persuasion, 291
Straw argument, fallacy of, 151–52
Structural blame, in policy analysis, 242
Structures, definition of, 242
Subclaims, 55
Subculture, 31–32
Sufficient condition, reasoning from, 120–21
Syllogism, definition of, 109
Systems perspective, 237–39

Terminal values, 213
Terministic screens, 274
Testimony
    reliability, 79
    reluctant, 307
Times Index, 92
Topicality, 323–24

Toulmin model
    parts of, 179–87
    usefulness of, 184–87
Toulmin, Stephen
    on argument fields, 35–36
    Uses of Argument, 179
Tradition, appeal to, fallacy of, 150–51
Transitivity argument, as form of reasoning, 113–14
Tree Diagrams, 178
Triangle of Meaning, 268
Trustworthiness, 303–4
Two-sided analysis, 297

Value
    claims of, 66
    definition of, 66
    personal, 213
    social, 213
Value claims
    definition of, 66
    in fields, 66
Value emphasis, 216
Value hierarchy
    definition of, 126, 213
    the essence, 217
    the existent, 217
    the person, 217
    of quality, 217
    of quantity, 217
Value object, definition, 218
Value redistribution, 215
Value restandardization, 216
Value system, 213
Vertical file index, as evidence, 95
Vividness of language use, 281
Vocabulary, size of, 275

Warrant, in Toulmin model, 79. See also Inference, Reasoning
Wenzel, Joseph W.
    on argument contexts, 28
    on argument fields, 35
    on argument perspectives, 12
    on value claims, 66
Whately, Richard, on challenge, 62
Whorf, Benjamin, on language, 274
Windes, Russel R., on evidence, 74

Ziegelmueller, George W., on claims, 61